Reading
WOMEN
Writing

a series edited by
Shari Benstock and Celeste Schenck

Reading Women Writing is dedicated to furthering international feminist debate. The series publishes books on all aspects of feminist theory and textual practice. *Reading Women Writing* especially welcomes books that address cultures, histories, and experiences beyond first-world academic boundaries. A full list of titles in the series appears at the end of this book.

Penelope writing to Ulysses. From *Les Epistres d'Ovide*, by Octavien de Saint-Gelais. Bibliothèque Nationale.

Penelope Voyages

WOMEN AND TRAVEL IN THE BRITISH LITERARY TRADITION

Karen R. Lawrence

Cornell University Press

ITHACA AND LONDON

First published 1994 by Cornell University Press.

Printed in the United States of America

⊗ The paper in this book meets the minimum requirements of the American National Standard for Information Sciences—Permanence of Paper for Printed Library Materials, ANSI Z39.48–1984.

Library of Congress Cataloging-in-Publication Data

Lawrence, Karen, 1949–
  Penelope voyages : women and travel in the British literary tradition / Karen R. Lawrence.
     p.   cm.—(Reading women writing)
  Includes bibliographical references (p.) and index.
  ISBN 0-8014-2610-3 (alk. paper).—ISBN 0-8014-9913-5 (alk. paper)
  1. Travelers' writings, English—Women authors—History and criticism.   2. Women travelers—Great Britain—Biography—History and criticism.   3. English prose literature—Women authors—History and criticism.   4. Women and literature—Great Britain—Historiography.   5. Voyages and travels—Historiography.   6. British—Travel—Historiography.   7. Women—Travel—Historiography.   8. Travel in literature.   I. Title   II. Series.
PR778.T72L38   1994
820.9'355—dc20   94-20853

With gratitude I dedicate *Penelope Voyages*
to the centripetal forces in my life—
to a remarkable group of colleagues
in the English Department at the University of Utah
(transplants, like me),
who have helped make Salt Lake City home—
and, most of all, to Peter, Andrew, and Jeffrey,
who make a home of anywhere.

Contents

Preface

Historically, the discourse of absence is carried on by the Woman: Woman is sedentary, Man hunts, journeys; Woman is faithful (she waits), man is fickle (he sails away, he cruises). It is Woman who gives shape to absence, elaborates its fiction, for she has time to do so; she weaves and she sings; the Spinning Songs express both immobility (by the hum of the Wheel) and absence (far away, rhythms of travel, sea surges, cavalcades). It follows that in any man who utters the other's absence *something feminine* is declared: this man who waits and who suffers from his waiting is miraculously feminized. (Barthes, *A Lover's Discourse: Fragments*, 13–14)

Travel need not be seen in the context of love, as a leaving or an abandonment. In this fragment from *A Lover's Discourse*, however, Roland Barthes reinforces one of the most enduring narratives of the gendering of travel, a narrative that conflates travel and absence in the experience of Penelope, who is left behind. But then in writing "fragments," Barthes already instructs the reader to alter and play with the topoi of the discourse: "What we have been able to say below about waiting, anxiety, memory is no more than a modest supplement offered to the reader to be made free with, to be added to, subtracted from, and passed on to others" (5). And yet, as Barthes also knows, the "modest" supplement is such common currency that to alter it strategically, in the passing on, is no modest task.

For it is a Western cultural truism that Penelope waits while Odysseus voyages. Although Odysseus's story is cast in relation to the woman at home who waits, it is, as well as a "love story," an adventure, an epic, a romance, a story of exile. Away from home, Odysseus is preoccupied; even the stories he tells while on his journey are on subjects other than the beloved. But Penelope, with time on her hands, her hands at the loom, tells one story, if she tells at all. Indeed, one can say that despite their differences in energy and focus, adventure literature and the domestic novel share a powerful assumption: that "woman's place" is, first and foremost, at home. The woman as beloved is the "fixt foot" that "makes no show / To move," as Donne puts it; the male foot of the compass explores the world around it, tracing its journey as it goes ("Valediction forbidding mourning"). Graphically enacting the circular pattern of an exilic narrative like the *Odyssey*, Donne's conceit also provides a metaphor for the inscription of the male journey, for travel writing as well as travel.

What happens when Penelope voyages? What discourse, what figures, what maps do we use? Can Penelope, the weaver and teller of the story of male absence, trace her own itinerary instead? Furthermore, how is femininity constructed when its relation to the domestic is radically altered? For in the ahistorical abstraction Barthes articulates, there is a timeless permanence to the assignment of place in the narrative. But, as Joan Scott says, "the point of new historical investigation is to disrupt the notion of fixity, to discover the nature of the debate or repression that leads to the appearance of timeless permanence in binary gender representation" (94). In fiction and in history Penelope did voyage, at times contesting, reinventing, reinscribing the ideologies of domesticity. Women writers mapped these voyages in narratives that appropriated literary traditions developed by male writers to trace the itineraries of men. In the hybrid genres of travel literature—imaginary voyage, picaresque, letters, ethnographic narrative, sentimental romance, novel, fantasy—we encounter seekers of various kinds who chart their path of exploration while recognizing that they follow in someone else's footsteps. This anxiety of belatedness inflects the narrative account of travel as well as the voyage of discovery. "Questions of travel," to use Elizabeth Bishop's phrase, are also questions of travel writing, of departing literarily as well as literally from the beaten path.

In the last twenty years, feminist critics and feminist presses like Virago have rediscovered and republished forgotten texts by women travelers. Biographies and interpretations of the works of individual women travelers have done much to bring to academic and wider public attention the extent of women's travel and travel writing. Yet despite proliferating evidence of women's travel and travel writing, historians of travel literature and theorists of travel in its various forms have been slow to amend their accounts. Feminist critics have just begun to chart and theorize women's travel, most often in the context of imperialism (see, in particular, Mary Louise Pratt's *Imperial Eyes* and Sara Mills's *Discourses of Difference*).

In *Penelope Voyages* I range widely in order to explore multiple genres of travel literature in the British literary tradition in which woman is both writer and traveler. I consider the significance of gender for the imaginative possibilities of travel writing and the value of travel in testing out cultural freedoms and restraints. Emphasis shifts from the way in which the British cultural imagination has constructed and expressed itself centripetally in domestic fiction to its centrifugal impulses in the literature of travel—from the tradition of Richardson to that of Defoe. A study of this literature supplements Sandra Gilbert and Susan Gubar's important but partial view of how images of confinement dominate British women's writing in the eighteenth and nineteenth centuries and Rachel Duplessis's characterization of the restrictive romantic plots and forms of pre-twentieth-century literature. Travel writing reveals a set of alternative myths or models for women's place in society. Equally important, it provides a particularly broad spectrum of generic possibilities—realistic and fantastic, "scientific" and sentimental, epistolary and narrative.

Like the pleasures of travel, the pleasures of theorizing about travel include an encounter with that which resists domestication, even domestication by "theory." One senses what escapes, that is, what travels beyond the theoretical ground one has chosen to map. Yet, what does bind together the fictional and nonfictional examples highlighted here is their use of the figure of movement to explore pressing issues of personal and historical agency, problems of (and opportunities for) women's cultural placements and displacements. The narratives that most interest me all acknowledge in various genres that despite the generally liberatory impulse behind most voyages out, one cannot float above the cultural vehicles available for transporting the imagination, the "vessels of conception," as Christine Brooke-Rose calls them in her novel *Between* (442).

In *Penelope Voyages* I consider the imaginative and conceptual appeal of movement and border crossings yet at the same time attempt to retain crucial distinctions within what feminist and postcolonial critics have called "the politics of location." This "politics" involves a redefinition of notions of "home and family, community and liminality, self and other," as Teresa de Lauretis puts it (*Feminist Studies*, 16). In analyzing how women writers of travel semanticize cultural and geographic border crossings, I seek not merely to re-place a male traveler with a female traveler but to show the relational, discursive operations of identity in these women's texts. "Home," as Biddy Martin and Chandra Talpade Mohanty argue in "Feminist Politics," is not homogeneous but relational, the "self" is not a unitary entity but a construct defined by what it is not. The idea of home, Martin and Mohanty contend, depends on the "repression of differences even within oneself" (196). The topos of travel furnishes a testing ground for this relational notion of identity, exaggerating the politics of location which infuses all identity formation. The book is not intended, then, as a general overview or survey, since the very possibility of an impersonal, "distanced" view of travel would replicate the kind of static assignment of places my work seeks to dislocate. Nor is it a comparative study of travel by women of various racial, class, and national statuses; my examples are all travel narratives written by white, aristocratic or middle-class Englishwomen, whose race and class inform their expectations of mobility as thoroughly as they inform their domestic ideologies.

Throughout the book I have used the term "travel" loosely but deliberately to cover a range of historical practices and genres precisely because the term retains its historical associations with a Western, white, middle class and with a generally male, privileged ease of movement. For the very concepts of mobility and placement (as in the differing concepts of "traveler" and "native") carry ideological significance; Arjun Appadurai has pointed out that "travel" suggests "motion of the free, arbitrary, adventurous sort associated with metropolitan behavior" (35). English women travelers are situated within this general definition, under the "European heading," as Jacques Derrida calls it (*Other Heading*). Yet under this heading, the concept of "freedom" is variously construed and measured. Indeed, a schematic opposition between adventure and domesticity collapses in a nuanced treatment of travel writing, demonstrating something illusory within both the stabilities of domesticity and the freedoms of travel. Furthermore, travel, like domestic ideology, has a political history; as James Buzard demonstrates in his intellectual history of European tourism, the meaning of travel, even the traveler's solidarity with and difference from other travelers, changes over time (1–17).

I begin with a look at the way versions of travel produced by male writers, including theorists, have subsumed gender into geography, sometimes struggling to keep the "feminine" in its allotted place. From there I move on to examples of women's travel writing, from the seventeenth to the twentieth century, that remap (and destabilize) femininity in relation to the poles of travel/home, other/self, and foreign/domestic. From the cross-dressed heroine of Margaret Cavendish's Renaissance imaginary voyage to the wildly circulating libido in Brigid Brophy's "misprinted mistranslated . . . pornofantasy-narrative" (143), *Penelope Voyages* traces "Penelope" in the dual position of traveler and weaver of the tale.

An American Field Service scholarship inspired my love of travel when, at seventeen, I became an exchange student in Japan. More recently, participation in International James Joyce Symposia has fueled it. But *Penelope Voyages* was written, for the most part, at home. This is the place (a phrase particularly resonant in Utah) to recognize individually those colleagues who have helped me during the eight years it has taken to complete the book. Such a wide-ranging, perhaps even hubristic, project has required the help and honest criticism of a number of people with varied expertise.

Barry Weller deserves my deep thanks for being the most constant friend of *Penelope Voyages* from the beginning. Quite a few academics I know across the country would not consider publishing a book without Barry's erudite, meticulous, and generous help, and over the years of our friendship I have been one of the luckiest beneficiaries of his support. Srinivas Aravamudan offered insightful commentary on the early chapters of the manuscript, in particular, as well as canny suggestions and practical assistance regarding the illustrations for the book. Robert Caserio has read most of the book in one form or another, and I have profited from his ability to see steadily and whole. I thank Henry Staten, Steve Tatum, Meg Brady, Lee Rust Brown, Gillian Brown, Karen Brennan, Brooke Hopkins, Kathryn Stockton, Bruce Haley, and Christine Froula for taking the time to carefully critique individual chapters. I am grateful, as well, to Michael Rudick, who offered his excellent knowledge of German on more than one occasion. To John Rogers, Laurie Langbauer, and Jeanne Moskal, I owe a debt of thanks for discussions of their work and mine during their tenure as Humanities Center fellows at the University of Utah.

Shari Benstock and Susan Friedman read the manuscript at several stages for Cornell University Press and offered the most intelligent and detailed readers' reports I have ever received. Susan Staker served as my research assistant in the early years of the project, and Susanna Cowan saw it through to completion. I thank Susanna, especially, for making a list and checking it twice with such care. I am also grateful to Nancy Malone, my copy editor, and to Carol Betsch and Bernhard Kendler at Cornell University Press for their respective editorial roles with this book. It has been a genuine pleasure to work with them.

I would like to thank Frau Eva Scharf for her kind permission to reprint her Toulouse-Lautrec lithograph on the cover of *Penelope Voyages*. The Bibliothèque Nationale allowed me to use the illustration of Penelope writing, and Virago Press permitted me to reprint the cover of Mary Kingsley's *Travels in West Africa*. I gratefully acknowledge the support of the Guggenheim Foundation, which helped me to launch *Penelope Voyages*. An abridged version of my discussion of Woolf's *Orlando* first appeared in *Modern Fiction Studies* 38 (Spring 1992): 253–77 under the editorship of Ellen Carol Jones.

Karen R. Lawrence

Salt Lake City, Utah

Penelope Voyages

Introduction:
Hermes/Penelope

Hermes, God of Travel

In the multiple paradigms of the journey plot—adventure, pilgrim-age, exile, for example—women are generally excluded, their absence establishing the world of the journey as a realm in which man confronts the "foreign." Women (like Penelope) serve as the symbolic embodiment of home; often, however, a female figure (like Circe) may signify the foreign itself. Conrad's *Heart of Darkness* provides a modern example of woman in both symbolic positions for the male traveler—the "Intended" as faithful Penelope, the native woman as the embodiment of foreign territory.

Indeed, the plot of the male journey depends on keeping woman in her place. Not only is her place at home, but she in effect is home itself, for the female body is traditionally associated with earth, shelter, enclosure. Although the particular symbolic geography of the female as "home" may shift historically on a spectrum from nature to culture (at different times and in different literatures she may be variously figured as earth, cultivated garden, or domestic interior), she traditionally provides the point of departure and sometimes the goal for the male journey. This mapping of the female body underwrites not only travel literature per se, but the more general trope of the journey as well.

This dominance of man as subject and woman as object is manifested in the theoretical and critical discourse about travel and the plot of the journey as well as in the stories and myths themselves. It is striking that historical surveys of travel literature, such as Percy

Adams's *Travel Literature and the Evolution of the Novel*; psychoanalytic treatments of adventure, such as Paul Zweig's *The Adventurer*; structural typologies of narrative that take the journey as basic trope, such as the work of the Soviet semiotician Jurij Lotman; more Marxist-oriented studies that historicize the meaning of adventure, like Michael Nerlich's *Ideology of Adventure*; and theories of ethnography, such as Vincent Crapanzano's *Hermes' Dilemma and Hamlet's Desire*, all fail to theorize a place for woman as traveling subject. Indeed, Crapanzano's work is typical of many revisionary studies that confirm rather than interrogate the gendered paradigm. According to Crapanzano, the potency of ethnography is linked to the phallus, the transcendental signifier in the system of the symbolic. Crapanzano figures the ethnographer as Hermes, the god of travel, crossroads, and boundaries. "Hermes, etymologically 'he of the stone heap,' was associated with boundary stones":

> The herm, a head and a phallus on a pillar, later replaced the stone heap. The ethnographer, if I may continue my conceit, also marks a boundary: his ethnography declares the limits of his and his readers' culture. It also attests to his—and his culture's—interpretive power. Hermes was a phallic god and a god of fertility. Interpretation has been understood as a phallic, a phallic-aggressive, a cruel and violent, a destructive act, and as a fertile, a fertilizing, a fruitful and creative one. (44)

To varying degrees, all the studies of adventure and travel cited above encode the traveler as a male who crosses boundaries and penetrates spaces; the female is mapped as a place on the itinerary of the male journey. Teresa de Lauretis demonstrates that this sexual mapping of the journey has great persistence in mythic and narrative structures, as well as in the theoretical discourse on narrative. Both in narratives and in their structural analyses, woman's body is itself spatialized. In this "mythical-textual mechanics," as de Lauretis calls it, the traveler penetrates spaces that are "morphologically female" (*Alice Doesn't*). Summarizing an essay on plot typology by Lotman, de Lauretis finds that the "hero, the mythical subject, is constructed as human being and as male; he is the active principle of culture, the establisher of distinction, the creator of differences. Female is . . . an element of plot-space, a topos, a resistance, matrix and matter" (119). De Lauretis maintains that myth, psychoanalysis, and semiotics all exemplify this coding of the journey.

Norman O. Brown's *Love's Body*, which anticipates by many years Crapanzano's ethnographer as Hermes, is representative of the phallocentrism of typologies of the journey. In Brown's psychoanalytic model, the male attempts to leave the mother's body behind when he lights out for the territory: "Fraternity comes into being after the sons are expelled from the family; when they form their own club, in the wilderness, away from home, away from women. The brotherhood is a substitute family, a substitute woman—alma mater" (32). But the body of the mother returns as the world: "Geography is the geography of the mother's body" (36). "The wandering heroes are phallic heroes, in a permanent state of erection; pricking o'er the plain. The word coition represents genital sexuality as walking; but the converse is also true: all walking, or wandering in the labyrinth, is genital-sexual. All movement is phallic, all intercourse sexual. Hermes, the phallus, is the god of roads, of doorways, of all goings-in and comings-out; all goings-on" (50).[1]

Indeed, it is just such an experience of the male's reencounter with the maternal body he has tried to flee that provides an important trope for Freud's essay "The 'Uncanny.'" To exemplify the experience of the uncanny, Freud refers to a persistent male dream of travel that reveals both the repression of the mother's body and its unexpected reappearance. "There is a joking saying," he remarks, "'Love is homesickness'; and whenever a man dreams of a place or a country and says to himself, while he is still dreaming: 'this place is familiar to me, I've been here before,' we may interpret the place as being his mother's genitals or her body. In this case too, then, the *unheimlich* [unfamiliar] is what was once *heimisch*, familiar; the prefix 'un' is the token of repression" (245). The uncanny here is the sudden involuntary awareness of the repetition of the familiar in the foreign; it is nothing new or foreign but something "old-established in the mind [that] has become alienated from it only through the process of repression" (241). Although Freud's essay posits several different kinds of uncanny repetitions, not all of which depend on a rediscovery of the female body, it is just such a rediscovery that he narrates in connection with an uncanny experience of his own. Here, it is not a symbolic dream of travel that Freud recounts but an actual travel experience, a trip to a provincial town in Italy. As he is walking in the deserted streets, he "finds himself" in a quarter of town with "nothing but

[1]For Brown's more extensive treatment of Hermes, see *Hermes the Thief*.

painted women" in "the windows of the small houses." Although he tries to leave this section of the city, he inadvertently keeps returning, to the point that his presence begins to "excite attention" (237). Tellingly, Freud fails to link this experience of travel with his previous analysis of the unheimlich female body in the dream of travel. Curiously unanalyzed in the passage is his own "excite[d] attention." Freud fails to comment on the content of the repeated scene, stressing only its involuntary repetition. At the end of his experience, he says he was "glad enough to find myself back at the piazza I had left a short while before, without any further voyages of discovery" (237). As Susan Sage Heinzelman points out, in his narrative, as in his journey, Freud tries to avoid the significance of the female body (70).[2]

The uncanny terrifies because it collapses the distance between the familiar and the foreign in a way that the traveler (in these narratives, the male traveler) does not anticipate. In a sense, the idea of adventure depends on this distance; the physical distance between the poles of familiar and foreign figures the desire to separate the two. This structure of difference between here and there by necessity oversimplifies the opposition between home and the foreign, until difference is intentionally mediated by the traveler in the acts of travel and travel writing (I will return to this act of mediation and translation in much more detail). In the Oedipal narrative of travel, home represents the safe, feminized space to be left behind for the terrain of adventure, home's own potential disturbances homogenized. The nineteenth-century "angel in the house," as Nina Auerbach points out, was such a figure for tamed female sexual energy at home (72–73). In this scenario, female libido and power are exiled to a foreign land, as in Rider Haggard's Amazon community in *She*.[3]

---

[2] In *Haunted Journeys: Desire and Transgression in European Travel Writing*, Dennis Porter cites Freud's essay on the uncanny to introduce the notion of the "haunting" quality of travel narratives but does not explicitly link it to gender. He does, however, argue for the relevance of Freudian theory to the analysis of travel writing, because it offers a vocabulary and paradigm for understanding movement in terms of desire and transgression. Porter identifies his work as in the tradition of "masculinist studies," which pursue "extended commentary on a question Freud never explicitly asked . . . 'What does man want?' "(17). "To deal adequately with the complex motivations that drive women to travel or at least to write about it would, therefore, require a separate book that would have to be theorized differently" (17).

[3] Ronald R. Thomas discusses the relation between Freud's development of the theory of psychoanalysis and the trope of adventure, citing Haggard's *She* as a formative influence on Freud's theory of dreams and the "plot" of the family romance. Thomas analyzes a dream that Freud recounts in *The Interpretation of Dreams*, in which Haggard's

In *The Adventurer*, Zweig theorizes the "unrelenting masculinity" of adventure and the defensive strategy behind the exclusion of women that many other critics merely take as a given in their analyses. Particularly in the chapters "The Flight from Women" and "The Myth of Odysseus," Zweig exposes the flight from women as a motive force behind the plot of adventure. The adventure "represents a poignant male fantasy: moved by his desire to vanquish the many faces of woman, he reinvents the shape of manhood itself so as to free it from its multiple attachments to the feminine" (79). Explaining the harshness of the masculinist adventure in Oedipal terms, Zweig says the male traveler represses his longing for the body of the mother and must separate almost violently from it. Zweig notes that in his anxiety, man tries to "exile this frightening female energy to far away" (68), but it reappears in the form of obstacles that the hero must vanquish in the course of his journey. He sees the caves and dragons encountered on the journey as essentially feminine survivals of great mother religions, the hero somehow enacting patriarchy's overthrow of matriarchal power.

Yet if female energy returns unexpectedly to be battled on the journey, its most terrifying avatar is not the antagonist who fights but the seducer who threatens to return the traveler to a womblike oblivion. In Zweig's analysis, Calypso, whose name derives from *kaluptein*, "to hide," serves as an important figure for the way the uncanny female body threatens the whole enterprise of adventure. "To be kalypsoed is to fall outside the poem, as Odysseus does for seven idle years." He goes on to say, "The 'Apollonian' clarity which Nietzsche admired in Homer, is the clarity of remembered acts" (26). If going home is the impetus for Odysseus's particular journey, staying home (even the premature, illusory resting place that mimics home for the exhausted voyager) ends the story altogether. The power of woman, both at home and on his journey, may subvert adventure and fame. A Delilah, woman threatens to sap male energy for adventure.[4]

---

novels provide the plot for Freud's own "journey" toward authorship. Thomas goes on to say that "increasingly, Freud's own life story becomes interchangeable with this novel of adventure and empire building," as Freud anticipates his "adventure of building the empire of psychoanalysis" (40).

[4]One might think here of the erotics of narrative theorized in Peter Brooks's *Reading for the Plot*. Basing his narratology on Freud's *Beyond the Pleasure Principle*, Brooks defines "narrative" as a vehicle of desire that seeks its own end but in its own time. Hence, plot is seen as a kind of "squiggle" that separates beginning and end or holds

The value of Zweig's analysis is that he provides a theory for what isn't in the story as well as what is. His psychoanalytic reading theorizes a return of the repressed "feminine" which reveals that the female body is not so easily kept in one place. Paradoxically, if in Zweig's schema the motive force for adventure is the flight from women (61), he also posits a "feminine" presence haunting the ethos of adventure that inheres in the hero's receptivity and adaptability. Because adventure is meant as a time-out from the everyday world of work and the adventurer is receptive to what befalls him, Zweig posits a feminizing spirit at work in the genre: "The lady herself is bound, on the one hand, by her powers, but on the other she remains the presiding spirit of the knight's adventures, the gateway through which he must pass into the domain of the magical" (68). Although Zweig fails to question his own reinscription of this spirit in traditional gender categories (woman as receptive and passive, woman as gateway), his analysis usefully suggests the way woman disturbs the male narrative of travel, her energies refusing to stay put, either at home or on the path of adventure.[5]

One could say that this attempted "flight from women" is repeated in many histories and theories of travel. Although not all the paradigms of the journey are psychoanalytic, the oedipalized journeys typical of the psychoanalytic treatments exemplify the elision of female subjectivity evident in most of these analyses.[6] Even in so sophisticated a work as *Hermes*, a collection of essays concerned with the journey as a trope for narrative crossings and displacements, Michel

---

off the premature collapse of life and death (104). In the case of adventure, the "energy for adventure," as Zweig describes it, depends on eluding female power in order to survive. The oblivion of Calypso's cave is one example of what Brooks sees as the threat of short circuit, a return to the womb of the mother that the adventurer attempts to escape.

[5]In identifying a particularly feminine spirit in adventure, Zweig resembles Northrop Frye, who also posits the genre of romance as female in spirit. Frye describes this spirit as guile and *froda*, or "craft," often associated with women who must use their wits rather than force (68–69). The *Odyssey* (as opposed to the *Iliad*, for example) serves as an important example for this analysis because its hero, aligning himself with Athena, substitutes craft and ingenuity for physical prowess.

[6]Stanford Lyman and Marvin Scott's essay "Adventures" is an example of a non-psychoanalytic treatment of adventure that maps it according to the cultural paradigm of male sexual conquest (153), thus ignoring female subjectivity. Michael Nerlich's *Ideology of Adventure* assumes a strictly male model as well. See also Martin Green's excellent discussion of the deliberate masculinism of adventure, which he sees as a purposeful swerve from the more androgynous (though still implicitly androcentric) tradition of the domestic novel (*Dreams of Adventure*).

Serres stops short of examining the problematic of gender. *Hermes* is a magnum opus in which Serres attacks nothing less than the conceptualization or "mapping" of knowledge in Western thought. In his analysis of certain prototypical texts from different ages (for which the *Odyssey* functions as the prototype of "literature" itself), he examines different "ideologies of knowing." Serres makes us radically rethink the model of the journey, subverting the idea of a linear journey and replacing it with multiple crossings, displacements, and connections between discourses. Hermes presides over this conceptual reorganization, although not as transcendental phallic signifier, as he appears in the work of Brown. In Serres's analysis, Hermes is the figure for a journey across discontinuous spaces. He is the guide of travelers and protector of boundaries, trickster, translator, messenger (and ancestor of Odysseus). As Josué Harari and David Bell put it in their introduction to Serres's work, Hermes as guide "keeps moving; he connects, disconnects, and reconnects the endless variety of spaces he traverses" (xxxiii).

For Serres, the *Odyssey* is paradigmatic of literature because in it "original spaces proliferate on the map of the journey, perfectly disseminated, or literally sporadic, each one rigorously determined. The global wandering, the mythical adventure [of Ulysses], is, in the end, only the general joining of these spaces, as if the object or target of discourse were only to connect, or as if the junction, the relation, constituted the route by which the first discourse passes" (49). In Serres's discussion the journey of Odysseus functions allegorically as the journey of discourse.

But in his subtle and fascinating analysis, one sees a rather strange elision of the problem of gender. Serres points out that Hermes twice intervenes to protect his hero—when his adventure is threatened by the magic of Calypso and of Circe. As Harari and Bell observe in their introduction, "Twice in his wanderings Ulysses is hopelessly stranded, twice the narrative of the *Odyssey* starts faltering, twice Hermes appears—to break Calypso's and Circe's magic—in order to revitalize the narrative. Ulysses departs and with him literature sets off again" (xxxiv). Thus Hermes protects his traveler from the female magic that would threaten the narrative itself. He guides Ulysses across the juncture in the narrative, that which Zweig has also mentioned in reference to the threatening oblivion of Calypso. The magical power of the female is here antagonistic to the power of Hermes—and it saps the energy of adventure and narrative.

And yet, at one point in Serres's analysis, Hermes curiously metamorphoses into the female figure of Penelope. Of this formulation, Serres says:

> Thus we have Penelope at the theoretical position: the queen who weaves and unweaves, the originally feminine figure who, become male, will be Plato's Royal Weaver. . . . Penelope is the author, the signatory of the discourse; she traces its graph, she draws its itinerary. She makes and undoes this cloth that mimes the progress and delays of the navigator, of Ulysses on board his ship, the shuttle that weaves and interweaves fibers separated by the void, spatial varieties bordered by crevices. She is the embroideress, the lace-maker, by wells and bridges, of this continuous flux interrupted by catastrophes that is called discourse. In the palace of Ithaca, Ulysses, finally in the arms of the queen, finds the finished theory of his own *mythos*. (49)

The formulation resembles Zweig's idea of the essential feminine spirit of adventure; here, the stops and starts of Ulysses' adventure and of the narrative enterprise are presided over by the woman who waits at home. She is author who first and foremost protects the energies of narrative, at the occasional expense of her desire that her husband's exilic route be shortened. Unlike her sisters Calypso and Circe, she prolongs rather than preemptively blocks the narrative— until her protagonist and husband can be led home in the *Nostos*, his circle ending where it began, in the arms of the queen (those arms, those weaving hands). As weaver and unweaver, she is the spirit of narrative repetition, defending against the premature closure of the story.

Serres notices something important about Penelope's power in Homer's epic.[7] Yet what does it mean to place Penelope at this theoretical position, to see her as the "originally feminine figure" who, sometime between Homer and Plato, changes sex like Woolf's Orlando (although in the opposite direction)? It is clear that the mythically feminine craft of weaving provides the perfect metaphor for text

---

[7]That the mythos of Odysseus is completed in the arms of Penelope is suggested within the *Odyssey* by Antikleia, Odysseus's mother, in the final line of her speech to him in Hades. She says, " 'Note all things strange / seen here, to tell your lady in after days' " (192). In the mother's advice, the wife completes Odysseus's journey as it is transformed into narrative—Penelope becomes the final and best audience of his travel tale.

making itself (elsewhere Serres also mentions Ariadne in this context); but in a work that so imaginatively, even compulsively, analyzes displacements from discourse to discourse, it is surprising to find so little about this sexual displacement. In an important sense, the significant "border" crossing now for Hermes is that between genders; Hermes becomes hermaphrodite, but Serres fails to elaborate on just how this works.[8] Harari and Bell, without theorizing, compare Serres's own "linguistic journeys" to the arts of those "bad" female magicians, Circe and Calypso. They say, "One is touched by the magic wand of Circe and the seductive charms of Calypso: vocabularies diverge and bifurcate, are transformed and concealed, and finally disappear precisely when one begins to appreciate their savor" (xxxvii). Circe's, Calypso's, Penelope's, Homer's, Hermes', and Serres's crafts all come together (female arts and crafts and male craftiness) in a figure that, although untheorized, suggests the disruption of the opposition between familiar and foreign, inside and outside. Penelope is a kind of wild card; outside the narrative "at the theoretical position," she nevertheless is *in* the narrative as well. Circe's and Calypso's magic now appears to be hers, but in a larger sense, the text itself is her praxis, material evidence of her craft. Penelope is in two places at once.[9]

   We can extract from Serres's Penelope/Hermes a figure for the slip-

[8]Indeed, despite this once important link between female craft and Hermes' craftiness, Serres seems to posit maleness as constitutive of the journey, particularly in its modern incarnation. In his essay "The Apparition of Hermes: *Dom Juan*," he identifies Don Juan as "the first hero of modernity . . . a fickle voyager in search of an impossible (unique) love" (3). Calling him a "three-headed devil," Serres sees him as "a character with three roles: as a ladies' man, he seduces; as a man of ideas, he discourses; as a man of money, he defers his debt" (4). In this essay, which maps the intersection of science, myth, and literature, it is the male who occupies the exclusive position at the crossroads. One might look at Alexander Gelley's *Narrative Crossings: Theory and Pragmatics of Prose Fiction* to see Serres's ideas about Penelope extended to a discussion of a female Hermes who traces an itinerary—the Widow in Goethe's *Wilhelm Meister* (134).

[9]It is just such a place for woman, inside and outside the narrative, that Samuel Butler proposed in his *Authoress of the Odyssey* and Robert Graves went on to fully imagine in *Homer's Daughter* based on Butler's theory. It was not Circe, Calypso, or Penelope, but Nausicaa whom they imagined as an "honorary Daughter of Homer," to use Graves's phrase (9). In this reading, Odysseus's unwitting, naked intrusion into the space of the young girls' play is placed within the context of the narrative told by a female voice, as if the native turned the tables on the ethnographer, writing her own ethnography. Without making the leap with Butler and Graves to seeing a woman as possible author of the *Odyssey*, Northrop Frye suggests that Penelope's weaving might have played a greater role in an earlier version of the Odyssey story. He suggests that the motif of Penelope's crafty loom work may be a vestige of a more "primitive" tale in which Penelope's games with the suitors were "central to the story" (70).

periness of boundaries between inside and outside, male and female, domestic and exotic. Penelope/Hermes destabilizes these borders and remaps the geography of narrative and narrative theorizing. Weaver and unweaver, constructor and deconstructor, woman as traveler and storyteller might be said to break the law of boundaries. Derrida has spoken of the "joyous disturbance of certain women's movements . . . [that has] actually brought with it the chance for a certain risky turbulence in the assigning of places within our small European place. . . . Is one then going to start all over again making maps, topographics, etc.?" he asks, "distributing sexual identity cards?" ("Choreographies," 69). And in "Penelope at Work," Peggy Kamuf focuses on the troubling potency of the female "weaver" and recognizes the power of Penelope to elude attempts to fix her place within the poem (attempts that begin with her son Telemachus, who twice tries to banish her to her room, away from the domain of male discourse). Cleverly, Kamuf sees Penelope "as a shuttling figure in power's household," a figure for the poet himself who weaves and unweaves his text (7).[10] One might urge a certain caution, however, about the deconstructive "use" of Penelope, for the topos of Hermes/Penelope as destabilizer is itself a cultural product and might take on varied significances, as Brown implicitly points out in his discussion of the difference the attributes of changeableness and stealth take on when transferred from Hermes to Pandora under the "misogynist" pen of Hesiod (*Hermes the Thief*, 55).[11]

We might return to Serres's placement of Penelope at the "theoretical position," which I take to mean, among other possibilities, the position of theory. In his analysis she thus serves as figure not merely for the author/weaver but also for the theorist, whose *distance* from the discourse enables her privileged position. She occupies a place outside narrative, elsewhere, displaced from the scene of action. According to Serres, "theory" thus begins and ends at home with Pe-

---

[10]One can see the appeal of the Penelope trope as an organizing metaphor and source of theory for feminist critics in work such as Susan Stanford Friedman's *Penelope's Web* and Rachel Blau Duplessis's *H.D.* For a feminist reading of Homer's Penelope as a figure of indeterminacy in the poem, see *Penelope's Renown: Meaning and Indeterminacy in "The Odyssey"* by Marylin A. Katz.

[11]Some feminist critics, such as Nancy K. Miller, also highlight the slippery "politics" of reading this shuttling figure. See Miller's fine essay "Arachnologies: The Woman, the Text, and the Critic." In "Feminism and Deconstruction, Again: Negotiating with Unacknowledged Masculinism," Gayatri Chakravorty Spivak discusses how theorists of deconstruction use woman as the "name that is the non-truth of truth" (215).

nelope; the traveler "finds the finished theory of his own *mythos*" in the waiting arms of the queen. But the slippery role of Hermes within Serres's (and his commentators') analysis compromises this distance, for Hermes' narrative identity meets Hermes' theoretical position as Penelope. The idea that theory can stand outside narrative, patiently waiting at a distance for the completion of the narrative trajectory, is belied by the destabilizing figure of Hermes/Penelope shuttling between the roles of traveler and homebody. Theory itself is both situated and yet mobile. As theorists such as Edward Said have pointed out, theory provides no universal vantage point from which to survey narrative (and other) topographies,[12] but participates in its own politics of location.

Theories of travel and those of narrative in which travel serves as central trope most vividly betray their politics of location through a certain blindness to the role of gender in their topographies. Surprisingly, this blindness is also evident in revisionary theories of ethnography, otherwise so attuned to the position of the observer. It is to Hermes as "translator," the one who writes the other in the language of home, that I now turn. Here, too, in the theoretical discourse, one can find a hidden fault line of gender.

Hermes, the Translator

The series of essay collections that James Clifford has edited and authored since the eighties provides one of the most ambitious efforts (by a Western intellectual) to reenvision the project of Western ethnography.[13] Continually revisiting the problem of ethnographic authority in the representation of the other, Clifford focuses on the ways in which ethnographers battle "the pull of authoritative representation of the other" by attempting to hold in view the "specific contingencies

[12]See Said's "Traveling Theory" in *The World, the Text, and the Critic.* Also see the collection *Traveling Theories, Traveling Theorists,* edited by James Clifford and Vivek Dhareshwar.

[13]More radical critiques of Western ethnography, however, have been launched by writers from within the neocolonial cultures themselves, such as Samir Amin in *Eurocentricism* and V. Y. Mudimbe in *The Invention of Africa: Gnosis, Philosophy, and the Order of Knowledge.* The whole Eurocentric project of Western ethnography has come under fire from many of these critics, who view it as inextricably linked to the imperialist project, despite its increasing sophistication about the links between knowledge and power.

of the exchange" ("Ethnographic Authority," 135). In all his work, Clifford seeks both to acknowledge and to resist the mystification of ethnographic authority. The "very activity of ethnographic *writing*—seen as inscription or textualization—enacts a redemptive Western allegory [that] needs to be perceived and weighed against other possible emplotments for the performance of ethnography" ("Ethnographic Allegory," 99). Clifford's essays suggest various possibilities, that is, for resisting the complex of power and knowledge that inevitably marks ethnographic writing. Focusing first on the representational (and, indeed, fictional) techniques for "textualizing" the other in order to demystify ethnographic authority (see *The Predicament of Culture* and *Writing Culture*), Clifford later discovered in the idea of travel itself a new possibility for redeeming the ethnographic project. He describes "an emergent culture-as-travel-relations ethnography" ("Traveling Cultures," 102) that demystifies the writing of culture by avowing the transits and traversals—the itineraries of both subject and ethnographic object—which eventuate in each particular encounter at a cultural crossroads. But within these rewritings of ethnographic problems there is little attention to gender, although Clifford has noted the necessity of more focus on this issue. In his essay "On Ethnographic Authority," Clifford influentially summarizes important changes in the performance of ethnography, but the essay nonetheless serves as a revealing example of the occlusion of gender even in revisionary ethnography.[14]

The essay begins with two emblems of the ethnographer: one, the frontispiece of Father Lafitau's *Moeurs des sauvages* (1724), which "portrays the ethnographer as a young woman sitting at a writing table amidst artifacts from the New World and from classical Greece and Egypt"; the other, the frontispiece of Malinowski's *Argonauts of the Western Pacific*, a photograph of a Trobriand chief (118). Clifford's main purpose is to allegorize the difference between these two images as telling the story of ethnographic evolution, from the role of the ethnographer as transcriber, at work thousands of miles away from the culture she studies, to the activity of the ethnographer as participant/observer, a definite presence in the cultural encounter. What strikes one in reading Clifford's analysis, however, is his failure to mine the richly gendered representations. Although Malinowski's portrayal of

---

[14]See Deborah Gordon's critique of the collection *Writing Culture*, edited by Clifford and George Marcus, in "Writing Culture, Writing Feminism: The Poetics and Politics of Experimental Ethnography."

the male ethnographer in the field seems perfectly understandable, why in Lafitau's frontispiece is it a woman writer who stitches together a text from the presence of the artifacts? And why does Lafitau, who, as Clifford points out, did spend five years in the field, displace the image of his own experience onto the scene of the woman writing?

A footnote in Clifford's article cites an essay by Michel de Certeau that analyzes Lafitau's frontispiece in great detail. The footnote refers to de Certeau's analysis, however, for its insights about the "suppression of dialogue in Lafitau's frontispiece and the constitution of a textualized, ahistorical, and visually oriented 'anthropology' " (143 n. 9). Clifford, who presumably has read the essay, never mentions de Certeau's fascinating inquiry into the transgendering of Lafitau's anthropologist. For, in discussing Lafitau's picture of ahistorical reconstruction in the laboratory, de Certeau does indeed focus on the gender of the ethnographer/writer and addresses Lafitau's act of displacement. In describing the frontispiece, Lafitau speaks of "a person in the posture of one writing"; and de Certeau notes that "the subtle ambiguity of the expression Lafitau uses in his text hides what in the image is manifest: This writer is a woman" ("Writing vs. Time," 49). De Certeau goes on to speak of the artifacts in the frontispiece as a network of references around the writer that reinforce her gender (Astarte, Diana of Ephesus, a picture of Eve and Mary); he then claims that Lafitau's work is "celebrated in particular for having identified a 'gynecocracy' or 'empire of women' in the Iroquois or Hurons . . . an originally matriarchal and matrilinear system" (49). The mother/writer is the representative of the author in the frontispiece. He is there, de Certeau claims, "as a *transvestite*": "A dream of being a mother in order to engender?" de Certeau asks, and goes on to propose that Lafitau, a celibate missionary, envisioned himself as the mother of a new science of anthropology (50).[15] The new importance of writing in constructing history and, specifically, textualizing the absent other, is related in de Certeau's analysis to the woman/writer as fabricator, the one who sews together the fragments

[15]Both Clifford and de Certeau fail to address the iconographic convention that portrays abstractions, such as fields of intellectual inquiry, as female. One might argue that Lafitau depicts Anthropology as feminine, rather than the anthropologist as a woman. However, the conventional aspect of Lafitau's representation does not obviate the analysis of gender. The contrast between feminine abstraction and masculine participation is itself significant. De Certeau's analysis of the iconography surrounding the female figure and of the displacement of Lafitau's own experience suggests fruitful possibilities for a more gender-inflected reading than Clifford's.

of culture, the debris of the fathers, to create a text (de Certeau refers to "the feminine work with texture" [62]). De Certeau allegorizes this frontispiece to show the historical and scientific gesture by which the writer, rather than the traveler, missionary, or explorer, becomes the hero of the story, and fabrication, rather than authentication, becomes the heroic act.

Yet, curiously, in his own earlier work on what he calls "a primal scene in the construction of ethnological discourse," the writing of Jean de Léry's *Histoire d'un voyage faict en la terre du Brésil* (1578), de Certeau, like Serres in *Hermes*, fails to note the disturbing effect of gender within his own analysis of the West's writing of the primitive other. Indeed, he philosophically opposes a position of self-analysis, even as he says that "in letting words, references, and reflections freely associate with the reader that I am, I must wonder what this analysis will hide or reveal in me" (*Writing of History*, 211).[16] De Certeau describes native speech as the "missing precious stone. It is the moment of ravishment, a stolen instant, a purloined memory beyond the text" (213). These moments threaten the Western narrative, creating what he calls "a lapsus in Western discourse"; they "rend holes in the fabric of the traveler's time" (227). The travel writer struggles to reserve (and conserve) for the West something of this mystery, to make "a return to the Christian and French text through the exegete's and the voyager's combined efforts. Productive time is sewn back into the fabric, history is generated anew, after the break precipitated by the throbbing heart that was going back over there, toward that instant when, 'totally ravished,' fascinated by the other's voice, the observer forgot himself" (214). Not only does de Certeau collapse, without acknowledgment, the "native" other with the female other, but he also grafts onto the story of ethnology—again, without notice—an Odyssean narrative: Odysseus, in danger of being permanently "kalypsoed" on his travels, becomes Odysseus lashing himself to the mast to escape the lure of the Sirens' voices. De Certeau writes, "It is the 'un-heard' that purloins the text or, more precisely, is stolen from the thief [Hermes, the thief as ethnologist and historiographer]" (227). The native, the woman, is that which cannot be contained by the narrative. Yet the labor of traveler/historiographer seems split in two

[16]De Certeau continues: "For what dream, or what lure, is my writing a metaphor? There can be no answer. Self-analysis has been disenfranchised, and I would not know how to replace a text with what only another voice could reveal about the place in which I am writing" (212).

along the fault line of gender, for if de Léry is Odysseus, ravished by the voice of the "native," female other, he is also Penelope (although, again, not named as such), for in his act of writing, "productive time is sewn back into the fabric, history is generated anew" (214).[17] Here Odysseus, the traveler, captivated by the female/native other, suddenly metamorphoses into Penelope, the ethnologist as fabricator, whose strategies of containment seek to suture the narrative (and history). In de Certeau's fascinating analysis, as in Serres's, gendered assignments begin to slip and slide; women's work goes uncontained, despite the strategies of narrative and (de Léry's) historiography, despite the strategy of de Certeau's own theorizing.

Penelope Voyages

If mapping the female body in fictional and theoretical versions of man's exilic wandering covertly but resoundingly keeps woman in her place, the literary tradition is full of more explicit representations of male fears about female wandering.

> "Would thou hadst hearkened to my words, and stayed
> With me, as I besought thee, when that strange
> Desire of wandering this unhappy morn,
> I know not whence possessed thee; we had then
> Remained still happy, not as now, despoiled
> Of all our good, shamed, naked, miserable."
> (*Paradise Lost*, bk. 9, ll. 1134–39)

Milton's Adam bemoans the consequences of Eve's "wandering"; the implication of errancy couples movement and straying. The very "desire of wandering" seems to come from abroad, from beyond Adam's

---

[17]De Certeau leads the reader through a twenty-page analysis of scenes of "ethnological eroticism" (229), at which point, in an act of writing almost imitative of the orgiastic pleasure he describes, he unveils the native other as Woman: "This conquering and orgiastic curiosity, so taken with unveiling hidden things, has its symbol in travel literature: the dressed, armed, knighted discoverer face-to-face with the nude Indian woman" (232). He then elaborates: "The repressed returns: with the image of nudity, 'an exorbitant presence'; with the phantasm of the *vagina dentata*, which looms in the representation of feminine voracity; or with the dancing eruption of forbidden pleasures. More basically, the native world, like the diabolical cosmos, becomes Woman. It is declined in the feminine gender" (233).

xenophobic domain ("I know not whence possessed thee"); this dangerous breach of inside and outside "despoils"—the woman's desire of wandering contaminates and shames the body at home.[18]

Such suggestions that the circulation of women is dangerous continue to mark descriptions of women's travel. From nineteenth-century reviews of the respectable Mrs. Trollope, which link women's travel to sexual promiscuity through a play on her name,[19] to recent anthologies of women's travel writings, such as Lisa St Aubin de Téran's *Indiscreet Journeys* and Leo Hamalian's *Ladies on the Loose*, the unrestrained circulation of women is cast in sexual terms. (The latter title is meant as a tongue-in-cheek reference to the circulation of proper Victorian ladies yet capitalizes, nonetheless, on the suggestion of movement as promiscuity.) It is this typecasting that has led some feminist writers to doubt the applicability of the Odyssean plot to women's travels. For example, Hélène Cixous and Catherine Clément view the plot as a literary dead end for women and certainly for the "newly born woman" (from the title of their book). Addressing the twentieth century's most famous rewriting of the Odyssean plot, Joyce's *Ulysses*, they cite the following line from the novel's third chapter as emblematic of the circumscription of female wandering in male narrative: "Bridebed, childbed, bed of death." They continue:

> Thus woman's trajectory is traced as she inscribes herself from bed to bed in Joyce's *Ulysses*. The voyage of Ulysses with Bloom standing constantly at the helm as he navigates Dublin. Walking, exploring. The voyage of Penelope—Everywoman: a bed of pain in which the mother is never done with dying, a hospital bed on which there is no end to Mrs. Purefoy's labor, the bed framing endless erotic daydreams, where Molly, wife and adulteress, voyages in her memories. She wanders, but lying down. In dream. Ruminates. Talks to herself. Woman's voyage: as a *body*. (66)[20]

---

[18]Of course, this link between movement and straying from the path is as old as the Bible and is found throughout the literary tradition, in Dante's and Spenser's woods of error, for example. Generally, the wanderer is opposed to the pilgrim, who engages in a purposeful quest. But the female traveler's particular baggage includes the historical link between female wandering and promiscuity.

[19]An American reviewer wrote: "There is much in a name. . . . The name of Mrs. Trollope, therefore, may be, at least, the shadow of a thing" (quoted in Fussell, 295).

[20]Interestingly, Cixous and Clément do not mention a counterimage to this image of Penelope in bed that is also represented in *Ulysses*. In the "Proteus" chapter of the novel, which deals with changes of all kinds, the following passage appears in which

Lillian Robinson doubts the viability of the plot for either women writers or women characters: "I find it impossible to imagine *The Odyssey au féminin*," she says, "because, in the travels of any female, the sexual question looms larger and creates new difficulties of its own. Whom Does She Sleep With? becomes so central as to block out all the other questions such a myth is supposed to answer.... Meanwhile, for most women writers, the Ulysses myth has ... remain[ed] essentially external to any central female project" (29).[21]

Can women writers revise the various plots of wandering (in romance, adventure, exploration, and travel narratives) without succumbing to the traditional pitfalls of these plots for a feminine protagonist? Such a question intersects feminist concerns about whether women will "get caught" in their own imitation of patriarchal discourse and myth, unable to repeat with a difference. As Mary Jacobus asks in "The Difference of View," "Can women adapt traditionally male dominated modes of writing and analysis to the articulation of female oppression and desire?" (32). Adding fuel to these anxieties about the appropriateness of adventure for a woman writer/protagonist is a study such as Nerlich's *Ideology of Adventure*. Nerlich examines the ideological uses of adventure from a Marxist perspective but categorically dismisses the idea that women are of much use to adventure or that adventure can be of use to women.[22] Yet women write the mythos of adventure and, more significant, transform it. The gender of the viewer affects the ideology of seeing as well as the tropes projected onto the foreign landscape.[23] Take, for example, Patrick

---

woman is the symbol of change and movement, not rootedness: "Across the sands of all the world, followed by the sun's flaming sword, to the west, trekking to evening lands. She trudges, schlepps, trains, drags, trascines her load. A tide westering, moon-drawn, in her wake" (3:391–93). One can say that this image also figures women in negative terms, as changeable, hence fickle. Here, however, Joyce gives it a twist by making the woman figure the changing tides of language usage, so that the female represents the protean powers of language rather than feminine duplicity or artifice. See Lawrence, *The Odyssey of Style in "Ulysses"* and "Joyce and Feminism."

[21] In *Daisy Miller*, Henry James shows the danger to women when they cross cultural boundaries and are misread by those around them. The question of Daisy's sexuality obsesses the narrative of Winterbourne, an American expatriate who treats the traveling American girl like an anthropological subject of study. One could say that Daisy, her circulation in society subject to crushing suspicion, is one "poetical" subject (as James describes her in his "Preface," 269) who doesn't "translate" well from one culture to another and ultimately dies of the fact.

[22] Nerlich's focus is on class—specifically, the appropriation of one class's myths by another, for example, the bourgeois appropriation of courtly culture as a weapon against the feudal nobility (1:135).

[23] Annette Kolodny discovered in her important research on the pioneer narratives

Brantlinger's description of British conquest: "In British literature from about 1830 to the 1870's, white heroes rarely doubt their ability to tame various geopolitical mistresses—Africa, the sea, the world"—a description that borrows the gendered rhetoric typical of the Victorian period (44). But gender complicates issues of racial and cultural confrontation, altering, for instance, the sexual paradigm of the "penetration" of darkest Africa in the nineteenth century or the sense of the traveler as pioneer in a no-man's-land. Female oppression is itself complicated when the European white woman traveler confronts colonialism's other, sometimes another woman.

In this book I explore, in Nerlich's terms, how the genres, plots, and tropes of travel and adventure have been "useful" for British women writers in supplying a set of alternative models for woman's place in society. These myths or models cohere in an *expansion* of women's sphere and *extension* of their itinerary, that is, they seek both to allot more (and new) territory to women's province and to replace the static mapping of women as space (which we have seen in male configurations of the map of travel) with a more dynamic model of woman as agent, as self-mover. Similarly, travel *writing* has provided discursive space for women, who sometimes left home in order to write home, discovering new aesthetic as well as social possibilities. This metaphor of travel into new territory manifests itself in Sandra Gilbert and Susan Gubar's brief discussion in *No Man's Land* of the relation between women's exploration and an invasion of a no-man's-land that is both geographic and literary, social and aesthetic. (And it influences the study's unwarranted assumption of a correspondence between women's travel to unknown places and their support for women's suffrage.) Indeed, the trope of the journey underwrites utopian impulses within French feminist theory that seek to project an "elsewhere" for women's writing. Cixous and Clément project such a plot in *The Newly Born Woman*. As Sandra Gilbert says in her introduction to the book (relying on the geographic metaphor in the title of her own book on twentieth-century writing), "Like many other women's, her [Clément's] imaginative journeys across the frontier of prohibition

---

of American women that male writers imagined the unknown territory as female, a virgin wilderness to be possessed and tamed, whereas women had a different imaginative response to the foreign, one that did not enact the male desire for possession of the female body. Kolodny focused on actual records of women travelers; my own account includes fictional representations of travel.

are utopian voyages out into a no place that must be a no man's and no woman's land" (xiv).[24] Even experimental writers who mistrust the very notion of the purposeful quest for a destination (about which I say more presently) rely on the trope of crossing borders—often forbidden borders—into new territory. Christine Brooke-Rose says she finds herself "on the frontier of something and I must twist language in some way to pass the frontier, and that's the pleasure" (quoted in Turner, 31).

Travel literature, however, by both men and women writers, explores not only potential freedoms but also cultural constraints; it provides a kind of imaginative resistance to its own plot. In flights of the imagination, as well as on the road, home is, of course, never totally left behind. Indeed, the very search for the new in the literature of travel is itself conventional; in romance, picaresque, adventure, exploration, and ethnography, surprise is expected. That is why travel literature explores a tension between the thrilling possibilities of the unknown and the weight of the familiar, between a desire for escape and a sense that one can never be outside a binding cultural network. Just as more recent work has shown the shadowy (and often repressed) presence of the foreign in domestic fiction, so *Penelope Voyages* explores the way travel writing by women creates a permeable membrane between home and the foreign, domestic confinement and freedom on the road. Both strategies of expansion and those of containment have a certain fragility; even in the more fantastic forms of travel narratives, including proto–science fiction (such as Cavendish's imaginary voyage or Woolf's staging of Orlando's spatial and historical mobility), which would seem most exempt from the demands and contingencies of real travel, a sense of cultural obstacles and blockages seeps in.[25]

[24]See Gillian Brown's discussion of the persistence of an expansionist rhetoric in feminist thought, even French feminism, which ostensibly renounces the rhetoric of possession central to liberal feminism. Her astute remarks occur in an essay on anorexia and the way it literally "embodies the often contradictory connections between consciousness, self-determination, and freedom in the liberal humanist logic of individual entitlement" (191).

[25]The complicated topic of how English domestic fiction either expresses or represses the foreign, including the imperial foreign, is beyond the scope of this book. I refer the reader to the work of Patrick Brantlinger and Ronald Thomas, who have shown how the "exoticism of the colonies" intrudes on domestic literature as "a shadowy realm of escape, renewal, banishment, or return for characters" (Brantlinger, 12) or exotic states of mind (see Thomas). Both critics focus on male examples; Brantlinger, for example, discusses the convention of the male traveler who brings back stories to charm a largely

So, what is the difference of women's writing? Although throughout I resist sweeping statements about generic differences between travel literature by men and that by women, in general, women writers of travel have tended to mistrust the rhetoric of mastery, conquest, and quest that has funded a good deal of male fictional and nonfictional travel. In its various permutations, the *"Odyssey au féminin"* includes a strong sense of the constraints on self-propelled movement and mistrust of the quest and its purposeful destination. Miriam Henderson, Dorothy Richardson's traveling heroine in her thirteen-volume modern novel *Pilgrimage*, thinks of it this way: "A man's job perhaps. Yet to have a distinct end in view endangers both end and means. To know beforehand where you are going is to be going nowhere" (*Dawn's Left Hand*, 4:171–72). Richardson shares with a writer such as D.H. Lawrence both a pilgrim's sense of the importance (even sacredness) of a journey that transfigures one's familiar being and a skepticism of confident blueprints for travel into the unknown. Yet throughout *Pilgrimage* (and in the representation of Miriam's thoughts), she emphasizes the way gender inflects the mistrust of quests and destinations. Again and again in travel writing by women, both fictional and nonfictional, one finds that this skepticism marks the writer's sense of agency, including the agencies of traveler and writer. This awareness, of course, is historically inflected as well—for example, by the potentially conflicting discourses of imperialism and femininity in nineteenth-century women's travel writing analyzed by Sara Mills. Indeed, the trope of travel—whether in its incarnations as exile or adventure, tourism or exploration—provides a particularly fertile imaginative field for narrative representations of women's historical and personal agency. Women travel writers often deconstruct the opposition between activity and passivity, self-willed and compelled movement. From Cavendish's and Burney's representations of the seemingly forced exiles of their heroines to two different assessments of postmodern "mobility" in travel novels by Brooke-Rose and Brophy, these women writers use travel to figure an oscillation be-

female audience. In his work on modernism, Fredric Jameson argues that the formalism of modernist literature emerges from its repression of the world of the colonies. According to Jameson, modern fiction defensively forges aesthetic wholes as a strategy to repress the colonial absences in the text. Finally, critics such as Gayatri Spivak (in "Three Women's Texts") and Benita Parry have focused on the repression of the consciousness of the "subaltern" in a work like *Jane Eyre* and its very different rewriting in Jean Rhys's *Wide Sargasso Sea*.

tween chance and determination, between purposeful itinerary and errancy. Despite differences of historical period and gradations of class, these writers all represent constraints that bind both traveler and travel writer, whether in the romance figure of chance (in Cavendish's imaginary voyage, Woolf's *Orlando*, and Brophy's *In Transit*), the more novelistic representation of social fact (in Burney's *The Wanderer*, Sarah Lee's *The African Wanderers*, Woolf's *The Voyage Out*, or Brooke-Rose's *Between*), or the fidelity to the actual claimed in nonfictional travel narratives such as Wollstonecraft's *Letters Written during a Short Residence in Sweden, Norway, and Denmark* and Kingsley's *Travels in West Africa*.

In accounting for the risks and profits, surprises and accomplishments of travel, these narratives provide for a model of the self that in many cases prefigures the lessons of psychoanalysis and deconstruction: that agency is never entirely self-willed, never purely a question of conscious desire. As will become clear in the first chapter, which focuses on fictions of exile, the ambiguities of agency are explored in the way movement is initiated and continued. To my mind, Paul Fussell's prefatory statement in *The Norton Book of Travel* that "to constitute real travel, movement from one place to another should manifest some impulse of non-utilitarian pleasure" (21) too strictly polices the borders between self-motivated and forced movement, and between use and pleasure. Fussell's generalized treatment of the topos of travel ignores the different cultural freight that the woman traveler may carry.

In choosing a range of imaginative representations of women's foreign travel, I argue that one of the interests of travel literature lies precisely in the flexibility of its cultural images and hybrid forms.[26] Travel can accommodate the ambivalent impulses of Florence Nightingale's radical individualism and her service as handmaiden to the British Empire (the "Angel out of the House," as this image is named by Elizabeth Helsinger, Robin Lauterbach Sheets, and William Veeder [xv]). Nina Auerbach points out that for Victorian spinsters who emigrated, women's travel represented an attempted escape from family (124); in the case of the "sisters of empire," like Anna Buchan (John

---

[26]This flexibility, of course, applies to male as well as female travelers, but because the domestic roles for women were more circumscribed than those for men, the flexibility provided by the topos of travel is more striking and, perhaps, more liberating in women's writing.

Buchan's sister) or Emily Eden, however, it could represent a new filiation of brother and sister abroad, in the larger "family" of British colonial life. It could be antisocial, a lighting out for the territory, or imperialistic, a "mission" undertaken in the service of the state.[27] Suspicious of the entire Enlightenment dynamic of change through foreign travel, Carole Fabricant emphasizes the conservative tendencies of eighteenth-century travel abroad. She says, "Along with the literature (both fictional and nonfictional) that recorded it, [foreign travel] allowed the English to indulge their appetite for the bizarre and the primitive in a 'safe' manner, without its having any necessary effect upon the internal workings of English government and society; it encouraged the illusion of cultural diversity while permitting—indeed, reinforcing—the continued ethnocentricity of English culture" (256-57).

For each of the examples of travel literature in this book, I try to ask the question, What is at stake in the movement of the travel and in the excursion of the writing? What is the relation between personal transformation through travel and social and political order? Victor Turner addresses this issue in his nuanced discussion of the pilgrimage. Turner emphasizes the pilgrim's liberation from "the obligatory everyday constraints of status and role" (207), while acknowledging the social processes involved in the journey itself. The pilgrimage, he says, is a "liminal" experience (i.e., of occupying a threshold space), an "interval between two distinct periods of intensive involvement in structured social existence" (175). He points out that the journey, which in this case is communal, has its own structure, what he terms an "antistructure." In comparing liminars (pilgrims, for example, who deliberately cross thresholds into a different order of experience) with marginals (people habitually on the margins of society, a category in which he includes women in a changed, nontraditional role), Turner observes that the journey for the liminars is a "ritual preceding cultural absorption" and often a "symbolic movement into a higher status," whereas the marginals have "no cultural assurance of a final stable resolution of their ambiguity" (233). Turner's analysis suggests that the question of status intersects that of gender—the rel-

---

[27]The collection *Western Women and Imperialism: Complicity and Resistance*, ed. Nupur Chaudhuri and Margaret Strobel, confirms the spectrum of positions occupied by women travelers vis-à-vis imperialist projects. Essays on Flora Shaw, wife of Lord Lugard, the architect of the British policy of indirect rule in Africa, and Annette Akroyd Beveridge reveal the way some women played a role in legitimizing conquest.

ative position of the traveler in his or her own society affects the significance of the journey undertaken. This issue of the journey's private and public "profit" surfaces, for example, in the story of Rachel Vinrace, the young female traveler in Woolf's first novel, whose trajectory ends in death rather than cultural reabsorption in England, and in the varied political uses made of Mary Kingsley's travel writings on Africa.

In dealing with the various liminal experiences recorded in women's travel literature in the British tradition, in *Penelope Voyages* I embrace a host of genres that make up the hybrid and ambiguous literary kind called the literature of travel. My progression through examples from the seventeenth to the twentieth century liberally crosses boundaries between fiction and nonfiction. Although I do take up differences between the authority of fictional creation and the responsibility of recording actual, contingent experience, I am fundamentally concerned with the way both fictional and nonfictional travel engages the contradictions foregrounded in travel and travel writing, between intention and surprise, authority and adjustment, calculation and risk, and the role and representation of the foreign.

Recent critical work has confirmed the complex relation, both technical and historical, between the categories of fiction and nonfiction in regard to the literature of travel. This work has demonstrated the paradox that it is often the successful use of fictional techniques that establishes ethnographic credibility. Furthermore, critics like Johannes Fabian have shown how technical issues such as the representation of temporality become ideological, inscribing certain relations of power. In a sense, all travel writing, from the imaginary voyage to ethnography, involves what Brigid Brophy calls "those vertical take-off flights directly out of the present into the never-never tense: fictions" (24). And if contemporary ethnography has rigorously explored its own reliance on fiction, recent studies of the novel have likewise stressed the interdependence of fiction and actual travel narratives. Michael McKeon's *Origins of the English Novel*, Percy Adams's *Travel Literature and the Evolution of the Novel*, and William Spengemann's *The Adventurous Muse* all explore the influence of travel literature on the development of the novel. These studies establish the aesthetic and ideological importance of travel literature in the English literary tradition.

More interesting for my purposes, however, than the mutual influences of travel literature and the novel is the way travel literature expresses and represses fundamental anxieties. The search to make it new is crucial to travel writing, from voyages of exploration to tourism. Even voyages of discovery betray anxiety that someone else's marker has preceded the explorer both geographically and textually. Michel Butor cites as itself a kind of writing the voyage of discovery, saying it "demonstrates most strikingly the phenomena of marking and writing. Crosses, monuments, tombs are erected and inscribed. The first thing that Americans do upon walking on the moon is to raise a flag, and no one even dreams of being surprised" (10). The desire to chart the territory inflects both the voyage of discovery and its narrative account. And yet, even if the territory has not actually been colonized, it probably has been in the imagination of the explorer, for the terra incognita may be mapped in literature and myth. As Peter Knox-Shaw demonstrates in *The Explorer in English Fiction*, Columbus's account of the New World was already, in a sense, belated. His description of the mouth of the Orinoco, which he thought to be the entry into Paradise, echoes both the description of Eden in the Bible and the representation of Paradise in *Mandeville's Travels*, books that he took with him on his voyage. If the traveler's footsteps were off the beaten path, the traveler usually was still aware of treading on someone's imaginative territory (1–2).

I make this point because I believe it is misleading to say, as do some nostalgic analyses of adventure, that there is such a thing as wholly "original" travel or travel writing, that there is ever a place from which the sound of echoing footsteps is entirely absent or a scene of writing that doesn't acknowledge a previous scene. As Evelyn Waugh once pointed out, everything is already labeled. The almost desperate attempt in eighteenth-century travel writing to make it new, to find a new angle from which to cast a travel book recognizes that it was getting harder and harder to be first. Walter Bagehot makes the anxiety of influence explicit in his review of Lady Mary Wortley Montagu's *Letters and Works*:

> The second traveller [is] always in terror of the traveller who went before. He fears the criticism,—"this is all very well, *but* we knew the whole of it before. No. 1 said that at page 103." In consequence, he is timid. He picks and skips. He fancies that you are acquainted with all which is great and important, and he dwells, for your good and to your pain, upon that which is small and unimportant. . . . Lady Mary made good use of her position in the front of the herd of tourists. She told us what

she saw in Turkey,—all the best of what she saw, and all the most remarkable things,—and told it very well. (221)

Bagehot may well be projecting a nineteenth-century anxiety onto the
eighteenth century, for as Buzard points out, it was only in the mid-
nineteenth century, when Cook's Tours made travel available for the
masses, that the distinction between traveler and tourist became significant (109–10). Yet his remarks underscore the relationship between
the traveler's quest to be different from other travelers and the travel
writer's anxieties of belatedness. The mistrust of crass tourism might
be viewed as an intensification of the anxiety of influence that marks
all travel writing.

Indeed, countless nineteenth-century English travelers to the Continent searching for the sublime with *Childe Harold's Pilgrimage* in hand
or Americans carrying *The Marble Faun* to Rome are only two examples of the way fictional travel impinges on actual travel. Much travel
writing self-consciously places itself in a tradition with aesthetic fore-
bears, a tradition of mixed parentage of travel narrative and fiction.
W. H. Auden and Louis MacNeice begin their own generic hybrid,
Letters from Iceland, with a letter/poem to Lord Byron, their precursor
as poet and traveler. Lady Montagu read with enormous pleasure
Mrs. Lennox's *The Female Quixote*, itself, of course, a rewriting. Sybille
Bedford's *A Sudden View*, a twentieth-century novel about the narrator's trip to Mexico, quotes many passages from Madame Calderon
de la Barca's *Life in Mexico*, a travel book the narrator takes along to
read, consciously eschewing Prescott's more famous narrative of Cor-
tez's exploits. George Eliot leaves England with George Henry Lewes
and writes that she is taking off for "La Bassecour" (the fictional Bel-
gian city of Brontë's *Villette*). And, as the following quotation from
Byron's Letters and Journals suggests, almost everyone who set sail for
unknown parts felt the ancestral presence of Defoe's traveler: "By this
time tomorrow evening we shall be embarked on the vide world of
vaters vor all the world like Robinson Crusoe" (208). Indeed, Frances
Burney refers to her woman protagonist in *The Wanderer* as "a female
Robinson Crusoe" (836). *Penelope Voyages* tracks the way travel literature by women engages this fundamental sense of belatedness and
the question of literary appropriation.

Whatever the particular genres or models of travel literature, in the
discussion here I explore the links between the itinerary of the sign
and the traveler, between travel as reading and writing and writing

as travel.[28] Rather than a typology of travel literature genres, then, this study is more in keeping with what Butor has called an "iterology of travel," focusing, that is, on the various types of "conversations with culture" in which travel writing engages. In making the reading and writing of culture their central concern, travel narratives allow for a demystification of both cultural and literary conventions for representing the self and the other. Transferred to a new semiotic network, the traveler is a sign to be deciphered and a reader and writer of signs. One could say that the semiotic stakes are raised by travel and travel writing, for the transfer of meaning across cultural and often national boundaries means that what might be regarded as a "natural" construction of subjectivity and objectivity in a domestic setting is now staged in the mode of self-conscious confrontation and interrogations of cultural convention. A cultural exaggeration occurs, an emphasis added. In his *Letters from Iceland*, Auden describes this process of cultural defamiliarization in jaunty couplets:

> Now home is miles away, and miles away
> No matter who, and I am quite alone
> And cannot understand what people say,
> But like a dog must guess it by the tone;
> At any language other than my own
> I'm no great shakes, and here I've found no tutor
> Nor sleeping lexicon to make me cuter. (16)

But if the male poet breezily captures the loss of linguistic and cultural security that attends foreign travel, I want to close this chapter with an example of a woman's more frightening, if still exhilarating, crossing of borders, in travel and in writing. Charlotte Brontë's *Villette* functions as almost an allegory of both the promise and the risks of the voyage out from domestic fiction set in England, a rewriting of *Jane Eyre* in a foreign key.[29] The first hundred pages of the novel, set

[28]Individual discussions of texts do address the genres and conventions of travel writing, both fictional and nonfictional. The spectrum of examples includes anthropology and ethnography at the nonfictional, "scientific" pole (Kingsley); nonfictional travel writing (Wollstonecraft); the realistic novel (Burney, and Woolf's *The Voyage Out*); the adventure novel (Lee); romance and imaginary voyage (Cavendish, Woolf's *Orlando*); and the adventures of the signifier in postmodern fantasy (Brophy) and fiction (Brooke-Rose) at the opposite pole of fictionality.

[29]The movement out from England in *Villette* seems to address the unsatisfied yearnings with which Brontë ends *Jane Eyre*. By this I refer not to the madwoman in the attic, about whom Gilbert and Gubar have written eloquently, but to the novel's lingering

in England, offer the domestic as a kind of annihilating setting, as the narrative increasingly robs Lucy Snowe of her ability to signify, to mark her place. Unlike Jane Eyre, who moves from orphan to governess to lady, Lucy Snowe loses rather than gains ground in England. Her journey to Brussels is both her and the narrative's attempt to enhance her narratability, to give her a story worth telling. In a sense, *Villette* stages the necessity of a voyage out of the domestic novel, as if the centripetal impulse of the genre threatened to collapse the narrative, causing it to cave in on itself as around a black hole.

As she lands in Labassecour, Lucy's habitual sense that she is powerless and inarticulate is intensified. As an English girl in Belgium, she is literally deprived of her language. Her situation is emblematic: she is the image of the powerless female, without the keys to the culture or the power of its privileged discourse. After losing her luggage as well as her language, Lucy is forced to appeal to a young, good-looking Englishman who can converse both in French and, as Lucy puts it, in "the Fatherland accents" (123). When he speaks to and guides her, Lucy's response is, "I should almost as soon have thought of distrusting the Bible" (124). Travel alters the terms of the traveler's role as both reader and text. On the one hand, Lucy's silence and anonymity are increased in this strange land as is the threat of annihilating loneliness; on the other hand, both as decoder and as sign she is animated into more active existence. Lucy, the foreigner, is likely to be scrutinized, to be "read" by others, and to impress them with her foreign character. The spying, reading, and decoding that are the major activities conducted at Madame Beck's give Lucy greater existence and power, as interpreter and as sign; yet as the semiotic stakes increase in the foreign country, Lucy is likely to misread and to be misread. The novel traces Lucy's increasing ability to signify as writer and traveler. Still an unlikely and reluctant heroine by novel's end, Lucy, like Penelope, takes her place in the dual "theoretical position" of traveler and signatory of the discourse, discovering in her voyage out from England a new language of passion in which to inscribe her own desire.

---

interest in the missionary St. John Rivers, who voyages out to India. It is he on whom the epilogue focuses, even after Jane Eyre has resoundingly (and rightly) rejected his offer of marriage. Rivers is Jane's surrogate here, the traveler who actualizes the excursive possibilities of her imagination. For a fuller discussion of Lucy Snowe's travel in *Villette*, see Lawrence, "The Cypher: Disclosure and Reticence in *Villette*."

1

Exilic Wanderings:
Cavendish and Burney

If travel is a potent metaphor for the imagination's access to an else-where, exile introduces the alibi of necessity, an estrangement from home initiated by circumstances beyond the traveler's control. We begin the study of women's travel and adventure in the British literary tradition with two fictions of exile in which reluctant heroines are propelled into the world of adventure, when the security of "home" is destroyed— by civil war, in the case of Margaret Cavendish's imaginary voyage, "Assaulted and Pursued Chastity" (1656), and by the French Revolution, in the case of Frances Burney's novel *The Wanderer; Or, Female Difficulties* (1814). In both fictions, personal wandering is linked to national fate, although the English Civil War is only a shadowy topical allusion in the undifferentiated space-time of Cavendish's romance geography, whereas the French Revolution is a significant part of the Real in the more verisimilar space-time of Burney's novel. Both fictions were in fact produced under the painful conditions of exile caused by war: Cavendish, later the duchess of Newcastle, along with other English nobility, spent the interregnum in Antwerp; Burney, or Madame D'Arblay, spent more than ten years in France during the war between England and France. In both fictions, "home" is no longer hospitable, and the protagonist is catapulted into the realm of adventure, a refugee at the mercy of her host's hospitality. As emphasized in the title of Burney's novel and the name of Cavendish's protagonist, Travelia, travel and travail are particularly linked when it is women who wander far from home, attempting to uphold their virtue.[1] The preamble to Cavendish's tale might serve

---

[1] This topos of the unfortunate female traveler differs from the narrative tradition famously named by Nashe's *Unfortunate Traveller*, in which Jack Wilton eventually dis-

both fictions as a cautionary preface about the dangers of female travel: "Virtuous Women, if they wander alone, find but very often rude entertainment from the Masculine Sex, witness Jacob's Daughter Dinah which Shechem forced" (394–95). The biblical allusion suggests a link between female wandering and a transgression of boundaries (the Hebrews are in Canaan when the violation occurs) as well as between the fate of a woman and that of a nation.

These treacherous paths, however, occasion ingenuity on the part of the fleeing protagonist, manifested in physical disguises and rhetorical persuasiveness. As a strategy of survival, both female protagonists travel incognito, Cavendish's heroine Travelia cross-dresses as a male page and then a male warrior, and Burney's "Incognita" (as she is called) first appears in the novel in ragged clothes, with a patch over her eye, made up to appear scarred and dark-skinned. Although I've focused on the pain involved when women travel, the projection of the heroine into a new place, however fraught with danger, is in itself an opportunity to imagine new possibilities, new relationships of power and authority. In his study *Exile and the Narrative Imagination*, Michael Seidel says that "in the exilic plot the extraneous becomes foundational, the blighted and ill-fated from one sphere become instigators and originators in another. The powers of exilic imagining represent desired territory, lost or found, as narrative fate" (8). Seidel's comment comes closer to describing Aeneas than Travelia or Incognita; indeed, the posture of the two female exilic travelers seems more reactive than foundational. Yet, in Cavendish's appropriation of the genre of the romancelike "imaginary voyage" and Burney's picaresque revision of *Robinson Crusoe*, both writers exploit the alibi of exile to lay some claim to the "desired territory" in Seidel's description. The topos of exile provides fictional opportunity to explore new forms of women's agency and power.[2]

---

covers that travel is supererogatory when everything to satisfy desire can be found at home. As an older and wiser man asks Wilton: "Countryman, tell me, what is the occasion of thy straying so far out of England to visit this strange nation? If it be languages, thou may'st learn them at home; nought but lasciviousness is to be learned here. Perhaps, to be better accounted of than other of thy condition, thou ambitiously undertakest this voyage: these insolent fancies are but Icarus' feathers, whose wanton wax, melted against the sun, will betray thee into a sea of confusion" (341). Cavendish does write a tale that could be classified as belonging to the "antitravel" tradition of Nashe's narrative, but "The Tale of a Traveller," which immediately follows Travelia's story, involves male rather than female travel.

[2]For a critical examination of the trope of exile in contemporary feminist discourse, see Caren Kaplan, "Deterritorializations: The Rewriting of Home and Exile in Western

Margaret Cavendish (1623–73), one of the earliest English women writers to rewrite the plot of adventure *au féminin*, hardly seems a candidate for the description "blighted and ill-fated." As a woman from a well-to-do family who married the Marquis of Newcastle, she possessed both social and financial security, without which the publication of her writings would have been exceedingly difficult.[3] Indeed, the talented Cavendish was the most prolific and best-published woman writer of her day, disseminating her poems, letters, essays, plays, and natural philosophy. Her status enabled her to meet many of the finest scientific and literary minds around, and although her natural philosophy was, for the most part, disparaged by others engaged in scientific inquiry, she was the first woman to be invited to attend a meeting of the Royal Society.

Despite Cavendish's privileged position, she experienced very keenly the paucity of active, public roles for women. In an epistle to the Universities of Oxford and Cambridge, she wrote that women "are kept like birds in cages, to hop up and down in our houses, not suffered to fly abroad to see the several changes of fortune and the various humours ordained and created by nature" (Grant, 214). Not surprisingly, movement serves as a metaphor for freedom and the satisfaction of intellectual curiosity. Yet, paradoxically, movement at home is also the sign of women as agitated, almost hysterical in their domestic confinement, separated as most were from the world of intellectual as well as physical exploration. The "security" of domesticity produces its opposite—agitation and movement, a phenomenon also explored by Montaigne in his essay "Of Idleness": "And there is no mad or idle fancy that [idle minds] do not bring forth in this agitation" (21). Thus movement is a complex figure for Cavendish that deconstructs the simple opposition between stability "at home" and the uncertainty of a journey into the unknown.

In the prefatory materials that introduce her various writings, Cavendish herself presents the "errancy" of her prolific writings as a re-

Feminist Discourse." I argue that for Cavendish and Burney, exile provides both a general metaphor for a woman's homelessness and a plotted terrain of specific cross-cultural encounters.

[3]In "Women's Published Writings, 1600–1700," Patricia Crawford points out that women of aristocratic and gentry origin could pay for publication, whereas other women could not (214).

sponse to the social and imaginative constraints placed on women. For example, in the preface to *Natures Pictures Drawn by Fancies Pencil to the Life*, the collection in which her imaginary voyage "Assaulted and Pursued Chastity" appears, Cavendish excuses her prolixity in the following manner: "That my ambition of extraordinary Fame, is restless, and not ordinary, I cannot deny: and since all Heroick Actions, Publick Employments, as well Civil as Military, and Eloquent Pleadings, are deni'd my Sex in this Age, I may be excused for writing so much; for that is the Reason I have run, more busily than industriously, upon every Subject I can think of." Her ambition is "restless," not merely "uneasy" but (according to the *Oxford English Dictionary*) "continually moving or operating, never ceasing or pausing." Domestic retirement induces discursiveness, even ec-centricity (as in its root meaning of a movement out from the center). Prolixity both mirrors and serves as outlet for excess energy; it functions as both symptom and as strategy. Although the image is defensive—she "excuses" her writing by invoking the self-deprecatory concept of flightiness—Cavendish also implies that the busy bee might be a gadfly that disturbs intellectual complacency. Invention is born of necessity. The volumes of her work on a vast range of topics in almost every available genre—poetry, story, philosophical and scientific treatise, letters, and drama—suggest a kind of unchanneled pleasure in "running on." Virginia Woolf, who wrote the first feminist essay on the duchess, says of her writings: "There they stand, in the British Museum, volume after volume, swarming with a diffused, uneasy, contorted vitality" (83). It's as if this errant, diffuse textual body cannot even be contained within the authoritative shelves of the venerated patriarchal institution.

"The danger raised by idleness is that of the loss of one's bearings, that is to say, the loss of the property or properness of the *oikos*" (the Greek for "home" from which "economy" is derived), Georges Van Den Abbeele comments in *Travel as Metaphor from Montaigne to Rousseau* (14). Paradoxically, in the case of Cavendish, flamboyant, excursive writing (and publication, which circulates this writing abroad to readers) becomes a strategy to recuperate the "property" lost in the dispossessing idleness of home. This recuperation under the signature of the author is a form of compensation, a mastery that enables creation of a new space, a new world of words. In some of her prefatory writings where she addresses the reader, Cavendish emphasizes this process of writing as mastery. In her address "To All Noble and Worthy Ladies," which prefaces the utopian fiction *The Description of a New*

World, Called the Blazing-World, Cavendish speaks of authoring as an establishment of just such an authority as she has been denied: "Though I cannot be Henry the Fifth, or Charles the Second, yet I will endeavour to be Margaret the First; and although I have neither power, time, nor occasion, to conquer the world as Alexander and Caesar did; yet rather than not to be Mistress of one, since Fortune and the Fates would give me none, I have made a World of my own."

In her article on the politics of the female subject in the seventeenth century, Catherine Gallagher emphasizes the connection between the topoi of exile and dispossession and an absolutist, monarchical view of the power of authorship. Gallagher sees an important imaginative link between the exiled monarch Charles II, "himself the ruler of a kind of fantasy kingdom," and the private woman, the "site of true sovereignty" (29). "During the years when the Cavendishes, like the rest of the English court, were exiled in France and Holland, Charles II . . . [t]he real king had become the ruler of what amounted to a microcosm, had almost been reduced to a private kingdom, and hence had practically enacted the metaphorical equivalence of sovereign monarch and sovereign private person. . . . The monarch in the interregnum, then, serves as a convenient historical pivot for a metaphoric reversal in Cavendish's work: the private woman, completely retired, turns into a figure for the emperor" (29).[4]

But I have argued that property and authority are linked to an eccentricity and excursiveness in Cavendish's self-representations rather than to monarchic self-rule. This excursiveness materializes in the narrative trajectory of her imaginary voyage. The utopian mapping of a new world that Gallagher explores in Cavendish's *Description of a New World, Called the Blazing-World* represses this fascination with movement and risk that is, to my mind, one of Cavendish's most characteristic enactments of writing as a form of travel. This delight in movement, as I have noted, is a feature of Cavendish's textual corpus as a whole. For example, John Rogers points out that it is crucial to

---

[4]Cavendish's poetic preface to the collection *Natures Pictures Drawn by Fancies Pencil to the Life* (hereafter cited as *Natures Pictures*) illustrates the way the court's banishment from England could provide a metaphor for a surrogate court of the literary imagination, a sympathetic audience whom the author could summon into being in her writings: "Yet Banishment to my dear Lord, was then / A dangerous Rock, made of hard-hearted men. / And hearing of such dangers in my way, / I was content in Antwerp for to stay; / And in the Circle of my Brain to raise / The Figures of my Friends crowned with Praise."

Cavendish's natural philosophy, in which problems of historical and personal agency and action emerge "as the scientific categories of impulsion and motion" (217).[5] In Cavendish's use of the imaginary voyage, however, a hybrid genre of travel narrative that combines conventions from allegory, romance, and utopian fiction, risky movement serves as the master trope.[6] This form, fictional and fantastic, enabled her to explore problems of women's agency and authority in the intricacies of the plot of movement, both forced and self-propelled.

In the long tale "Assaulted and Pursued Chastity," forced exile from a war-torn mythical country, the Kingdom of Riches, propels the young Travelia into a romance geography full of adventures. She finds herself in the Land of Sensuality, where she encounters a prince who threatens to rape her. Using her wits and a stolen gun, Travelia eludes him. Realizing she must disguise herself to evade assaults on her chastity, she dons the clothes of a male page, boards a ship bound for "new Discoveries towards the South" (418), and the heart of the imaginary voyage begins, as she travels to different islands full of an extraordinary mixture of peoples, social organizations, beasts, and plants. On the way, she befriends an old man who treats her like a son. Adventures ensue, culminating in Travelia's service as commander of the queen's forces in the Land of Amity against the more powerful army of a king, led by none other than the prince who has searched for Travelia since she escaped from him. The tale ends with the unmasking of Travelia as a woman and the subsequent marriages of king and queen and Travelia and the regenerate prince.

The tale suggests an alternative to Gallagher's view of Cavendish's autotelic absolutism—a more mobile, improvisational imagination displayed by exiled heroine and author. This exilic voyage, with its romance wanderings through space, engenders for its protagonist and its author alike both mastery and surprise, imaginative projection and response to contingency. In the heroine's responsiveness to the workings of chance, the opposition between passivity and activity and between hapless victimization and absolute control is deconstructed— enforced movement occasions action, intentional movement produces surprise. I use the term "improvisation" to specify qualities that are

[5]In "New Castles in the Air: Margaret Cavendish and the Ethics of Self-Motion," Rogers discusses the analogy between the role of physical motion in Cavendish's natural philosophy and her ideas on the social motion of human beings.
[6]See Philip Babcock Gove's *Imaginary Voyage in Prose Fiction* for the most extensive treatment of this genre, which reached its height of popularity in the eighteenth century.

both generic and historical-political. For improvisation is both a persistent feature of the genre of romance, whose protagonists must respond to the workings of chance with wit and agility, and what Stephen Greenblatt identifies as the hallmark of the emerging mobile modern personality (*Renaissance Self-Fashioning*, 227). Travelia in "Assaulted and Pursued Chastity" displays a craftiness that is not only an aspect of romance inventiveness—the traveler as Hermes the trickster—but also a more distinctly modern improvisational ability that allows her to respond to circumstances on the road and to capitalize on what fortune throws her way.[7] Greenblatt shows how this improvisation is linked historically to the exercise of power in England's imperialist expansion and how physical mobility translated into a "mobile" personality (I will return to this point later). Thus, in using the topos of exilic wandering, Cavendish explores the link between imagination and power in various cultural encounters, verbal and physical, between the traveler and her antagonists. Although Cavendish creates a landscape of the mind, thereby eliminating the contingencies of real travel, her fictions build in obstacles to the mind shaping its own desires. Gallagher's stress on the private, autotelic domain of female subjectivity and metaphoric sovereignty of authorship potentially short-circuits Cavendish's representations of the workings of power in cultural confrontation, thereby muting the more extroverted, social interests in Cavendish's fictions of exile and exploration.

Thus the improvisation of the explorer, rather than the creation *ex nihilo* of the godlike monarch of the imagination, provides a more appropriate model for the traveling protagonist of Cavendish's imaginary voyage and a more general metaphor for the flexibility of a writing in which accommodation is the form of power. Cavendish takes what she inherits of cultural traditions and improvises; specifically, she refashions gender roles and limitations (and, to a lesser extent, explores the imperialist encounter when the traveler is female), and reappropriates romance conventions to alter the mostly passive role of women in romance. As Elaine Hobby points out, Cavendish was not alone among women writers of the period in improvising on

---

[7]See Northrop Frye's *Secular Scripture: A Study of the Structure of Romance* for a description of the importance of craft and guile (or *froda*) over force as the "animating spirit" of the comic romance form. Frye associates this *froda* with female craft and deception in the romance (67–72).

established tradition. Lady Mary Wroth and Anna Weamys rewrote male romances, particularly Sidney's *Arcadia*; eschatological and prophetic writings of women, particularly during the interregnum, display a similar fascination with radically different "worlds"—if not "elsewhere," then in England in the future. I want to suggest both that Cavendish is not anomalous in her improvisations and yet that she made eccentricity and excursiveness hallmarks of self-presentation and governing tropes in her work. Although improvisation and eccentricity are not synonymous, they are linked in Cavendish's work in the topos of wandering—improvisation suggests the more conscious, strategic elements of this mental and physical movement; eccentricity suggests a deliberate deviation from the customary but also the possibility that wandering brings genuine surprises, not fully under the traveler's control.

Just how much of a departure from tradition Cavendish's work represents is itself a concern the duchess reiterates in the rather anxious discourses that frame her writing. In constructing her work as property that offsets her dispossession, she insists, for example, in the frontispiece to *Natures Pictures*, that the reader should "Then read those Lines which Shee [Cavendish] hath writt, / By Phancy's Pencill drawne alone / Which Piece but Shee, can justly owne." Indeed, in her preface to *Natures Pictures*, she maintains that she has read neither much history nor romance: "Though some of these Stories be Romancical, I would not be thought to delight in Romances, having never read a whole one in my life." Despite these disclaimers and their representation of an absolute geographical separation between her world of words and the rest of literary tradition, the boundary between what is hers and what is their territory is repeatedly put into question. The characterization of the duchess in the frontispiece of *Natures Pictures* contradicts her contention of originality, for it represents her in a toga, flanked by Apollo on one side and Minerva on the other. Is she associated with the apparently self-sufficient, generative energy of Apollo, or is she better understood as an avatar of Minerva, subtly resourceful and creative but defined by the fact that she has sprung, fully formed, from the male brain of Jupiter? In an epistle that precedes his wife's preface to *Natures Pictures*, the duke figures the duchess's writing as perceived by men to be a kind of territorial intrusion into the male province of literature. Male readers, he hopes, will not fear that the woman who writes "does strive / T'intrench too much on Man's prerogative." Even imaginary travel for a woman is a form of trespass, for heretofore the imaginary voyage as a genre had been almost entirely a male province.[8]

In the romance geography of "Assaulted and Pursued Chastity," the civil war serves metaphorically to introduce the uncertain boundaries between invasion and excursion, home and the foreign, peaceful property and usurped territory. Cavendish's heroine is forced to leave her home, the Kingdom of Riches, after the body of the state becomes diseased when "Feverish Ambition" breaks out "into a Plaguy Rebellion, killing numbers with the Sword of Unjust Warr; which made many flye from that Pestilent Destruction, into other Countreys" (395). Interestingly, it is the women and children who are expelled from this diseased body by the husbands and fathers: the men who choose to stay rather than flee to another country "sent their Daughters and Wives from the Fury of the Inhuman Multitude; chusing to venture their Lives with the hazzards of Travels, rather than their Honours and Chastities, by staying at home amongst rough and rude Soldiers" (395–96). The syntax of the sentence is confusing (what is the subject of the verb "staying"?), but the line suggests that it is the *men* who choose to hazard the lives, rather than the chastity, of their women. We are meant, of course, to see this as a topical allusion to the forced exile of aristocrats such as the Cavendishes precipitated by the unjust Civil War. In addition, the expulsion of women from the arena of the action suggests a dispossession based as much on gender as on class.[9]

---

[8]One has only to consult Gove's index for confirmation.

[9]In the eleventh section of *Natures Pictures*, titled "A True Relation of My Birth, Breeding, and Life," the duchess describes the effect of the Civil War on herself and her husband. The dispossession of women in particular is more directly articulated in Cavendish's play *Bell in Campo*, in which Lady Victoria addresses her army of women: "But the Masculine Sex hath separated us, and cast us out of their Companyes, either out of their loving care and disire of preserving our lives and liberties, lest we might be distroyed in their confusions, or taken Prisoners in their loss, or else it must be out of jealousy we should Eclipse the fame of their valours with the splendor of our constancy. . . . besides, those women that have staid at home will laugh at us in our return, and their effeminate Lovers . . . will make Lampoons of us for them to sing of our disgrace, saying, our Husbands, Lovers, and Friends were so weary of us, as they were forced to take that pretence of affectionate love to be rid of our Companyes; wherefore if you will take my advise, let us return, and force those that sent us away to consent that we shall be partakers with them, and either win them by perswasions, or lose our selves by breaking their decrees" (quoted in Moira Ferguson, 326). Crawford points out that during the war many women did take on increasing responsibilities as male family members traveled with the war: "With husbands, fathers and sons away fighting or in exile, women were defenders of their homes, petitioners for estates and generally responsible for their families' survival" (213). In both *Bell in Campo* and "Assaulted and

Yet the grammatical ambiguity is potentially revealing—although the grammar indicates the male subject, the sense would suggest the opposite. We teeter between male and female agency, as if this strange construction poised the adventure somewhere between travel and exile (self-determined and forced).

Both the sudden outbreak of war and the equally abrupt restoration of peace are effected in typical romance fashion—products not of political and social events but of chance.[10] Travelia tries desperately to return to the restored patriarchy at home, but "fortune" prevents it. Her life becomes one of wandering and exile; her chastity is threatened and her virtue tested. Thus begins a tale of the specifically "female difficulties" associated with wandering; a century and a half later, Frances Burney would conjoin these notions in the title of her novel *The Wanderer; or, Female Difficulties.*

The motif of exile yokes adventure to necessity; if Travelia engages in adventures that only men usually encounter, it is because her situation is dire and her physical survival depends on it. It is true that the necessity to provide an alibi for adventure is not confined to women writers; as John Richetti has pointed out, in the most compelling exilic narrative of the next century, *Robinson Crusoe,* forced exile provides opportunities for self-assertion and creativity *and* an excuse for exercising such powers. Defoe, in other words, needs to rationalize Crusoe's will to power by allying it with necessity, to channel the restlessness that landed him on the desolate island in the first place into productive ingenuity ("Robinson Crusoe," 209). The situation of exile, despite its trauma, provides fictional capital. But the need to *disguise* self-assertion and will to power which Richetti finds in Defoe and which Martin Green finds in adventure stories from the late seventeenth century on applies doubly for a woman writer. For the injunction to silence and modesty, so essential a part of the behavior prescribed for seventeenth-century women, militated against self-assertion in action and in the recording of action. Even in the genre of romance, which has a tradition of female authors (in the French romances, in particular, which were read by many of the seventeenth-century women writers) and was, as a genre, receptive to

---

Pursued Chastity," the abjection of the women is strongly suggested, despite the narrator/speaker's seeming acceptance of the protective intentions of men.

[10]See Bakhtin's discussion of early Greek romance in "Forms of Time and of the Chronotope in the Novel" in *The Dialogic Imagination* (84–130).

female heroines, the protagonist was expected to "carry out her tactics in low profile, that is, behave with due modesty" (Frye, 79). One could say that Cavendish conforms to this dictate to the extent that the title of the tale and a number of incidents emphasize the involuntary aspect of Travelia's travels—she runs from her lascivious pursuers rather than to a new land. And, as in many romances, the preservation of virginity propels the plot; the story promises to end if this virginity is violated before the tale concludes in the conventional marriage. Yet, of love and adventure, the two chief elements of romance, the latter rather than the former occupies the space of Cavendish's narrative.[11] It's as if consummation of the love interest were deferred to enable the plot of ambition and adventure to be written. The narrative has less to do with keeping sexuality under wraps, as the title implies, than with cloaking female ambition. The ostensible plot, with its emphasis on maintaining the heroine's chastity until the major love interest in the story develops satisfactorily, enables the plot of ambition to be written.[12] Travelia's tale is a "cautionary tale" because women's reputations need the protection of fathers and husbands, as Cavendish knew. Yet, out of the exigencies of exile, Travelia is forced to adapt, to change, to take on authority. Like her creator, whose exile seems to have fueled her desire for self-inscription, Travelia's sudden propulsion out of one land of conflict into others unleashes her imagination. With all the hardships and near disasters Travelia suffers, it is clear that Cavendish's exuberant writing is intoxicated with the possibilities of adventure and power for her heroine.

Cavendish, then, writes a narrative that is thoroughly conventional in its reliance on what M. M. Bakhtin calls the space-time chronotope of early romance, which adapts "adventure-time," a "highly intensified but undifferentiated" time (90) in which contingency reigns. As such, it draws heavily on the expected motifs of romance: chance occurrences and meetings in time and space—abductions, flight, storms, shipwrecks, pirates, miraculous rescues, disguises, recognitions, and failures of recognition. The action of the plot, according to Bakhtin, "unfolds against a very broad and varied geographical background. . . . There are descriptions, often very detailed, of specific features of countries, cities, structures of various kinds . . . the habits and customs

---

[11]See Frye's generic discussion of these two elements of romance in *The Secular Scripture* (24–26).

[12]See Nancy Miller's "Emphasis Added: Plots and Plausibilities in Women's Fiction."

of the population, various exotic and marvelous animals and other wonders and rarities. . . . Large portions of these novels are taken up with speeches of the characters—relevant or otherwise" (88). In these early Greek romances, which Bakhtin argues provided a model for many romances up through the eighteenth century, the love plot structures the narrative in providing its beginning and end. Lovers meet, are separated, and finally reunite.

Surprise is expected in romance, and improvisation—response to contingency—is a necessity. Yet Cavendish innovates on these topoi through gender reversals. The war that turns the world upside down at the beginning of the story seems almost a mild reversal compared with those generated as Travelia travels to unknown and fantastic "elsewheres" where powers are reassigned. Although Travelia is initially "like a Ship at Sea that is not anchored nor ballasted, or with Storm tost from Point to Point" (402), her adventures increasingly put her in positions of authority, mostly over men, and the love plot itself has little importance. On the contrary, Travelia's most important relationships are with the old man she encounters while she is disguised as a young male page—he virtually adopts her as a son and they participate in adventures together—and with cannibals, pirates, even fantastic purple people who live in what seem like gingerbread houses. The other significant same-sex relationship occurs in the last and most important episode of the story, in a land where two rival male and female kingdoms are separately governed by a king and queen in battle with each other because she has refused his love. The prince who has pursued Travelia throughout the story is the chief commander of the king's army, and Travelia, still dressed as a young man, helps defend the queen, who falls in love with her, thinking that she is a he. It is this charged relationship with the queen that supplies most of the final episode's interest.

Cavendish's treatment of these episodes constitutes an exception to the androcentric model in Northrop Frye's description of "the exciting adventures" in romance, which are "normally a foreplay leading up to a sexual union" (24). In Cavendish's appropriation, however, one might say the foreplay is all. This erotics of narrative, however, runs the risk of obscuring the "nonfrictional" homosocial patterns in the text. Although the potential assault on Travelia's sexual purity propels the plot until the desired "love match" allows for lawful intercourse, single-sex bonding seems to suit Travelia just fine (in the platonic "male-male" relationship with Travelia's sidekick in adventures, his/

her adopted father, and the "female-female" relationship with the queen). Indeed, the bond between adopted father and son and that between warrior queen and woman warrior suggest alternative ways of conceiving relationship other than heterosexual love.

The strategy of cross-dressing is crucial to this enterprise. First as male page, then as warrior, Travelia's cross-dressing enables her not only to elude her pursuers but also to shape events by assuming power. Travelia's masquerade allows her both to enter and to control certain patriarchal spaces and to elude, for the duration of this serious game, the structures governing sexual identity. One could say that by means of this romance topos of cross-dressing, Cavendish smuggles her heroine into the genre of adventure, just as the heroine smuggles herself in drag onto the ship bound for unknown parts. In this way Cavendish's seventeenth-century imaginary voyage becomes a fitting emblem for the cross-gendering aspect of adventure and adventure writing—to write and to live adventure was to make an incursion into a no-man's-land, to play the role of a man. Travelia becomes a woman warrior, a peacemaker, a speechmaker, an explorer and discoverer, a female Odysseus by virtue of a transvestite masquerade. Cross-dressing thereby displaces and transposes the ordeals of Travelia's chastity into judicial and rhetorical trials more common to male protagonists of romance. As many commentators have observed, cross-dressing in early romance is predominantly concerned with the main erotic plot; it is impelled by the heroine's desire to seek out her lover or remain faithful to him in the face of rival suitors.[13] Cavendish's use of cross-dressing precipitates a gender confusion more concerned with issues of power than love, at least until the relationship with the queen combines them.

The climactic episodes in the Land of Amity combine complications

---

[13]In *The Secular Scripture* (78), Frye discusses this topos, and in *Still Harping on Daughters: Women and Drama in the Age of Shakespeare,* Lisa Jardine comments on Shakespearean comedy and its sources. Remarking on the use of the topos of the male page in Shakespearean sources such as Barnaby Riche's tale "Of Apollonius and Silla" and Thomas Lodge's *Rosalynde,* Jardine notes the relation between gender and class: "In each of these tales a virtuous woman adopts male disguise (the disguise of a page or serving lad) out of loyalty to lover or husband, to escape an unlooked for sexual affront at home. . . . The loyal woman preserves her 'chaste' self by transposing female dependency into male dependency: page instead of wife or daughter. In this guise she manages to retain her attractive submissiveness, whilst engaging in fantasy 'adventures' which culminate in her triumphantly revealing her true self (and sex) to the beloved, and being reinstated as loving spouse" (24–25).

of cross-dressing with the topos of the woman warrior in an exploration of female power and authority. As much work on sixteenth-century romance and ballad traditions has revealed, the motif of the Amazon warrior occupies a place in travel narratives as well as in literature of the period.[14] According to Percy Adams, the episode in Cavendish's tale involving the rival kingdoms was probably based on a story Columbus passed on about an island "inhabited only by Amazons, who mate annually with the inhabitants of another island inhabited only by men" (116). Louis Montrose says that sixteenth-century travel narratives "often recreate the ancient Amazons of Scythia in South America or in Africa. Invariably, the Amazons are relocated just within the receding boundary of *terra incognita*." (66). Montrose goes on to discuss the Amazon mythology as symbolically embodying and controlling "a collective anxiety about the power of the female not only to dominate or reject the male but to create and destroy him" ("Shaping Fantasies," 66). The "collective anxiety" here seems largely male.

What happens when a woman writer uses a topos that expresses male cultural anxieties about female power? How does she or can she transform these narratives of anxiety into protofeminist representations of female authority and power? If a mixture of fascination and horror led male imaginations to banish Amazon culture to the boundary between the known and the unknown, in her version of female sovereignty Cavendish displaces the barbarism associated with the Amazon story onto other elements of her tale. (In naming the Land of Amity, she retains the first syllable of Amazon, suppressing the potentially more threatening representations of female sovereignty and aggression.) The more terrifying aspects of the Amazon legends, such as women's cannibalizing young boys, are split off in Cavendish's tale, displaced onto other islands where Travelia encounters cannibals. In the Land of Amity, female aggressiveness is portrayed as a response to male threat—it is couched in the mode of self-defense (although there is a hint that the queen of Amity doesn't need or is not interested in the king of the rival community, perhaps ultimately a bigger threat to sexual politics than the sex war that is represented).

[14]See Dianne Dugaw's *Warrior Women and Popular Balladry* and Julie Wheelwright's *Amazons and Military Maids: Women Who Dressed as Men in the Pursuit of Life, Liberty, and Happiness.* For a fascinating discussion of the complex significance of the figure of the Amazon in eighteenth-century literature, see Laura Brown, "Africans and Amazons: Gender, Race, and Empire in Daniel Defoe."

Even in the case of Spenser's Britomart, the obvious prototype for Travelia as woman warrior, important differences exist. For one thing, as Montrose points out about both Britomart in *The Faerie Queene* and Elizabeth as warrior queen in Ralegh's *Discoverie . . . of Guiana*, "the woman who has the prerogative of a goddess, who is authorized to be out of place, can best justify her authority by putting other women in their places" ("Shaping Fantasies," 79). Loyalty and affection, rather than rivalry and assertion, mark Travelia's relationship with the queen; there is no defeat of Radigund by Britomart for the sake of Artegall.

For Travelia, first as male page, then as male warrior in service to the queen, the role of servant camouflages the exercise of her power. The tale is couched conservatively in terms of the alibi of exigency, but the use of masquerade, like exile, allows great imaginative license in regard to gender and sexuality. There is a time-out before the inevitable unveiling and reconciliation at the story's end. The topoi of the imaginary voyage and the masquerade allow Cavendish to stage what Terry Castle has called "a gynesium," a place that "cannot, in the end, be reconciled with only patriarchal geography" (258). When she reveals her gender, Travelia explains, "Necessity did enforce me to conceal my Sex, to protect my Honour" (509). Yet the explanation is not wholly convincing, given the obvious delight the heroine takes in playing various male roles. Like the tendency of exile to drift into self-determined travel, the motif of cross-dressing takes on a pleasurable life of its own.[15]

The battle between the sexes culminates in the Land of Amity, where complications of love and sovereignty unravel. Armed conflict begins when the queen refuses to marry the king of the rival kingdom. Leaving Travelia in charge at home, the queen goes into battle and is subsequently captured by the king's forces, led by the prince who has pursued Travelia across the seas. Travelia's confused blend of identification with and affection for the queen surfaces in the narrative. When the queen is captured by the king, Travelia's anger at the

---

[15]In his essay "Fiction and Friction," Greenblatt argues that travel and exile enable transvestite complication "on the road" while ultimately serving a conservative end of restoring normative structures after the travel is done. This seems to me to ignore the fact that the complications of gender are not so easily suppressed, even by the resolution of the marriage plot. For an argument with Greenblatt's reading of Shakespeare, see Stephen Orgel's discussion of the anxieties about gender that linger—for example, in the epilogue of *As You Like It*—in "Nobody's Perfect: Or Why Did the English Stage Take Boys for Women?"

queen's imprisonment induces "a Masculine and Couragious Spirit in her: for though she could not have those Affections in her for the Queen, as a Man; yet she admired her Heroick Virtues" (476). (This is a world in which the queen acts like a king, so Travelia's feudal response is already complexly gendered.) Leaving "women and children behind" (477) as advocates to the gods and entrusting part of her command to her aged father (another wonderful reversal of convention), Travelia goes to do battle with the prince, the commander in chief of the king's armies, prefacing her efforts with a rousing prebattle speech. She wins the love and admiration of both her soldiers and the queen, who respond to her outwitting of the prince and defeat of his army. But if wit is androgynous, strength is not; in hand-to-hand combat with him, Travelia's physical prowess is no match. In defeating her, the prince discovers her identity. It is as if reality has leaked into fantasy, so that the authority of brute strength leads to Travelia's forced unmasking.

The battle over and the sides reconciled, however, the tale takes a potentially comic turn in which erotic complication increases with Travelia's martial defeat. The queen refuses the king's advances, this time because she's in love with Travelia. The prince allays the king's anxieties by telling him that Travelia is a woman. Everyone seems pleased except the queen, who is still in love with her/him. The queen prays to God to quench the fires of her heart "unless a Woman to a Man can turn" (506), and, again, the gender confusion hints at amatory desire. "Since I cannot marry her, and so make her my Husband," the queen says, "I will keep her, if I can, and so make her my Friend" (507). Whatever erotic comedy arises from Travelia's cross-dressing locates itself at the boundary between female friendship and love. Gender resistance combines here with the hint of sexual fantasy.[16]

[16] For a good discussion of how feminist criticism often overlooks the role of homoerotic fantasy in the use of cross-dressing, see Lisa Moore's review of Felicity Nussbaum's *Autobiographical Subject: Gender and Ideology in Eighteenth-Century England*. Moore focuses on cross-dressing in *A Narrative of the Life of Mrs. Charlotte Charke*. Many examples of cross-dressing in fictional and nonfictional travel narratives of the seventeenth and eighteenth centuries, however, do not display the intrigue or the complications of gender found in Cavendish. Two eighteenth-century travel texts, Eliza Haywood's masquerade novel *Idalia* (1724) and Louis de Bougainville's *Voyage round the World* (1772), provide interesting contrasts. The beautiful and male-disguised eponymous heroine of Haywood's novel becomes the object of another woman's affection, but the situation merely leads to more vengeance and jealousy on the part of the woman rather than to any real play with issues of gender boundaries and roles. In contrast to the fantasies of power and assimilation acted out in Cavendish's tale, female powerlessness and ex-

Furthermore, although female power is tempered at the end of the story, it is reluctantly renounced. After confessing to the army that she is a woman forced to disguise herself to protect her virtue ("as the love of Soul and Body is inseparable, so should the love of Chastity and the Feminine Sex" [509], Travelia tells them), Travelia insists that "a Sword becomes a Woman when it is used against the Enemies of her Honour" (510). The soldiers respond that she should be blessed by Heaven "what Sex soever you be" (510). Travelia addresses her friends and tells them that "thus with my Masculine Clothes I have laid by my Masculine Spirit; yet not so, but I shall take it up again, if it be to serve the Queen and Kingdom, to whom I owe my Life so many Obligations" (511). A verbal sparring then occurs, with the soldiers clamoring for Travelia as their vice-regent to the prince's viceroy. Permission is granted, "to pacifie" the soldiers, but the prince tells them that she should also govern him. "She answered, That he should govern her, and she would govern the Kingdom" (512), thus slyly revising the domestic ideology of the time, that man is monarch over his wife, but she is monarch over the kingdom of the domestic sphere; the symmetry in Travelia's retort to the prince suggests that the love relationship might not be a wholly adequate substitute for the power that she has already wielded. (This verbal sparring is echoed by the king and queen when he tells her that she will be worshipped and she retorts, "I had rather have what I adore, than to be adored my self" [474].) The prince concludes: "And in her [Travelia's] Eyes, new

---

ploitation are expressed in *Idalia*. The devices of cross-dressing and travel lead only to more humiliation and pain. See *Idalia*, reprinted in *Masquerade Novels of Eliza Haywood*. In his nonfictional travel record, Louis de Bougainville records what he calls "a very singular fact," namely, the long-delayed revelation that a male servant on board ship is a woman. This revelation is particularly hard to accept, de Bougainville says, because the servant to a naturalist had proven himself/herself to be an expert botanist as well as an "indefatigable" traveler. The most interesting aspect of the anecdote is that although the fellow European travelers suspected the man was a woman, the sexual identity was confirmed only when the ship docked in Tahiti and the natives immediately recognized the man as a woman and wanted to present her with the customary honors accorded her sex (300–301). In this case, the unmasking is displaced onto the natives, as if they had a more "natural" sense of sexual identity than the easily fooled European males. The story has a further twist—the naturalist, Commerson, who marries his manservant/maid when her identity is exposed by the Tahitians, also names a flower after him/her for exhibiting morphological characteristics that are sexually ambivalent. The name in French is *Barre* which means "bar" and "barrier." The incident is just one of many in de Bougainville's narrative and is not accorded particular significance. I am indebted to Stephen Orgel for acquainting me with this episode and to Srinivas Aravamudan for his insights about it.

Worlds you there might see, / Love-flying Cupids there as Angels be" (512). Donne rather than Shakespeare is invoked here, as the blazing new worlds imagined during the course of Travelia's travel are replaced by the trope of the world in the lover's eyes.[17] Ambition and love are domesticated; after marriage, the prince and Travelia "had Masques, Playes, Balls, Pageants, Shews, Processions, and the like" (514), thus safely containing the role playing in proper aesthetic form. The gods rejoice and Zephyrus blows Travelia's name "into the glorious Trumpet of good fame" (513).

"Assaulted and Pursued Chastity" implicitly raises the question, to whom does adventure belong, whose "territory" is it? It is a question to which both gender and class are relevant. In meeting the test of adventure, the main character "performs a series of exploits which makes him/her a hero, eminent in virtues such as courage, fortitude, cunning, strength, leadership, and persistence" (Green, *Dreams of Adventure*, 23). Although the pronouns are inclusive, the definition seems to all but eliminate a female protagonist, whose main virtue, according to both social and literary convention, was chastity. In cross-dressing adventure through her imaginary voyage, Cavendish displays the protofeminist possibility that women can be the actors and aggressors, not merely the objects, in adventure. The element of masquerade suggests that masculine courage, like costume, is something one can put on, impersonate, thus yoking prowess and ingenuity.

But Travelia's wittily successful cross-dressing is only one example of how improvisation leads to power on her travels. It is in her confrontations with the "native" populations of various islands that improvisation is historically inflected by Renaissance exploration narratives, taking on a political character that imbricates gender politics with those of national identity. In these episodes, Travelia's foils are

[17]In 1668, Cavendish wrote an even more bizarre fantasy tale called *The Description of a New World, called the Blazing-World*, which Douglas Grant says owes something to Francis Godwin's *Man in the Moone* (206). Cavendish's imagination and fantasies of power are let loose in this tale, in which a young woman sails out of the world to a "Blazing World," where she marries the emperor and rules the kingdom. The soul of the duchess of Newcastle is fetched from earth for consultation on spiritual mysteries. Many more fantastic things happen, ending with the soul of the duchess promising the emperor and empress that she will design a theater that is suitable for the production of her own plays. In *Voyages to the Moon* Marjorie Nicolson disparages the story, the only example of this proto–science fiction genre by a woman writer that Nicolson cites (221). It is this tale of supreme fantasy, which begins as a journey (to the North Pole) and then becomes an exploration of another realm beyond the planet, that Gallagher discusses in her essay on Cavendish.

not lustful males but natives. It is here that Cavendish makes use of the colorful and exciting travel literature that she had read to transform her incognita into a version of the brave English explorer. As Marjorie Nicolson points out, even in her most fantastic utopian fiction (for example, *The Description of a New World, called the Blazing-World*), Cavendish probably made use of the contemporary literature of discovery, such as accounts of the exploration of Australia, as well as the writings of Sir Francis Drake (221–22). In considering the link between improvisation and power in the formation of the modern European personality, Greenblatt discusses the Europeans' ability to establish power over native populations they encountered in their travels by adopting forms of identity that allowed them to enter the preexisting political, religious, and even psychic structures of the natives while turning those structures to European advantage (*Renaissance Self-Fashioning*, 227). Greenblatt revises the work of the sociologist David Lerner, who stresses that the Western "mobile" personality, fostered by the physical mobility initiated in the Age of Exploration, bred empathy toward the other; instead, Greenblatt emphasizes the power politics concomitant with Western adaptability (225).

In "Assaulted and Pursued Chastity" Cavendish represents such a crafted identity for her heroine, whose ingenuity is tested vis-à-vis the bizarre "others" that she encounters on her journey and learns to master. Travelia's craftiness begins before she meets these others, as when she tricks a servant into giving her a pistol or steals the clothes of a male page, but it culminates in her encounters on the islands. For example, Travelia and her adopted "father" are to be sacrificed by the cannibals, who plan to cut out their hearts and eat them. The old man advises Travelia to learn the language of the people so as to convince them the gods would be angered if the two white visitors were slain. "Since my Life lyes in my Learning," Travelia valiantly announces, "I will learn for my Life" (432). This reluctant exercise of mastery over the natives is unusual in exploration narratives and encodes a characteristic apology for female learning and writing found throughout women's writings in the seventeenth century. Rhetorical prowess becomes life-sustaining—Travelia must speak or be eaten. She meets the test of the situation and makes a powerful speech to the cannibals about their offending the gods by killing their captives. She cannily uses the natives' own ideology to achieve survival. The speech alone is not sufficient, however, for modern technology as well as verbal ingenuity is required. (Again, despite the power of words, the narrative acknowledges the realities of contemporary tools of aggression.) Travelia and her sidekick make gunpowder out of "Salt-peeter and brimstone" (433). She then shoots the priest of the cannibals with the pistols and gunpowder she and the old man have made (435). In a later episode, Travelia delivers an eloquent sermon to the natives: "Thus Preaching every day for some time, forbidding Vain and Barbarous Customs, and Inhuman Ceremonies; teaching and perswading them to believe," Travelia "tames" the natives, "by which Doctrine they were brought to be a Civilized People" (442). At a time when, to Cavendish's mind, England itself had lapsed from true English values, she depicts Travelia as an avatar of British civilization in bringing the word to the heathens. In this way the undifferentiated romance geography of the tale (which, as Bakhtin points out, in early romance focuses on the heroism of an individual rather than the public, political man) is shaped to a more political semiotics despite the lack of specificity of the representation of place, in defining either home or the foreign.

Indeed, Travelia's talents are a curious combination of modern savvy and aristomilitary ability, as if Cavendish were, on the one hand, writing an adventure story that reasserted the power of the aristomilitary class and, on the other, ushering in the changing modern world of technology and scientific discovery. Her tale is a hybrid, a Janus-faced tale that looks back to the archaizing impulse of romance (appealing, when even the English monarch had proved expendable) and forward to the modern project of exploration that increasingly glorified scientists as well as military men as discoverers. I call this former impulse "archaizing" because Cavendish's tale reinforces the aristomilitary ethos of adventure at a time when the cast (and caste) of adventure was changing. Both Green and Michael Nerlich locate the seventeenth century as a transitional phase in the ideology of adventure, one involving the appropriation of the ideology by the merchant class. Although Nerlich is wary of fixing the "origins" of various phases of adventure, he discusses the 1640 revolution in England and its aftermath as an important time of transition, citing particularly 1651, the year of Cromwell's Navigation Act (and the year in which Defoe has Robinson Crusoe set out on his journey) (262). The bourgeoisie was usurping the ideology of adventure, just as the Civil War in England had forced into exile aristocrats such as the duke and duchess of Newcastle, depriving them of their power. In terms of adventure, members of the aristocracy such as the duke were out of work, bereft of the opportunities to display their courage, fortitude, and leadership. The "Heroick Actions, Publick Employements, as well Civil as Military, and Eloquent Pleadings" that the duchess mentions in the preface were denied to both husband and wife; in this regard, she identified with her class's predicament and the aristocracy's loss of its rightful public role. The tale offers social legitimation for dispossessed monarchists.

Yet Cavendish's tale is not purely nostalgic. In remythologizing adventure for women, she drew on more "modern" writings of the Age of Discovery and fashioned a female heroine canny enough to meet the challenges of this unfamiliar world. As Adams observes, in her tale of Travelia, Cavendish combines the "fantasy of Lucian with the realism, often marvelous but based on fact, of Renaissance travel accounts" (116). Mixed with descriptions of imaginary beasts are details of flora and fauna that reflect the accounts of botanists and scientists, the new breed of seventeenth-century travelers.

This habit of cataloguing specimens that could be seen in the travel accounts of these scientists seems to have resonated with Cavendish's own intellectual energy. In reading her biography, one can see her exorbitant desire to map out fields of knowledge, such as the new geographical and intellectual areas being conquered by seventeenth-century scientists and explorers. The volumes after volumes in the British Museum that Woolf speaks of stand like so much "booty" brought back from Cavendish's wide-ranging intellectual adventures, as if she, like the traders in Hakluyt's *Principal Navigations Voyages & Discoveries of the English Nation*, could circle the globe and return with treasure. Indeed, in her preface, Cavendish describes the development of the English language almost as an act of successful plunder. She speaks of her preference for a simple English but then goes on to revel in a description of just what riches are found in the English language as a result of its expropriation of other languages: "And when I use any forreign words, do not, I beseech you, attribute it to affectation, or to the vanity of being thought skilful in those Languages from whence they are taken: for I have never learn'd any, besides my Mother-Tongue, which is (at this time) extreamly enrich'd with the wise and lawful Plunder of others; and is like Mithridate and Cordial-waters, which are much the better for being compounded of the choicest Ingredients." Even the mixed provenance of tropes in "Assaulted and Pursued Chastity"—from romance, travel, and fantasy literature—suggests a kind of ransacking of literary resources for what might be recoverable by the woman writer. One senses a pleasure in accumulation (worthy of Crusoe) that signals a general seventeenth-century acquisitiveness as well as the construction of a specifically authorial "property." In *Sociable Letters*, Cavendish writes: "I wish . . . I had a Thousand, or rather Ten thousand Millions [of readers], nay, that their number were Infinite, that the Issue of my Brain, Fame, and Name, might live to Eternity if it were possible" (163).

I invoke this image, both imperialistic and improvisational, because it is not only significant for Cavendish's self-representation as a female English writer but also emphasizes why the genre of the imaginary voyage provided such a suitable vehicle for a modern female fable of adventure. One is struck in reading Cavendish by the extravagance, the lavishness of her imagination—as if it needed to construct the most outrageous eccentric realms to represent. Purple people, rare animals—half-bird, half-squirrel—houses made of spices (an updated gingerbread house?), imaginative rearrangements of gender and race (societies where men sacrifice to male gods and women to female gods, societies in which all those with royal blood are of a different color)—this is the inventory of the fantastic realms represented in a travel tale, so conventionally labeled "Assaulted and Pursued Chastity," about a fugitive heroine "forced" to wander the world. There is something wildly flamboyant in Cavendish's use of her paint box to color, an excess and ostentation antithetical to the stated cautionary purpose of the tale. In her imaginary voyage, Cavendish created an overdetermined, exaggerated structure of mobility—including exile, adventure, male impersonation, and encounters with an alien outrageously "othered" by color and species. Imaginary travel was one strategy by which she could dress up the world while conforming, in the end, to a pattern of female chastity. The lavishness of the writing is thus wonderfully at odds with the chasteness so coveted in the plot. The fugitive and cross-dressed female traveler provides the alibi for the more grandiose female explorer/writer; the baroque imagination of this cautionary tale about female travail and travel suggests that the fear of losing one's moral compass has been replaced by a pleasure in drifting.[18]

[18]At a session on Margaret Cavendish at the annual meeting of the Modern Language Association in 1993, Judith Kegan Gardiner and Carol T. Neely drew on psychoanalytic paradigms to explain the mixture of bashfulness and exhibitionism that marks Caven-

This expansiveness, prodigality, and improvisation help to link the wandering represented in the writing and the plot of Cavendish's imaginary voyage with her often-noted sartorial display. The duchess was legendary for her eccentric "dress-up"; indeed, her bizarre dress and gesture were read by men of her time as male impersonation. Sir Charles Lyttelton wrote of Cavendish that her behavior was "very pleasant, but rather to be seen than told. She was dressed in a vest, and, instead of courtesies, made legs and bows to the ground with her hand and head" (quoted in Grant, 184). With what Evelyn referred to as "the extraordinary fanciful habit, garb, and discourse of the duchess" (Grant, 17), she invented herself and the blazing new worlds in her writings. Turning female constraints to imaginative advantage (by seizing on such limits as boundaries to be transgressed), she made "fantasticall motion" the trope of her art, including the text of her person. In the epistle "To All Noble, and Worthy Ladies," which prefaces her *Poems, and Fancies*, she writes:

> *Poetry*, which is built upon *Fancy*, *Women* may claime, as a *worke* belonging most properly to themselves: for I have observ'd, that their *Braines* work usually in a *Fantasticall motion*; as in their *severall*, and *various dresses*, in their many and singular choices of *Cloaths*, and *Ribbons*, and the like; in their *curious shadowing*, and *mixing of Colours*, in their *Wrought workes*, and divers sorts of *Stitches* they imploy their *Needle*, and many *Curious* things they make. (A3)

Stitching together fabrics of fantastic motley, Cavendish demonstrates the diverse energies of women's errant imaginations.

————

On the final page of her 836-page novel *The Wanderer; or, Female Difficulties*, Frances Burney's narrative "comes home" to Defoe's *Robinson Crusoe*.

> Here, and thus felicitously, ended, with the acknowledgement of her name, and her family, the DIFFICULTIES of the WANDERER;—a being who had been cast upon herself; a female Robinson Crusoe, as unaided and

dish's personal and textual style. Gardiner argued for the applicability of the model of narcissism to Cavendish's representation of the self; Neely employed the model of the fetish to explore the psychological satisfactions of Cavendish's lavish utopic imagination.

unprotected, though in the midst of the world, as that imaginary hero in his uninhabited island; and reduced either to sink, through inanition, to nonentity, or to be rescued from famine and death by such resources as she could find, independently, in herself.

How mighty, thus circumstanced, are the DIFFICULTIES with which a FE-MALE has to struggle! Her honour always in danger of being assailed, her delicacy of being offended, her strength of being exhausted, and her virtue of being calumniated!

Yet even DIFFICULTIES such as these are not insurmountable, where mental courage, operating through patience, prudence, and principle, supply physical force, combat disappointment, and keep the untamed spirits superiour to failure, and ever alive to hope. (836)

This metafictional Odyssean return to an interpretive home in the British literary tradition mirrors the trajectory of the narrative, in which the wandering and, for much of the novel, anonymous heroine finally claims her rightful inheritance and her patrimony. Like its wandering protagonist, the excursive narrative defers the assertion of its family inheritance, only to resolve itself, at the end, in the *oikos*, the "domestic economy."[19] As Van Den Abbeele has shown, return to this domestic economy is a crucial part of the voyage; the traveler brings her accumulated capital (money, knowledge, experience) back home (8). The final summing up by Burney's narrator functions as just such an accounting, one produced after considerable expenditure of narrative (and readerly) energy.

It may seem paradoxical that the narrative would claim as archetype the ur-story that has launched a thousand male adventures (and a whole subgenre called the Robinsonade).[20] Yet the use of Defoe's novel as an exemplary text for women would not have surprised eighteenth-century readers. Indeed, in their *Practical Education*, the Edgeworths specifically recommended *Robinson Crusoe* to female students, for two complementary reasons. First, as Nancy Armstrong explains it, "they thought women were likely to learn to desire what Crusoe accomplished, a totally self-enclosed and functional domain where money did not really matter" (16). Secluded from the market-

---

[19]See Alastair Fowler's discussion of family resemblance as the basis for a theory of literary genres in *Kinds of Literature: An Introduction to the Theory of Genres and Modes* (40–44).

[20]See Green's discussion in *The Robinson Crusoe Story* of this tale as paradigmatic of male adventure for the French, German, and English literary traditions.

place on his desert island, Crusoe lives like a middle-class "domestic" woman. And, second, according to the Edgeworths, "to girls this species of reading cannot be as dangerous as it is to boys: girls must soon perceive the impossibility of their rambling about the world in quest of adventures" (111). The pedagogic importance of the novel buttresses Armstrong's argument about the feminization of the middle-class subject in the eighteenth century. As she sees it, it was the literary representation of domesticity that helped to forge the link between femininity and the middle-class subject (4–5). Even for boys, as Green points out, the story was "the most edifying and improving kind of adventure, the one that had the most to do with work and the least to do with war, and so was the one most recommended by teachers and preachers and incorporated into moral culture" (*Robinson Crusoe Story*, 2).

Crusoe as a figure of middle-class "domestic" values is how Virginia Woolf interprets the character. Defoe's adventure tale, she says, belies the reader's expectations of adventure at "the limits of the world" (54), representing instead the quotidian, commonsensical sensibility of the middle class: "Everything appears as it would appear to that naturally cautious, apprehensive, conventional and solidly matter-of-fact intelligence" ("Robinson Crusoe," 56). Building on Woolf's interpretation, Paul Zweig makes what would otherwise seem the surprising move of disqualifying *Robinson Crusoe* from the genre of adventure, identifying it instead as a counterexample, that is, an example of "anti-adventure." "Wherever Robinson Crusoe looked, whatever the cost he paid in suffering, exhaustion, and fear, he discovered a profoundly domestic, ultimately familiar world," Zweig notes (123).[21]

Although these readings minimize the risk inherent in Crusoe's wanderings, they nevertheless rightly capture the way the novel exemplifies a domesticity independent of the family. Although Crusoe aggressively flees society to seek adventure on the high seas and later

[21]Because Zweig defines adventure as a flight from women, he might well be expected to include in the category the story of Robinson Crusoe, who, even on the island for so many years, yearns more for a slave than for a woman. Furthermore, Zweig's theory also accounts for a certain feminine spirit presiding over adventure despite the male adventurer's desire to escape it, so one might expect him to theorize his exclusion. I think Zweig neglects to discuss the relation between domestication and gender in Defoe's novel partly because his main interest in his analysis of the novel is the issue of class.

ponders the original sin of his wanderlust, he progressively cultivates his exilic garden and, through the resources of his intelligence and labor, turns the uninhabited island into a home. Paradoxically, a centripetal rather than centrifugal impulse dominates the story. The testing of the hero on his island fortifies and consolidates; the novel stages the joys of unpacking, of arranging, of settling into a home: "But I was gotten home to my little tent, where I lay with all my wealth about me very secure. It blew very hard all that night, and in the morning, when I looked out, behold, no more ship was to be seen; I was a little surprised, but recovered myself with this satisfactory reflection, viz., that I had lost no time, nor abated no diligence to get everything out of her that could be useful to me, and that indeed there was little left in her that I was able to bring away if I had had more time" (50).[22]

Burney's "cross-gendering" of the Crusoe figure is complex, given the varied gender inflections in the original. But the narrator's own analogy between *The Wanderer* and Defoe's original urges us to interpret both stories as triumphs of bourgeois resourcefulness and moral imagination. The analogy suggests that the Incognita represents the same values of self-sufficiency, industry, and self-possession that characterize Crusoe. Significantly, it asserts that a woman in the midst of English society is "as unaided and unprotected as" a single, isolated man in the middle of the ocean. The Wanderer's story emerges from this simile—her position in society is metaphorically equivalent to that of Robinson Crusoe. It is interesting that Defoe's original for a moment flirts with a similar figurative equivalence—one that might have produced an entirely different narrative, exploring male isolation in the midst of an alien society. Early in the novel, when living in Brazil and a stranger to those around him, Crusoe observes: "I used to say, I

[22]This is not meant to ignore the element of mastery and domination also at work in the text, the kind of ideology that suggests it as an allegory of colonial domination. James Joyce, the Irishman, constructed an overtly political reading of the novel as prophetic of English imperialism. "The true symbol of the British conquest is Robinson Crusoe. . . . He is the true prototype of the British colonist. . . . The whole Anglo-Saxon spirit is in Crusoe" ("Daniel Defoe," 24). This perspective is shared by Green and other contemporary critics. Indeed, as Zweig's study, among others, illustrates, *Robinson Crusoe* has served as a paradigmatic text for interpretations of class as well as gender ideologies. All these fascinating readings unmask the "fiction" of escape from culture in the novel, revealing how English (and male) fears and expectations are transplanted to the island. Just as a discourse of domesticity is constructed in the absence of the family, a related discourse of class is constructed in the absence of society, even before Friday's appearance.

lived just like a man cast away upon some desolate island that had nobody there but himself. . . . I say, how just has it been, that the truly solitary life I reflected on in an island of mere desolation should be my lot" (30). The "mere desolation" in society, Crusoe implies, is a pale anticipation of his subsequent struggle for physical and spiritual survival on the island. But it is precisely an inverted hierarchy of suffering that the narrator of *The Wanderer* suggests by analogy. In calling Crusoe Defoe's "*imaginary* hero on his uninhabited island" (emphasis added), she suggests that her own narrative is more "real" by virtue of being more explicitly social. In lieu of a fiction of escape from culture, Burney represents her "female Robinson Crusoe" in the middle of British institutions and mores. She takes the topoi of exile, vulnerability, and social uprooting and rewrites them with a female protagonist whose wandering occurs in the midst of a society in which she has no "place." Burney translates Crusoe's distance from home into the Wanderer's erasure within the symbolic order. The female sojourner is as cut off from power, property, and material resources on the island of Britain as the male castaway on a deserted island.[23]

Thus, the difference that gender makes in the tale of wandering is both repressed and acknowledged on the final page. This eleventh-hour recovery of a patronymic text (like the deferred inheritance of the Wanderer's patronymic) offers to resolve the complicated questions the protracted narrative raises concerning identity and the relations between movement and female virtue—an ideological *nostos* or homecoming that casts the text in terms of the middle-class domestic virtues that Defoe extols in his novel.[24] Yet, it also retains a

[23]In "An Island of Her Own: Heroines of the German Robinsonades from 1720 to 1800," Jeannine Blackwell discusses Robinsonades that have female protagonists, written largely by anonymous or male German writers. She points out that female Robinsonades differ from male in their constructions of more social environments for their heroines. "While the male Robinson character often goes it alone, against all odds, the woman castaway survives through communal effort and nurtures long, deep female friendship" (17). In listing the common topoi of this genre, Blackwell shows that they often drew on conventions of romance such as cross-dressing, sea voyages, shipwrecks, and the like and often maintained the same kind of "alibi" for travel to be found in both Cavendish's and Burney's fictional voyages. "In order to be a sympathetic heroine, she cannot willfully desert duty for desire and therefore must be driven to it. Her act of escape then ceases to be personal choice and becomes unavoidable" (10–11).

[24]In *Acts of Naming: The Family Plot in Fiction*, Michael Ragussis discusses the importance of naming and inheritance in emplotting characters in the bourgeois family in novels from the eighteenth to the twentieth century. He discusses certain gender differences in these novels, including the greater difficulty for women of escaping the

sense of difference between the wanderer fictionally "cast" as a woman, "cast upon herself; a female Robinson Crusoe," and that of the imaginary male castaway. The narrator's summary emphasizes the importance of specifically "female difficulties" (a reference to both physical and gender differences). If Defoe makes his male adventurer cross over into the realm of the domestic and private, Burney propels her castaway into the public realm of the marketplace: her female Crusoe circulates as a commodity, an unwilling and pained participant in the economy of travel. As I will argue, the "return" of the prodigal narrative offers a fiction of closure that does not completely resolve the difficult issues of gender and class articulated in the novel.

Burney's novel begins with the colorful romance topos of a sea crossing, also drawing (like Cavendish's tale) on the romance conventions of disguised identity and "assaulted and pursued chastity." The novel opens during Robespierre's reign of terror as a nameless heroine, dark-skinned and bedraggled, a patch over one eye, begs passage on a boat carrying English refugees back to their homeland from France. The protagonist seems to be a young Frenchwoman, traveling incognito, who spends the duration of the novel "wandering" in England. For much of the novel, the heroine refuses to divulge her identity; we discover that although she has been raised in France, she is the daughter of a secret marriage between an English commoner and an English lord. She is escaping from an unscrupulous French husband, a commissar of the Revolution, who manipulates her into marrying him by threatening the life of her guardian, a French bishop (the marriage is never consummated and the husband subsequently dies). The Wanderer awaits a mysterious letter, addressed to "L.S.," that is to contain a message of the bishop's safety and thereby allow her to reveal her identity (the deferred letter, then, is an emblem of the larger deferral of her "proper" name). In the course of the narrative, this anonymous heroine is variously called "the Wanderer," "the Incognita," "Ellis" (a distortion of "L.S."), and, finally, Juliet Granville (her proper name).

Although other Burney novels, like eighteenth-century novels in general, are concerned with issues of identity, authority, and inheritance, in *The Wanderer* Burney posits a kind of limit case for women—a foreign protagonist without access to the props of English patri-

---

"family plot," even in "wilderness" fictions that hold out the possibility of namelessness (235).

archal civilization while forced to live in its midst. Without name or money (she has even lost her purse on the passage over), she is a nobody, forced to work for her living, using her wits and talents and avoiding the potentially ambiguous patronage of men. Although the narrator's contention that the Wanderer might "sink, through inanition, to nonentity, or . . . be rescued from famine and death" by her own resources might seem melodramatic, the eight hundred pages that chronicle the protagonist's "wandering" reveal the potentially drastic consequences of such an unprotected situation for a woman. Indeed, the protagonist's painful condition is enacted as physical exposure in the final volume of the novel, when the wanderer becomes a fugitive, fleeing her French pursuers in the English countryside.

Armstrong calls Burney "a homebound author" (48), but in her reappropriation of Defoe's exilic narrative, Burney turns domestic fiction inside out, paradoxically making "home" a hostile environment for a woman and revealing, among other things, the implicit xenophobia of "Englishness," a fiction of purity that depends on the exclusion of the foreign. In emphasizing this environing hostility to the "outsider" and the lowly status of the heroine and its threat to her survival, Burney draws on the flexible genre of the picaresque, with its "episodic, open-ended narratives in which lower-class protagonists sustain themselves by means of their cleverness and adaptability during an extended journey through space, time, and various predominantly corrupt social milieux" (Bjornson, 4). As this loose definition suggests, the picaresque is more fully rooted in the details of the daily labor to survive than is romance. Burney's eighteenth-century tale of wandering is much more concrete in its depiction of social space than is Cavendish's romance; the protagonist's wandering is now seen as a disadvantageous circulation in the marketplace of English society.[25] Burney shows how the mercantile cast expressed in Defoe's adventure story menaces the woman traveler, particularly a foreigner in whom recognizable signs of English class are absent. Such a wanderer may be perceived as selling the one commodity she possesses—her body. She is forced not only to earn a living but to market her talents in public as well (at one point even launching a career as a paid ac-

---

[25]Travelia's short sojourn as a male page is more a use of stock convention than an occasion to explore the implications of class for the plot of adventure, whereas Burney's realist novel does engage such issues.

tress)—a risky business for a late eighteenth-century woman whom the "private" realm should protect from such public exposure. She runs the risk of commodification, whether through being "kept" by male patrons or through displaying her talents publicly for money.

Relying on the kindness of strangers is different for a female wanderer, as Defoe himself had shown in *Roxana* and *Moll Flanders*. If one wonders why these novels didn't provide a more directly relevant model for Burney, one has only to look at the very different moral implications of Defoe's treatment of the relationship between female movement and virtue. He developed the roguish implications of the female picara, whose ability to survive leads her into criminal behavior. Burney herself represents femininity as well within the law; her heroine remains "proper" even without her proper name. Defoe develops the comic strand of the picaresque in emphasizing freedom of invention and the delights of roguish wit, and although Burney's narrative does indeed take some pleasure in the exercise of the Wanderer's "talents" as they help pay her way in society, it more indelibly inscribes the pain involved for the wandering picara. One could say that Burney draws on a possible derivation of the word "picaresque" in the Spanish literary tradition, that is, its etymological link to the Spanish verb "picar," meaning to prick, puncture, or bite (see Sieber, 5). According to Bjornson, the name of the "first" Spanish picaresque hero, Lázaro (the hero in the anonymous *Lazarillo de Tormes* [1554]), is phonetically linked to one of the key recurrent words in the text, "laceria," meaning misery and poverty (21).

In representing the radical ambiguity of an "unclassed" and unclassified female body circulating through time and space, the narrative exploits the potential for humiliating "misreadings" of the Wanderer which would link her, in society's eyes, to the image of a Moll or Roxana. The potential for drastic misreading is exaggerated in the area of women's work. The Wanderer has developed the type of talents expected of a "lady," such as embroidery and playing a musical instrument; but when these skills become the source of her livelihood, in the occupation of music teacher or milliner, her already ambiguous class status falls further. Margaret Doody captures the uncertainty of the Wanderer's economic and symbolic status, including the potential for her being misread as selling herself rather than her honest labor: "Juliet is a Wanderer, like a beggar, like a Romantic poet, or—in a woman's case—like a prostitute" (329). Even without a "name," the Incognita still runs the risk of losing her "good name." One can see the wandering female body in Burney's novel as a text on which characters project their own readings of class.[26]

In a sense, Burney's allusion to Defoe's text on the final page of her novel attempts to resolve this issue, emphasizing character instead of class connections. The ambiguity of the female traveler—is she a wanderer, lady, beggar, prostitute?—is "resolved" by appeal to the solid middle-class English virtues displayed by Crusoe (and from which the English "society" within the novel seems to have lapsed), just as the protagonist, despite her French upbringing, is revealed to be English. The difficult foreignness of the character (Juliet seems to be French but turns out to be English) and, potentially, of the narrative (French politics are "imported" into the British novel) is put to rest. Yet the unclassed Incognita creates a disturbance in the text not wholly resolved by this return of the prodigal narrative to the English tradition. Moreover, this return belies the way in which Burney "crosses" French politics with the British novel just as she smuggles the Incognita aboard a British vessel. The only Burney novel to be published after her ten-year exile in France with her French husband, M. D'Arblay, *The Wanderer* "imports" from France a discourse of equality that attended the revolutionary struggle. Another way to say this is to observe that in the novel the aristocrats' unjust treatment of those who work activates the revolutionary potential in the idea of the "bourgeoisie": it stands for alliance between the middle and working classes.[27] Although the protagonist behaves better than the women with whom she works at the haberdashery, her rock-bottom economic position allies her with them rather than with most of the aristocracy and the gentry, who survive on private incomes. Despite the fact that woman's paid work is disparaged by the "good" male character, Al-

[26]The importance of class in this fiction of wandering might be usefully compared to the situation in a much older fiction of wandering, *The Golden Ass* of Apuleius. Bakhtin discusses this novel as the next permutation in classical literature after Greek romance of the chronotope of the road. If Cavendish's use of wandering is fruitfully compared with the type of action found in the Greek romance, Burney's is closer to this "adventure novel of everyday life," in which the wandering protagonist is transformed into an ass, thus "descending" to a humiliating role in day-to-day existence. "In all these situations Lucius performs not as Lucius but as an ass. At the end of the novel he casts off the appearance of an ass and . . . reenters the highest, most privileged spheres of life" (121).

[27]See Nerlich's reading of *Robinson Crusoe*, which restores just such a revolutionary potential to Defoe's own story (263–74).

bert Harleigh (whom the Wanderer will eventually marry at story's end), there is something noble about those who survive by their labor, even in its menial forms. As Doody points out, in documenting the lives of workingwomen of various kinds, Burney followed a tradition of radical women writers of the 1790s (318). And, in restoring this more potentially revolutionary sense of "bourgeois," she followed a 1790s tradition of Jacobin novels as well.

One could say that the novel represents a "hazardous crossing" between the discourse of equality that came out of the French Revolution and the tradition of British fiction. Indeed, the opening scene is a figure for this hazardous crossing; the young, foreign woman with a dark scarred face begs to be taken aboard the small boat returning English travelers to their homeland. The scene is an emblem for a crossing and a crossing out, for the political and French dimension of Burney's text is both acknowledged and repressed. This tension lies behind Burney's own equivocal disclaimers about the politics of her novel and the disappointed response of some of Burney's contemporaries, who found her novel either too French or not French enough.[28]

Burney's unfinished manuscript, begun in England, accompanied her to France in 1802, where she and her husband expected to remain for a year or so, only to find themselves exiled from England for ten years when the Peace of Amiens broke down in 1803 and Napoleon blockaded the ports. In the dedicatory letter to her father, "Doctor Burney," that prefaces the novel, Burney refers to the manuscript's double "traversal" of the ocean: after ten years the finished manuscript returned with her to England. The border crossings of the text (from one "hostile shore" to another) are presented in the letter as unproblematic: "The voluminous manuscript was suffered to pass, without demur, comment, or the smallest examination" (xviii). Here,

---

[28] A review in the *British Critic* began with the following: "Her long residence in a foreign country, it was conjectured, would have opened sources of information, of which her inventive powers were so well enabled to take a due advantage both in portraiture of character and the description of events" (quoted in Burney, *Journals and Letters*, 7:478n). Although the review goes on to agree with the author's delicacy in approaching such matters, the fact remains that the reception of the novel included the overriding sense that it was neither as good as nor different enough from her previous novels written before her exile. Indeed, in the same review, the critic suggests that Burney's travel seems to have had only a pernicious effect on her language, as she had "forgotten the common elegancies of her native tongue" (565). (In the novel, Juliet herself is called at one point "a frenchified swindler.") Like some of the novel's reviewers, certain characters within the narrative clamor for information from Juliet about her native France and its political condition, a pressure that Juliet continually resists.

in a textual act of passing without comment, Burney edits out of her account the perilous journey of the manuscript itself from Paris to Dunkirk in 1812, which preceded her departure for England. In her journal, she describes the anxious events surrounding this trip. While Burney waited in Dunkirk for a ship to take her back to England surreptitiously, she had the manuscript of *The Wanderer* sent from Paris so that she could pass the time in writing. To send the manuscript, M. D'Arblay had to assure the police that it was neither "political, nor even National, nor possibly offensive to the Government" (*Burney: Selected Letters*, 159), but when the manuscript arrived at the customs house, the police officer there grew irate at "a sight so unexpected & prohibited" that it took the help of an English merchant to assuage his anger ("This Fourth Child of my Brain had undoubtedly been destroyed ere it was Born, had I not had recourse to an English Merchant, Mr. Gregory" [160]).

This volatile English-French import, like the woman traveler smuggled aboard the English ship in the novel's opening scene, is greeted at the border as contraband. The mixed parentage of the novel, born of political events in both England and France, almost leads to its demise. The trope of the border crossing resonates in the preface to suggest a link between travel, travel writing, and transgression. This acknowledgment of danger and prohibition that appears in Burney's journals, however, is elided in the material space of the novel. It is as if the borders of the novel could keep at bay the potentially more disturbing aspects of Burney's and her manuscript's own border crossings, with all their implications for her own double identity as English and French (Frances Burney and Madame D'Arblay).

The novel as a genre is defined here as a safe space, a refuge from politics that offers domestic shelter. Thus, the distinguishing mark of domestic fiction, its supposedly private and nonpolitical character, is underscored. The preface's disclaimers hammer home this point: "I have felt, indeed, no disposition,—I ought rather, perhaps, to say talent,—for venturing upon the stormy sea of politics; whose waves, for ever either receding or encroaching, with difficulty can be stemmed, and never can be trusted" (xviii). Early in her career she has turned, she says, from the "tempestuous course" of political writing. Political topics, Burney contends, are "without my sphere, or beyond my skill" (xix); she is anxious, she says, to "steer clear, alike, of all animadversions that, to my adoptive country, may seem ungrateful, or, to the country of my birth unnatural" (xix). She assures us that during her ten years of exile in France, she was "perfectly *a stranger to all personal disturbance*; save what sprang from the painful separation that absented me from you my dearest Father, from my loved family, and native friends and country" (xx: emphasis added).

Because of her disavowals, Burney's preface reads like Freudian denegation, her very metaphors ("tempestuous course," "stormy sea") returning us to the scene of political danger that opens her novel. The representation of politics as a crossing of boundaries imports the topos of the foreign journey. Even as she avers her personal distance from conflict and danger during her French exile, the negative ("a stranger to all personal disturbance") includes rather than expels an aura of suffering and reminds us of the suffering stranger in her novel. Elsewhere in her preface, Burney rewrites this denial, in a different, more ambiguous formulation of the relation between French politics and her fiction (and between politics and fiction in general). In this passage Burney seems to acknowledge the disingenuousness of her own figure of separate realms or countries: in one of the rhetorical turns that makes the text of the preface itself a sinuous road to travel, she says:

> Nevertheless, to avoid disserting upon these topics as matter of speculation, implies not an observance of silence to the events which they produce, as matter of [f]act: on the contrary, to attempt to delineate, in whatever form, any picture of actual human life, without reference to the French Revolution, would be as little possible, as to give an idea of the English government, without reference to our own: for not more unavoidably is the last blended with the history of our nation, than the first, with every intellectual survey of the present times. (xix)

The confusingly circuitous looping of French and English in the sentence syntactically mirrors the inextricability of the two "realms," partly because the personal pronoun used to refer to Burney's own allegiances is problematic for this woman of two countries. After "swearing" that the novel is, by its very nature, separate from politics, Burney instead suggests that it is permeated by "reference" to the French Revolution. The spirit of the Revolution pervades the text and is not so benignly blended as Burney here would indicate.

This slippage is important, for the trope of the border crossing bridges the supposed separation between the private sphere of domestic fiction and the public sphere of politics. But what exactly is transplanted from French to British soil? How does Burney, with her Royalist sympathies and explicit endorsement of Edmund Burke's conservative *Reflections on the French Revolution*, succeed in representing the politics of the Revolution in her novel? What is the relation between the private wandering and suffering of the protagonist and the historical discourses of the novel?

Revolutionary violence and blackmail propel the initial journey that begins the novel: the shadowy Gothic/French pursuer/husband is himself a commissar of the March 1793 Convention. The novel represents the tyranny that accompanied the reign of Robespierre. Furthermore, in the commissar's act of sexual blackmail, Burney astutely recognizes that despite the new rhetoric of equality, women might be more powerless in revolutionary times than during the monarchy.[29]

Yet despite this critique of revolutionary violence, Burney's novel is rife with representations of the conditions of class and gender oppression that might spawn resentment and violence. These conditions become visible largely because the foreign sign of the Wanderer disrupts the semiotics of gender, class, and even race in the English community, thus revealing turbulent instabilities beneath its surface. First appearing in the novel as a dark-skinned servant, then forced to work for a middle-class living, and finally revealed as the daughter of an English nobleman, the Incognita presents an interpretive puzzle. In her penurious condition, with servant's clothes and upper-class manners, bearing, and accomplishments, she stymies an English society accustomed to associating class with virtue. "The French Revolution has opened our eyes to a species of equality more rational . . . than that of lands or of rank" (612), says Gabriella, Juliet's French friend, who goes on to bemoan the topsy-turvy social world in which all classes are forced to earn a living. Yet it is precisely this disordered world that the Wanderer imports into English society. Although Castle demonstrates that Burney plays with the mixing of classes through the trope of the masquerade in earlier novels (266), here class confusion circulates with the Wanderer throughout the plot rather than be-

[29] In *Women and the Public Sphere in the Age of the French Revolution*, Joan Landes discusses just this paradox. She maintains that the rhetoric of equality in the revolutionary period depended on sexual difference. By her account the initial impetus to extend the discussion of equality to women, represented by Condorcet's efforts in 1790, soon gave way to the masculinist values of the bourgeois public sphere, from which women were barred (95).

ing "aestheticized" in contained scenes of performance. Nor can these ambiguities be contained by the "resolution" of identity at novel's end. Does Juliet Granville's heritage as the daughter of a commoner and a lord confirm middle-class ideology, which supports a separation between class and virtue, or the more conservative ideology of birth and family romance, which reinforces the relation between class and virtue after all? I would argue that the disturbing presence of the Wanderer as circulating and enigmatic sign is not resolved in an unambiguous and coherent "political" reading, that it is precisely the instabilities and contradictions that remain. When Giles Arbe asks the Wanderer why it is better for her to take charity from a poor family than from a rich bachelor, his question resonates through the novel, exposing her refusal of male help as a moral luxury, dictated by the codes of middle-class femininity, codes that lead her to exploit the poor.

Thus the enigmatic Wanderer functions as a disturbing "parasite" in the narrative, destabilizing the social system and creating discomfort in the text. She is the guest who disrupts the economy of hospitality—Hermes, the traveler, as parasite. Michel Serres describes the parasite: it enters a system unobtrusively but disrupts it, like static (*Parasite*, 14). The Wanderer enters English society and the novel cloaked and disguised, trying to pass without observation. Yet, in Burney's gendered version of this disruption, beauty makes the parasite noticeable; both men and women are drawn to the Wanderer as a mysterious and beautiful sign and are unsettled by her ambiguities. If by the end of the novel she is revealed as a beautiful pearl, for its duration she is society's irritant, so that irritation itself becomes an important category of response in the novel.

Indeed, the Wanderer is perceived as a foreign body, particularly by the women in the story, who understand the power of the parasite and seek to expel it. Mrs. Marple, one of the female Furies whose heartless comments prick the surface of the narrative as well as the composure of the Wanderer, complains of the presence of the Wanderer at the inn where the passengers sojourn for the night: "Are we to go on any farther as if we were to live all our lives in a stage coach? Why can't that body as well stay in the kitchen?" (15). Mrs. Marple seeks to separate the "body" of the Wanderer from the rest of the social body, containing her in the kitchen as a "domestic" rather than allowing her to circulate dangerously abroad. Thus, early on in the novel, Mrs. Marple calls into question one of the most familiar topoi of the travel narrative and the one with which the novel begins: that strangers brought together through travel are all in the same "boat."

The passengers' anxieties about the foreignness of the traveler's "body" are emphatically figured in the characters' recourse to contemporary cultural discourse that conflates racial and sexual categories to create an "anatomy of difference."[30] Addressing Harleigh, the solid and chivalrous Englishman who defends the stranger's presence on the boat and later falls in love with her, a woman passenger taunts him: "I wonder what sort of a dulcinea you have brought amongst us! though, I really believe, you are such a complete knight-errant, that you would just as willingly find her a tawny Hottentot as a fair Circassian" (4). If the Englishmen tend to name her a "fair Aenigma," these references to her as "Hottentot" and (later in the text) as Creole suggest that enigma is really stigma, of a particularly sexual and racial kind. As Sander Gilman has pointed out, "By the eighteenth century, the sexuality of the black, both male and female, becomes an icon for deviant sexuality in general" (209). Yet the particular reference to Hottentots and Creoles suggests the importance of the idea of racial mixing, of mediation of a frightening kind.[31] That the Wanderer is finally revealed to be "one of them," her foreignness virtually dissolving in the rational explanation of her straitened circumstances and the restoration of her rightful inheritance, does not mitigate her function as a cultural wild card. The dark scarred woman at the beginning of the text, whose eyepatch ultimately conceals nothing, catalyzes the fears about the rampant sexuality of society's others and attaches those fears to the image of the circulating woman traveler "on the loose." Fears about the Wanderer's status—economic, racial, and sexual—go beyond the discourse of equality imported with the novel's historical placement during the French Revolution, as if the discourse, once let

---

[30] Londa Schiebinger discusses this conflation in "The Anatomy of Difference."

[31] As Mieke Bal notes in her review, Gilman's own discourse has a problematic subtext, which betrays the fact that there is a "contamination" of the critic by the discourse he aims to critique. Symptomatic of this slippage, Bal contends, is Gilman's tendency to equate Hottentots with blacks (28–30). Laura Brown's work on contemporary accounts of race and gender in the eighteenth century shows that how to categorize the Hottentot was itself a subject of debate. Buffon, for example, "argues that the Hottentots are not true Negroes, but rather whites who make themselves dirty by wallowing in filth" (Brown, "Imperial Disclosures," 191). The references in Burney's narrative seem to draw on both the mapping of sexual onto racial difference and the ambiguities of "passing" and mixing that were current in eighteenth-century discourse on race.

loose, produced mutants beyond the realm of the imagination. One can see a fascinating, unintentional illustration of the way this racial "danger" was perceived as overflowing the borders of the novel in Macaulay's critique of Burney's language in *The Wanderer*. Virtually echoing the invective hurled at the novel's foreign protagonist, Macaulay called Burney's prose "a sort of broken Johnsonese, a barbarous *patois*, bearing the same relation to the language of *Rasselas*, which the jibberish of the Negroes of Jamaica bears to the English of the House of Lords" (306).

Name-calling, as in the above examples from the narrative, is one response to the Wanderer's frightening namelessness, a strategy for verbally putting the stranger in her place. Even more benign attempts by the characters and the narrative to "interpellate" the stranger (to use Althusser's term), to "hail" her into society rather than exclude her from it, emphasize the ambiguity of her status. Throughout the narrative, the stranger's "marker" keeps changing disconcertingly, from the "Wanderer" of the title page, which alludes to her exilic and aimless journey, to the "Incognita," which emphasizes her symbolic placelessness as an unknown social quantity. The temporary name "Ellis," assigned by the other characters, who confuse the initials of the addressee of the letter from France ("L. S.") with the surname, emphasizes her lack of roots in patriarchal society. Like her general victimization by circumstance, the naming of Ellis is dictated by the frivolities of chance. Doody suggests in her biography of Burney that the name Ellis rings with the phrase *elle est* (she is) and is thus emblematic of the novel's quest for female identity, what Doody calls the "riddle of Womankind in various metamorphoses" (324). I would emphasize, however, the other side of the Wanderer's victimization, that is, the particularly disturbing effect of her anonymity. Moreover, the French "elle est" yokes gender identity to larger political disturbances of assigned places that erupt with the French Revolution.

The only character who overtly welcomes the destabilizing influence of the Revolution is Elinor Joddrel—as her name suggests, a double for the Wanderer (Ellis-Elinor). The discourse of equality enters the novel in Elinor's speeches, where it is given a distinctly feminist twist. Elinor, the Wanderer's fellow escapee on the boat from France, gives voice to the revolutionary ideas she has encountered there and offers a strident critique of patriarchal society, which Juliet's fate concretely exemplifies. For Elinor, the personal situation of a woman and the political injustice toward women in society are inseparable. (It is a discussion over *The Rights of Man* that causes Elinor to break her engagement with Albert Harleigh's brother, Dennis.) It is through her that the politics of the French Revolution enter the novel as an explicit topic and the collective condition of women is most powerfully articulated. Elinor argues that the world was "shaken by the French Revolution," and extending the discourse of equality to women, she offers a vindication of their rights. As I'm suggesting, the figure of Mary Wollstonecraft as a mediator between French ideas and British society haunts the representation of Elinor. Recently, critics such as Judy Simons, Doody, and Julia Epstein have developed this obvious parallel. Wollstonecraft went to France, ardently supported the revolutionary cause, and appropriated the language of Enlightenment reason for women, and one hears echoes of her commitments in Elinor's impassioned plea for "the Rights of human nature; to which the two sexes equally and unalienably belong." The conflicts between Elinor's philosophy of rationality and her passionate sensibility as well as her melodramatic and suicidal nature evoke more personal aspects of Wollstonecraft, including her tragic romance with Gilbert Imlay and repeated suicide attempts.[32]

Recent critics have pointed out that Elinor's speeches are partially discredited by her hysterical, even self-destructive outbursts, as if in the novel Burney were drawing back from the more radical implications of her own sympathies. Burney does represent the emotional cost of such anger and unbridled passion as Elinor's, and the extremes of Elinor's romantic passion qualify our reading of her character. Other characters are embarrassed by her harangues, a context that mitigates the power of her words. Yet it seems to me that Burney undermines Elinor's political rhetoric more out of cynicism than resistance to change. When, in a rare outburst against her fate, Juliet complains of the "severe DIFFICULTIES of a FEMALE . . . without fortune or protection," Elinor retorts, "Forget that you are a dawdling woman . . . [and] remember that you are an active human being, and your FEMALE DIFFICULTIES will vanish into the vapour of which they are formed" (377). On the one hand, Elinor's plea for drastic change feels cathartic in the midst of the often silent and interminable suffering of Juliet. We long

---

[32]See Doody's discussion of the parallels between Elinor (and even Burney) and Wollstonecraft (342–43, 350–51). One aim of Doody's fine biography is to place Burney in a tradition of radical women writers of the 1790s. Judy Simons develops this parallel as well (107–10).

for some action—some response—in this tale of female travel and travail. Yet Elinor's advice to Juliet about taking an active role in her destiny and the importance of a change in her consciousness proves utopian, for the weight of social convention is too great. The whole book teaches us that "female difficulties" do not "vanish" into thin air but retain an alarming and almost unremitting solidity in the text. One could say that the ideology of change, manifested in the idea of physical movement as liberating, is questioned in this insistently obstacle-laden narrative. Burney's problematic "feminism" is, in a sense, too skeptical for Elinor's brand of almost magical thinking. And, indeed, although Elinor discourses on suicide and even attempts it, she, like the narrative, goes on and on.

I contend that the protraction of the narrative, with its deferrals and sudden aggressive outbursts, is a formal embodiment of Burney's feminism and directly linked to the trope of wandering. Narrative wandering is both diagnosis and strategy. It is through pain that feminism, like revolution, is invented. But Burney's is both a nonrevolutionary and nonprogressive mode of textualizing antagonisms, a mode of narration that prolongs pain and defers resolution. Her skepticism of a "quick fix" is played out in the use of narrative delay. Indeed, if all the suffering could be dissipated by the female assertiveness that Elinor proposes, the narrative would conclude in one volume rather than five. "I have neither time nor humor for narratory delay," says Elinor, who encourages quick resolution, commanding Juliet to reveal her identity, but the narrative itself proceeds at a slower tempo. Both Burney's contemporaries and some recent feminist critics have questioned this strategy of narrative wandering. In a highly unflattering and now infamous review, William Hazlitt links narrative deferral to feminine etiquette: "The difficulties in which she involves her heroines are indeed 'Female Difficulties';—they are difficulties created out of nothing. . . . The whole artifice of her fable consists in coming to no conclusion. Her ladies 'stand so upon the order of their going,' that they do not go at all" (124–25). (This reference to "female difficulties" is a masculine dig at what is perceived as women's monthly hypochondria.) In her introduction to the novel, Margaret Drabble also seems critical of unnecessary delay in the narrative, which she attributes to the illogical demands society places on women: "It cannot have escaped her creator's notice that Juliet, in order to remain pure and uncompromised and to evade the insulting and threatening attentions of various lascivious pursuers, is obliged to expose herself to all sorts of unnecessary dangers and to roam the wild countryside, a wanderer indeed, when a word of rational explanation might have brought the whole plot to a sudden and simple end" (xiv).

It appears that both approving, feminist readers such as Drabble and disapproving male readers like Hazlitt find difficulty explaining the rationale for the protracted narrative. But it is precisely in resuscitating the link between the picaresque and pain in a gendered context that the shape of the narrative finds its purpose. The topos of wandering, rather than the progress of the quest, underwrites the narrative movement. It is instructive to contrast Burney's gendered version of wandering with Norman O. Brown's description in *Love's Body* of the masculine mode of adventure in which narrative impetus is equivalent to phallic thrust. Brown's male adventurer goes "pricking o'er the plain" (50). Instead, in Burney's model, the female protagonist (the picara) is "pricked" by external events, goaded on from adventure to adventure, trying desperately to avoid exposure and confrontation. *The Wanderer* presents an interesting challenge to the "erotics of plot" posited in narrative theories such as those of Brown, or Peter Brooks, who see desire as the narrative motor, desire that resists any agent which brings premature closure or short-circuiting.[33] Protagonist and plot in Burney's novel are goaded by irascibility and even violence; in response, the Wanderer moves on, fearing exposure, display, and erotic violation. The irritation is noted in a sense by Mrs. Ireton (appropriately named), who says to Juliet: "You may be a person of another century. A wandering Jewess. I never heard that the old Jew had a wife, or a mother, who partook of his longevity; but very likely I may now have the pleasure of seeing one of his family under my own roof?" (462). According to Mrs. Ireton, anonymity becomes equivalent to the mark of the outcast—although Burney roots the Wanderer's suffering in specific social conditions, there is something almost ritualistic about the disruption of safety and her traveler's forced return to the "road."

Thus some of the pleasures we expect from genres with the journey as their central trope—adventure, romance, epic—are withheld in this novel. And despite Burney's use of picaresque narrative rhythms, the

---

[33]In *Reading for the Plot*, Brooks relates extension of plot to the pleasure principle, which, although ultimately seeking the discharge of tension and a state of quiescence, looks to do so "in its own fashion," that is, in its own time and way (102). Although Brooks discusses the pleasure of both the reader and the narration (the storytelling), he focuses first on the desire of the protagonist that informs the dynamic of plot.

pleasures of roguish wit are largely absent from the Wanderer's movement to escape humiliation and discovery. Female wandering as represented by Burney is a narrow lot (Juliet can't even benefit from the accumulation of capital that is Robinson Crusoe's reward for his Puritan self-sufficiency and hard work). Like Odysseus, another famous exile who must often travel incognito, the Wanderer dons disguises and plays roles when necessary, forced as she is to rely on the hospitality of her hosts. But whereas Odysseus establishes his identity through courageous battles against adversity, the Wanderer very reluctantly, painfully, uses her talents, dreading any notice of her person or identity. In the fourth volume of the novel, in which Juliet travels in the countryside, the model of *The Odyssey* is clearly evoked, as she stops to share "libations" with various hosts. But although her hosts may expect a story in recompense for their hospitality, Juliet cannot afford them the pleasure of storytelling that is one of the hallmarks of travel as well as epic and romance literature. In this regard, the female Wanderer violates even the law of the parasite. "The parasite is invited to the *table d'hôte*; in return, he must regale the other diners with his stories and his mirth. To be exact, he exchanges good talk for good food; he buys his dinner, paying for it in words. . . . Each society allows a linguistic specie that can be exchanged advantageously for food" (Serres, *Parasite* 34). But Juliet's reticence, her refusal to tell her story, disrupts even this substitution. The garrulous exchange Serres describes is chastened by the Wanderer's vow of silence.

Indeed, at every turn, the display of her talents is cramped by the sense that only self-effacement will avert suffering. Although, as Julia Epstein suggests, there are moments when Juliet is flushed with her accomplishments, acknowledgment always brings more painful exposure (*Iron Pen*, 183). Although Juliet's aristocratic education has permitted her to turn her abilities into work for pay, talents tarnish when exposed. In the preface to *The Wanderer*, Burney cites her own refusal to sign her name as author of *Evelina*, her first novel. She refers to the novel as "wrapt up in the mantle of impenetrable obscurity" (vi). The reference suggests connections between Burney's anonymity, the novel's "cover story" (as a nonpolitical text), and the protagonist's disguise. Wrapping herself in a "brown" paper wrapper, so to speak, Juliet desires to avoid notice, to mark time until the crucial letter arrives from France. Unlike Zweig's male adventurer, who fears being buried in oblivion in Calypso's cave, Juliet seeks safety in oblivion and the narrative seeks to minimize "event" as much as possible.

Yet the narrative is punctuated by moments designed to goad the Wanderer into revealing her identity, moments that disrupt the narrative surface as they disrupt the protagonist's composure. Interestingly, the anger and frustration beneath the decorous surface of English society find sarcastic voice in the invective of its middle-aged women, for example, in the epithets hurled by Mrs. Ireton. Female aggression does boil over in the narrative at certain moments and, paradoxically, it is often directed at Juliet. Brutality in Burney's novels is often perpetrated by aristocratic men on women of other classes, but some of the most stunning moments in *The Wanderer* involve other women humiliating Juliet. Such a scene of verbal violence occurs between Juliet and Mrs. Ireton.

"So you had disfigured yourself in that horrid manner, only to extort money from us upon false pretences?"

.   .   .

The stranger did not dare risk any sort of reply.

.   .   .

"Nay, you are in the right, I own. What business is it of mine to confine your genius to only one or two methods of maiming or defacing yourself. ...O, I am diving too deeply into the secrets of your trade, am I?... You have been bruised and beaten; and dirty and clean; and ragged and whole; and wounded and healed; and a European and a Creole, in less than a week. I suppose, next, you will dwindle into a dwarf; and then, perhaps, find some surprising contrivance to shoot up into a giantess. There is nothing that can be too much to expect from so great an adept in metamorphoses." (36–37)

The disfigured image of Juliet that Mrs. Ireton creates (and Elinor uncannily repeats when she calls the Wanderer a "maimed and defaced dulcinea") is emblematic of the text itself, ingeniously transforming and maintaining itself, but marked by defacing moments of cruelty. The litany of the Incognita's false identities that Mrs. Ireton sarcastically recites is striking in its nastiness, mauling the surface of the narrative as well as Juliet. There seems to be almost a breach of fictional as well as social decorum, for the narrative has managed for the most part to contain this verbal assaultiveness. Mrs. Ireton refuses to be stopped by the "mantle of obscurity," exposing Juliet's self-effacement as defacement. In hurling epithets at the unnamed stranger, she in a sense refuses to accept the Wanderer's "fictions" of identity and remarks instead the pain that underwrites such self-constructions. The thrust of her antagonism seems to be that Aldonza is parading as Dulcinea, her anger typical of the kind of aggression that the well-to-do heap on lower-class characters in Burney's novels. Juliet's refusal to assume her social position by identifying herself enrages Mrs. Ireton, who is invested in keeping everyone in her place. It is Juliet's protean identity rather than her social climbing that excites Mrs. Ireton's wrath, as if Juliet's paradoxical and lonely "freedom" from a place in patriarchal society threatened Mrs. Ireton with its contrast to her own unchanging condition. Mrs. Ireton's own power, as a widow, depends on a stable private income and the possession of property; Juliet's *portable* self-possession seems particularly frightening to her. Sir Jaspar points to Mrs. Ireton's frustration when he conjectures that her sarcasm is the only outlet for her wit (518). This "reading" of Mrs. Ireton implicitly suggests that the tongue-lashing of such angry female characters curiously repeats (with a difference) Juliet's defacements, revealing anger as another response to the narrow confines of female identity. On a continuum of responses to "female difficulties," female invective lies at the opposite pole from female silence but expresses the same impotence and frustration.

Epstein maintains that the scenes of aggression in Burney's novels are a strategy of exposure, of ripping the surface of convention. She says that these moments enable Burney to represent "female fear and the forced loss of control that constantly lurks beneath society's polite forms and coerces women into self-suppression . . . violence cracks the surface of polite and acceptable social engagement and raises the specter of exposure" ("Writing the Unspeakable," 132). What this theory doesn't explain, however, is the excessive brutality of female characters toward the heroine. The misprisions of the protagonist by some of the female characters are more interesting than the misreadings by male characters, who tend to cast the "Fair Aenigma" as either object of adoration or sexual bait. Mrs. Ireton and Mrs. Marple, on the other hand, articulate the real difficulty of fixing the circulating sign of the female Wanderer. They expose her self-creations as successive defacements, unveiling the politics of sexuality that force her into increasingly more humiliating roles.

As an agent of narrative goading and painful exposure, Mrs. Ireton is one aspect of the female writer, the other represented by Juliet: if

Juliet is the magician of identities that Mrs. Ireton thinks she is and therefore a figure for the writer's own negative capability, Mrs. Ireton stands in for the writer who unmakes the fiction of the novel's supposedly "safe space." Indeed, because Juliet becomes, in Mrs. Ireton's interpellations of her, a "disfigured" heroine, the two figures collapse into one—the narrative includes both the self-creation of Juliet and the defacement and de-creation of Mrs. Ireton. This textual weaving and unraveling returns us to Penelope's canny deferral, the woman artist who intentionally staves off premature closure until the "proper" closure of Odysseus's return home. I would suggest, however, that Burney's Penelope is indeed in two places at once in this fiction of wandering; she is Serres's Hermes/Penelope at the theoretical position, both the writer "at home" and the exiled traveler.

Despite the novel's ultimate reclamation of patriarchal legacies at its end in what seems like the acquiescence of a journey home, *The Wanderer* denies that sense of the accumulation of capital the voyager usually brings home from his journey. The "booty" of experience cannot recompense the suffering; the scarring of the narrative is not magically healed. "[Odysseus] dines with Alcinous, paying for his meal with his edifying stories; he frees himself from the song of the Sirens; he eliminates from his house the 'pretenders,' who themselves act like parasites" (Serres, *Parasite*, 9). Although the Wanderer's difficulties are resolved and the narrative "felicitously" concluded (836), the "summing up" cannot sufficiently account for the pain in the narrative.

Thus, Cavendish's "Assaulted and Pursued Chastity" and Burney's *The Wanderer* exemplify two very different treatments of the link between women's travel and travail. Whereas Cavendish converts the risks of romance wandering into the rhetorical capital of speeches and performances, turning drift into an element of pleasure, Burney eschews such an exchange, leaving us with the residue of pain. As I have argued, these differences are in part generic and historical. For Cavendish, the romance geography of the imaginary voyage provided an opportunity for baroque reinvention of women's agency in the social world. In the topos of exilic wandering, Cavendish discovered a lexicon of impulsion, motion, and reaction with which to explore ambiguities of agency. If the imaginary voyage enabled her to try out the pleasures of various social hypotheses, she used the genre to circumscribe action in a nexus of power relations. Foucault's formulation of the workings of power seems apposite to Cavendish's own representations. Power, he says, is "a total structure of actions brought to bear upon possible actions; it incites, it induces, it seduces, it makes easier or more difficult; in the extreme it constrains or forbids absolutely; it is nevertheless always a way of acting upon an acting subject or acting subjects by virtue of their acting or being capable of action" (789). Exile provides the alibi of necessity, the initiating condition of the plot of romance wandering—it absolutely forbids, in Foucault's terms, continued dwelling at home. But once on the road, the opposition between consent and resistance is deconstructed in "worlded," if bizarre, social engagements.

In Burney's novel, as in Cavendish's imaginary voyage, exile is a metaphor for women's dispossession in English society; but in the more verisimilar geography of the eighteenth-century novel, the destabilization of the traveler's social "place" is concretely represented, making her both more exploited and more powerfully disruptive of the "foreign" social economy she enters. If chance occurrences impel the movements of Travelia, beginning with the vague disturbance of the civil war, the social antagonisms, fueled by the specific historical circumstances of the French Revolution, propel the movements of the unclassed and declassed wanderer in Burney's story. Yet, as in Cavendish's tale, agency in *The Wanderer* is conceived in terms of neither absolute activity nor passivity. In the more populated world of Burney's novel, where women characters are individuated, one finds women as goads to movement and women as circulating objects— impelling and constraining each other's trajectories. The painful deferral of narrative closure thus represents both the humiliations visited on and the responsive energies mobilized by the woman who wanders.

2

Composing the Self in Letters: Wollstonecraft's *Letters Written during a Short Residence in Sweden, Norway, and Denmark*

"If ever there was a book calculated to make a man in love with its author, this appears to me to be the book," William Godwin wrote of Mary Wollstonecraft's *Letters Written during a Short Residence in Sweden, Norway, and Denmark* (*Memoirs*, 249). This unusual travel book was cast in the form of letters to a lover, unnamed in the text but clearly Gilbert Imlay, who sent Wollstonecraft (accompanied by their illegitimate daughter) as his agent on a business trip to Scandinavia in the summer of 1795. Imlay's motive, however, was complex, for at the same time as he requested his lover/agent to try to recover some lost and probably embezzled cargo on a Swedish vessel he had commissioned to sail to France, he also wanted her out of the way so that at home in London he could establish a liaison with another woman. Claire Tomalin aptly summarizes Imlay's instigation of Wollstonecraft's travel: "There is an almost sublime effrontery about sending off a discarded mistress, newly recovered from a suicide attempt and accompanied by a small baby, on a difficult journey into unknown territory, to recoup your financial disasters for you and leave you free to enjoy the company of her rival without reproach: in his way, Imlay was a man of resource" (175).[1]

[1]Wollstonecraft's journey to Scandinavia was quite unusual for a British traveler, even at the end of the century. Jeremy Black points out that few eighteenth-century British travelers chose Scandinavia as their destination. William Benson, the son of an iron merchant, traveled to Sweden at the beginning of the century because it was Britain's principal source of iron; a few aristocrats, such as Lord and Lady Effingham, Lord Clinton, and Lord Bruce, made brief tours; in 1786 Sir Henry Liddell embarked on a

Addressed to an absent lover who failed to respond in the way she desired (the romance ended when she returned to England), ironically, the travel letters contributed to the development of Wollstonecraft's relationship with Godwin, whom she subsequently married. In *Letters*, Wollstonecraft writes both a travel book addressed to the public about a sublime northern landscape that few Englishmen and women had ever seen or read about and, at the same time, a "lover's discourse," to use Roland Barthes's term, a discourse that transforms the beloved's absence into an aesthetic "ordeal of abandonment" (*Lover's Discourse*, 13). Her epistolary discourse is thus double: it is amorous—like a host of abandoned female lovers before her, she attempts to renew a response—and it is educational—like Smollett's Humphry Clinker, she writes as travel guide.

One might object at the outset that to introduce Wollstonecraft's text by way of Godwin's response is already to reinforce certain stereotypes about women and letters. For one thing, his projection of "calculated" intention might seem to cast Wollstonecraft as a designing woman whose main agenda was some kind of seduction. Furthermore, in circumscribing her travel letters as amatory, Godwin reinforces the narrow idea of women's epistolary writing as a vehicle for private emotion. Seventeenth- and eighteenth-century male editors of epistolary collections regarded emotion as the "natural" sphere of the female letter.[2] This framing of epistolary discourse in terms of emotion is particularly problematic in the case of Wollstonecraft, whose works repeatedly explore the vexing relation between sensibility and rationality and seek to uncouple women and emotion.

Instead of confirming stereotypes about women and letters, Woll-

---

three-month tour of Scandinavia to fulfill a wager that "he could go to Lapland and return with two reindeer and two Lapp women" (31). In the final section of this chapter I compare Wollstonecraft's cultural analysis of Scandinavia with William Coxe's in his authoritative, three-volume travel record, which Wollstonecraft read before undertaking her own journey.

[2] Essays in *Writing the Female Voice* document the widespread tendency, in the seventeenth and eighteenth centuries, to circumscribe female epistolarity within the sentimental tradition. In "Authority, Authenticity, and the Publication of Letters by Women," for example, Elizabeth C. Goldsmith traces critical response to Madame de Sévigné, whose travel letters to her daughter made her one of the most famous female letter writers of the seventeenth century. She maintains that the standard view of Sévigné's letters, even into the twentieth century, was of her "natural, feminine affinity to the letter genre" (53–54).

stonecraft's text challenges both androcentric and feminist "gender-
ings" of travel and epistolarity.[3] Even Godwin's response to these
letters reverses the gendering of a typical fictional scene in literature
involving travel, from Shakespeare to Elizabeth Gaskell, of women
romantically fascinated by the storytelling of the male traveler—Dido
listening to Aeneas, Desdemona eliciting Othello's biography, the ladies of Cranford responding to Mr. Peter's colorful stories of his military career in India. Godwin reacts to Wollstonecraft's travels as if
entranced by her prowess as both traveler and writer, responding to
a new kind of exotic—a romance of the ice—and to a new type of
traveler, who manages to transfer to herself as observer and writer
some of the power of the sublime northern landscape. This response
he shared with a whole generation of male readers inspired by Wollstonecraft's book, which, according to Richard Holmes, "entered into
the literary mythology of romanticism within a single generation"
(41). Coleridge, Southey, Wordsworth, and Hazlitt praised it, and Robert Louis Stevenson took a copy of the first edition with him to Samoa
(Holmes, 36).[4] Southey wrote that the book "caused him to fall in love
with the cold climate and the moonlight of the North" (Nyström, 45).
Powerfully revising the topoi of both sentimental traveler and epistolary lover, this discourse inspired texts as well as love.

Furthermore, although *Letters* constructs the writer in relation to an
absent and potentially unfaithful lover, its plot performs a twist on
the Barthesian "lover's discourse," in which the woman gives shape
to absence while *she* stays home and the lover departs ("the Spinning
Songs express both immobility . . . and absence" [Barthes, *Lover's Discourse*, 114]). Here, Wollstonecraft herself takes to the road. Movement

---

[3]Wollstonecraft was not alone in expanding the province of the female epistolary
tradition beyond domesticity. In this enterprise, she continued the work of Madame de
Sévigné, Lady Mary Wortley Montagu, and Wollstonecraft's immediate predecessor,
Helen Maria Williams. However, most letters written by women in the eighteenth century "reinforce[d] literary and social restrictions on female enterprise" by linking the
private letter and domestic confinement (Spacks, "Female Resources: Epistles, Plot, and
Power," 64).

[4]Arctic exploration occurred throughout the nineteenth century, augmenting the Al-
pine literature of the sublime from the previous century and further establishing the
northern sublime as a masculine realm of arduous adventure. Chauncey Loomis says
in "The Arctic Sublime" that Coleridge's "The Rime of the Ancient Mariner" was in-
fluenced by his reading of accounts of Arctic exploration (98–99). It makes sense to
consider the sublime in Mary Shelley's *Frankenstein* as owing something to her mother's
representations in *Letters* as well as to Coleridge's poem. I will discuss more fully below
the possibilities of a "female sublime."

replaces the endless waiting of Penelope; the business of travel and travel writing competes with the preoccupation of abandoned love. Indeed, Wollstonecraft's journey geographically and textually blurs the opposition between excursus and domesticity and their typical gender assignments of masculine and feminine, respectively. Traveling on Imlay's business, encountering hosts who bluntly tell her that she is "a woman of observation" who asks *"men's questions"* (*Letters*, 248; parenthetical citations are to Todd/Butler ed.), she nevertheless carries "domesticity" with her in the form of Imlay's illegitimate child, Fanny, and a nursemaid, in tow for part of the journey. *Letters* reflects the mixed agenda of its writer, as topics of commerce and nursing intersect in the text. Distance both attenuates and strengthens the ties between traveler and lover. On the one hand, the travel book was envisioned by Wollstonecraft as a means of achieving financial independence from Imlay: "I have begun [*Letters*], which will, I hope, discharge all my obligations of a pecuniary kind.—I am lowered in my own eyes, on account of my not having done it sooner" ("Letters to Imlay," 422). At the same time, both her role as his business proxy and the epistolary genre of the travel record tighten the cord of connection between them by making him the absent addressee. The *oikos* (Greek for "home") of the journey is renewed, so to speak—painfully—on every page, with every salutation and farewell. An attempt at once to forget the pain of home and to renew domestic ties, a project dedicated to "composing" the self in letters, poignantly framed by two suicide attempts, *Letters* conflates the poles of home and abroad.

Thus, Wollstonecraft's epistolary travel book graphs both centrifugal and centripetal impulses. Furthermore, it embodies and materializes the philosophical idea of female liberty that dominates Wollstonecraft's writings. For in her arduous voyage to Scandinavia (and its record in writing), Wollstonecraft gives spatial extension to one of the central figures of her philosophy of liberty: that strength of body and mind come from their exercise. Reprising crucial issues from *A Vindication of the Rights of Woman* (as does *The Wrongs of Woman, or Maria; a Fragment*, which in many ways it resembles), the travel book gives substance to philosophical debates about liberty, particularly women's liberty. Repeatedly in *Vindication* she juxtaposes the image of the cramped body and mind of girls and women with the exercise of the "locomotive faculty of body or mind" (141) so nurtured in most boys and men: "To preserve personal beauty, woman's glory! the limbs and faculties are cramped with worse than Chinese bands, and the sedentary life which they are condemned to live, whilst boys frolic in the open air, weakens the muscles and relaxes the nerves" (41). She says, "For man is so constituted that he can only attain a proper use of his faculties by exercising them, and will not exercise them unless necessity, of some kind, first set the wheels in motion" (141). *Letters* is the record of such an exercise, a venture into the world that records both the profits and losses, pleasures and pains of such movement. "I cannot praise a fugitive and cloistered virtue unexercised and un-breathed, that never sallies out and sees her adversary, but slinks out of the race where that immortal garland is to be run for, not without dust and heat" (Milton, 247–48): these are Milton's words in "Areo-pagitica," not Wollstonecraft's, yet her precursor in the analysis of liberty provides a fitting statement of the risky and strenuous enter-prise of her travel text. Wollstonecraft's idea of liberty demonstrates her Enlightenment faith in the acquisition of moral knowledge through travel. Her liberal feminism builds on the spatial phenome-nology of individualism that is Locke's legacy—a philosophy of the self's expansion through the senses.[5]

But Wollstonecraft's conception of a woman's sphere expanded be-yond the cramped confines of domesticity emphasizes the possibility that knowledge brings pain as well as pleasure. In a private letter to Imlay written after she visited the town of Beverley, England, where she had lived for six years as a young girl, she says: "The town did not please me quite so well as formerly—It appeared so diminutive; and, when I found that many of the inhabitants had lived in the same houses ever since I left it, I could not help wondering how they could thus have vegetated, whilst I was running over a world of sorrow, snatching at pleasure, and throwing off prejudices" ("Letters to Im-lay," 410–11). Self-extension involves risk; if exercise is a strengthen-ing discipline, it does not inure the adventurer to the chance or penalties of sorrow.[6] Indeed, as opposed to the security of philosoph-ical observation, travel writing is particularly alive to the vicissitudes encountered on the road. Wollstonecraft more than once describes her

---

[5]See C. B. MacPherson's discussion of the development of the theory of possessive individualism from its origins in the seventeenth century. See also Gillian Brown's anal-ysis of this spatial phenomenology in "Anorexia, Humanism, and Feminism."

[6]In "Setting Byron Straight: Class, Sexuality, and the Poet," Jerome Christensen pres-ents a more conservative view of Wollstonecraft's idea of exercise. What he refers to as "Wollstonecraftian exercise" is "aimed at defending against chance, and devoted to the proprietarial conservation of a self anxiously possessed" (140). I view Wollstonecraftian exercise, particularly as represented in *Letters*, as a more risky deployment of the fac-ulties.

letters as "desultory," conflating the wanderer and her writing, importing into the process of composition the contingencies of travel. In *Letters*, Wollstonecraft replaces the more secure and impersonal vantage point of "speculation" in *Vindication* with the presentation of a more labile viewpoint. At one point in *Vindication* she figures herself as calmly surveying the scene from her promontory: "Let me now as from an eminence survey the world stripped of all its false delusive charms. The clear atmosphere enables me to see each object in its true point of view, while my heart is still. I am calm as the prospect in a morning when the mists, slowly dispersing, silently unveil the beauties of nature, refreshed by rest" (110). In *Letters* this image of the masterful and clear-eyed survey of the world gives way to an itinerary of responsiveness and encounter: "I shall continue in my desultory manner to make such observations and reflections as the circumstances draw forth" (260). These "circumstances" pertain both to travel and to travel writing; the "risks" involve the reception of the text as well as the circumstances of the traveler abroad.

Godwin's response as a reader suggests the way Wollstonecraft's text deliberately constructs both its writer/traveler and reader in relation to their very capacity for response. The fiction of addressing the travel book to a lover promotes the question (and problem) of feeling to a central position in the writing and reading of the travel text, both as topic and performance. As in her previous works, the problem of sensibility almost obsesses the travel text, since sentiment for Wollstonecraft is like a difficult lover—one can't live happily with or without it.

I have spoken of the "fiction" of address to a lover partly because there is some ambiguity surrounding the status of this text as actual letters. The original manuscript of *Letters* has been lost, and there seems to be no actual record that the letters were ever sent or intended to be sent. In her introduction to a 1976 edition of the book, Carol Poston says, rather ambiguously: "Wollstonecraft's chronicle of that summer of 1795 spent in the northern countries, in the form of letters written to Gilbert Imlay in London, was published in 1796 by Joseph Johnson as *Letters Written during a Short Residence in Sweden, Norway, and Denmark*. Because the letters were written to an actual person, they are lively and vivid, and for the most part avoid the artificiality that can sometimes be limiting in the epistolary form" (xi). It seems more likely, however, as Holmes conjectures in a footnote to his tandem edition of Wollstonecraft's travel book and Godwin's memoirs, that they were intended as a travel journal, addressed to Imlay, rather than as letters to be sent (279n). Supporting this theory is a fascinating textual "double" in the form of letters that *were* sent to Imlay and that overlap the writing of the travel book, letters that were not intended for publication but were posthumously published by Godwin. (These letters shocked many readers with their open representation of Imlay and Wollstonecraft's adulterous relationship.) Thus, the travel book represents its audience as both an absent beloved (Imlay) and a public readership.

A sympathetic chain of response between traveler and reader is projected—the travel writer represents her response to the landscape of Scandinavia, which, in turn, is meant to evoke a response in the reader. This affective chain, rather than leading to entrapment in the realm of private feeling, is meant to reinforce the social vision delineated in the text; one could say that the erotic and pedagogic are linked, for the traveler is a philosopher who creates a kind of pedagogy of feeling and taste.[7] The traveler becomes representative, her experiences generating philosophical meditations on response and sympathy. Travel "views" lead to cultural views about the importance of taste (sensibility allied with judgment) in society as a whole: "If we wish to render mankind moral from principle, we must, I am persuaded, give a greater scope to the enjoyment of the senses, by blending taste with them. This has frequently occurred to me since I have been in the North" (*Letters*, 307). Like Coleridge and Wordsworth, poets who attach the love of nature to the development of a social sense, Wollstonecraft treats aesthetic response as moral and social. Sometimes the relation between social vision and private suffering is uneasy—the confident tones of these pedagogic, abstract pronouncements about the role of feeling coexist in the text with moments when sentiment threatens to arrest the narrative: "At present black melancholy hovers round my footsteps; and sorrow sheds a mildew over all the future prospects, which hope no longer gilds" (303). The reader is constructed as both a public who will learn from Wollstonecraft's

---

[7]In her study of the relation between letters and desire, Linda Kauffman tells us that theorists of epistolarity divide the genre into two major categories: erotic and educational (177). Janet Altman speaks of the travelogue or travel letters as one of three strands of educational letters (196). Wollstonecraft's text cannot be so neatly categorized.

travel "views," and a private, more intimate reader whose response to the traveler-in-writing is sometimes wistfully, sometimes defiantly solicited in the text.

This curious mixture of intimate address and philosophical meditation places Wollstonecraft's travel text in the emerging context of Romantic conversation poems such as Wordsworth's *The Prelude* and Coleridge's "Frost at Midnight" that construct their own sympathetic listener. Wollstonecraft casts her travel record in the mode of prophecy, in which "prospects" refers to a survey of time as well as space, a distant future about which one might warn others. She refers to herself as Cassandra: "Cassandra was not the only prophetess whose warning voice has been disregarded" (342). Part of the book's agenda is to evoke a response from both a lover and a public who haven't been listening. As in Romantic lyric, the natural landscape seems to initiate the conversation: "When fugitive feelings are taken seriously, when every sight and sound calls to the passing poet—'Nay, Traveler, rest!';—then the Romantic nature lyric is born" (Hartman, "Wordsworth, Inscriptions," 221). The foreign landscape "speaks" to the English traveler, who in turn urges her audience to pay attention.

The tone of urgency, then, responds to both the necessity and the absence of a sympathetic listener. The relation between travel and absence which Barthes explores in *A Lover's Discourse* and which I invoke at the beginning of this book on women's travel nowhere finds a more powerful emblem than Wollstonecraft's *Letters*. As Barthes puts it, "What is proposed here then is a portrait, but not a psychological portrait; instead, a structured one which offers the reader a discursive site: the site of someone speaking within himself, amorously, confronting the other (the loved object) who does not speak" (*Lover's Discourse*, 3)—in *Letters*, the writer is constructed in relation to an absent other. Barthes goes on to say, "An always present I is constituted only by confrontation with an always absent you" (13). The deictics of Wollstonecraft's text constantly remind us that she is here, now, in the place where he / the reader-lover is not: "And here I am again, to talk of any thing, but the pangs arising from the discovery of estranged affection, and the lonely sadness of a deserted heart" (*Letters*, 283). In this first-person record, as opposed to the third-person narratives of travelers by Cavendish and Burney, writer and traveler are on the road together; the textual "I" is constructed in relation to her distance from home base, which is both England and the place where the lover resides. Absence suffuses the text so that distance in space is also registered as a distance in time, a record of something passing. Gestures of preservation are found throughout the text, as if travel writing were inevitably a testimony of loss as well as distance: "Straying further, my eye was attracted by the sight of some heart's-ease that peeped through the rocks. I caught at it as a good omen, and going to preserve it in a letter that had not conveyed balm to my heart, a cruel remembrance suffused my eyes; but it passed away like an April shower. If you are deep read in Shakespeare you will recollect that this was the little western flower tinged by love's dart, which 'maidens call love in idle-ness' " (246–47). Like the unsatisfying letter from her lover, even hopeful nature is a text already inscribed with loss, reminding her, as it does, of the happier erotic promise of Shakespeare's *Midsummer Night's Dream*. Wollstonecraft as female Odysseus is an exile like Joyce's Leopold Bloom, a traveler whose "business" abroad always occurs in relation to a sense of estrangement at home.[8] For Wollstonecraft's traveler, as for Brontë's Lucy Snowe in *Villette*, "home" is a place already made strange: "I am weary of travelling," Wollstonecraft writes in a private letter to Imlay near the end of her journey, "yet [I] seem to have no home— no resting place to look to.—I am strangely cast off" ("Letters to Imlay," 426–27).

Travel arises at least in part from disappointed domesticity; it offers transport from the realm of disappointed love to a potentially happier place. In a private letter to Imlay, Wollstonecraft writes: "Before I left the shore, tormented, as I now am, by these North-east *chillers*, I could not help exclaiming—Give me, gracious Heaven! at least, genial weather, if I am never to meet the genial affection that still warms this agitated bosom—compelling life to live there" ("Letters to Imlay," 414). Travel, she seems to say, is initiated out of some kind of lack, an idea she repeats in *Letters* in a myth of the development of civilization: "Man must therefore have been placed in the north, to tempt him to run after the sun, in order that the different parts of the earth might be peopled" (263). But if the transfer from the lack of "genial affection" to a place of "genial weather" implies that travel is an escape from the pain of a disappointing love, it also suggests the way that writing can provide a space for transforming pain into something else. As Michel Butor reminds us, writing is a form of travel (15)— the transfer of the meaning of "genial" from affection to weather ex-

---

[8]Wollstonecraft set sail on June 16, 1795, 209 years before Joyce's Bloomsday.

emplifies a troping, or turning in writing, as a strategy for dealing with loss. It also suggests that travel writing may be an escape from the limits of the lover's discourse, in which distance is only absence (the absence of genial affection). It might allow a woman writer to write beyond the topos of sentimentality that has immured others while still allowing for an exploration of feeling and response.

Movement transports the traveler and narrative beyond the kind of emotional fixation that resembles being stuck in one place. This transport is threatened by the physical delay of Wollstonecraft's departure from Hull, England: a lack of wind forced her ship to remain off the coast of England for eleven days before setting sail for Scandinavia. Private letters to Imlay written while she awaited departure suggest that she "read" this delay allegorically, as threatening to imprison her in emotional stagnancy.

Here, a difference is apparent between the way Wollstonecraft composes her travel book, intended for publication, and her private letters to Imlay. For in the private letters, written before Wollstonecraft left England, she says of her imminent departure: "The quitting England seems to be a fresh parting.—Surely you will not forget me.—A thousand weak forebodings assault my soul, and the state of my health renders me sensible to every thing" ("Letters to Imlay," 412). Throughout these letters she evokes the image of herself as painfully "dwelling" on Imlay's abandonment, possessed by sadness, and awaiting his letters. "My hand seems unwilling to add adieu! I know not why this inexpressible sadness has taken possession of me. . . . I dread to meet wretchedness in some new shape" (412). In her next letter to Imlay, she laments:

> Why am I forced thus to struggle continually with my affections and feelings?—Ah? why are those affections and feelings the source of so much misery, when they seem to have been given to vivify my heart, and extend my usefulness! But I must not *dwell* on this subject.—Will you not endeavour to cherish all the affection you can for me? What am I saying?—Rather forget me, if you can. (413, emphasis added).

In the following letter she describes herself as "tossed about" by her own emotions: "It is indeed wearisome to be thus tossed about without going forward. . . . I will not, my dear ——, torment you by dwelling on my sufferings" (413–14). Like the ship, she is at the mercy of forces beyond her control. To be so tossed without moving forward is to lose control, not only over her emotions, but over her writing as well, for the letters themselves circle around their own predicament. It is as if both time and space were "blocked" by such fixation, for she can no longer imagine a future ("When going to [Lisbon], ten years ago, the elasticity of my mind was sufficient to ward off weariness—and the imagination still could dip her brush in the rainbow of fancy, and sketch futurity in smiling colours" [414]).[9]

In contrast to these private letters, the first letter in the travel book begins after the voyage is under way. Travel and travel writing serve as both strategies and metaphors for moving beyond the fixation of feeling. Providing transport, they counteract the mental obsession that freezes her in one "place," threatening to block all movement—physical, mental, emotional, and literary. Travel and travel writing convert mental circling or repetition into the lucid and energetic extension of the mind toward other observations—that is, they convert mental "dwelling" into narrative movement. In this letter's first paragraph, Wollstonecraft writes, "I adhere to my determination of giving you my observations, as I travel through new scenes, whilst warmed with the impression they have made on me" (243).

Yet the threat of painful repetition, indeed, of getting "stuck" in a groove, still haunts the discursive voyage of *Letters*, as though the writing keeps rediscovering the same "wretchedness in a new shape." The refrain of personal abandonment, as well as the more general complaint about women's powerless plight, echoes through the travel book; these refrains sometimes abruptly end in such phrases as "to return to the straight road of observation" (326) or "Whither do I wander?" (269). The wandering of conjecture and surmise, digression from the narrative, can sometimes lead to unforeseen distresses; the sally can begin to circle back on itself. At such moments, a straighter road of observation is sought in relief. It's as if there were two competing figures of travel in the text: one a more desultory and risky movement that promises new discoveries but sometimes threatens instead an enervating fixation, a dwelling on painful thoughts, and one, more purposive, intentional, philosophical—the more direct (and more comforting) route of observation. On the last page of *Letters*, purposeful movement is represented as coming to an end: "My spirit of observation seems to have fled—and I have been wandering round

---

[9]Wollstonecraft made her first trip abroad in 1785, when she traveled to Portugal to nurse her dying friend Fanny Blood.

this dirty place, literally speaking, to kill time" (345). The word "literally" here is fascinating—the physical "wandering round" is the opposite of healthy "exercise"; it is as if the body of the traveler were devitalized, even murdered, by the spirit's aimlessness. And time itself is murdered at the site of fixation, a murder that signals the death of the narrative. In the absence of spirit, the letter perishes as well. The above entry is the last in the book and is signed "Mary ——" in a final valedictory gesture (other letters end with a closing such as "God bless you!" or "Adieu," for example, but no other letter ends with a signature). The blank marks the site of the missing surname "Imlay" (letters of introduction Wollstonecraft took to Scandinavia identify her as "Mary Imlay," even though she and Imlay never married). With this painful excision, the travel writer terminates the correspondence.

———

The fear of emotional fixation, of being unable to proceed, raises the specter of sentimental fiction, in which emotional tableaux sometimes stop the narrative in its tracks. Speaking of Sterne's mid-century *Sentimental Journey through France and Italy by Mr. Yorick* (1768), which charts Yorick's physical and emotional itineraries, Janet Todd suggests that the episodic structure of the picaresque facilitates the hero's movement through the emotional moments of the narrative. She describes Yorick as a "feeling heart, fallible human being and resilient *picaro*, moving on unmarred by the tears of the world" (89). Further, the self-mockery and humor of Sterne's highly influential representation of the traveling man of feeling further insure against the possibility of getting stuck.

Wollstonecraft's writing strategy is very different, for her travel record does not adopt Sterne's self-mockery, nor is the figure of the picaro congruent with the responsible, authoritative image of the traveler that she wants to convey. But her narrative, in its own way, makes a point of the travel writer's authority to control the itinerary and choose topics of discussion; like a tour guide, the writer shepherds the reader over potential crevasses of emotion. That is, at moments she deliberately cuts off the figure of her own pain: "How I am altered by disappointment—When going to Lisbon, the elasticity of my mind was sufficient to ward off weariness, and my imagination still could dip her brush in the rainbow of fancy, and sketch futurity in glowing colours. *Now—but let me talk of something else—will you go with me to the cascade?"* (*Letters*, 310: emphasis added).[10] When the overwhelming sense of loss in the present moment threatens to arrest the narrative ("I cannot write any more at present. Tomorrow we will talk of Tonsberg" [272]), she assumes her prerogative as author and hurries us on. Painful topics become a space to be quickly traversed.

This sense of control over the itinerary of feeling is reinforced by the formal possibilities of the epistle; Wollstonecraft's use of new beginnings and endings to her letters not only provides convenient stopping places in the travelogue but also renews the contract of writer and reader at will. Like the *fort-da* game of Freud's grandson in *Beyond the Pleasure Principle,* which allows a rehearsal of the loss and return of the mother, the comings and goings of the letters give the traveler/ writer the illusion of control over the presence and absence of the lover. Not only is the reader of the text constructed as a lover, but the lover is constructed as a reader, as well. In a sense, the traveler/writer "reforms" the lover's silence in casting him as the interested reader of her travelogue.

In this regard, there are significant differences between the "private" letters to Imlay that Wollstonecraft actually sent and the fictional "letters" that constitute the travel book.[11] Like Lucy Snowe, Wollstonecraft composed two versions of her letters to her loved one, hence, two versions of both the woman traveler and the lover/reader. Whereas "Imlay" appears as cold, inattentive, and silent in the private letters, he is constructed as a more sympathetic, although still unsatisfying, reader in *Letters.* For in the fictional letters, she invokes him as an armchair traveler who *wants* to accompany his tour guide; she presumes his interest: "I almost forgot to tell you" (311), she says, as if he hangs on her travelogue. Addressing him as an interested member of her audience, she leads him through her own itinerary of sites and subjects: "But let me talk of something else. Will you go with me to the cascade?" Yet she does confess to her "dear friend" that she can no longer deny her sentiments even though she appears to control

---

[10]In her private letter to Imlay dated June 20, 1795 (quoted on p. 82), she does not so quickly abridge the suffering.

[11]Issues of "public" and "private" are complicated when one regards the dual texts, because the "public" travel book is addressed to Imlay as well as to a larger readership, and the "private" letters, not intended for publication, were published by Godwin. It was public response to Godwin's publication of the private letters that caused Wollstonecraft's reputation to plummet, whereas the travel book, widely read in England, Europe, and America, endeared her to the public, if not to Imlay.

the narrative itinerary: "For years have I endeavoured to calm an impetuous tide—labouring to make my feelings take an orderly course.—It was striving against the stream.—I must love and admire with warmth, or I sink into sadness." She even ventures to cast herself in a little dialogue as love-sick Maria, the sentimental heroine in Sterne's story: "Tokens of love which I have received have rapt me in elysium. . . . My bosom still glows.—-Do not saucily ask, repeating Sterne's question, 'Maria, is it still so warm?' Sufficiently, O my God! has it been chilled by sorrow and unkindness—still nature will prevail" (280). In this mock reenactment of Sterne's *Sentimental Journey*, Wollstonecraft both exposes the "warmth" of her emotion and controls its representation by playfully rescripting Sterne's novel. The genre and form of the travel letters allow Wollstonecraft to modulate between a sense of worthwhile risk (in responding to the contingencies of travel) and a sense of control (in the power of her writing to "compose" the self of the traveler and her itinerary).

Wollstonecraft's emphasis on responding to circumstance alludes to a whole tradition of male sentimental travel and its feminizing spirit. In this tradition, the faculty of responsiveness is an index of the male traveler's value. As Todd points out, Sterne's traveler helped define the mid-century concept of sentimentality ("the faculty of feeling, the capacity for extremely refined emotion and a quickness to display compassion for suffering" [7]), which during the century was increasingly associated with women (8). In Sterne's *Sentimental Journey*, to which Wollstonecraft refers several times in *Letters*, Yorick is as sensitive as a woman, and it is his responsiveness to, not his mastery of, foreign lands that recommends him as a traveler. On the other hand, this susceptibility and vulnerability disguise a manipulative potential that Robert Markley describes as part of a "masculinist complex of strategies" involving the superiority of the man of feeling, who lavishes his benevolence on mostly female victims (211). Promulgating the importance of feeling and responsiveness while also warning of the dangers of indiscriminate emotion, Wollstonecraft rewrites an already ambiguously gendered tradition of travel narrative.

Wollstonecraft's own relation to sensibility and sentimental fiction has been much debated by literary critics. Mary Poovey calls Wollstonecraft's attraction to sentiment "ambiguous," for although Wollstonecraft produced sentimental novels such as *Mary, A Fiction*, her *Vindication of the Rights of Woman* is seen by Poovey and other feminist critics as rejecting the potential traps in a definition which links women with emotion and which separates them from rationality (*Proper Lady*, 70–80). Poovey and Cora Kaplan, most notably, have interpreted Wollstonecraft as denying the role of sexuality and passion and pursuing the argument that women are essentially rational creatures, just like men except for their "feminine" educations.[12] They fault her for fostering a fatal split between intellect and emotion. Yet, *Letters*, Wollstonecraft's last published work before her tragic death in childbirth, has been read by some critics (including Poovey) as the piece that most successfully repairs this dissociation of sensibility through the flexible genre of travel writing, in which Wollstonecraft was able to wed intellect and emotion, personal reflection and social observation. Moira Ferguson and Janet Todd ascribe to the travel book a "golden mean" between intellect and emotion (91). In her introduction to the text, Carol Poston sees the book as "possibly the perfect fusion of the personal and intellectual selves of Mary Wollstonecraft" (xx).

I, too, find *Letters* important to consideration of Wollstonecraft's treatment of emotion. In it she both portrays a traveler who acknowledges the power of emotion and uses the narrative to control the itinerary of her own feelings. But an emphasis on the travel genre as a formal *container* for intellectual and emotional content ignores the way the dialogic structure of the travel record enacts, as well as rehearses, the philosophical problems it treats thematically. My argument focuses on gestures of address in the text as they contribute to a pedagogy of feeling. *Letters* is an argument for sensibility that tests eighteenth-century (as well as differently nuanced early Romantic) notions of "correspondence"—first, between the traveler and nature and, then, between the traveler's response to nature and the reader's response to the traveler's representation of experience. This thematics of "correspondence" is mirrored in the epistolary structure of the travel record (the epistolary correspondence between writer and reader). Participating in the discourse of both love and travel, the letter serves as envoi between traveler and reader, a transfer of felt emotion and experience, such that the letter moves its recipient. As in sentimental fiction and amorous discourse, the travel letters are textual bodies that function as "metonymic . . . displacement[s] of de-

---

[12]See Poovey's *Proper Lady and the Woman Writer: Ideology as Style in the Works of Mary Wollstonecraft, Mary Shelley, and Jane Austen* (48–81) and Cora Kaplan, "Pandora's Box: Subjectivity, Class, and Sexuality in Socialist Feminist Criticism."

sire," as Linda Kauffman puts it (38) (and hence are fetishized in sentimental fiction). The text bears the impress of the writer. In this regard, the illusion of immediacy is important. In *Letters*, Wollstonecraft insists on serving up her impressions of Scandinavia still warm on the page: "I adhere to my determination of giving you my observations, as I travel through new scenes, while warmed with the impression they have made on me" (243). It is as if the page itself received a bodily imprint from the writer's strongly felt impression.

The erotic body of the lover, the sentient body of the traveler, and the textual body of epistolary discourse merge. Although Wollstonecraft chooses to mute the erotic significance of the impress, emphasizing instead the intellectual and emotional responses captured in the word "impression," the body's trace remains. One might also say that the erotic body of Mary Wollstonecraft the traveler is displaced onto the body of the letter that is offered to the reader. This displacement allows for a revision of the trope of the female traveler's victimized body, which appears in *The Wanderer* and most sentimental fiction about women of sensibility alone in the world. As Todd says of women, as opposed to men, of feeling, in sentimental fiction "the sensitive body in women is inevitably sexualized for onlookers" (100). In recounting her travel experiences in Scandinavia, Wollstonecraft plays down her vulnerability as woman traveler. Only very occasionally in *Letters* does Wollstonecraft foreground the situation of a woman alone: "A woman, coming alone, interested them. And I know not whether my weariness gave me a look of peculiar delicacy; but they approached to assist me, and enquire after my wants, as if they were afraid to hurt, and wished to protect me" (269). Yet there is curiously little sense of the female traveler as a cynosure of erotic scrutiny. It is the romantic fate of the letter, its reception—cold or warm, welcomed or neglected—that bears the force of this sentimental drama; the circulation of the woman traveler herself in foreign society is represented as remarkably free of this sentimental concern.

The general emphasis on responsiveness—the traveler's to the landscape and the reader's to the traveler's account—is characteristic of a change in eighteenth-century travel writing during the latter half of the century. The shift to subjective descriptions of travel from the more impersonal "objective" accounts characteristic of the first half of the century accompanied an increasing emphasis on the traveler's response to the poetic qualities of landscape, as defined in the elaborate aesthetic discourse of the sublime and picturesque. Writing of eighteenth-century travel literature, Charles Batten describes a change that occurs after mid-century: "No longer loaded with facts, [travel writers'] accounts become collections of evocative descriptions focusing on the almost poetic qualities of mountains, forests, rivers, and lakes" (97).[13] The descriptions were meant to draw forth a corresponding response in the armchair traveler, the reader. Batten argues that by the end of the century, the prime objective of travel writers was to elicit the reader's emotion, "to open up sublime pleasures for their readers" (29). Batten's focus is on nonfictional travel writing, such as William Gilpin's "On Picturesque Travel" (1792), which Wollstonecraft had reviewed and which Batten calls "the most influential eighteenth-century statement about travel in search of the beauties of nature" (106). The emphasis in Gilpin is on landscape as emotionally stimulating; literature, including travel writing, could capture and confer duration on the emotions of the viewer and could cause, in turn, a similar response in the reader. This shift corresponds to a redefinition in the meaning of the sublime, from "the external cause of a particular aesthetic state in the beholder" to "that state itself," that is, from the object to the subject (Cohn and Miles, 296). In Batten's formulation of the "sublime pleasures of the reader," one can see that the language of the writer somehow migrates to the reader. Indeed, in the Longinian tradition, sublimity of language manages not only to transport but also to make the audience itself sublime.[14]

I want to emphasize here that Wollstonecraft's travel letters participate in a very prevalent eighteenth-century aesthetic discourse. The travel record makes a type of "argument" for responsiveness that draws on a complex chain of psychological reactions hypothesized by eighteenth-century aesthetics, a chain from object in nature to perceiver/writer to reader. Yet I also suggest that Wollstonecraft taxes this discourse by staging the *problems* of correspondence, including the difficulty of transferring the traveler's responsiveness to the lover/reader through representation on the page. In a private letter to Imlay (not published in *Letters*), Wollstonecraft elaborates on the link between social responsiveness and sensitivity to nature: love, she says, is "an affair of sentiment, arising from the same delicacy of perception

---

[13] In *The Adventurous Muse: The Poetics of American Fiction, 1789–1900*, William Spengemann describes a similar shift toward greater subjectivity in American travel writing of the same period.

[14] Steven Knapp discusses the principle of "identification" implicit in Longinus's remarks on the transport of the audience through sublime language (68).

(or taste) as renders them alive to the beauties of nature, poetry, etc., alive to the charms of those evanescent graces that are, as it were, impalpable—they must be felt, they cannot be described" ("Letters to Imlay," 418). Responding to the lover is like responding to nature, indeed has the same source in a "delicacy of perception"; yet even with the refined vocabulary of eighteenth-century aesthetics, the "charms of those evanescent graces," either in nature or in human nature, are almost impossible to convey. In *Letters* she says: "Yet we cannot find words to discriminate that individuality [in every prospect] so as to enable a stranger to say, this is the face, that the view. We may amuse by setting the imagination to work; but we cannot store the memory with a fact" (268). In reviewing Gilpin's picturesque travel books, Wollstonecraft had pointed out the difficulty of transmitting the traveler's response: "The observations of taste, which depend in a great degree on the organization of individuals, cannot, like more stubborn knowledge, be conveyed from one understanding to another, with precision and clearness; on the contrary, sentiments which are lively, in proportion to the sensibility of the person who feels them, are ever evanescent, and almost incommunicable" ("Review of 'Observations on the River Wye,' " 161). The relay of perception and feeling between writer and reader is riddled with difficulties. Impressions are evanescent, Wollstonecraft says, and in *Letters*, in particular, one senses the danger that the warmth of the traveler's "impression" will cool, the letter becoming a souvenir or trace.

The potential gaps in the chain of communication between traveler/ experiencer and reader are explicitly addressed in the "Advertisement" that prefaces the letters. Here, questions about sympathy between writer and reader and about the writer's ability to transmit responsiveness in writing are addressed to the "public" reader. Acknowledging that her first-person travelogue constructs her as "the little hero of each tale" (241), she goes on to say that it is the reader who must assess the value of spending time with such a traveler/ writer. She represents her hopes for a response in the reader, not in the affective discourse of sentimental philosophy, but in the drier tones of the rhetoric of entitlement she had used in *Vindication*: "A person has a right, I have sometimes thought, when amused by a witty or interesting egotist [Imlay?], to talk of himself when he can win our attention by acquiring our affection. Whether I deserve to rank amongst this privileged number, my readers alone can judge and I give them leave to shut the book if they do not wish to become better acquainted with me" (241). In *Letters*, Wollstonecraft constructs a female subjectivity for the reader's attention, a self in writing who deserves affection and respect. The author of *A Vindication of the Rights of Men* and *A Vindication of the Rights of Woman* now invokes the "rights" and entitlements—and a proper "estimation" or appreciation—leading to respect instead of rejection. Response and responsibility are linked in this rhetoric. The public reader is thus implicated in the process of judgment and feeling represented in the travelogue, but he/she is constructed as a reader wiser than the lover/reader, who fails to estimate the writer properly.[15]

In presenting her theory of reader response in this Advertisement, Wollstonecraft separates herself from the emotive rhetoric of sentimental journeys such as Sterne's, which seek affective persuasion, with the overwhelming force of the pathos generated in the tale. Instead, Wollstonecraft tells us, the reader is judge of this little hero and the quality of her "views" set down in travel writing—the reader can choose to accompany or not to accompany her, depending on his assessment. Kauffman regards the genre of amorous epistolary writing as "simultaneously a love letter and a legal challenge, a revolt staged in writing" (18). Basing some of her arguments on Bakhtin's idea of pathos as a surrogate forensic discourse, she goes on to show that texts within the genre are "structured around accusation, confrontation, trials, self-justification" (46); these are texts, Kauffman contends, that work not only by emotion alone but by argument as well. In his enormously influential "enquiry" into the topics of the sublime and beautiful, Edmund Burke maintains that rational argument has no place in regard to beauty, for "who ever said, we *ought* to love a fine woman, or even any of these beautiful animals, which please us? Here to be affected, there is no need of the concurrence of our will" (110). Yet, in a sense, this is precisely what Wollstonecraft attempts in her writing—to shift love to a more rational basis, transvaluing Burke's "beauty" by attempting to make it intellectual. The fusion in the Advertisement of claims to entitlement and appeals to emotion signals a shift in the basis of appreciation from pure sentiment to respect. As Wollstonecraft says in her introduction to *A Vindication of the Rights*

---

[15]In the private letters, Wollstonecraft focuses explicitly on Imlay's "misreading" of her character: "It is my misfortune, that my imagination is perpetually shading your defects, and lending you charms, whilst the grossness of your senses makes you (call me not vain) overlook graces in me, that only dignity of mind, and the sensibility of an expanded heart can give.—God bless you! Adieu" ("Letters to Imlay," 420).

of Woman, many women seem "only anxious to inspire love, when they ought to cherish a nobler ambition, and by their abilities and virtues exact respect" (7). This terminology makes clear that aesthetic responsiveness is a moral category.

Wollstonecraft's travel record implicitly revises Burke's "gendering" of the sublime and beautiful (and, thus, continues her critique of his politics in *A Vindication of the Rights of Men*). For in Burke's distinctions between beauty and sublimity, the former emerges as the "feminine" stimulus that elicits love, and the latter, the "masculine" stimulus that elicits awe and respect. For Burke, beauty is linked to those virtues which "engage our hearts, which impress us with a sense of loveliness" (100), whereas, on the other hand, the sublime virtues are those which evoke astonishment and admiration.[16] One can see Wollstonecraft's travel book as an attempt both to "toughen" the notions of beauty purveyed by Burke and to recoup for a female writer the province of the sublime.[17] She does this in two related ways: by representing the confrontation between the woman traveler and nature in sublime moments and by creating the representation of a sublime woman, her capacities expanded and enlarged through these transforming moments (the sublime, transferred from object in nature to perceiving consciousness). As Ronald Paulson notes, Wollstonecraft saw Burke's idea of the beautiful as part of a fiction created by men that binds women (84). Instead, Paulson suggests, Wollstonecraft described the sublime rather than the beautiful woman. He cites her *Historical and Moral View*, in which she refers to the "energetic character—A supple force, that, exciting love, commands esteem" (quoted in Paulson, 85).[18] This intellectual, or sublime, beauty is still, for Burke,

---

[16]Burke is most concerned with the sense of power and immensity in the sublime and its consequent production of terror and dread. In recording certain moments of her confrontation with nature, Wollstonecraft captures this sense of the self's confrontation with the vastness of nature, demonstrating that women could experience such a moment of transport. But in translating the sublime into more social terms, she is more like Kant in his *Observations on the Feeling of the Beautiful and Sublime*, who says that "sublime attributes stimulate esteem, but beautiful ones, love" (51).

[17]Terry Eagleton points out that Wollstonecraft felt Burke's distinction between love and respect "aestheticizes women in ways which remove them from the sphere of morality" (55).

[18]In a letter to Imlay from Gothenburg, Wollstonecraft reiterates these terms of energy and force: "Aiming at tranquillity, I have almost destroyed all the energy of my soul— almost rooted out what renders it estimable—yes, I have damped that enthusiasm of character, which converts the grossest materials into a fuel, that imperceptibly feeds hopes, which aspire above common enjoyment. Despair, since the birth of my child,

a social quality that causes love. In a sense, then, beauty becomes less familiar, less domesticated than it is in Burke, whereas sublimity, paradoxically, becomes more social. Martin Price posits two phases of the sublime: the "heroic ascent into transcendence" and the less dramatic, less heroic, yet radical domestic sublime in what he calls "the home epic" of *Middlemarch*, exemplified in the moment of Dorothea's connection with "involuntary, palpitating life" (47). Wollstonecraft's versions of the sublime cross more recognizably sublime moments of transcendence with the kind of social and moral human sympathy Price sees as that version available to women.

In the article "Toward a Female Sublime," Patricia Yeager calls the Romantic sublime "a genre lacking, for the most part, in literary foremothers" (198), a fact that would not surprise most "phallocentric" critics, who do "not expect women writers to be concerned with hypsos, with transport, with the grand discontinuities" (198). In many ways, Wollstonecraft's descriptions of her own confrontation with the lofty landscape of the imaginatively uncharted north qualify as the kind of "trespass" that Yeager sees in female appropriation of the sublime (199).

> Reaching the cascade, or rather cataract, the roaring of which had a long time announced its vicinity, my soul was hurried by the falls into a new train of reflections. The impetuous dashing of the rebounding torrent from the dark cavities which mocked the exploring eye, produced an equal activity in my mind: my thoughts darted from earth to heaven, and I asked myself why I was chained to life and its misery? Still the tumultuous emotions this sublime object excited, were pleasurable; and, viewing it, my soul rose, with renewed dignity, above its cares—grasping at immortality—it seemed as impossible to stop the current of my thoughts, as of the always varying, still the same, torrent before me—I stretched out my hand to eternity, bounding over the dark speck of life to come. (*Letters*, 311)

Wollstonecraft is concerned with the enlargement of the mind's capacity through a powerful and intimidating mirroring of natural objects. This view is close to the Kantian and the Romantic versions of the mind's confrontation with infinity, which produces an expansion

---

has rendered me stupid—soul and body seemed to be fading away before the withering touch of disappointment" ("Letters to Imlay," 418–19).

of the self. The sublime experience begins with a stimulus in nature, but response to it is internalized and psychologized; this view emphasizes the individual's particular capacity to apprehend such grandeur. As Alexander Gerard describes it in his essay of 1759 on taste (which Wollstonecraft would have known), the mind of the viewer responds to the large object in nature with a corresponding expansion. The mind "sometimes imagines itself present in every part of the scene which it contemplates; and from the sense of this immensity, feels a noble pride, and entertains a lofty conception of its own capacity" (12). Cascades are just such natural wonders to be reckoned in the repertoire of the sublime, and in this passage, Wollstonecraft comes closest to recording a sublime moment of transcendence: "I cannot tell why—but death, under every form, appears to me like something getting free—to expand in I know not what element; nay I feel that this conscious being must be as unfettered, have the wings of thought, before it can be happy" (*Letters*, 311). The trope of pioneering travel merges with the transport of the sublime to produce an image of intellectual and poetic freedom—unfettered flight of thought. Here, sublime nature tutors the traveler/poet's being. Sweden in particular figures as an aboriginal landscape of great power that promises renewal: "Approaching the frontiers, consequently the sea, nature resumed an aspect ruder and ruder, or rather seemed the bones of the world waiting to be clothed with every thing necessary to give life and beauty. Still it was sublime" (262).[19]

Yet if at rare moments a form of the heroic sublime is recorded, the dialogic structure of the epistolary travelogue, compounded by the haunting absence of the lover, creates the sense that the grand, solitary moments Wollstonecraft records in her narrative are directed toward a reader/witness whose own response is crucial to the completion of the scene. In her deconstruction of the opposition between domesticity and excursion, Wollstonecraft establishes a domestic center for the sublime, one that resembles Coleridge's evocation of domestic "geniality" in "Eolian Harp," "Frost at Midnight," and, in a more complicated way, "Dejection." The word "geniality," crucial to Coleridge's poetic lexicon ("my genial spirits fail," "principles of Genial

---

[19]As I have suggested throughout, the vocabulary of the sublime was highly developed by the time of Wollstonecraft's travels. But the more conventional setting for experiencing the sublime would have been Switzerland. Wollstonecraft's travels to Scandinavia *were* anomalous in the period.

Criticism"), also occurs in Wollstonecraft's text. "Genial" identifies an imaginative quality that is distinctly nonegotistical because it involves more than one person. As it applies to the conjugality in Coleridge's lyrics, it usually appears in terms of disappointment, as it often does in Wollstonecraft's *Letters*. But crucial to this concept of geniality is the establishment of a domestic center for the imagination (and for the sublime) as opposed to the excursive models of sublimity in the Miltonic epic tradition. Wollstonecraft produces a narrative of excursion in which travel to the north involves a solitary confrontation with a sublime, almost primitive landscape; nevertheless, contrary to experiences of the depopulated egotistical sublime most of the recorded moments look toward a process of social recuperation and integration.[20]

I said earlier that as Wollstonecraft's traveler/poet responds to the sublime landscape, she tests and unsettles the aesthetic discourse of correspondence. Wollstonecraft's own disappointed geniality makes her aware that the "correspondence" is imperfect, as it may not be fulfilled in the reader/lover. She sees, that is, the split between her "views" of the sublime and picturesque and the "looks" that she receives from the other.

Nature is the nurse of sentiment,—the true source of taste;—yet what misery, as well as rapture, is produced by a quick perception of the beautiful and sublime, when it is exercised in observing animated nature, when every beauteous feeling and emotion excites responsive sympathy, and the harmonized soul sinks into melancholy, or rises to extasy, just as the chords are touched, like the aeolian harp agitated by the changing wind. But how dangerous is it to foster these sentiments in such an imperfect state of existence; and how difficult to eradicate them when an affection for mankind, a passion for an individual, is but the unfolding of that love which embraces all that is great and beautiful.

When a warm heart has received strong impressions, they are not to be effaced. Emotions become sentiments; and the imagination renders even transient sensations permanent, by fondly retracing them. I cannot, without a thrill of delight, recollect views I have seen, which are not to be forgotten,—nor looks I have felt in every nerve which I shall never more

[20]See Frances Ferguson's essay "Malthus, Godwin, Wordsworth, and the Spirit of Solitude" on the relation between the Romantic notion of freedom and depopulation.

meet. . . . I cannot write any more at present. Tomorrow we will talk of
Tonsberg. (271–72)

The grammatical twists and turns, which make this such a difficult
passage to grasp, indicate the troubling implications of following
through with the logic of correspondences. In the first turn, signaled
by "yet" in the first line, Wollstonecraft acknowledges that harmony
with nature can just as easily produce melancholy as pleasure, depending on "the changing wind." This possibility of pain as well as
pleasure in the landscape is a feature of acute receptiveness—melancholy and "extasy" are but two sides of a sympathy with nature. At
the second turn, however (the "But"), she recognizes the pain this
correspondence brings to an "imperfect state of existence" when,
among other things, the traveler's response to nature is not recipro-
cated by the other (the reader/lover). If "affection for mankind" and
"a passion for an individual" logically unfold from the "love which
embraces all that is great and beautiful," pain is inevitable if the "individual" (or mankind at large) does not participate in the chain.
Here, the "exercise" of perception is labor unrepaid. The price (but
also the reward) of this disproportion will be memories etched indelibly on the heart and on the page. Reciprocity is broken; the "views"
recollected are not mirrored in loving "looks." "I cannot write any
more at present"—the writing itself ends abruptly.

A fundamentally elegiac sense of the self adumbrates a dialectic of
absence and presence that seems almost deconstructive. Indeed, in
both forms of the epistolary correspondence there is fuel for a Derridean reading. In a private letter to Imlay, Wollstonecraft writes: "The
last time we were separated, was a separation indeed on your part—
Now you have acted more ingenuously. [L]et the most affectionate
interchange of sentiments fill up the aching void of disappointment"
("Letters to Imlay," 411). In the space of their separation, Wollstonecraft hoped to use the exchange of letters as a way to fill the void
with writing; yet the letters, in a Derridean sense, never reach their
destination.[21] They reveal a correspondence that represents loss and
absence as constitutive. The overwhelming sense is that the discourse
is structurally posthumous, as if the writer and reader were already

[21]Derrida's discussion of the way letters of desire fail to reach their destination is
fruitfully apposite to Wollstonecraft's *Letters*. See his "Envois" in *The Post Card: From
Socrates to Freud and Beyond.*

dead. Again, this shadowy feeling is elaborated in the private letters: "I feel that I cannot endure the anguish of corresponding with you— if we are only to correspond. No; if you seek for happiness elsewhere, my letters shall not interrupt your repose. I will be dead to you" ("Letters to Imlay," 424). The power of *Letters* resides in the way it both performs and tests its own aesthetic and social ideas, in constructing a series of "responses," personal and cultural, that never quite "correspond" in the way it projects. In a letter to Imlay Wollstonecraft writes, "I must compose my tortured soul, before I write on indifferent subjects" ("Letters to Imlay," 427); the suggestiveness of the word "compose," as both self-integration and composition, points to the way the writer seeks to heal her fractured self. Mitzi Myers claims that *Letters* is a prototype of Romantic autobiography, recording the growth of the writer's self-identity: "The writing of the book quite literally holds her together, as she discovers her power to overcome fragmentation, the power of the self to create unity and make sense of its multiple roles and painful experiences" (173). Although Myers's statement aptly captures the suturing work of the travel book, it also too neatly covers over the deconstructive fault lines remaining in the text and the losses that can never be elided.

The economy of travel that Wollstonecraft considers in *Letters*—the profits of her exercise versus its unrecompensed labor—finds echoes in Wollstonecraft's analysis of the political economy of Scandinavia. This analysis depends on a calculus of exertion and reward, a balanced "economy" neither too profligate nor too frugal. In Norway she finds a liberal tradition of equality that prevents the massive accumulation of wealth: "The distribution of landed property into small farms, produces a degree of equality which I have seldom seen elsewhere; and the rich being all merchants, who are obliged to divide their personal fortune amongst their children, the boys always receiving twice as much as the girls, property has not a chance of accumulating till overgrown wealth destroys the balance of liberty" (*Letters*, 273). Wollstonecraft critiques both lavish expenditures and parsimonious accumulations—whether of money, knowledge, or feeling, arguing instead for a balanced economy. "It is this want of proportion between profit and labour which debases men, producing the sycophantic appellations of patron and client" (287). Rampant commerce squanders human relationships.

Throughout *Letters*, one finds an emphasis on use rather than on squandering, consolidation rather than dissemination, that clusters around metaphors of taste and digestion as opposed to the manifestations of unbridled appetite: "The captains acquire a little superficial knowledge by travelling, which their indefatigable attention to the making of money prevents their digesting; and the fortune that they thus laboriously acquire, is spent, as it usually is in towns of this description, in shew and good living" (274). Taste means knowledge digested; it regulates expenditure. Retaining the sensory as well as mental connotations of "taste," Wollstonecraft attacks indiscriminate, promiscuous "appetite," as evident in too much eating and drinking (meals, she comments, last interminably in Scandinavia) and in the frantic search for variety of experience. In a private letter to Imlay, she remarks a profligacy in the "common herd":

> The common run of men, I know, with strong health and gross appetites, must have variety to banish *ennui*, because the imagination never lends its magic wand, to convert appetite to love, cemented by according reason.— Ah, my friend, you know not the ineffable light, the exquisite pleasure, which arises from a unison of affection and desire, when the whole soul and senses are abandoned to a lively imagination. . . . These emotions, more or less strong, appear to me to be the distinctive characteristic of genius, the foundation of taste, and of that exquisite relish for the beauties of nature, of which the common herd of eaters and drinkers and *child-begeters* [sic], certainly have no idea. ("Letters to Imlay," 408)

In this more personal representation of the squandering of seed, Wollstonecraft attacks indiscriminate "appetite" and wasteful dissemination in spendthrifts of emotion and sexuality. If such descriptions clearly apply to Imlay, they are again part of the fabric of a philosophy that tries to unite freedom and solidarity in an image of architectural rootedness and balance (love is "cemented" by reason, responses that are, in turn, the "foundation" of a good relationship). Wollstonecraft states, "As the mind is cultivated and taste gains ground the passions become stronger and rest on something more stable than the casual sympathies of the moment" (*Letters*, 258), and "I never met with much imagination amongst people who had not acquired a habit of reflection; and in that state of society in which the judgment and taste are not called forth, and formed by the cultivation of the arts and sciences,

little of that delicacy of feeling and thinking is to be found characterized by the word sentiment" (251). Taste is the foundation of this
house of culture, just as it forms the basis of individual relationships.[22]

The cultural rootedness she figures here is seen as an antidote to
both a wayward and frantic travel and an "indiscriminate hospitality"
at home. To Imlay she writes: "How can you love to fly about continually—dropping down, as it were, in a new world—cold and strange!
every other day? Why do you not attach those tender emotions round
the idea of home, which even now dim my eyes?—This alone is affection—every thing else is only humanity, electrified by sympathy"
("Letters to Imlay," 407). Imlay's continual movement suggests promiscuity, a dissemination; he is figured as a pollinating bee (as Tomalin
puts it, Imlay was a traveler who thought he could always travel on
[143]). Conversely, the hospitality given to all travelers, usually a virtue praised in travel literature from Homer onward, is critiqued by
Wollstonecraft as part of an indiscriminate outlay of emotion: "Hospitality has, I think, been too much praised by travellers as a proof of
goodness of heart, when in my opinion indiscriminate hospitality is
rather a criterion by which you may form a tolerable estimate of the
indolence or vacancy of a head; or, in other words, a fondness for
social pleasures in which the mind not having its proportion of exercise, the bottle must be pushed about" (Letters, 251). We return to
the importance of labor and exercise; again one finds a theory of culture based on the strenuous labor and exercise of the faculty of taste.
And just as she has exposed the inequities within English economic
and cultural institutions in other writings, here she penetrates to contradictions within Scandinavian societies. "Still the men stand up for
the dignity of man, by oppressing the women" (253).

In analyzing cultural encounters she has experienced on her trip,
Wollstonecraft takes an evolutionary view of aesthetic and social development. "I am now more than ever convinced that it is intercourse
with men of science and artists, which not only diffuses taste, but
gives that freedom to the understanding, without which I have seldom
met with much benevolence of character, on a large scale" (302). Aesthetic experience is constituted by culture, not merely by the capacity
of the individual. And although Wollstonecraft chronicles the dangers

[22]See Gillian Brown, "Anorexia, Humanism, and Feminism," for a discussion of the
way Wollstonecraft "links woman's self-possession to a redefinition of food relations"
(198), according to which women protect themselves against the excesses of "glutton-
ous" male appetite.

of economic development, she documents the cultural limitations of the more "primitive" culture she visits. This evolutionary view of culture casts Wollstonecraft in the role of both time and space traveler, one visiting a less advanced society to analyze the benefits of civilization not yet in evidence there and to warn of the potential dangers that development may bring. Wollstonecraft measures the cultures she encounters with an English yardstick, and although she does not beat them over the head with it, as certain imperial travelers of the next century will do, her reflections on the lack of refinement implicitly assume a superior position. Rejecting Rousseau's primitivism, she views the Scandinavian peoples as a negative example for English aesthetic theory.

And yet if one compares Wollstonecraft's *Letters* with William Coxe's *Travels into Poland, Russia, Sweden, and Denmark*, a travel book that she read before her Scandinavian journey and cites in her book, one is struck not only by the different agenda of the books—Coxe's three-volume account means to describe very fully the history, politics, and culture of the countries he visits—but also by Wollstonecraft's greater interest in the less official, more plebeian segments of society. Coxe's chapter headings begin with lists of the topics covered, such as "Description of Stockholm—Presentation to the King—Court—New Swedish Dress" (3:94). His is a journey (and narration) that appeals to authority, both in its means of establishing credibility (the preface cites the sources on his journey as "persons of the highest rank and authority" [1:v], and he adheres "solely to those facts which appeared to me to be derived from the most unquestionable authorities" [1:vi]) and in the class-conscious representation of the rank of the travelers, who are flattered to be received by royalty throughout their travels. (Indeed, the volumes are dedicated to Coxe's sponsor and traveling companion, Lord Herbert.) We are told that the son of Linnaeus himself takes Coxe on a tour of the botanical garden in Upsala (3:218).

Alongside this authoritative, informative, and descriptive catalogue, Wollstonecraft's travel book attempts to offer a cultural analysis concerned with the workings of gender and class ideology as it operates throughout Scandinavian society. She concerns herself with often mundane details about ordinary people. It is not mere observation but analysis for which she strives, and at her best she anticipates a Gramscian unmasking of a culture's common sense as unanalyzed ideology. For example, she points out the labor and even violence disguised in the production of capital: "Contractors, and . . . the swarm of locusts who have battened on the pestilence they spread abroad . . . like the owners of negro ships, never smell on their money the blood by which it has been gained" (*Letters*, 344). If at times her penchant for generalization leads her to elide the individual differences of those she studies, it also enables her to see social structures operating in the drama of individuals (as she does in her analysis of her own personal situation). This ability to push observation to social analysis is an important component of Wollstonecraft's project of overturning assumptions about a female critic (and, in this case, female traveler). In *A Vindication of the Rights of Woman*, she had written: "The power of generalizing ideas, of drawing comprehensive conclusions from individual observations, is the only acquirement, for an immortal being, that really deserves the name of knowledge. . . . But this exercise is the true cultivation of the understanding; and every thing conspires to render the cultivation of the understanding more difficult in the female than the male world" (54). In representing and testing an aesthetic ideology, in rewriting the prototypical journey out from England—hers is in various measures part business trip, travelogue, love letter, prophecy—Wollstonecraft destabilizes our view of what the "female" and "male world[s]" signify at the close of the eighteenth century.

3

"The African Wanderers":
Kingsley and Lee

In the hundred years that separates Wollstonecraft's unusual "business" trip to Scandinavia and Mary Kingsley's travels to West Africa, women's travel burgeoned, much in relation to imperialist projects of church and nation. According to Dorothy Hammond and Alta Jablow in *The Myth of Africa*:

> The clearest indication that the British were now at home in Africa was the ubiquitous presence of the ladies. Previously these had been settlers' wives in South Africa, but they did not write of their lives, and it is only from the accounts of some of the early missionaries' wives that we learn something of the Englishwoman's situation. They were expected to share the work, hardship, and discomforts. . . . By the end of the century, however, administrators, traders, and even travelers were bringing their wives to Africa. The land was considered sufficiently tame for lady tourists to travel on safari. (84)

In an otherwise astute discussion of British imperialism in Africa, Hammond and Jablow find amusement in the feminization of colonial travel wrought by "the ladies."

This suggestion of the way the presence of white women on the imperial frontier not only mitigates the excitement of adventure but also impedes colonial relations among men marks even sophisticated meditations on British imperialism. For example, in O. Mannoni's and Ashis Nandy's seminal discussions of colonial psychology (in Africa and India, respectively), white women are viewed as the source of an exaggerated racism that inhibits colonial male-to-male relationships. Mannoni remarks that feminine "racialism" is often an "over-compensation" for a sense of "inferiority" (116). Nandy attributes white women's racism to their sexual anxiety. He maintains that white women in India "were generally more exclusive and racist because they unconsciously saw themselves as the sexual competitors of Indian men, with whom their men had established an unconscious homo-eroticized bonding" (9–10). The inscription of women in "plots" of sexual jealousy and powerlessness limits their roles in colonial situations to victimization in sexual relations and frustration in public action.[1]

To offset impressions of women as secondary agents of imperialism who frequently perpetuated English racism, other historians and critics have recuperated the roles of women in the colonial context in a discourse antithetical to Hammond and Jablow's generalized treatment of "the ladies." This other tradition of analysis seeks to recover the lost stories of "intrepid" women who did make it to the imperial frontier and who traveled alone rather than settling down with husbands on their missions of empire. This tradition (including some feminist analyses) makes its argument through biographies of rugged individualists, focusing on the courage and iconoclasm of women travelers to unknown parts. These very prevalent and in some senses revisionary representations of women's active roles as adventurers concentrate on the single woman rather than on woman as helpmate. Indeed, many of the women who traveled to Africa were either divorced or widowed. In the title of her book *Spinsters Abroad*, Dea Birkett emphasizes the social and sexual status of the unmarried and solitary woman traveler—a well-known Victorian type—transforming travel into the antithesis not only of domesticity but of heterosexual relationship as well. This view of travel as a flight from the oppressions of patriarchy supplies a counterpart to Paul Zweig's notion of adventure as a flight from women. In the hands of some male writers who consider women travelers, this iconoclastic image tends to become either threatening or comic. Leo Hamalian, whose book on eighteenth- and nineteenth-century women travelers applauds the

---

[1]Opposing the thesis of white women's unconscious racist response to colonial homoeroticism, Sara Suleri has recently analyzed the way Anglo-Indian women's writing unmasks the "disembodied homoeroticism" in colonial relations and intentionally revises the heterosexual paradigm of ravishment and possession typical of many male exploration and travel narratives (77).

"small but impressive library of first-person narratives that combined genuine learning with the spirit of individualism" (xii), nevertheless entitles his book *Ladies on the Loose,* a title that raises the specter of uncontained female sexuality. On the other hand, for Evan Connell, whose book *A Long Desire* presents various stories of travel and adventure, the solitary women travelers become comic freaks. Even Connell's admiration for their courage is tinged with condescension. In his characterization of Isabella Bird Bishop, who is "shaped like a penguin, holding court in gold-embroidered slippers and a petticoat decorated with gold and silver Japanese wheels," he transforms the traveler into a comic Miss Pickerel on her way to Mars. "They give the impression of being mildly batty," he says, "these upright, energetic, innocent, valorous, polite, intelligent, prim, and condescending British females in long skirts, carrying parasols ... and not infrequently clinging like a huge black moth to the back of a coolie who must have thought he had been engaged by a creature from a different universe." "No, no, I'll go along with Ibn Batuta or that Chinese whose name I can't remember, but this woman is too much" (24).

But it is the feminist analysis of nineteenth-century women's travel, including, significantly, travel to British territories and colonies, with which I am most concerned. These studies provide important acts of recovery and attention, often attempting to demonstrate how women travelers to the imperial frontier managed to escape the system of exploitation that underwrites male narratives. "With very few exceptions," Katherine Frank says in "Voyages Out," "all the women rejected the virulent racism that blights most of the male accounts of Africa" (73). Frank seems to acknowledge the complex social situation of these women travelers, in whom competing claims of gender, racial, and class discourses created both a sympathy with native populations and an assumption of superiority: "The entrenched Victorian conviction of white racial supremacy, then, was responsible for nineteenth-century women's extraordinary freedom in Africa, where their identity derived from their white skins rather than their female bodies. But at the same time, the legacy of sexual oppression paradoxically fostered these women's identification with the subjugated Africans whose lower station facilitated their own liberation in Africa" (72). In this passage, Frank appears to recognize, although not analyze, the "quest for liberation" as itself complicitous in the pattern of British imperialist domination. The danger of ignoring this complicity can be seen in Birkett's description of courageous women

travelers: "The Dark Continent, the Orient, the Savage Lands" provided "the stage upon which their new experiences as travellers could
be realized" (47). Birkett thus ignores the way the "native" land becomes merely a backdrop for the drama of female liberation, which
feminism in the 1980s seeks to recover. As Gayatri Chakravorty Spivak points out in a provocative essay on the relation between Western
feminism and women in the so-called developing nations: "Historically, it is well known that we in this country take our model of mil-
itancy from the British nineteenth century. For feminist individualism
in that age of imperialism, the stake was the making of human beings.
That meant the constitution and interpellation of the subject, not only
as individual but as 'individualist'" ("Political Economy of Women
as Seen by a Literary Critic," 219). Spivak's suggestive comments attempt to unmask the universalistic rhetoric of the Western quest for
self-realization, even women's self-realization, as the forging of an
imperial self whose definition depends on its difference from (and
domination of) others not so individuated. Spivak's essay helps us
recognize the ideological assumptions in much of the individualist
rhetoric in female travel writing and even its more contemporary recuperation in feminist criticism.[2]

An incident from Mary Kingsley's *Travels in West Africa* exemplifies
the complexity of racial, class, and gender discourses in British wom-

---

[2]Although I find Spivak's comments rightly suspicious of the rhetoric of aggressive
individualism that marks the descriptions of intrepid British women travelers, her conflation of "individualism" and "individualist" runs the risk of too reductively collapsing the significances of travel for different women, for example, Gertrude Bell and Mary
Kingsley, who resisted the label of "New Woman" and rejected the claims of the wom-
en's suffrage movement. Indeed, "the making of human beings" was variously nuanced
in women's travel (as demonstrated in Nupur Chaudhuri and Margaret Strobel's edited
collection *Western Women and Imperialism: Complicity and Resistance*). As Nandy says of
certain women travelers to India who there discovered alternatives to the male pattern
of political domination, they "found in Indian versions of religiosity, knowledge and
social intervention not merely a model of dissent against their own society, but also
some protection for their search for new models of transcendence, a greater tolerance
of androgyny, and a richer meaning as well as legitimacy for women's participation in
social and political life" (36). Nandy points to the way that Annie Besant, for example,
attempted to reconcile Western and Eastern spirituality in her study of theosophy and
travel to India, a reconciliation that displays a pattern different from that of the quest
for the imperial self. It is fascinating that although Nandy mentions that Besant and
Mira Richards (and others) were Irish, he neglects to follow up on the implications of
this anomaly: that their own colonial status might have combined with their gender to
produce a different sense of cultural mediation between West and East.

en's travel writing. Kingsley relates the story of her use of what is called "trade English," a type of pidgin English the grammar of which "has no gender." Kingsley tells a purportedly humorous story of being addressed as "sir" by her African carriers because of the lack of gender markings in the language. Her point is the comical confusion of genders, the way that she as traveler becomes androgynous, but ironically, Kingsley (who is generally an extremely astute reader of cultural roles) fails to recognize not only that the *generic* gender is masculine (and not really a third, neuter gender) but also, more important, that the class and race markers of the word "sir" signify her superiority.[3]

Kingsley's *Travels in West Africa* (1897) and Sarah Lee's *The African Wanderers; or, The Adventures of Carlos and Antonio* (1847)[4] provide instructive examples of how women writers recorded and imagined British confrontation with West Africans in two very different genres—narrative-ethnography and sentimental abolitionist novel, respectively—during two different periods of the English presence in Africa. My choice to focus on travel literature concerning Africa rests on a number of considerations. Throughout the nineteenth century, Africa represented a kind of limit case for the European imagination— the unknown Dark Continent on the other side of European enlightenment and the photographic negative of its civilization. As numerous critics have observed, this evocation of Africa is particularly gender-inflected. Despite different narrative stances and rhetorical topoi in different genres, changes in the European attitude toward Africa over the course of the century, and the previously mentioned presence of women in Africa by the late 1800s, travel literature on Africa is often coded in masculinist terms. A strongly gendered semiotics marks the multiple genres recording British encounters in Africa: fictional adventure writing ("the main form within literature" that inspired "the expansive imperialist thrust of the white race," according to Martin Green [*Robinson Crusoe Story*, 2]), nonfictional exploration narratives (using the "monarch of all I survey" rhetoric of the British explorer in Africa [see Pratt, *Imperial Eyes*, 201]), and imperial romance (with

[3]For a more recent, Foucauldian treatment of the competing discourses of femininity and colonialism in travel writing by women, see *Discourses of Difference: An Analysis of Women's Travel Writing and Colonialism* by Sara Mills. See in particular the chapter "Feminist Work on Women's Travel Writing."

[4]Lee is also known as Mrs. T. E. Bowdich, Mrs. R. Lee, and Sarah Lee Wallis.

its eroticization of the African landscape as the female body waiting for male penetration [see Brantlinger]).[5]

In selecting these two examples of women's writing about Africa in the nineteenth century, my purpose is neither to praise these representations for sensitivity greater than that of "male" narratives nor to damn them for their complicity with the dominant ideologies of their time.[6] I choose these texts as examples of two very different generic and narrative strategies for handling mediation between black and white and female and male on the imperial frontier. Lee's mid-century adventure tale deploys topoi of sentimental romance in a nondomestic, fraternal mode—themes of rescue and foster-parentage give way to the more modern themes of conversion and trade; in Kingsley's more skeptical, less sentimental version of cultural confrontation (conversion, as well as conquest, is treated with great suspicion), trade serves both as chief mechanism and as metaphor for a purported reciprocity between European and African. The two writers represent different forms of "passing" in their texts: Lee's dark-skinned Latino protagonists curiously mediate between white and black, and as I said above, Kingsley represents herself as a woman traveler addressed as "sir," a comical "error" that her text records with some degree of pleasure in gender neutrality. In examining these two texts, I am also concerned with the way two women who traveled in West Africa represented Africa as a product for a home audience.

Despite the homogenizing force of Africanist discourse, the epistemological project of the "invention of Africa," as V. Y. Mudimbe calls

---

[5]Dorothy Hammond and Alta Jablow identify a difference between British and French travel narratives in this regard: British adventure narratives project "a desire for freedom and withdrawal from the importunate demands of marriage, of women, and of love itself" and are therefore "less concerned with heightened sexuality" than the French narratives, which envision "some ultimate sexual experience to be found only in Africa" (154). As Zweig shows in *The Adventurer: The Fate of Adventure in the Western World*, displacement rather than absence of the feminine occurs in many British narratives, in which the woman left behind is reinvented on the other side of adventure, erotically displaced onto the foreign body of the foreign land. Recent studies of the eroticization of the discourse of African travel, such as Christopher Miller's *Blank Darkness: Africanist Discourse in French* and Dennis Porter's *Haunted Journeys: Desire and Transgression in European Travel Writing*, tend to focus on the French tradition of travel writing, which explores as Porter puts it, "opportunities not available in the same way in Europe to push beyond the limits of the pleasure principle" (175).

[6]Other narratives by European women who traveled to West Africa include those by Mary Falconbridge, Elizabeth Melville, Mary Gaunt, and May Mott-Smith. See Patricia Romero's *Women's Voices on Africa: A Century of Travel Writings* and Catherine Barnes Stevenson's *Victorian Women Travel Writers in Africa*.

it, encompasses many historical and geographical variations. My choice of narratives on West Africa is conditioned by the fact that, as Philip Curtin points out, West Africa supplied the earliest images of the continent because it represented the core of the slave trade (vi). It is also the source of the idea of the fetish, which the West found so powerful; I will discuss this idea in some detail in regard to Mary Kingsley's book.

By mid-nineteenth century, when Sarah Lee's novel was marketed, images of Africa were eagerly consumed by the British reading public. The commercial success of nonfictional records published earlier in the century had inspired the burgeoning of fiction about Africa, sometimes produced by explorers and travelers with firsthand experience of the continent. "By the 1850's," Curtin writes, "the image [of Africa] had hardened. It was found in children's books, in Sunday school tracts, in the popular press. Its major affirmations were the 'common knowledge' of the educated classes" (vi).[7]

Indeed, the relation between the circulation of British travelers and that of their Africanist discourse at home becomes especially pressing in a colonial context. As the preface to Henry Stanley's novel *My Kalulu, Prince, King, and Slave* (1874) indicates, questions of audience and ideological function are bound up with suppositions about gender. For many books about Africa, like Stanley's novel, were conceived as "food" for future male imperialists.

> This book has been written for boys; not those little darlings who are yet bothering over the alphabet, and have to be taken to bed at sundown, and who, when they awake, put civilised and respectable families into confusion with their cries . . . but for those clever, bright-eyed, intelligent boys, of all classes, who have begun to be interested in romantic literature, with whom educated fathers may talk without fear of misapprehension, and of whom friends are already talking as boys who have a promising future before them. These boys are the guests for whom I have provided a true Africa feast. The feast provided for them is not over rich, because Africa is not far enough advanced yet to furnish delicacies, such as puddings, cakes, confections, &c.; but what there is of it, plain rice

[7]The subject of the differences between narratives of East and West Africa, between orientalist and nonorientalist discourses, is too broad for consideration here. No few examples of travel writing concerning Africa can represent the totality of either Africa or travel writing. I have chosen to confine my examples to West Africa for the reasons stated above as well as to provide a control in my discussion.

and curry, dried meat of game, wild fruits of piquant flavour, &c., is healthy and good for such as you, and taken once in a while, between your own regular banquets, you might thrive and be better for it. (Stanley, v–vi)

Girls and mama's boys are excluded from this manly and healthy repast. The concept of ingestion, which Conrad so powerfully transforms in his portrait of Kurtz's devouring egotism, is suitably civilized in Stanley's preface. The novel, after all, is meant as juvenile literature; the men of the growing British empire are still boys. According to F. J. Harvey Darton, however, the difference between children's books earlier in the century (including the Robinsonades, with their "mixed conceptions about savages and nature and desert islands and morality") and the boy's adventure tale of mid-century is that in the new genre, there is an absence of "appeal to a dogmatic religious belief, or any *other* theory of conduct or education. . . . The explorer was no longer a mere missionary of religion. His travels were such stuff as dreams are made on. The English boy, like Drake in Darien, could look upon the unknown seas and vow that he would sail in an English ship upon them" (252–54). The simile is telling, for what Darton only indirectly suggests is the link between Britain's imperial "prospects," suggested by the magisterial survey of Drake in Darien, and the adventure of reading these boy's tales. If Robinson Crusoe was suitable literature for girls as well as boys, these boy's adventures were strictly for future male imperialists. The cross-cultural encounters represented in such fiction fueled and reflected the changing dynamics of Britain's increasing presence in Africa during Victoria's reign; the culminating scramble for Africa was codified at the Berlin Conference of 1884–85.

In his preface, Stanley conflates his roles as host and writer, blending the feasts partaken in Africa (of "plain rice and curry, dried meat of game") and the novel as "true African feast." As packaged in the boy's adventure story, the representation of Africa is a particular kind of product, nourishing to a certain type of reader. Michel de Certeau points to the "economy of translation" that underwrites such a venture of turning the "primitive" into a useful, edible commodity. In discussing Jean de Léry's *Histoire d'un voyage faict en la terre du Brésil* (1578), de Certeau speaks of the origin of this process in de Léry's writing: de Léry as writer/interpreter of the foreign translates the tantalizing appearances of things in Brazil into intellectual food for the readers back in France. Extrapolating from the act of discriminating between those plants and animals that merely look good to the eye and those that are truly "edible," de Certeau describes an ethnological "taste" that allows the traveler/writer to distill "an intellectual edibility," an "essence that has to be distinguished from ravishments" of the ear and eye. Such edibility is a measure of "utility"; the "double diagnostic of taste corrects seductions or repulsions of the eye; is it healthy or not to eat, raw or cooked? . . . From the baroque spectacle of flora and fauna to their edibility; from primitive festivals to their utopian and moral exemplariness; and finally from exotic language to its intelligibility, the same dynamic unfolds. It is that of *utility*—or, rather, that of *production*" (*Writing of History*, 224).

Stanley prepares a similar textual feast for his readers, serving them a healthy extract of Africa, cooking the raw material of the "primitive." Cooking and feeding are figures for the civilizing process itself. (They are usually women's work as well.) This feast, however, is prepared for boys only.

Such a feast is also prepared by Sarah Lee in *The African Wanderers*, which crosses *Robinson Crusoe* with African exploration narratives. This novel appeared in a series published by Griffith and Farran, which offered "Books for the Young of All Ages, Suitable for Presents and School Prizes" under the specific heading of "The Boys' Own Favourite Library." Other titles in the series include *Chums*, *Tales of the White Cockade*, *The Three Admirals*, *The Fiery Cross*, *Travel*, *War, and Shipwreck*, *The North Pole*, and *Harty, the Wanderer*. "The Girls' Own Favourite Library," on the other hand, includes *Shiloh*, *Rosamond*, *Fane*, *Simplicity and Fascination*, *Isabel's Difficulties*, *Millicent and Her Cousins*, *Aunt Hetty's Will*, and *A Wayside Posy*.

Despite the targeting of young audiences by gender, Sarah Lee's novel was found "intellectually edible" by future woman traveler and travel writer Mary Gaunt, who begins her first-person travel narrative *Alone in West Africa* (1912), by describing the scene in which, as a young girl in Australia, she first read about Africa. The book is not named in the text, but it is identifiable as *The African Wanderers*; Gaunt refers to this reading as an inaugural experience, "the first really exciting incident in my life" (2).

> It was a January morning, the sky overcast with smoke and a furious hot wind blowing from the north. The men of the household looked out anxiously, but I sat and read a story-book. It was the tale of a boy named Carlo who was wrecked on the coast of West Africa—nice vague location; he climbed a cocoa-nut tree—I can see him now with a rope round his waist and his legs dangling in an impossible attitude—and he was

taken by savages. His further adventures I do not know, because a man came riding in shouting that the calf paddock was on fire and every one must turn out. Everyone did turn out except my aunt who stayed behind to prepare cool drinks and those drinks my little sister and I, as being useless for beating out the flames, were sent to carry to the workers in jugs and "billies."

"Now little girls," said my aunt who was tenderness and kindness itself, "remember you are not to get tired."

I never finished the story of Carlo. Where he went to I can't imagine, but I can't think the savages ate him else his story would never have been written; and from that moment dated my deep interest in West Africa.

We grew up and the boys of the family went a-roving to other lands. . . . When we were young we generally regarded money as a means of lo-comotion. We have hardly got over the habit yet. Only for us two girls was there no prospect. Our world was bounded by our father's lawns and the young men who came to see us and made up picnic parties to the wildest bush round Ballarat for our amusement. It was not bad. (2–3)

If it is the brush fire that interrupts the scene of reading, which suggests that life might be more exciting than even art, it is the "fem-inine" preparation of food that definitely replaces the African feast of reading. In such a domestic economy, a boy's adventure tale is rendered useless to the little girl. Yet, the anecdote prefaces the nar-rative of Gaunt's own travels to West Africa twenty years later, in which she dubs her trip as a visit to "Carlo's land" (4). For Gaunt, following in Carlo's (and Lee's) footsteps, physically and textually, Africa is an alluring space of adventure rather than the actual geog-raphy found. As the destination of boys' adventures, "Carlo's land" symbolizes the girl child's never-never land of fulfilled desire. Gaunt's story suggests the appeal of boys' adventures for girls, notwithstand-ing Stanley's for-boys-only hospitality. As Green says: "Adventure tales were written about, and for, boys, but they were *read* by girls. For a girl to identify with boys was always, within certain limits, ac-knowledged as an advantage" (*Robinson Crusoe Story*, 6). But as Clau-dia Nelson shows, even in the hardy genre of adventure, manliness may be subtly imbricated with womanliness—the description of girls "identifying with boys" may not account for the overlap and entan-glement of manliness and womanliness in mid-Victorian texts, even those of adventure. Lee created a boy's adventure tale that represents the homosocial ethos of adventure, in which kindness and courage combine in her male heroes.[8]

Gaunt never mentions the title or author of the adventure story she read, but her description of "Carlo," shipwrecked on the coast of West Africa, climbing a coconut tree with a rope around his waist, precisely captures the events and evokes a particular illustration in Lee's novel. It is possible that Gaunt forgot the author of the tale, just as she drops the *s* from the name of the hero; it is also possible, however, that she anxiously represses the gender of the author to emphasize her own originality and daring.[9]

The illustration that Gaunt must have known is reproduced here; it depicts Carlos shimmying up a coconut tree "in the manner of the natives" (*African Wanderers*, 100) while his friend Antonio watches from below. In Lee's adventure, the two protagonists have just been abandoned on an island off the coast of Africa. Later editions of *The African Wanderers* were called *The African Crusoes* (Greenstein, 134); the thematics of the castaway combine with African adventure, thus emphasizing (like Burney's redaction of Defoe in *The Wanderer*) dependency and vulnerability rather than the confident mastery of exploration. In the complex appropriation of adventure by women writers, Lee's novel exemplifies strategies of mediation—in this case, between "masculine" confidence and "feminine" dependency. Although she herself made three trips to West Africa and spent much time alone on the coast while her first husband, T. E. Bowdich, negotiated a treaty with the Ashanti,[10] Lee "cross-genders" her own Af-

---

[8]That Gaunt herself was an Australian colonial, the daughter of an English prospector who went out to the colony, might have encouraged her identification with the spirit of adventure on the frontier.

[9]Gaunt dates the inception of her interest in West Africa from her reading of the story of Carlo and goes on to relate how fascination with it was "put on hold" during her twenty-year marriage. Premature widowhood led to her renewed interest in traveling to Africa, but she says she first wrote books about Africa to earn the money to travel there. Her story stresses the way Africa becomes a textual product that is a blend of citation and personal record, desire and necessity. There is a certain irony in the fact that Gaunt marketed Africa as a means to travel there.

[10]For a narrative of T. Edward Bowdich's "missions" in West Africa, see *Mission from Cape Coast Castle to Ashantee with a Statistical Account of That Kingdom and Geographical Notices of Other Parts of the Interior of Africa* and *Excursions in Madeira and Porto Santo, during the Autumn of 1823, While on His Third Voyage to Africa*, the latter of which contains an appendix by "Mrs. Bowdich" that offers her view of the voyage, along with details of her husband's death in Africa.

Carlos climbs a Cocoa-nut tree.—*Page* 100.

rican experience—not by cross-dressing her adventure heroine, as does Cavendish, but by representing the adventures of boys. Yet as the illustration from her novel makes clear, Lee replaces the stalwart blond sons of England, who serve as protagonists in the typical stories of English adventure that Darton and Green discuss, with some dusky, rather hairy Latinos. Lee's heroes supply a middle term between black and white, for Carlos is a Spanish orphan, raised by a British soldier who rescues him on the battlefield during the Carlist War of the 1830s, and Antonio, an Italian, is a former gondolier turned soldier. Both the oppositions between masculine and feminine and the Manichean oppositions between black and white are destabilized by a curiously shifting scale of European as well as African difference. The somewhat roguish and protean Spanish orphan hero (like the archetypal picaresque protagonist) is dark enough to be mistaken for an African.[11]

By introducing her plot of African wandering with the Spanish civil war of the 1830s, Lee, like Burney, crossed the topos of wandering with contemporary politics and placed African exploration within a larger European political framework. The Carlist Wars were part of a broader European ideological battle among absolutism, liberalism, and expansionism. The first Carlist War, the setting for *The African Wanderers*, was waged from 1833 to 1839 between two factions—the Carlist counterrevolutionaries, aristocrats and defenders of the Church led by Don Carlos, and the followers (called Cristinos) of Maria Cristina, queen regent of Spain, who initiated parliamentary reforms.[12] Although sympathy in Britain was somewhat divided between the two sides in the conflict, British foreign policy officially sided with the liberal Cristinos rather than the reactionary Carlists and sanctioned the British Legion (a voluntary, nonregular army) to fight on the Cristino side. As Carlos Marichal notes, "The English and French bourgeoisies supported the Spanish Liberals because they feared the possible consequences of a Carlist victory, which would not only be a victory for Metternich and the European aristocracy, but also a blow against English and French commercial expansion in the Mediterranean" (57).

In Lee's novel, the Spanish civil conflict functions as a sign of the "real," of Continental political turmoil and potential chaos, of a world the English (and adventure fiction) cannot ignore. The British fighting on the Spanish battlefields are described in the narrative as "strangers

[11]In an essay on Renaissance exploration to the New World, Louis Montrose says: "For the Englishmen in the New World, the Spaniards are proximate figures of Otherness: In being Catholic, Latin, and Mediterranean, they are spiritually, linguistically, ethnically, and ecologically alien. . . . The sign of the Spaniard in English discovery texts simultaneously mediates and complicates any simple antinomy of European Self and American Other." This "mediation," however, occurs in the context of "manly rivalry," in which "England and Spain" vie in a "contest to deflower the new-found lands" ("Work of Gender and Sexuality in the Elizabethan Discourse of Discovery," 161). In Lee's abolitionist novel, there is no triangular relationship between manly rivals and feminized land; instead, the heroes, rather than rivals, are Latinos, adopted sons of an Englishman, who thus mediate between white traveler and African other.

[12]See John Coverdale's *Basque Phase of Spain's First Carlist War* and Carlos Marichal's *Spain (1834–1844): A New Society* for an understanding of the ideological stakes of the conflict, and *The Carlist Wars in Spain* by Edgar Holt for details on British participation in the wars.

to the vengeance which men of the same country feel towards each other in civil war" (2). The novel begins with a scene of battle. Colonel Lacy, a British soldier, and his sidekick, Sergeant Brown, who are fighting on the momentarily victorious side of the Carlists, discover two crying children next to their dead parents. The aristocratic family of Carlos and Henriquez, the two orphans rescued and subsequently adopted by the British soldier, is pro-Cristino, that is, on the liberal side. The specific ideologies at war are muted in Lee's adventure tale, which foregrounds instead the chaos and cost of war: "The Carlists robbed the Christinos [*sic*], the Christinos plundered the Carlists, and the banditti stripped them both. . . . Numbers of British soldiers who had been serving in the Spanish armies of either party, without pay, and rendered utterly insensible to every good feeling by the lives of bloodshed, rapine, and cruelty, which they had been leading for several years; without any one to superintend them . . . crowded to the port in order to obtain shipping for their native country" (7–9). Overtly, the British are ideologically aloof from the factions in the Spanish war. Yet the generational differences between Captain Lacy, an Englishman of the old school, Carlos (named by Lacy for Don Carlos) and Henriquez represent the inevitably changing face of adventure, from an aristocratic, military genre to one that could capture the spirit of bourgeois European expansionism.[13] The more liberal, capitalistic ethos predominates in the remainder of this abolitionist novel, which finds Carlos, the more restless of the brothers—as shipwrecked sailor, pupil of African culture, and entrepreneurial trader—finally returning to England to develop an import business.[14]

[13]Historically, a Colonel Lacy served as an English commissioner with the Cristino armies in the center of Spain (Holt, 121), but in the novel, Lacy fights for the Carlists, providing an older generation more in keeping with the aristocratic-chivalric assumptions of the traditionalist Carlist cause. These assumptions retained their appeal to a writer such as Conrad, who became a gunrunner for the Carlists in a subsequent war. Conrad fictionalizes this involvement in both *The Arrow of Gold* and *The Mirror of the Sea*. Frederick Karl says of this involvement: "That Conrad should have been involved in such ventures had little to do with belief. . . . The venture itself—hopeless, adventurous, anti-establishment—would have an appeal for its very futility" (132).

[14]Curtin calls the period of African exploration from the 1830s to the 1850s the "Age of Humanitarianism" (287), during which the act of 1833 was passed, emancipating the slaves in the British colonies (290). Patrick Brantlinger astutely observes the connections between the abolitionist literature of this period, which Lee's novel exemplifies, and the general project of imperialism in *Rule of Darkness: British Literature and Imperialism, 1830–1914*.

The cross-cultural rescue that begins the novel establishes a recurring pattern of paternalism in the narrative—Captain Lacy rescues the Spanish orphans, just as Carlos will rescue a Negro child in Africa. When Lacy and Brown discover the two crying infants by the side of their dead parents, a gentle fatherhood is established. The confusion and brutality of war are contrasted to the Englishmen's manly tenderness. Englishmen are first represented in the novel as helpfully intervening in the internecine battles of their more "passionate" European brothers, so that English adventure is seen against the more militaristic legacy of the conquistador tradition of adventure. This scene of paternalism serves as a prototype for the English experience in Africa.

English paternalism establishes a sympathetic circle of decidedly male geometry, a gathering of fathers, sons, and, later on, brothers. After he rescues the orphans, Captain Lacy brings them to an Irishwoman, the wife of an English soldier, who agrees to be their nurse: "But her fair face and hair, and her blue eyes, in addition to the surrounding scene, so bewildered the poor little things, that they shrieked, clung to each other, and imperfectly called for their parents. Kathleen, their new nurse, could not speak a word of Spanish; but the Sergeant and Captain Lacy caressed and soothed them in their native tongue" (5–6). In this fairy-tale rescue, Kathleen is the fairest and yet the most terrifying, the most "other" to the Spanish orphans. If Kathleen's feminine kindness ultimately overcomes cross-cultural mistrust and she helps mother them for a time back in England, it is noteworthy that the English soldiers combine a masculine (and more worldly) command of languages with feminine tenderness. In the specific paternalism of this rescue, a feminizing influence is at work that is not, however, encoded as effeminate. This liberal sympathy, combining feminine virtues with a manly spirit of adventure, is played out in a male milieu that excludes pure domesticity. Kathleen is both too feminine and, somehow, too starkly fair to participate fully in this messy, yet tender scene of male bonding. Her Irish stereotype (with its overtones of lower-class status) relegates her to a subsidiary and servantlike role,[15] but her Irishness also acts as a reminder of England's

---

[15]See George Stocking's discussion of the class dimension of Irishness in English discourse and of the way Irishness increasingly during the century provided "a mediating example for both attitude and policy in relation with 'savages' overseas" (225–35).

colonial responsibilities elsewhere, hence, of other claims of manly duty.

All women are excluded from the charmed circle of adventure. Indeed, in fairy-tale fashion, it is the cruel behavior of the boys' stepmother, Mrs. Lacy, that impels Carlos's sea adventures in the first place. At the end of the book, Antonio (Carlos's Venetian companion in Africa), Carlos, and Henriquez live happily ever after together, with the "fairer sex" only occasionally asking Carlos for his autograph (*African Wanderers*, 358). Although "fairer sex" is a cliché, in a book that so insistently refers to complexion, the phrase implies how very male this ethos of cross-cultural camaraderie is. The mix of paternalism and "brotherhood," first represented as the mediation between wholly European differences, will be extended to the Africans that Carlos and Antonio encounter.

The structure of rescue that begins with the orphans' terrified encounter with the English—soon tempered by humane behavior—is repeated when Carlos and Antonio land on an island off the coast of Africa. The two men, who have formed a bond on ship because both speak Spanish, make their way along the coast after being abandoned by the rest of the crew. They first come upon the body of a dead Negro and surmise that a slave ship has passed by; they then find a deserted child who has been left behind by the "inhuman brutes," the slave dealers. Traces of the most heinous cruelty to the Africans are everywhere apparent in the novel, but here the terrifying difference involves the confrontation between well-meaning Europeans and an African child: "Frightened and bewildered, [he] screamed, and, after one look at his preservers, obstinately hid his face in his hands, not daring to glance at them again" (120). The child is momentarily comforted by the food Carlos offers, but on seeing Antonio, he again screams and clings to Carlos as if for protection. " 'It's my beard and whiskers,' observed Antonio" (120). If Kathleen is too female and white to soothe the young Spanish infants, Antonio is too masculine and hairy (later we learn the Africans are unused to facial hair) to mollify the fearful Negro child. This mirroring repetition of the Spanish orphan's fear of Kathleen suggests that neither the most "feminine" nor the most "masculine" visage can bridge the difference between the races.

By repeating the topos of paternal rescue, first with the Spanish children and then the African child, Lee establishes a curiously shifting scale of difference, as the narrative plays out a series of racial substitutions. On the one hand, these shades of difference may seem merely a reflection of the "close articulation . . . between the domestic and the colonial spheres of otherness," as George Stocking puts it (234), and a strategy for mediating the foreignness of Africa for Lee's domestic readers. But in choosing to make Latinos the heroes of her novel rather than figures of a cruder form of masculinist adventure meant to contrast with English liberalism, Lee disturbs the European color "scale," which favors the whiter, more northern agent of civilization.

Indeed, Antonio's and Carlos's Latin complexions allow them to "pass" for native, a masquerade that both protects and endangers them. "It must be owned also that the Europeans were now so bronzed in complexion, that they might very easily have passed for Arabs, who occasionally approached that part of Africa, and stragglers from whom were seen even upon the coast" (239). The wanderers are thus confused with "the aristocracy of savages," as the narrator puts it (277). Therefore a curious instability exists in the racial discourse. On the one hand, the word "savages" and the idea of a racial scale among Africans bespeak a perfectly confident moral typing according to race; on the other hand, the confusion of the protagonists with their usual foils creates a potential identification with the position of the "other." Latin "blood" seems to enable Antonio, in particular, to adapt to the African heat, as if it brought him closer to the indigenous population. On board their ship, the *Hero,* before they are abandoned, Carlos admonishes Antonio for sleeping out in the open air, but " 'Never fear for me, sir,' said the faithful Italian, 'my Venetian blood does better in these countries than that of the English, and so will your Spanish; but what must be done now?' " (89). Curiously, Lee's use of rather conventional ethnic stereotypes leads to a subtle representation of difference that subverts the neat opposition of primitive and civilized, black and white. The lexicon for designating the travelers constantly shifts during the narrative, depending on the particular system of difference invoked: when Carlos and Henriquez are among the English, they are called the "young Spaniards" (24); in Africa when he is alone with Antonio, Carlos is referred to as "the Spaniard"; on the ship, when he remarks on his difference from the English, Antonio is called the "faithful Italian"; in one episode the Europeans suddenly become "the white slaves" (282). Even the title *The African Wanderers,* with the ambiguities of its adjective, creates some confusion as to whether the wanderers are African or Europeans in Africa. This complication of racial position is different from the "harmoniously unbalanced antithesis" between black sidekick and white hero in works such as Marryat's *Mr. Midshipman Easy* (Brantlinger, 58) or the fear of "going native" that marks Conrad's novels.

Although Carlos's and Antonio's abilities are never seriously questioned, their status as wanderers relegates them to a dependent position in which they are forced, like Burney's wanderer, to rely on the kindness of strangers, in this case, African strangers. "This man receives us, poor, defenceless, destitute wanderers; never asks whence we came, how we got here, or whither we are going; gives us the best of everything, and suffers us to go to rest without a single inquiry. It is sufficient for him that we are strangers, and in need," Carlos comments to Antonio (138). This emphasis is different from the use of the Crusoe story in Marryat's *Masterman Ready* (1841), in which the Seagrave family develops their desert island into a little colony, thus illustrating the resourcefulness of the English character and its natural mastery of its environment. One could compare Lee's blurring of the racial politics of her novel with what Abdul JanMohamed calls the "syncretic" desires of certain colonialist fiction, such as Kipling's *Kim*, in which an emotional identification with the "native" land occurs in the context of the ultimate security of a stable racial division that is reaffirmed by story's end (78–79). JanMohamed points out that before the novel's conclusion recovers the "paternal function," Kim's orphanhood and dusky skin color allow him considerable play with the boundaries of racial and cultural difference: "As an orphan (a fact that is inconsequential to him), [Kim] has no origins and therefore no familial, social, political, or teleological constraints either" (78). Ultimately, according to JanMohamed, the narrator restores Kim to his natural racial identity (as Irish), thus reinforcing the manichean allegory that seems to be disrupted during the course of the fiction. (It is curious, however, that JanMohamed says nothing of Kim's Irish, rather than English, origin, that is, the difference of colonial status within the European "white" realm.)

Ultimately, however, these syncretic desires and the subtle and interesting slippages of difference give way to more predictable models of mediation of European and African positions through conversion and enlightenment. In *The Invention of Africa*, Mudimbe offers a Foucauldian analysis of the episteme that characterizes mid-nineteenth-century representations of Africa. He describes a dualistic anthropology that posits homologous antitheses between primitiveness and civilization, pagan and Christian, naked (child) and civilized (adult), among others, and an "ideological model of conversion" that mediates the terms of the oppositions. Thus, conversion is the overall model of mediation, with education serving as a more secular version (50). Mudimbe speaks here specifically about missionary discourse but applies this general ideological model to the nineteenth-century European encounter with Africa.

Mudimbe's model does not seem to acknowledge the kind of surprises within Western textual representations of Africa that I have argued appear in Lee's fiction. But his model is helpful for understanding how, despite destabilizing racial difference, Lee's novel recurs to an Enlightenment faith in education and the secular religion of commerce as forms of mediating cultural conflict. In this kinder, gentler form of colonialism, European "magic," consisting of education, Christianity, and capitalism, counteracts the fetish of the African. In an episode entitled "The Power of Education," the narrator describes the force of European Enlightenment philosophy, which, in place of violence, will convert the Africans to more rational and productive beings.

> They [the Africans] began to listen to him [Carlos] as to a being of a higher nature than themselves—to believe that he was right in all things, because they found him to be right in a few. They loved both the white men—sported with both alike—shared their meals, their society, their labours with equal affection; but there was a feeling of respect and deference towards Carlos which they could not themselves define or understand. It was the power of education which thus told upon them; the *spell* which a superior and well-informed mind exerts over its inferiors, even though the influence may be unfelt by itself. (165: emphasis added)

Interestingly, the superiority here is not purely racial, that is, associated with the whiteness of the skin: it depends on the moral worth that presumably comes with a certain kind of education.

This "education" combines the teaching of capitalism and of Christianity. As Patrick Brantlinger says of *Dawn Island*, Harriet Martineau's abolitionist novel of the same decade, commodity fetishism replaces the "unprogressive fetishism" of the Africans (31) and commercial trade replaces the barbarity of slavery. Reciprocal trade becomes the model of mediation.

> The precious treasures from Africa were passed through the Customhouse . . . and as it pleased God to bless their [Carlos and Henriquez's]

endeavours, they were the channel through which many blessings
flowed upon their fellow-creatures. Commerce with the western coast of
Africa was a principal feature in the transactions of Carlos, in the hope
of benefiting a country in which he took an undying interest; and when
he reflected on the immense riches of that beautiful land, and the universal spirit of traffic which pervades its inhabitants, he hoped that
sooner or later its natural productions would wholly supersede the de-
grading and inhuman slave-trade, which stamps it with the seal of barbarity. (*African Wanderers*, 356)

The fiction here is one of equal partnership rather than coercion,
projecting onto the Africans the "universal spirit of traffic." In this
version of the boy's adventure story, the violence and aggression in
the colonial adventure are suppressed in a vision of reciprocal trade.
The vision is emblematized by the commercial city of Liverpool. Early
in the story, Captain Lacy returns to the city after fighting in the Spanish civil war but finds that "the air of Liverpool, impregnated by the
smoke of many chimneys and factories, did not agree with [his]
health, accustomed as he had been for years to live almost entirely in
the field" (11). This response exemplifies a pastoralism in the "older"
generation, and indeed, Lacy moves out of the city of industrial revolution to a quieter existence in the outlying area. By the end of the
novel, however, the image of Liverpool functions as a sign of the
English ability to absorb and harmonize difference. The presence of
Carlos and Antonio and their African servant fails to create a ripple
on the surface of this industrial Mecca: "The good inhabitants of this
great commercial city are too much accustomed to foreign men to
spend much time in gazing at strangers; and although most of them
turned their heads as the bronzed passengers, with their black servant
carrying weapons, passed hastily by them, they offered no interrup-
tion" (341). The earlier suggestion that industrialism is unhealthy van-
ishes in this more optimistic resolution, just as the frightening
cross-cultural confrontations are replaced by the blending of black,
brown, and white skins in this urban landscape.

This "blending," ultimately used in the service of a Western ideal
of reciprocal trade, functions in Lee's novel as a topos of mobility and
freedom, despite the sometimes dangerous and harrowing adventures
faced by her wandering heroes. In a nonfictional account of her own
travels to West Africa, appended to her *Stories of Strange Lands*, Lee
in her self-portrait offers a very different image of circulation, as ev-

eryone on the boat stares at the "lady passenger mad enough to go
to Africa" (254). The ethos of free circulation, of blending, is unavail-
able to the "lady passenger," who constantly serves as the object of
others' gazes. In the same autobiographical notes, she describes her
meeting with the real-life Antonio, whom she met on the boat and
whose "qualities as a *buffo*" she praises. "His powers of mimicry extended even to his voice," she says, "his gestures were perfectly ir-
resistible; and the instant he displayed his brilliant white teeth,
contrasted with his black beard and rich brown complexion, no one
could avoid joining in his mirth" (256). Lee transforms Antonio into
a stereotype of male charm, and in so doing, she creates an image of
the traveler who can blend, mimic, and circulate freely, none of which
the woman traveler can do. This figure fulfills the "syncretic" desires
of the fiction. The roving, adaptable Latin orphans experience what
Lee describes as "the constant excitement afforded by a life which
often presents danger, and constantly requires contrivances for comfort and enjoyment" (311).[16]

In her brief discussion of Lee's *Stories of Strange Lands*, Mary Louise
Pratt points to Lee's text as an example of "the gendered division of
labor around travel and writing."[17] Pratt discovers biographical cor-
relates for this division of labor: She observes that Lee dutifully edited
her husband's writings but failed to produce a full account of her own
years in West Africa. Pratt regards Lee's stories as a cover for her real

[16]In the short stories collected with her autobiographical narrative, Lee displaces her
cultural analysis of women's restricted movement in society onto the African heroines
of her fairy-tale-like stories. Adumissa, the beautiful and tragic heroine of one of her
stories, plots to save herself from marriage, which she realizes will curtail her freedom.
To her would-be suitor she says: "I have been an only child; I have been the principal
person in my family; every one has obeyed me; and, free and happy, I have never
known what it was to submit. If I were to marry, I should become as nothing; I should
lose my rank and my freedom, and be mingled with the multitude" (*Stories*, 11). If the
vision of a totally free woman is ultimately negated by the rebellious heroine's tragic
death, it seems to have been totally unthinkable in a European fictional
setting.

[17]The focus on gender in Pratt's book represents something of a departure from her
work on travel that had earlier appeared in *Critical Inquiry* and the collection *Writing
Culture*. In those essays Pratt seemed wary of drawing a dividing line between travel
writing produced by men and women. In the book, however, she discusses differences
in men's and women's travel writing, finding "a division of labor" between "male
travelers . . . driven by curiosity, which legitimates their every move" and certain
women travelers who refuse the rhetoric of mastery (104). Yet, as Pratt goes on to say,
despite their different rhetoric and stances, these texts often participate in the same
agenda as texts by men which belong to the genre of "anti-conquest" narratives, a genre
that paradoxically sustains rather than overturns the imperial project.

desire to write a nonfictional account of her own journey. She notes: "As it turns out, however, Lee ingeniously makes her stories an occasion rather than a substitute for her own account of Africa. Each comes accompanied by an enormous string of footnotes, some of them pages long and complete with illustrations. It is here in the notes that we find the makings of the travel book Lee never wrote: explanatory commentary, ethnographic descriptions, observations on flora and fauna, personal anecdotes. The notes seem to be Lee's main source of pride in the book" (*Imperial Eyes*, 106). But I would argue that her fiction was more than simply compensatory; rather it gave Lee room to imagine her own adventurous circulation and to explore the complexities of racial encounter. It provided a form of displacement, a realm of possibility, that licensed a going out from experience, a textual circulation. Mary Kingsley's nonfictional *Travels in West Africa*, as we shall see, more directly represents the African wanderer as female, a traveler who is also a mobile, improvisational "trader" on the market. In her hybrid and voluminous narration—part natural history, part ethnography, part travel narrative—Kingsley, like Sarah Lee before her, found the liberal image of trading partners a fruitful figure for the woman writer of adventure. In her text, as in Lee's, Hermes, the god of travel, is also Hermes, the patron of trade.

A distinguished male scientist offered this bit of advice to his friend Mary Kingsley before her departure for West Africa in 1893: "Always take measurements, Miss Kingsley, and always take them from the adult male" (*Travels in West Africa*, 244–45). It encapsulates some of the prevalent assumptions about gender, race, and science at the end of the nineteenth century, when Kingsley produced her enormously popular book. The admonition succinctly embodies the Western cultural assumption that the male is the generic norm. As Donna Haraway writes of museum taxidermy and collecting safaris in colonial Africa, the typical animal "in its perfect expression" had to be an adult male. The particular "tone of perfection could only be heard in the male mode. It was a compound of physical and spiritual quality judged truthfully by the [male] artist-scientist in the fullness of direct experience" (41).

As Haraway suggests, natural science is a tissue of cultural assumptions about sexuality and gender. But the avuncular advice offered to Kingsley on her departure for Africa must also be considered in the context of racial discourse (which Haraway likewise addresses in her analysis of modern science). The mania for measurement was characteristic of late Victorian anthropology. Kingsley was going out to study, as she put it, not only "fish" but also "fetish," African law and religion as well as "nature." Her study of African culture, then, must be seen in the context of late nineteenth-century anthropological discourse, a mixture of racialist and evolutionary doctrines that sought to fix "the measure of man." If, from a feminist point of view, white women were the domestic "other" for the male norm, this norm's other "other" was the dark-skinned "primitive," encountered and studied beyond the borders of the European map. The perfection of the adult white male was to be seen in marked contrast to this primitive self. The African became the object of inspection for white anthropologists and ethnologists, a specimen measured by a European yardstick and found wanting. In *The Mismeasure of Man*, Stephen Jay Gould chronicles the history of such procedures in physical anthropology (particularly craniology), showing how science in the latter half of the nineteenth century was obsessed with the idea of measurement and discovered in numbers a confirmation of racialist and racist assumptions. Cranial indexing, the ranking of races by the size of their skulls, was a respected intellectual practice in the post-Darwinian nineteenth century.

The "Miss Kingsley" addressed by the scientist is thus not only a woman in a predominantly male world of natural scientists, ethnographers, and explorers but also a white woman who is welcomed into a fraternal circle of European measurers. As I will discuss, the feminist foregrounding of gender difference should not occlude the woman traveler's own relation to an objectivist epistemology, in which knowledge and power were indissolubly linked. The difference of race cannot be divorced from the gendering of the scientific "hunt," as Haraway calls it.[18]

Indeed, as de Certeau argues, Western historiography itself is a result of travel and the colonial encounter, the voyage out and the return that provide a perspective on one's "home." In this sense, ethnography and history are the discursive equivalents of the cultural construc-

---

[18]See Cynthia Eagle Russett's *Sexual Science: The Victorian Construction of Womanhood* as well as Haraway's *Primate Visions: Gender, Race, and Nature in the World of Modern Science* for a discussion of the intersection between categories of sexuality and race in the development of scientific discourse. Also very useful for an understanding of the development of the ethnographic imagination in the nineteenth century is Christopher Herbert's *Culture and Anomie: Ethnographic Imagination in the Nineteenth Century.*

tions of "other" and "self"; "departure" and "return" signify places on the itinerary of the voyage as well as topoi in the discourse of the self and other. As Arjun Appadurai illustrates, the binary opposition between the mobility of the traveler/ethnographer and the stasis of the "native" to be studied establishes a power differential that puts "natives . . . in one place, a place to which explorers, administrators, missionaries, and eventually anthropologists, come" (35). Appadurai is particularly interested in the way anthropological discourse links "intellectual and spatial confinement" (36), so that "natives" are "confined" to a mode of thought, which the mobile Western observer freely travels to see.

In this cautionary mode I want to interrogate the figure, which remains very popular even today, of intrepid Victorian women travelers and their appeal for feminist recuperation. For the image of these Victorian women striding in long skirts through the bush, stopping to eat manioc, constructs the female counterpart to the British male explorer and empire builder. The important Virago/Beacon Traveler Series, which republished neglected travel texts by Victorian women, displays some of the problems of this feminism in relation to colonialist discourse. The attractive cover of the 1988 Virago/Beacon reprint of Kingsley's *Travels* illustrates what I mean. One sees a black-and-white photographic insert of Mary Kingsley, a bust that shows her looking properly buttoned up and Victorian, with a firm but perceptibly humorous gaze. This photograph is superimposed on what seems to be a color painting of an African scene, replete with towering palm trees, river, five Africans perched on or standing before a big rock that looks like a large white molar, and a canoe that resembles a banana. The caption printed above this scene reads, "The witty and highly readable classic about African culture by one of the most intrepid adventurers." The back cover refers to Kingsley as "larger than life."

Here, the white woman individual is foregrounded against what Johannes Fabian has called an "ethnographic present" that effaces history from the African scene and represents instead a timeless, primitive landscape (80–87). Africa becomes a generalized setting, even a theatrical set, for the drama of female liberation that a 1980s white Anglo-American feminism seeks to recover. This iconic representation mirrors Birkett's contention that "the Dark Continent, the Orient, the Savage Lands" provided "the *stage* upon which their new experiences as travellers could be realized" (47: emphasis added). Both the cover

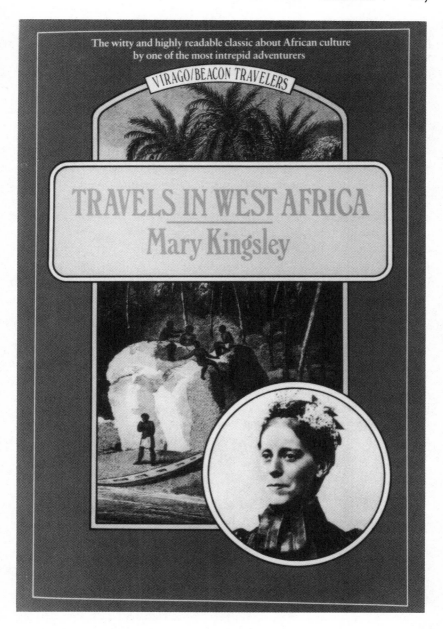

The witty and highly readable classic about African culture
by one of the most intrepid adventurers

VIRAGO/BEACON TRAVELERS

TRAVELS IN WEST AFRICA

Mary Kingsley

and the critical study proffer an ideologically loaded iconography—a photographic portrait of the white Western woman and a landscape painting of the exotic stage. A celebration of aggressive individualism, albeit in "feminine" form, is repeated in the semiotics of cultural confrontation on the cover of Kingsley's book.

Kingsley's own complex relation to imperialism and the individualism of adventure is obscured by the cover. The iconography and rhetoric of feminist recuperation, for example, ignore Kingsley's own resistance to the lexicon of self-discovery. Although Kingsley constructs a narrative "I" in her text, she deliberately eschews the search for identity thematized in much nineteenth-century travel literature. Although it is tempting to see in the topos of travel a route to self-discovery, Kingsley's hybrid narrative in fact frustrates our attempts to chart the narrator or traveler as a unified psychological "self." In a stimulating discussion of types of British colonial travel narratives, Pratt argues that experiential narratives of travel on the cultural frontier produce subjects defined by the bourgeois realm of the private individual: "This sentimental, experiential subject inhabits that self-defined 'other' sector of the bourgeois world, the private sphere—home of desire, sex, spirituality, and the Individual" (*Imperial Eyes*, 78). But Kingsley's protean narrative performance resists the coherence and self-revelation that are major "products" of both domestic fiction and sentimental travel narratives of the Victorian period. One of the most telling insights into Kingsley's resistance to self-revelation is "On Not Writing a Novel" by Rosellen Brown. After spending five years researching and planning a novel with Kingsley as protagonist, Brown explains that she abandoned her attempt because she had no sense of introspection, of an "inner life" (20), in Kingsley's writings.

Furthermore, foregrounding the intrepidity of the British traveler against an exotic background obscures the crucial significance Kingsley attributed to representing African culture to a British reading public. Kingsley's travels led her to recognize the political stakes of representation. She opposed both the blatantly aggressive policies and rhetoric of imperialism practiced by the Belgians and the more ostensibly liberal but still aggressive ethos of the British, who sought to "civilize the natives." The crucial point is that the effectiveness of Kingsley's arguments against existing imperial policy depended on the power of her narrative to represent the rich and complex African cultures that were being trampled by such policy. Although she never questioned the British presence in Africa, she argued that its Crown colony ideology and practice were both stupid and insensitive. Describing this system in the preface to her other tome on West Africa, *West African Studies* (published in 1899), Kingsley wrote that the Crown colony system "brought with it suffering to the native races and disgrace to English gentlemen, who are bound to obey and carry out orders given them by the system" (xii).[19] The very terms of her rhetoric ("native race" versus "English gentlemen") confirm her implication in colonial discourse, yet one must recognize the nuances of her textual "productions" of Africa, as well as their complicities.

Kingsley's enormously popular travel books and the series of speeches she subsequently delivered back in England made her an important public and political figure. A late twentieth-century consciousness observes just how much her critique of British colonial policy still locates itself within certain imperialist assumptions; yet as a cultural figure she fascinates, as does her narrative, because her relation to the cultural and political ideologies of the 1890s is complex enough to admit diverse interpretations. Indeed, her own relation to mainstream British intellectual culture was ambivalent. The daughter and niece of eminent Victorian men of letters George and Charles Kingsley, respectively, she felt marginalized as a woman by the educational system that helped "interpellate" the young men of England into its ideological systems (including the "muscular Christianity" that her uncle Charles espoused throughout his life). In this respect she can be fruitfully compared with Virginia Woolf two decades later.

The interest of Kingsley's ambiguous status in relation to the dominant culture's imperial ethos increases when one looks at the way her writings were appropriated by political and intellectual figures of radically divergent views, such as J. A. Hobson and Michael Davitt, on the one hand, and Rudyard Kipling, on the other. In his book *Imperialism* (1903), Hobson, the British anti-imperialist economist and social philosopher, mentions Kingsley approvingly and relies on the "testimony" of her travel writing to reveal the folly of the Crown colony system in Africa (121n); Davitt, the Irish patriot and politician who fought for land reform and home rule in Ireland, argued before Parliament against a poll tax in Ireland, citing Kingsley's writing against a hut tax in Africa. Yet Kipling, who knew and admired Kingsley,

[19]In *The English Novel in the Twentieth Century*, Green takes 1897, the year when Kingsley's *Travels* was published and the year of Queen Victoria's diamond jubilee, as an exemplary time of British pride in its imperial potential (1–15).

could also write a tribute to her indomitable "British" spirit, representing her as belonging to the freemasonry of the male adventurer: "Being human, she must have feared some things, but one never arrived at what they were. . . . At her own wish her body was delivered to the sea from a little torpedo-boat, off Simonstown. And, as the Quartermaster of that uneasy craft used to say in after years: 'That was how we buried Mary' " (4–5). Neither of these views of Kingsley is "mistaken." Both were available as "readings" of her cultural image and her texts. This double reading of Kingsley has been updated in the very divergent assessments of Mudimbe, who uses her to illustrate a particularly crude late Victorian misunderstanding of African fetish (10), and Sara Mills, who in her "case study" of Kingsley argues that the clash between femininity and colonialism in Kingsley's travel narrative produces a text both inside and outside the dominant discourse (see 153–74).

Kingsley both identified with the masculine voyages of exploration and science and exposed the masculinist hubris that often attended exploration, colonization, and anthropology conducted by men. Insofar as she identifies with the ethos of masculine adventure, Kingsley appropriates conventions of adventure, as if deliberately breaking with a female domestic literary tradition. As a woman who spent the first thirty years of her life at home with her mother, while her writer/physician/adventurer father toured the world, Kingsley read voraciously, including exploration narratives and adventure. One of her favorite books was Defoe's *A General History of Robberies and Murders of the Most Notorious Pyrates* (Frank, 68). When her parents died within six months of each other and she decided to go to Africa, she seems to have embraced male adventure and a certain mischievous iconoclasm that she found in her book of pirates.[20] In *Travels* she continually praises the "old Coasters," salty traders whom she met on her voyage and generally preferred to both missionaries and colonizers.

In the self-representation with which she begins her narrative, Kingsley implicitly places herself in relation to the mercantilist tradition of adventure through the figure of speculation. Prefacing the

[20]This book about pirates, attributed to Defoe, contains the narratives of "the Remarkable Actions and Adventures of the Two Female Pyrates, *Mary Read* and *Ann Bonny*." The narratives, which record "the odd Incidents of their rambling Lives" (117), might have provided Kingsley's imagination with a particularly interesting adaptation of a masculine model. Like Cavendish's Travelia, both women cross-dress as men to gain passage aboard the pirate ships.

introduction with the type of capsule summary often found in eighteenth-century picaresque novels (the introduction "relateth the various causes which impelled the author to embark upon the voyage"),
Kingsley begins the text proper rather jauntily, with the following: "It
was in 1893 that, for the first time in my life, I found myself in possession of five or six months which were not heavily forestalled, and
feeling like a boy with a new half-crown, I lay about in my mind, as
Mr. Bunyan would say, as to what to do with them" (1). Both the
monetary figure and the cross-gendering in this self-representation
place Kingsley's story within the tradition of travel as investment. The
coin metaphor is fascinating; leisure time in her "possession" is like
capital just waiting to be spent. The root meanings of "adventure" are
tapped metaphorically: both "venture," as in the risking of money,
and "future" (*l'avenir*) are implicitly evoked—the thirty-year-old
Kingsley is like a boy about to embark on his future. The "half-crown"
prophesies the importance of the marketplace in Kingsley's journey,
for she subsidizes her travels in Africa by bartering from village to
village. She thus deliberately aligns herself with the merchant/adven-
ture tradition of British travelers, fictional and nonfictional, including
Robinson Crusoe, whose own trip to Africa is described (unlike Kingsley's) as the most "unfortunate of all enterprises" (*Robinson Crusoe*,
15). Although a more serious, scientific persona is fashioned in the
narrative—the "Miss Kingsley" who takes measurements—this trope
of speculation predominates, combining associations of fortune, risk,
and investment. "If there is a great investment in travel, it is perhaps
because travel models the structure of investment itself, the *transfer* of
assets that institutes an economy, be it political or libidinal, 'restricted'
or 'general,' " says Georges Van Den Abbeele (xvii). In various ways,
Kingsley's narrative emphasizes this general economy of travel, but
its images and themes also align it with a particular version of mercantile, masculine adventure.

Narratives in this venture/adventure tradition often begin with a
sense of domestic dead end. Historically, this tradition of adventure
often appealed to the second sons of English families or to non-English
sons of Britain (Scotsmen, for example), who lacked the benefit of
patrimony entailed upon their older brothers and had no reason to
remain at home.[21] Even when this particular sociological scenario does
not apply, the tradition of venture/adventure often acknowledges that

[21]In "The Invention of Tradition in Colonial Africa," Terence Ranger discusses the

the protagonist has nothing to lose: think of Melville's Ishmael, who explains his wandering by saying, "Some years ago—never mind how long precisely—having little or no money in my purse, and nothing particular to interest me on shore, I thought I would sail about a little and see the watery part of the world" (1). Kingsley's narrative borrows this studied casualness, which often marks the venturing/adventuring tradition, as well as the sense of England's diminished possibilities: there seems to be nothing better to do than to go exploring. Yet her adaptation of this jaunty, "masculine" tone submerges an exhausted past that has been differently shaped by gender—that of a Victorian spinster who selflessly nursed her parents and suddenly found herself alone with her life when her parents died in 1893 (a classic topos for other Victorian women travelers, such as Marianne North and Mary Taylor).[22] More like Lucy Snowe in Brontë's *Villette* than Huck Finn or Ishmael, Kingsley begins her narrative with her departure from England because England cannot support her story. In her memoirs, Kingsley figures this "bankruptcy" of the domestic situation with a vacant interior, both of "home" and the self: "The fact is I am no more a human being than a gust of wind is. . . . It never occurs to me that I have any right to do anything more than now and then sit and warm myself at the fires of real human beings" (quoted in Gwynn, 26). Domesticity and coherent identity are decentered here—Kingsley imagines herself as vaporous, empty, unfixed; the familiar motif of the Victorian hearth is displaced, located elsewhere, with "real human beings." If domestic fiction "invested common forms of social behavior with the emotional values of women" (Armstrong, 29), Kingsley, like Lucy Snowe, seems ill-suited to such "investment." Yet the pathos of blighted domesticity figured in her memoir is muted in the travel narrative, which launches itself breezily by invoking boy's adventure, a tradition that also falls short of a perfect fit.

Early on, Kingsley's narrative plays through a series of tropes borrowed from male textual traditions. In the first chapter, she adapts the heterosexual erotics so prevalent in African travel narratives writ-

---

way primogeniture created a whole class of insecure second sons of England, for whom the colonies provided one of the few hopes for advancement.

[22]See Mary Russell, *The Blessings of a Good Thick Skirt: Women Travellers and Their World*, 150, 156.

ten by male explorers—the romantic figure of the mysterious foreign land, both seductive and pitiless: "The West Coast of Africa is like the Arctic regions in one particular, and that is that when you have once visited it you want to go back there again; and, now I come to think of it, there is another particular in which it is like them, and that is that the chances you have of returning from it at all are small, for it is a *Belle Dame sans merci*" (11). Sandra Gilbert and Susan Gubar make much of this image in nineteenth- and twentieth-century literature, reading its pervasiveness as a sign of male anxiety about the sexuality and power of women and of the dark and mysterious others men encountered: "And She is there in continents that during the nineteenth century became increasingly accessible to European explorers, 'underdeveloped' continents where ordinary trade and comparatively ordinary geographical research inevitably became entwined with Her extraordinary existence. Rider Haggard located Her under a mountain in the heart of an African darkness" (10). Margery Perham and J. Simmons suggest that these works produce an underlying analogy between the body of the "dark slave, ravished, beautiful but untamable" and the land (*African Discovery*, 16). In Keats's poem, La Belle Dame speaks a "language strange"; she enthralls the poet, seduces him with her enigmatic otherness. The question is, How can the female traveler and travel writer make use of a topos that links racial and sexual otherness? What happens to the equation of the power of the foreign with the power of a female "language strange" that spellbinds and threatens the male traveler, like the music of the Sirens?

"I succumbed to the charm of the Coast as soon as I left Sierra Leone on my first voyage out" (11): Kingsley identifies herself with the men who choose the seductive danger of Africa rather than the boredom of "being home in England." Later on in the narrative she extends this idea, employing the image of the African forest to signify an uninterpretable mystery. Describing a night in this forest, she says:

> Unless you are interested in it and fall under its charm, it is the most awful life in death imaginable. It is like being shut up in a library whose books you cannot read, all the while tormented, terrified, and bored. And if you do fall under its spell, it takes all the colour out of other kinds of living. Still, it is good for a man to have an experience of it, whether he likes it or not, for it teaches you how very dependent you have been, during your previous life, on the familiarity of those conditions you have

been brought up among, and on your fellow citizens; moreover it takes the conceit out of you pretty thoroughly during the days you spend stupidly stumbling about among your new surroundings. (102)

Kingsley represents herself as a "man" who encounters the "spells" and "charms" of a feminized land—the feminine seductions of La Belle Dame now complicated by African magic, which implicitly invokes the idea of fetish (about which I will say much more). Africa "takes the colour out of" normal living—suddenly European culture seems impossibly bleached and vacant. African travel becomes obsession, bewitchment. Yet worth noting is the way that Kingsley's rather conventional metaphor of Africa as unreadable text is offered as an *alternative* to the topos of seduction—unless a man is spellbound and seduced, he will feel as though he is imprisoned in a library, tormented by the totally opaque foreign text. It is as if Kingsley divides two normally congruent tropes of African mystery—seductiveness and illegibility—into separate images: the male traveler on the scene, seduced by the feminine power of Africa, and the daughter back in her father's library, tormented by the foreign mysteries that present themselves as maddeningly inaccessible. The latter metaphor may evoke Kingsley's frustration in her own father's library, where she read Cook, Hakluyt, and other travel literature while her father roamed the world.

But it is in the way she demystifies seduction and de-eroticizes the cultural encounter that Kingsley's canny alteration of this heterosexual cultural trope can best be seen. For example, after aligning herself with the male travelers who hear the call of La Belle Dame and sneak back to her shores, she writes: "So I warned the Coast I was coming back again and the Coast did not believe me; and on my return to it a second time displayed a genuine surprise, and formed an even higher opinion of my folly than it had formed on our first acquaintance, which is saying a good deal" (11–12). The "language strange" that haunts the romantic male traveler is transformed into a polite, if sometimes judgmental, conversation between equals. Although she speaks of her "folly," Kingsley's mode of presenting this conversation rationalizes it—converting it into a model of exchange and reciprocity that will shape both forms and themes of the succeeding narrative. Furthermore, in the transformation, the ungainly European body becomes visible. The acts of "stupidly *stumbling*" in the new surroundings of Africa and *"fall[ing]"* under its charm" (emphasis added), are literalized in the text as physical comedy. The narrative is full of a slapstick that de-eroticizes the body of the traveler, making it the sort of de-humanized object Henri Bergson observes in his analysis of comedy. The traveler's body and mind caught by surprise provide a comic fall into knowledge quite different from the tragic Ancient Mariner-like fall that, for example, Marlow experiences in Conrad's *Heart of Darkness*. By virtue of these representations, the power of the European is undermined in actual physical pratfalls equivalent to slipping on a banana peel.

This fall into knowledge "trips up" the traveler's confident intellectual schemas of understanding. Instead of purposeful male "quest" to the interior, Kingsley's travels and travel writing display an interest in having one's interest thwarted as part of the risk of travel. The white traveler's encounter with difference produces surprise that undermines his or her system of rationality and superior orientation: "The truth is, the study of natural phenomena knocks the bottom out of any man's conceit if it is done honestly and not by selecting only those facts that fit in with his pre-conceived or ingrafted notions" (*Travels*, 441). If this comment conforms in some ways to the Western representation of Africa as enigma, that kind of projection of mystery analyzed in studies such as those by Brantlinger and Christopher Miller, the writing is far removed from the imperial gothic or romantic exoticism that usually attend this topos. Kingsley's is low mimetic representation in which intellectual reconsiderations are figured physically as reversals, upheavals, bottoms knocked out—things falling apart. The traveler's awkwardness as intruder in a foreign culture metamorphoses into slapstick when she slips and falls through the roof of an unprotected hut, "dropping in" unexpectedly, as she says. She represents herself as amusing the African villagers by "diving headlong from a large rock . . . they [the observers] applauded my performance" (170). The effect of this comedy is to dis-spell the romantic aura; the traveler represents herself, rather than the foreign culture, as spectacle.[23]

Although Kingsley's ever present wit allows her to cope with almost every situation, the stories she tells on herself repeatedly stage a loss of mastery for the European body. As opposed to the command of a

[23]See Pratt's discussion of the way Kingsley takes pleasure in play rather than aesthetic beauty. She comments on how Kingsley seeks to separate knowledge from control (*Imperial Eyes*, 215).

Stanley, we get at times a blow to the traveler's equilibrium that knocks stable ideas, as well as the body of the traveler, upside down. When she describes an episode in which her African guide suggests she proceed first to a very dangerous town on their path because she was "something queer" enough so the others "might not shoot [her] at sight," she remarks, "It is at such a moment as this that the Giant's robe gets, so to speak, between your legs and threatens to trip you up" (295). One could say that the image represents an emasculation of the great white male traveler, a limp phallus between the legs, like the tail of a dog that is ashamed. Again, knowledge is represented, not as confident mastery, but as a groping toward understanding.

The "Giant's robe" is a costume, and the theatrical metaphor in the two preceding examples appears repeatedly in the representation of Kingsley's encounters and reveals her canny grasp of cross-cultural theater and mastery as performance. One of the most interesting aspects of *Travels in West Africa* is the way in which Kingsley represents cross-cultural confrontation as theater on both sides, often substituting for a discourse of the essential and natural a rhetoric of masquerade and self-conscious cultural performance. In *Blank Darkness*, Christopher Miller elevates Conrad's *Heart of Darkness* (1899) to the status of an "allegory of all other Africanist texts" (170) because it is "a self-conscious meditation on misunderstanding, and its self-consciousness is what places it at a highly significant crossroads between an old and a new mode of Africanist expression, between the projection of a corrupt and ignoble Africa and the later critique of that projection and its political outgrowth, colonialism" (171). Kingsley's *Travels*, published two years before Conrad's novel, deliberately resists the impressionist mode of philosophical meditation that makes Conrad's text so haunting.[24] But Kingsley also self-consciously explores the power-knowledge complex in cross-cultural confrontation. Let me state this carefully: Kingsley, like other late Victorian ethnographers, is not free from polygeneticist, racist assumptions about the difference between Africans and Europeans. And, as Pratt points out, her "comic irreverence" itself could be seen as a form of mastery (*Imperial Eyes*, 215). Yet in her narrative she continually satirizes an imperialism of the intellect in ethnography and travel. Unlike most of her male contemporaries, she examines how the dynamics of power between African

---

[24]I can find no evidence that Conrad read Kingsley's book, although she mentions reading his *Nigger of the Narcissus*.

and European is gendered. She pokes fun at the project of European mastery, of Hermes the ethnographer as phallic interpreter.

The complex interaction between knowledge and power, particularly that involved in the ethnographic pursuit of Africa, is apparent in a passage in Kingsley's text that allegorizes the difficulties of what James Clifford calls "ethnographic subjectivity" ("On Ethnographic Self-Fashioning," 93–94). It occurs in a very important and even suspensefully delayed chapter on African "fetish," which is the object of Kingsley's ethnographic research.

> The difficulty of the language is, however, far less than the whole set of difficulties with your own mind. Unless you can make it pliant enough to follow the African idea step by step, however much care you may take, you will not bag your game. I heard an account the other day—I have forgotten where—of a representative of her Majesty in Africa who went out for a day's antelope shooting. There were plenty of antelope about, and he stalked them with great care; but always, just before he got within shot of the game, they saw something and bolted. Knowing he and the boy behind him had been making no sound and could not have been seen, he stalked on, but always with the same result; until happening to look round, he saw the boy behind him was supporting the dignity of the Empire at large, and this representative of it in particular, by steadfastly holding aloft the consular flag. Well, if you go hunting the African idea with the flag of your own religion or opinions floating ostentatiously over you, you will similarly get a very poor bag. (434–35)

In borrowing this story of the imperial white hunter (Her Majesty's representative), Kingsley creates a parable of the imperial Western intellect. Her "allegory" exposes the folly of the European's confident machismo and links it to the nationalistic ideologies that inhibit cultural encounters on the frontiers of empire. As Haraway has shown, the image of the hunt in narratives on African travel, particularly those recounting scientific enterprises, often buttresses the threatened manhood of the white traveler. African exploration of various kinds provided the white male traveler with "resources for restoring manhood in the healthy activity of sportsmanlike hunting"—"hunting" here includes capturing the African "image" in photography or gathering scientific information (53). In interrupting her description of African "fetish" with this story of the flag as trussed-up phallus,

Kingsley shifts the difficulties of interpreting African culture to the mind of the adventuring ethnographer and uncannily recognizes a form of fetish worship peculiar to Western patriotism.[25]

Although in some ways her narrative participates in the typical representation of Africa as insoluble mystery, figuring the African intellect as unfathomable terrain ("I must warn you also that your own mind requires protection when you send it stalking the savage idea through the tangled forests, the dark caves, the swamps and the fogs of the Ethiopian intellect" [440]), her emphasis falls on the cultural baggage of the Western consciousness. Anticipating Marlow's warnings in *Heart of Darkness* about the "few ideas" the European must take with him to Africa, her perspective is nevertheless more ironic and skeptical; for the moly to which this Hermes-ethnographer must cling is the recognition of "the untrustworthiness of human evidence regarding the unseen, and also the seen, when it is viewed by a person who has in his mind an explanation of the phenomenon before it occurs" (440). There is a sophisticated awareness, not only of knowledge as a kind of violence done to things, but of the reflexive limitation of vision as well—in seeing the other through Western eyes, we tend to project ourselves.

Kingsley advises that "the wisest way" to study the natural and cultural phenomena of Africa, particularly the fetish, is "to get into the state of mind of an old marine engineer who oils and sees that every screw and bolt of his engines is clean and well watched, and who loves them as living things, caressing and scolding them himself, defending them, with stormy language, against the aspersions of the silly, uninformed outside world, which persists in regarding them as mere machines, a thing his superior intelligence and experience knows they are not" (441–42). Again, this advice anticipates Marlow's speech

---

[25]In *Culture and Anomie*, Christopher Herbert praises a similar recognition of the dangers of prejudice and projection on the part of the traveler in Harriet Martineau's *How to Observe Morals and Manners* (1834), a much earlier text than Kingsley's. Showing that the narrative that dates the "invention" of modern ethnography from Malinowski falsely erases early nineteenth-century precursors such as Martineau, Herbert unearths a potential "mother" of ethnography early in the century. His excellent discussion, however, does not mention that Martineau's observations concern her travels to America rather than cross-cultural and racial confrontation on the imperial frontier. Furthermore, he does not account for the differences between cultural observation in the 1830s and imperial confrontation and observation at the end of the century, after post-Darwinian evolutionary discourse had changed anthropology and European imperialism had transformed the political scene of cross-cultural confrontation.

about the saving possibilities of concentrating on "rivets," a utilitarian, English antidote to the African mystery. Yet Kingsley does something quite different in her narrative by drawing an analogy between the Western form of fetishism, which attributes divinity to technological, material objects, and African fetish, which also views material objects as embodying religious and social value. The idea and discourse of the fetish, as William Pietz thoroughly demonstrates, was developed by eighteenth-century travelers to the West African coast and was produced by a specifically mercantile cross-cultural interaction ("Fetish, II," 45). Kingsley offers the idea of the fetish not as evidence of the Africans' irrationality and perversity—as it was often presented in Western discourse—but as an intelligible nexus of social, economic, and religious investments in the material object. Whereas much Western discourse on the fetish disparages what was viewed as a confusion of religious values with material objects, said to exemplify the African mentality (Pietz, "Fetish IIIa," 109), Kingsley, herself a thoroughgoing materialist, views it as a comprehensible, even valuable idea.

Yet "pursuit of the African idea," even when this phrase designates a cautious endeavor to understand the complex idea of fetish worship, entangles Kingsley in the language of mastery, even as she attempts to dissociate herself from it. As she persists in using the metaphor of "sport," she implicates herself in the discourse of mastery and capture. She calls "stalking the wild West African idea" a "pursuit" of "high sporting interest," "as beset with difficulty and danger as grizzly bear hunting" (430). Here, her analogy between the dangers of ethnography and those of hunting is meant to aggrandize intellectual pursuit.[26] The "pursuit," like the "hunt," must be approached with great caution. The long-deferred chapter entitled "Fetish" is summa-

[26]This theme of the real dangers of intellectual "pursuit" is repeated throughout her narrative, echoing that of one of her favorite books from her father's library, George Craik's *Pursuit of Knowledge under Difficulties*, a Victorian, intellectual *Profiles in Courage* that classifies different types of daring mental enterprises. Craik's study testifies to a liberalism of the intellect; it ratifies the idea that the pursuit of knowledge is available to all. The stories he tells are, he reminds us, "striking proof of how independent we really are, if we choose, of those external circumstances which seem to make so vast a difference of situation between man and man" (67). Although there are few women in this compendium of courageous individuals, Craik's point is that this pursuit is open to anyone, to "both sexes" and "young and old" (281). For Kingsley, the autodidact and female descendant of such an illustrious Victorian literary family, this book and its liberal fictions of possibility provided another plot in which to place herself: the scientist, rather than the pirate or explorer, could be the peripatetic hero.

rized as a narrative "in which the Voyager attempts cautiously to approach the subject of Fetish, and gives a classification of spirits, and some account of the Ibet and Orundas" (429). Can the ethnographer truly be divorced from the imperialist adventurer? In implicit recognition of the difficulties of figuring ethnographic activity, Kingsley varies her metaphors. The hunt becomes a gentler zoological expedition; ideas are "netted" rather than captured as prey, and the narrative also mentions "netting" a reason for a particular practice. It's as if all the professional activities of African explorers were encompassed by these sets of metaphors, implicated in one enterprise, yet different from one another—hunters, explorers, naturalists, ethnographers.

Whatever the particular occupation of the traveler, however, Kingsley's metaphors privilege the active "pursuit" of Africa on the frontier as opposed to a secondhand, more purely speculative approach. The narrative establishes a dichotomy between on-site ethnographic activity and the musings of armchair ethnologists comfortably at home in Europe, unwilling to risk the adventure. "Bagging" the game, which stands figuratively for achieving some satisfactory understanding of African culture, fetish in particular, is contrasted with "tagging" the stories somewhere back home. The image of the sportsman is meant to suggest some wit and ingenuity in the ethnographer, qualities that are missing from the mere collector of facts. Kingsley writes:

> African stories are of great interest when you know the locality and the tribe they come from; but I am sure if you were to bring home a heap of stories like this, and empty them over any distinguished ethnologist's head, without ticketing them with the culture of the tribe they belonged to, the conditions it lives under, and so forth, you would stun him with the seeming inter-contradiction of some, and utter pointlessness of the rest, and he would give up ethnology and hurriedly devote his remaining years to the attempt to collect a million postage stamps, so as to do something definite before he died. (439)

Kingsley constantly disparages the intellectual and physical safety of the "collector" that fosters such European misconceptions of the African and his or her culture. Her armchair ethnologist is defenseless against the "trick" played by the fieldworker, who physically "stuns" him with a cascade of African "facts." In Kingsley's scenario, these "facts" become so much garbage dumped over the distinguished ethnologist's head. She chooses philately as the proper occupation for this failed and frustrated ethnologist, for collecting *stamps* serves as the emblem for the sedentary rather than for risk-taking activity. Ticketing the "heap" of stories is implicitly compared with hoarding African objects, as opposed to promoting their circulation and exchange in the field.

Thirty years before Malinowski introduced twentieth-century standards of scientific participation-observation for the ethnographer, Kingsley contrasts the traveling scientist with the armchair egghead, representing proper ethnography as movement and adventure. Although she has a high regard for "experts" such as E. B. Tylor and Dr. Nassau, she regards with suspicion various kinds of "professionals"—government administrators and ethnologists alike—who fail to combine interpretation with experience and to consider the local context of the details of culture they analyze.[27]

Kingsley in her narrative rhetorically signals skepticism about taxonomy and rigid classification (i.e., "tagging" the game), juxtaposing it with the practical, the contingent, the nonsystematic. Digressions puncture her own discourse of classification. For example, her allegory of hunting the African idea interrupts the summaries of information on African fetish. Storytelling, that is, disperses her more "scientific" descriptions and catalogues of fetish; it is the storyteller, not the scientist, who "forgets" the source of information of the story ("I heard an account the other day—I have forgotten where"). In the midst of a crucial chapter on African custom and belief, her little parable (of the flag-bearing hunter) intrudes to disrupt classification and taxonomy. The folkloristic, the serendipitous (she *happened* to hear of this story which serves as a perfect allegory) enter the picture of knowledge. The hybrid forms within Kingsley's text—the "word swamp," as she called it, of narrative, diary, ethnographic facts, and stories quoted from African and European sources—formally imitate the mixed tones and textures of the Africa she encountered, while somehow, in their entirety, attempting to give an "idea" of Africa. It is as

---

[27]Earlier in the century, in *How to Observe Morals and Manners*, Martineau had also stressed the importance of field experience and cautioned against "hasty generalisation" (19) in interpreting "the social state of a nation" (17). But Martineau's narrative account of the intellectual difficulties that attend the traveler's sociological enterprise is itself very systematic and prescriptive, as indicated by her title. Kingsley, on the other hand, made of her narrative a farraginous mix of storytelling, description, and ethnographic summary that resists master narrative and system as it purports to come to terms with the "idea" of Africa.

if the African "story" cannot be told within the confines of any one tradition. Within the narrative, Kingsley often refers to her "goings on" (351), or errant behavior, and this same kind of wandering marks the narration as well as the events. Such language emphasizes the image of the wayward, risk-taking traveler who deliberately refuses the too neat summaries of African culture as well as the more aggressive, imperial "quests" of male exploration.

It is around the concept of "fetish" that Kingsley focuses her discussion of the recalcitrance of West African culture to Western systematization—there are fetishes for everything in African culture, Kingsley says, rebuking Western attempts to integrate African "religion" into a coherent whole. On the one hand, this interpretation might be read as exemplifying the European tradition of seeing Africa as the sign of the indecipherable, the unsystematic. As Gayatri Chakravorty Spivak and Christopher Miller have observed, Africa frustrated Western attempts to reify it even more thoroughly than had the Orient. Hinduism and Islam could be read as an intelligible code, but "fetish" could not. Spivak says:

> Part of my work is to notice what kinds of distinctions were made among the so-called others of the West. I have used the example of the codification of law. In this situation the Islamic code was taken as a real code, since it was a monotheistic code, but it was seen as incorrect. . . . And anything that was not either Hindu or Muslim—tribals and so on, and in a wider context, non-Islamic Africa and the Aboriginals of Australia— did not have a code, and was made the place of magic and fetishism. It is in this kind of context that one has to see the othering of the other of the West, in actual imperial practice. (*Post-Colonial Critic*, 39)

Yet, although most nineteenth- and early twentieth-century travelers and scientists considered fetish a "puerile cult of idolatry" (Christopher Miller, 44), Kingsley's treatment, as I have already noted, is quite different. She is fascinated—and captivated—by what she considers the local and pragmatic wisdom of African "charms" and "fetish." In a section titled the "Uncertainty of Charms," she tries to convey the practical and concrete aspects of belief: "Charms are made for every occupation and desire in life—loving, hating, buying, selling, fishing, planting, travelling, hunting, &c" (448). And, "I often think it must be the common-sense element in fetish customs that enables them to survive, in the strange way they do, in the minds of

Africans who have been long under European influence and education" (490). Although in this way Kingsley domesticates the uncertainties of African practice, by doing so she attempts to show that the imposition of Western moral schemas is irrational and bizarre.

Whereas the conventional Western discourse of the fetish treats the irreducible materiality and the contingent nature of African fetish as debased, unsystematic, and unspiritual, Kingsley's account gives them values. Her narrative tries to retain the sense of the foreignness of Africa not as Conradian mystique but as the stubborn resistance of the specific, the local. Kingsley records particular encounters in which the ethnographer literally bumps up against stubborn material or cultural facts and is made to recognize they have a life of their own, a fetish power. Interestingly, the twentieth-century ethnographer Steven Webster prescribes just such an immersion in the "contingencies" of everyday life: "Ethnography must hang on in good faith to the myriad contingencies and opaque personalities of reality, and deny itself the illusion of a transparent description, a luxury reserved for less reflexive sciences" (111). Webster's metaphors only inadvertently retain the physicality of Kingsley's prosaic comedy—one pictures the ethnographer literally clinging to ("hanging on" to) the "real," the quotidian detail. It is this comic, de-eroticized body of the traveler that Kingsley's narrative represents again and again which suggests one aspect of fetish that intersects with Bergsonian comedy, its "subversion of the ideal of the autonomously determined self" (Pietz, "Fetish II," 23). Thus, fetish is invoked in the narrative both as a charm, or moly, to aid the traveler and as the kind of fateful chance that leads to her sometimes humbling (and physical) confrontation with the African "fact" she has not anticipated. The narrator complains that "the worst of charms and prayers" is that the "thing you wish of them may, and frequently does, happen in a strikingly direct way, but other times it does not" (448). Again, this difficulty becomes the source of comedy: "Finding, we will say, that you have been upset and half-drowned, and your canoe-load of goods lost three times in a week, that your paddles are always breaking, and the amount of snags in the river and so on is abnormal, you judge that your canoe-charm has stopped. Then you go to the medicine man who supplied you with it and complain. He says it was a perfectly good charm when he sold it you and he never had any complaints before, but he will investigate" (449).

The iterative mode and present tense, the hypothetical exchange of European writer and European reader in the use of the second person (it is the "you" who experiences this bewilderment rather than the "I" of the writer), and the transformation of the medicine man into a local shopkeeper—all serve to domesticate the mystery and translate the foreign into terms intelligible (and ingratiating) to the English reader. The narration here suggests that African spirits are busy thwarting European travelers and that African charms produce the necessity of English "charm" and wit in the encounter between African and European. Yet here again Kingsley's narrative represents a crucial aspect of fetishism—its relation to and origin in mercantile transactions between different cultures. Fetish is a key phenomenon in her text not only for what it reveals about African custom but also for the commercial exchange it enables. The meaning of the African "fetish" becomes linked to the particular commercial transactions in face-to-face encounters.

But Kingsley shows how the element of surprise, of risk, of chance upsets the supposedly rational Western notion of economic exchange. As Pietz observes about the fetish trade between Europeans and Africans in early narratives of African travel, trading led to "a perversion of the natural processes of economic negotiation and legal contact. Desiring a clean economic interaction, seventeenth-century merchants unhappily found themselves entering into social relations and quasi-religious ceremonies that should have been irrelevant to the conduct of trade" ("Fetish II," 45). Kingsley, on the contrary, welcomed the "messiness" of commercial transaction and its two-way process, for the economic transfer was a means, not an end, leading as it did to ethnographic encounter. The transformation of cross-cultural confrontation into a series of particular "exchanges," even consumer exchanges, is linked to the important image of circulation to which I have alluded and thus leads back to the venture/adventure tradition I mentioned earlier.

I want to return to the topoi of circulation and exchange in an attempt to explain the importance of trade not only for Kingsley's overt political support of British trading concerns in Africa (at the expense of the Crown colony system of direct control) but also for what I would call the politics of representation in her text, that is, the representation of intercultural exchanges on the frontier. According to J. E. Flint, on her return to England, in her writings and speeches Kingsley became "the intellectual and philosophic spokeswoman for the British traders to West Africa" (96). As she acknowledges in the first chapters of her book, her journeys to Africa made her totally revise her impressions of traders, and she admits owing much to the trading company of Hatton and Cookson, which helped facilitate her journey. In an appendix to *Travels* called "Disease in West Africa," she lauds the "heroes of commerce, the West Coast traders" and praises England as "the greatest manufacturing country in the world." The trade carried on in West Africa "enables thousands of men, women and children to remain safely in England, in comfort and pleasure, owing to the wages and profits arising from the manufacture and export of the articles used in that trade" (691).

This tribute to men of trade is clearly an endorsement of England's expansionist policy as well as of alliance between expansion and capitalism (Kingsley contrasts capitalistic expansion, through free trade, with colonization, which is ultimately a drain on the mother country and destructive of the indigenous culture). But if Kingsley served, in part, as an apologist for the English free-trade companies, her interest in trade would be too narrowly interpreted as an idealization of capitalism. Flint reassesses Kingsley through a revisionary reading of the "real purpose" (i.e., ulterior motive) of her intense interest in African culture—to support the trader's position and to undermine that of the missionaries—yet only in a footnote does he concede that self-interest was not involved. Because he divorces the "politics" from the narrative enterprise, Flint is at a loss to explain Kingsley as a "fanatical supporter of [trade] interests" (97, n. 7).

Trade literally underwrote much of Kingsley's journey, for she partially supported herself by bartering Western goods, such as liquor and tobacco, in exchange for food, guides, conversation, and information. These exchanges are paradigmatic of mediation on the cultural frontier. Speaking of the exchange on which anthropology itself is based, Webster points out that the anthropological account usually represses this quid pro quo. Ethnography, he comments, treats as "unspoken promises" the "honorary cultural membership" for the ethnologist and the "sanguine hope of Western advantages" for the African hosts: "The impossibility of such unspoken promises is both the tragedy of cultural difference-domination and the ground of its understanding" (92). Webster is interested in demystifying and de-idealizing this cultural encounter between the object of study and the Western investigator. Kingsley frankly acknowledges the role that self-interest and material exchange play in cross-cultural confrontation. What she hoped to "purchase" through African transactions was not a commodity but participation in a male intercultural social commerce facilitated and emblematized by barter—the face-to-face exchange of goods and material as well as stories, information, and access. The benefits of commodity fetishism that those at home derive from the "heroes of commerce" differ from the anthropological trade sought by Kingsley, in which the market is infused with theater, personality, and risk. If Africans and English traders are depicted as serving each other's interests, Kingsley has a strong sense of the mutual manipulations that attend the maneuvers of exchange. For her, as for Sarah Lee, this fiction of mutuality involves projecting onto the Africans a relish and pleasure in the process of trade. She calls this process "the great affair of life" for the mainlanders, who "take to it as soon as they can toddle, and don't even leave it off at death, according to their own accounts of the way the spirits of distinguished traders still dabble and interfere in market matters" (56–57). Although there is much in *Travels* to confirm the difference between Africans and Europeans, trade functions to naturalize the difference by presenting both Africans and British travelers as having needs that are satisfied in the marketplace (and this marketplace is broadly conceived as the place of exchanges of various kinds, not only of material goods).

If this sense of the Africans' willing participation licenses the presence of British traders in Africa, it also sanctions participation of the female traveler and ethnographer. The marketplace offers Kingsley a neutral ground on which to encounter Africans and Africa. She finds an emblem of this genderless mediation in "trade English," which she describes as useful not only "as a means of intercommunication between whites and blacks, but between natives using two distinct languages. . . . It is by no means an easy language to pick up—it is not a farrago of bad words and broken phrases, but is a definite structure, has a great peculiarity in its verb forms, and employs no genders. There is no grammar of it out yet; and one of the best ways of learning it is to listen to a seasoned second mate regulating the unloading or loading, of cargo, over the hatch of the hold" (432). A whole series of cultural assumptions are embedded here; Kingsley wants to see the language of trade as a model of parity rather than mastery, a terrain on which different groups meet and spar and engage in a battle of wits. The most striking emphasis in her representation of trade English is on the fact that it is ungendered. Elsewhere, when this lack of gender results in her being called "sir," one begins to realize that the idea of "genderlessness" really denotes a generic maleness and a certain class and racial status. For in stressing the idea of parity, Kingsley ignores the markers of status evident in the address "sir" as well as the fact that the lingua franca of trade has its norm in an English the "natives" speak only imperfectly. We can recognize Kingsley's investment in affirming this fraternal system, for it significantly allows her neutral participation as woman traveler, trader, and scientist.

Thus, the woman traveler circulates within a male economy centered on the marketplace. Nancy Armstrong analyzes the way nineteenth-century English novels created an ideology of the domestic that gendered the spheres of private and public, producing the private sphere as the realm of the middle-class woman. The cultural exchange that occurs in this sphere, as represented in novels, is sexual.[28] Kingsley's travel narrative provides a counterexample to this tradition—it represents the female self not as sexual commodity but as a mobile, improvisational "trader" on the market. Putting herself in circulation is not the same as discovering the self so popular in accounts of intrepid Victorian women travelers, for to equate such circulation with self-discovery is to reinvest Kingsley's story with the value of a coherent, private subjectivity from which, even at home, Kingsley withheld belief. Her awareness of the theater of the self was heightened by the sense of cross-cultural encounter and audience. Sitting and warming herself "at the fires of other human beings" (Gwynn, 26): this is how Kingsley described her selfhood in general. It is no accident that the image evokes scenes of African fires where she warmed herself on her travels. As Gwynn says, this circulation was made possible through trade (48–54).

The economy of the traveling self on the cultural frontier, if capitalistic, is protean, risky, and infused with the personality of the circulating trader. It is thus more suited to the ethos of early modern capitalism and exploration, characterized by Stephen Greenblatt as "self-fashioning," than to the anonymity of capitalist exchange at home. Face-to-face barter and improvisational encounter in the male economy of cross-cultural confrontation may seem anachronistic in the 1890s. Flint accuses Kingsley of being reactionary rather than progressive, as she is often regarded. According to him, she attempted to "re-create and fossilize the conditions of the 1880's, when government was rudimentary, and the traders untrammelled by taxation, regula-

---

[28]Biographies of Kingsley rarely mention her reading the types of domestic novels that Armstrong cites as central to this "homebound" tradition. Instead, they cite her as reading picaresque novels such as Smollett's or tales of pirates.

tions, and official control" (104). As an example of her antipathy to change, he cites her opposition to introducing coinage into the British territories. Indeed, Kingsley's positive representation of face-to-face encounter does bespeak a resistance to the anonymity of both British bureaucracy and late nineteenth-century and early twentieth-century capitalism. In speeches he delivered around the time that Kingsley wrote her book (and that were published in book form in 1900), George Simmel diagnosed this anonymity and linked it with the institution of money itself (79). Kingsley's vision of the marketplace retained the sense of personal encounter and "face."

But this "face," to return to the theatrical metaphors that abound in the narrative, is represented by Kingsley as a construction for the benefit of an audience. In this regard, Kingsley's book looks forward rather than back to an earlier time. Applying Greenblatt's idea of self-fashioning to the situation of the ethnographer in a postmodern context, Clifford describes the late twentieth-century ethnographer as a self-fashioner, conscious of the way cross-cultural exchange is always a question of dress-up and presentation ("Ethnographic Self-Fashioning," 95). Rather than the sentimental heroic dramas found in many experiential travel narratives of the century, Kingsley gives us theatrics, the performance of the ethnographer and traveler as Hermes the trickster. Kingsley's references to her "goings on," her self-representation as an errant (wandering) traveler and writer belong in this context. Indeed, Kingsley's narrative is strikingly unsentimental about cross-cultural encounters. Her advocacy of trade and exchange must be distinguished from the ethos of a work such as Harriet Martineau's mid-century travel tale, *Dawn Island*, in which the expansion of economic activity is yoked to salvation and humanitarianism. Christianity and commerce go hand in hand to liberate the "savage" from the error of his ways. Kingsley recognizes manipulations, hustling, and self-fashioning on both sides of the cross-cultural divide. The trickster in folklore, it is well to remember, is a figure of the crossroads and the marketplace (Babcock-Abrahams, 159).[29]

[29] Although it is true that the major representational improvisations belong to the Western traveler's narrative "I" rather than to the African, Kingsley does present many scenes of verbal and material exchange where the African host and the European guest take pleasure in sparring and hustling each other. For a discussion of the trickster figure in West African myth and folklore (specifically, among the Ashanti, Fon, Yoruba, and Dogon), see Robert D. Pelton's *Trickster in West Africa: A Study of Mythic Irony and Sacred Delight*. His general description of the trickster suits the kind of comic persona Kingsley

Kingsley went to Africa, she says, to collect fish and fetish, that is, to study specimens and species. Much of the narrative is taken up with reporting what she discovered. But her narrative self-representation acknowledges that the Western observer is the observed as well, both performer and makeup artist. The Latin root of "species," Alexander Gelley reminds us, signifies the visual—that which is seen and that which is a spectacle in the sense of theatrical illusion, but it also implies the "mirroring or reflecting back on itself of the viewing instance" (27). This reflexivity, the acute sense of the viewer viewed, characterizes Kingsley's double vision. (Hence, these implications of "species" differ dramatically from those of the related word "specie," that is, metal coinage, which would apply to the anonymity of the market.)

This double vision bespeaks Kingsley's awareness of the theatrics that characterize not only macho European exploration but also the dyad of masculinity and femininity itself. Gender in her narrative involves masquerade and in the cross-cultural encounter is imbricated in the masculinist posturing of a Stanley. Imperialistic superiority is figured as theater—the imposing European male "Giant" wears a costume ("It is at such a moment as this that the Giant's robe gets, so to speak, between your legs and threatens to trip you up" [295]). Kingsley represents her traveling and writing as participating in such masquerade. In one scene, Kingsley and her men are trapped in a swamp by the rising tide that separates them from solid land. "No need for an old coaster like me to look at that sort of thing twice to know what it meant, and feeling it was a situation more suited to Mr. Stanley than myself, I attempted to emulate his methods and addressed my men. 'Boys,' said I, 'this beastly hole is tidal, and the tide is coming in'" (298). Here is dress-up twice over: Mary Kingsley, Victorian woman, masquerading as a salty old coaster who affects the hyper-virile swagger of a Stanley-like explorer. The "punchline" (including the representation of the "natives" as undifferentiated "boys") is vaudevillian. The travel writer as well as the African traveler must "dress up," for writing, like trading, demands a successful

---

adopts in her narrative: "It is precisely the trickster's earthiness, his popular inelegance, and his delightful inconsequence that have made our intellectual equipment for dealing with him look as ponderously inept as a steam shovel grasping for a grasshopper" (19). Kingsley's tome on West Africa disarms the compulsive thoroughness of the narration with this folkloric mask of casualness.

performance, a witty line for every occasion. Traveler and writer must be able to meet particular situations with dialogue that works.[30]

From the theatrics of gender and race in Kingsley's text, one gets a distinct sense not only that brands of masculinity are exposed as facade or performance but also that femininity, too, is shown to participate in masquerade. When she receives a note addressed to "Dear old Man" that offers her some clean men's shirts and trousers (a mistake caused by the ambiguities of gender in "trade English"), Kingsley mugs:

> Had there been any smelling salts or sal volatile in this subdivision of the Ethiopian region I should have forthwith fainted on reading this, but I well knew there was not, so I blushed until the steam from my soaking clothes (for I truly was "in a deuce of a mess") went up in a cloud and then, just as I was, I went "across" and appeared before the author of that awful note. (502)

Here Kingsley represents herself as representing the English lady. The extent to which she *feared* being taken for such a typical creature can be gauged by her anxiety about encountering a French nun at a Roman Catholic mission on the Rembwé River:

> Moreover I learnt she could not speak English, and I shrank in my condition from attempting to evolve the French language out of my inner consciousness; feeling quite certain I should get much misunderstood by the gentle, clean, tidy lady, and she might put me down as an ordinary specimen of Englishwoman, and so I should bring disgrace on my nation.

[30] At times quotation can also function as such dress-up. For example, in the footnote she supplies to her own rendition of ascending the Great Cameroons, Kingsley quotes Sir Richard Burton's account of his attempt to reach the summit in 1862. Burton describes, in dramatic, even gothic, terms the huge crater he encounters: "Not a blade of grass, not a thread of moss, breaks the gloom of this Plutonic pit, which is as black as Erebus, except where the fire has painted it red or yellow." Kingsley comments: "This ascent was made from the west face. I got into the 'Plutonic pit' through the S.E. break in its wall, and was the first English person to reach it from the S.E., the third of my nation, all told, to ascend the peak, and the twenty-eighth ascender according to my well-informed German friends" (595n). Clearly, her double quotation of Burton's "Plutonic pit" suggests first her appropriation, then her rejection of his more dramatic terms of description. Her own authoritative claim is deliberately stated in less heated terms, the sheer "facts" of her place in the line of mountaineers ostensibly allowed to speak for themselves. This understated way of claiming authority is characteristic of the narrative and seems intended to contrast with what Brantlinger calls the "imperial gothic" (227) of much European travel writing on Africa.

If I had been able to dress up, ashore I would have gone, but as it was I wrote her a note explaining things and thanking her. (350–51)

The "audience" for her persona is European as well as African. To be an "ordinary specimen of Englishwoman" is a terrifying fate; although Kingsley is willing to spar with African traders in "trade English," she is unwilling to be disadvantaged in French with another European woman, for without her wit she might too readily be mistaken for a walking (or traveling) cliché. Indeed, some of the rare anger in the narrative vents itself against a "lady passenger" who insists on playing the role of European lady to the hilt: "Yesterday I met a lady on the shore who asked me if I would take her to Gaboon. I said, as any skipper would, 'delighted, my dear'; and here she is sitting on the top of the cargo with her head just exactly in the proper position to get it bashed in, or knocked off by the boom; and her five bundles, one tin box, a peck of limes and a husband" (412). Kingsley goes on to say:

> My lady passenger is quite the lady passenger, frightened of the sea, and dissatisfied with the accommodation. I have stowed her with every care in the bottom of the boat . . . and she is grateful for the attention; but says "the vessel is not big enough," and goes on eating excruciatingly sour limes in a way that sets my teeth on edge. Half her sufferings arise from her disastrous habit of falling asleep; and then her head goes flump off the seat she is leaning it against, and crack against the ribs of the boat's side; I put my leather photograph case in her usual striking place, but she dodges it in her descent seven times in ten. (413–14)

What befalls the lady in the narrative is not the reversals and tumbles of the comic "I" but a more "fitting" physical punishment—a smack on the head for her brainlessness.

In Kingsley's case, the "difference" gender makes to her travel writing seems to me to lie importantly in this recognition of the theatrical dimension in cultural encounters and the problems of ethnographic representation. I do not mean to claim for Kingsley an anachronistic postmodern consciousness about representation; but I do want to suggest the way in which her often comic narrative functions, in particular, to acknowledge both the way European and native "dress up" to confront each other and the way in which textual forms often imply certain ideologies. Her sense of her own life as mediated and imagined through the books in her father's library gave her an especially strong sense of the need "to prepare a face to meet the faces that you meet," to quote T. S. Eliot. "When there were no more odd jobs to do at home, I, out of my life in books, found something to do that my father cared for, something for which I had been taught German, so that I could do for him odd jobs in it. It was the study of early religion and law, and for it I had to go to West Africa, and I went there, proceeding on the even tenor of my way, doing odd jobs, and trying to understand things, pursuing knowledge under difficulties with unbroken devotion" (Oliver, 78). This language comes from a narrative she fashioned in 1899, when the African exploration was all finished. An odd combination exists here: on the one hand, she seems to accept the patriarchal legacy of the name Kingsley, which included her traveler father and her two famous writer uncles, who celebrated British expansionism and adventure; on the other hand, she is aware that in this tradition she is the daughter who, running out of domestic housework, must make a project of finding some service to be done outside the home. She emerges "out of [her] life in books" in two senses—her travel is both a liberation from the confines of her father's library and a product of that same library, where her reading empowers her to cast herself in the multiple roles of adventurer, scientist, and pursuer of knowledge.

Mary Kingsley both used and transformed male models of adventure and commerce to represent her interaction with African culture and fashion herself as a participant in a male economy. But occasionally, particularly in private letters, she identified herself with a feminized Africa. To Nathan, the man to whom she was probably most attached, she wrote: "I will import to you, in strict confidence, for if it were known it would damage me badly, my opinion on the African. He is *not* 'half devil and half child', anymore than he is 'our benighted brother' and all that sort of thing. He is a woman . . . I know those nigs because I am a woman, a woman of a masculine race but a woman still." Elsewhere she calls herself an "African" and says, "We Africans are not fit for decent society" (quoted in Deborah Birkett, 16). Perhaps it is not surprising that in writing to her potential lover, Kingsley figures her own neediness and (indecent) sexuality by identifying with the African. Yet this self-description also suggests the fact that it was increasingly difficult to figure herself without recourse to this "other" being with whom she was so intensely involved in her travels and writings. The feminine domestic tradition, the masculinist tradition of imperial adventure, the self-effacing topoi of scientific writing—none of these provided the conventions for representing her differences from and resemblances to the people she came to study. *Travels in West Africa* offers more than another white woman's quest for herself in the mirror of the Dark Continent. In her seven hundred–page narrative/ethnography, Kingsley attempts to record how the awkward body of a white woman traveler both collided and colluded with West African cultures.

4

Woolf's Voyages Out:
The Voyage Out and *Orlando*

Near the beginning of *The Voyage Out*, Virginia Woolf's first novel and a travel story, we find a description of the ship, the *Euphrosyne*, that is transporting a group of English tourists to South America.

> But, on the other hand, an immense dignity had descended upon her; she was an inhabitant of the great world, which has so few inhabitants, travelling all day across an empty universe, with veils drawn before her and behind. She was more lonely than the caravan crossing the desert; she was infinitely more mysterious, moving by her own power and sustained by her own resources. The sea might give her death or some unexampled joy, and none would know of it. She was a bride going forth to her husband, a virgin unknown of men; in her vigour and purity she might be likened to all beautiful things, worshipped and felt as a symbol. (32)

This is a prose passage (and the term itself reminds us how narratology depends on the trope of travel) deliberately freighted with significance, the ship, like the novel's allegorical title, an overloaded vessel of meaning. As virgin bride, the ship figures the launching of the narrative. Epithalamic suspense marks the journey of this first novel, as well as that of Woolf's woman traveler, the cliché of the "maiden voyage" doubly revived. The *Euphrosyne* (the name refers to one of the three Graces) figures the trajectory of the female traveler, herself viewed as a symbol of mystery, beauty, and power. From the beginning of the novel, the topos of the journey is explicitly gendered.

The gendering, however, implicitly burdens the narrative, as evidenced in the compulsive figuring and refiguring of the initial metaphor. *She* is lonely, mysterious, self-propelled, vigorous, pure, worshipped, and she may encounter death or joy. The difference that gender makes creates a narrative difficulty, for the proliferating figuration suggests a problem in finding adequate terms of comparison—the ship is "more" lonely and mysterious than a caravan, the joy she might face is "unexampled." In the production of a mini-narrative from this exfoliating metaphor, the possible plots seem radically disjunctive (death or joy), as if the trajectory of the plot could not be clearly envisioned. Just how much cultural freedom and private agency the traveler enjoys is ambiguous: she moves, we are told, under her own steam, sustained by her own resources, yet at the mercy of nature (the sea) and culture (the marriage contract). The passage ends with a further intensification of metaphor, as the already figurative ship serves as a trope for the signifying power of the aesthetic, its ability to transport the viewer to the realm of the symbolic. Metaphor, Derrida reminds us in his meditation on and deconstruction of the rhetoric of metaphor, derives from the Greek root *pherein*, meaning "to carry, to transport" ("White Mythology," 231n). Derrida describes how the *Odyssey* has "traditional recourse to the ship, to its movement, its oars, and its sails, in order to speak figuratively of the means of transport that the metaphorical figure is" (241). Quoting Aristotle, Derrida says, "From metaphor . . . we can best get hold of something fresh" (238).

The sense of exploration and revivification is both fitting and cruelly ironic to the particular voyage out of its ingenue protagonist, Rachel Vinrace (alias Cynthia, in early versions of the novel), whose journey from virgin to bride is aborted by her premature death. Betrothed to the would-be novelist Terence Hewet, with whom she falls in love during her travels, Rachel dies of a disease she contracts in the jungle of South America. Ironically, the wedding veil becomes a shroud, as travel, typically a topos of liberation, becomes instead a dead end.[1] "The sea might give her death or some unexampled joy, and none would know of it"—but the narrative does indeed record and commemorate Rachel's journey into the extremity of death. One could say

---

[1] In a letter to her sister, Virginia envisioned the writing of her first book as a ship's passage into new territory, a journey that parallels the fate of her heroine: "Cynthia [Rachel] will not speak, and my ship is like to sink" (*Letters of Virginia Woolf*, 1:341).

again that Penelope is at the dual theoretical position as signatory of the discourse and traveler, this time weaving her own shroud in the form of the text. Woman's corpus and corpse form the body of the writing.[2]

Twenty years after she began *The Voyage Out*, Woolf again used travel to figure a woman's emergent identity in another novel, although with a definite turn of the screw. Partway through the three hundred–year evolution of his/her psyche, Orlando serves as ambassador to Turkey and miraculously awakens as a woman after a seven-day sleep. His/her sexual metamorphosis occurs "behind the veil" in the libidinous East, a change that "orientalizes" and parodies the veiling/unveiling of the "Truth" of femininity.[3] The metaphor of the ship's passage with "veils drawn before her and behind" in the first novel anticipates the "unveiling" in *Orlando*. The image of the veil is charged with varied significances (and these in turn have different nuances, depending on whether they are linked to East or West), but veiling always concerns concealment and revelation, hence, knowledge and truth, as Ludmilla Jordanova points out: "We can focus on what it either conceals or reveals—woman/nature/truth—that is, on what lies behind the veil" (91).

In both novels, then, travel is linked not only to female identity but also to its mystery and elusiveness, its likelihood of being cast as symbolic. Travel raises epistemological questions concerning women as both subjectivities and semiotic signs. And it signals imaginative transport: the exotic locations of Rachel's journey and Orlando's sex change function as resources for a new type of female adventure. One senses that transplantation is necessary for a new writing, especially in the representation of female identity. Particularly in *The Voyage Out*, England is portrayed as the common*place*, the *topos* out from which the narrative must go. On the first page of the novel, we read that England does not tolerate "eccentricity," and it is precisely eccentricity, a movement out from the center, that is required (as it is, in an-

---

[2] My reading of the novel is indebted to Garrett Stewart's excellent discussion in *Death Sentences: Styles of Dying in British Fiction*.

[3] The image of the veil in its metaphysical and epistemological, as well as its psychoanalytic and sociological/political significances, has been much discussed in recent criticism. See in particular David Shaw's *Lucid Veil: Poetic Truth in the Victorian Age*, Mary Ann Doane's "Veiling Over Desire: Close-ups of the Woman," Malek Alloula's *Colonial Harem*, and Ludmilla Jordanova's *Sexual Visions: Images of Gender in Science and Medicine between the Eighteenth and Twentieth Centuries*.

other way, in Cavendish's imaginary voyage). This centrifugal force not only represents the "desire of wandering," to quote the language Milton's Adam applies to Eve, but it also suggests that wandering poses a necessary risk to the development of feminine subjectivity. Yet even in traveling, this subjectivity cannot escape the Englishness that has sustained foreign voyages throughout British history. Indeed, Woolf's first novel, in particular, presents the irony that in voyaging out from England, the travelers recapitulate an "Englishness" constituted by the very desire to found new colonies oceans away from the fatherland. " 'Being on this ship seems to make it so much more vivid—what it means to be English,' " says Clarissa Dalloway chauvinistically (*Voyage Out*, 50), and even those travelers more ambivalent about "what it means to be English" find that they cannot entirely escape their national characteristics.

It is worth distinguishing, however, the terms of travel in *The Voyage Out* and *Orlando,* for, significantly, Rachel Vinrace's travel becomes a one-way trip, whereas Orlando has a round-trip "ticket." Although Rachel suffers a premature death abroad, Orlando as woman finds a way to repatriate, to return to the fatherland. In the case of round trips, Michel Butor tells us: "We depart, but leave behind our possessions, our roots; we keep our rights. It is well understood from the beginning that we will return" (7). Such rootedness is crucial for an understanding of Orlando's excursus, whereas Rachel's foray never resolves itself into the arc of return. Rachel Vinrace's voyage out gives way to a voyage in from which she does not awaken; Orlando, on the contrary, emerges from the intense interiority of a seven-day slumber in Constantinople, her awakening as a woman ultimately followed by her return to England. In *Orlando,* textual corpus as corpse is revised as the erotic body of the narrative. I will argue that the *nostos* (homecoming) of the journey is crucial to this formation.

The terminus of Rachel Vinrace's journey is a specific place with a specific history—the South American colony of Santa Marina. Although she had visited Italy, Greece, and even Turkey by the time she completed her novel, Woolf chose a destination for her protagonist that she herself had never seen. The title and plot of *The Voyage Out* invite allegorical readings that focus on the journey rather than the destination of the English travelers, and the novel eschews the precise description of place found in travel narratives for a more symbolic geography instead. Critics have pointed out the lack of specificity in the description and refer to the "mythical" community of Santa Marina because a place by that name has never existed. E. M. Forster, for example, praises this mythical topos: "It is a strange, tragic, inspired book whose scene is a South America not found on any map and reached by a boat which would not float on any sea, an America whose spiritual boundaries touch Xanadu and Atlantis."[4]

Yet if the novel plots a journey to a place of the imagination, as Forster says, the destination has more particular mythological and historical significances than Forster suggests. South America becomes a symbolic New World based on a historical New World, a space discovered on voyages spurred by European expansion. Santa Marina represents the vision of a New World of virgin promise that helped fuel European exploration. It is a place of the imagination historicized by Woolf in its colonial European context. Her turn-of-the-century tourists, out to recover the "new," evoke imperial adventure. Like Elizabeth Bishop's poem "Brazil, January 1, 1502," which begins, "Januaries, Nature greets our eyes / exactly as she must have greeted theirs"(91), Woolf's narrative telescopes colonial and sexual aggression, reminding us that Europe's "voyages out" to the New World were male penetrations of virgin spaces.[5] In *The Voyage Out* we read that when the English came three hundred years ago, the country "was still a virgin land behind a veil" (88), an undefiled female body that invited the European male's imagination.

Curiously, the history of colonialism is both written and effaced in the narrative in a process that mirrors the markings and remarkings of colonial invasion, including England's own belatedness in the region. This history is represented as a piece of information Mr. Pepper declines to convey to his fellow travelers as they approach the land.

As nobody said 'What?' he merely extracted a bottle and swallowed a pill. The piece of information that died within him was to the effect that

---

[4]This quotation serves as advertising blurb for the jacket of the Harcourt Brace Jovanovich edition of *The Voyage Out*.

[5]This aggression is most vividly evoked in the final stanza of Bishop's poem:

> Directly after Mass, humming perhaps
> *L'Homme armé* or some such tune,
> they ripped away into the hanging fabric,
> each out to catch an Indian for himself,—
> those maddening little women who kept calling,
> calling to each other (or had the birds waked up?)
> and retreating, always retreating, behind it.

three hundred years ago five Elizabethan barques had anchored where the *Euphrosyne* now floated. Half-drawn up upon the beach lay an equal number of Spanish galleons, unmanned, for the country was still a virgin land behind a veil. Slipping across the water, the English sailors bore away bars of silver, bales of linen, timbers of cedar wood, golden crucifixes knobbed with emeralds. (88)

The sly newcomers emasculate their Latin predecessors (the Spanish ship is "unmanned" in more ways than one) as they subtly penetrate the veil of the virgin, uncovering her secrets and snatching her treasure by dint of their wits rather than by force. England and Spain are coded as manly rivals for the prize of the virgin territory, as they are in Elizabethan travel narratives such as Ralegh's *Discoverie of the Large, Rich, and Beautifull Empire of Guiana* (1596), a work Woolf not only read but studied and reviewed as well. As Louis Montrose points out in an analysis of gender and sexuality in Ralegh's important narrative, it is "by constructing and reiterating a moral opposition between Spanish lust and tyranny, on the one hand, and English continence and justice, on the other . . . that the discourses of Englishmen such as Ralegh and Keymis obscure the fundamental *identity* of English and Spanish interests in Guiana" ("Work of Gender and Sexuality," 170). With ironic inflection, the narrator of *The Voyage Out* adopts the tone of English chauvinism; the story of conquest continues, with the "hardy Englishmen," who, fresh from their sea voyage, overcome the bloated and decadent Spaniards, reduce the natives "to a state of superstitious wonderment," and establish settlements. "All seemed to favour the expansion of the British Empire, and had there been men like Richard Dalloway in the time of Charles the First, the map would undoubtedly be red where it is now an odious green." But "the political mind of that age lacked imagination," we are told, and the English "dwindled away" (89).

"English history then denies all knowledge of the place," we read; the founding of a new colony within the last ten years owes more to tourism, the modern form of exploration (and exploitation), than to adventure. "The movement in search of something new was of course infinitely small, affecting only a handful of well-to-do people. . . . The country itself taxed all their powers of description, for they said it was much bigger than Italy, and really nobler than Greece. . . . The place seemed new and full of new forms of beauty, in proof of which they showed handkerchiefs which the women had worn round their heads, and primitive carvings coloured bright greens and blues" (90).

In this arch description, which conflates Renaissance exploration and the tourist's search for souvenirs of the primitive, history is both given and erased: it is deliberately withheld from the community of travelers while it is just as purposefully imparted to the reader. Virginity and hopes of a new world give way to the piercing of the veil and the plunder of resources; then, strangely, another dispensation of the new occurs. The slate is wiped clean and a new search begins for something unmarked, authentic (this search for the "new" finds its modern avatar in Mrs. Flushing, the self-confessed tourist and collector). The contemporary travelers come to the place without full knowledge of its history even as they repeat that history. If the semiosis of the "map" displays the colored signs of Spanish rather than English success in this region, the more important sign emitted by this virgin land is what Butor has called the "mythology of whiteness" (3). In these brief references to the colonial past of Santa Marina, far from establishing a concrete, historical sense of place, Woolf represents the function of South America as a continual resource for the European imagination. The "history" includes the colonial legacy of conquest (including English belatedness) and the perpetually renewable promise of authenticity that the myth of virginity extends, even to the modern explorer, the tourist (see MacCannell). Richard Dalloway's perspective of self-evident British superiority, a fantasy which envisions a perfect fit between native and imperialist desire and which offers chauvinistic reasons for England's colonial failure, is presented parodically in the narrative.[6]

Yet despite the irony toward conquest and exposure of imperialism's history of violation, the topos of the New World and the plot of exploration underwrite a quest for someplace authentic and untainted. That is, the novel appropriates the model of Renaissance exploration to explore the possibilities of a specifically feminine quest for new models of desire.[7] As Rachel and Terence climb to the top of

[6]The chauvinistic conception of England's diplomacy abroad is ironically revised in *Orlando*, which comically subverts Dalloway's macho swagger, presenting a very different kind of "man" in the age of Charles I. Men "like Richard Dalloway" are represented as men/women like Orlando, who sleep on the job rather than attend to international business.

[7]This geography of Elizabethan travel coexists with an older Homeric geography that maps an *Odyssey au féminin*. Much is made of Pepper's and Ridley's study of Greek—Pepper, Rachel tells Helen, has "turned Persian poetry into English prose, and English prose into Greek iambics" (he also quotes a Greek passage), and he is on the voyage "either to get things out of the sea, or to write upon the probable course of

a hill that gives them a survey of land and sea, the narrator describes their reaction: "Looking the other way, the vast expanse of land gave them a sensation which is given by no view, however extended, in England; the villages and the hills there having names" (210). Of course, the villages of South America, too, have names and histories; this blindness is part of the European survey. But the possibility that Rachel and Terence can forge a new "plot" for themselves outside London's convention-bound world buoys their voyage out. For the English, the blank page of South America provides an exhilarating and sometimes frightening escape from the already-written English script.[8] The book begins with the "very narrow" streets of London (9), where the Ambroses walk arm in arm, an act that angers others in the crowd who feel they take up too much room. Helen Ambrose, we are told, "knew how to read the people who were passing her" (11). The trope of the uncharted territory anticipates the hope of a new reading and writing and is represented first by the sea ("free of roads, free of mankind" [27]) and then by the new world of South America. As in early narratives of exploration, the separation between home and elsewhere, over here and over there, first appears as "an oceanic division: it is the Atlantic, a rift between the Old and New World" (de Certeau, *Writing of History*, 218).

In *Virginia Woolf and the Literature of the English Renaissance*, Alice Fox argues for the importance of exploration narratives to Woolf's writing, especially to her first novel. Particular scenes in Woolf's novel recall specific descriptions in the narratives of exploration that she read first when she was fifteen or sixteen, and then again when she came to write reviews. Woolf read Elizabethan travel literature avidly, and *Hakluyt's Voyages: The Principal Navigations Voyages & Discoveries of the English Nation*, a compendium of narratives, was one of her

---

Odysseus, for Greek after all was his hobby" (19). Helen at her embroidery is like Helen of Troy in the *Iliad*, weaving events into a tapestry: "She was working at a great design of a tropical river running through a tropical forest, where spotted deer would eventually browse upon masses of fruit, bananas, oranges, and giant pomegranates, while a troop of naked natives whirled darts into the air" (33). Helen, who is upset by the "naked natives" she observes, tries to weave them into a fabric she can control. In an earlier version of the manuscript, Woolf wrote that "Helen sat and looked at him [Hirst] with her needle in her hand . . . [;] her figure possessed the sublimity of a woman of the early world, spinning the thread of fate"(19:5) (quoted in DeSalvo, 85).

[8]The semiotic strangeness of the new world, as well as the uncharted emotions it elicits, frightens many of the English characters. Helen, we are told, dislikes the "unclassified emotions" swirling about her (277).

favorite texts. Fox shows that Woolf consciously suffused her first novel with allusions to this literature of discovery. For example, after she surveys the prospect from the hilltop, Rachel lies down in the grass and looks down at the water: "So it had been at the birth of the world, and so it had remained ever since. Probably no human being had ever broken that water with boat or with body" (211). Fox says that this scene recalls Drake's first view of the Pacific Ocean, a description Woolf encountered in her reading of Hakluyt (24). The survey of the indigenous land is thus linked to the colonial "prospect" of discovered territory. Yet, significantly, Rachel seeks to preserve rather than conquer. She identifies with this "virgin land behind the veil" (*Voyage Out*, 88) and longs for an "unbroken," uncolonized body, an Edenic territory unpenetrated by male exploration. This new world, which is at the same time the first world, is a text on which a new plot might be written, without violence, without invasion. The new topography represents a desire for a new topic of discourse, a twist on the narrative of colonization.

Woolf's woman explorer is doubly positioned in the geography of the narrative, curiously situated both as explorer, mapping an uncharted territory ("Even before the conqueror," Butor says, "the explorer seizes with his language the land he crosses" [10]), and as virginal territory. This double status, this problem of both marking and being the blank page, is telescoped in Rachel's dream, which follows Richard Dalloway's exciting and terrifying kiss. In this episode, Woolf revises the topos of "assaulted and pursued chastity," the threat of rape for the woman traveler on a sea voyage. At first Rachel envisions herself walking down a long tunnel that "grew so narrow by degrees that she could touch the damp bricks on either side. At length the tunnel opened and became a vault; she found herself trapped in it" (77). Rachel's voyage out uncannily maps a voyage into the spaces of her own body; her passage through a long tunnel (as if she were the phallic voyager) suddenly dead-ends in a narrow vault, collapsing female womb and tomb. One could see this as a frightening revision of the male version of the "uncanny" in Freud's essay, in which the Oedipal voyage out from the mother's body results in his unexpected (yet familiar) arrival at the destination of the female body in a foreign town. Rachel's adventures, too, bring her back to the female body, her own vaginal passages. "A voice moaned for her; eyes desired her. All night long barbarian men harassed the ship; they came scuffling down the passages, and stopped to snuffle at her door"

(77). Rachel loses her sense of agency; the men threaten now to invade her.

In staging a voyage to Rachel's own body, the novel reveals some of the difficulties for women writers of appropriating exploration narratives, perhaps the kind of difficulties which feminist writers and critics have noted. For example, Fox argues that despite the influence of such stories on her creation of *The Voyage Out*, Woolf believed that "Elizabethan literature was a male preserve, [hence] the women were consistently less associated with it in successive drafts" (26). Fox proceeds to say that "Woolf consistently divested females of the patina conferred by rich associations with Elizabethan literature," particularly travel narratives (27). But Woolf's "use" of the "rich patina" of exploration, including the exhilarations of its plot, is both more creative and more ambivalent than Fox suggests. Woolf formulated for herself the idea of a certain imaginative "profit" from reading male adventure narratives that parallels (and substitutes for) the material treasures the men discovered. In other words, she reformulates the erotics of discovery found in male travel narratives and transforms them into textual discoveries. In Woolf's diaries as well as her many reviews of modern editions of Renaissance travel texts, adventure and the reading of adventure produce an erotic pleasure of reception that binds together traveler, writer, and reader. While acknowledging the problematic politics of conquest, Woolf aestheticizes the motif of discovery. In a 1906 essay entitled "Trafficks and Discoveries" (her first of two reviews by that title), she reviews *The English Voyages of the Sixteenth-Century* by Professor Walter Raleigh (first published as an introduction to the last volume of *Hakluyt's Voyages*, commenting on the narrative of Drake's voyage. She likens it to "some coloured opium dream," whose "intoxication does not spring solely from the material glitter of the words. The profusion of the earth itself seems typical of the whole age, and the grosser counterpart of that opulence of the imagination which was now yielding treasures of another sort" (*Essays*, 1:122). Woolf transfers her own perception to Hewet in her novel: " 'That's where the Elizabethans got their style,' he mused, staring into the profusion of leaves and blossoms and prodigious fruits" (268). Travel to the new world feeds the imagination.

In a 1929 diary entry, Woolf recorded her first reading experience of travel literature in an Oedipally charged language of erotic initiation:

It was the Elizabethan prose writers I loved first & most wildly, stirred
by Hakluyt, which father lugged home for me—I think of it with some
sentiment—father tramping over the [London] Library with his little girl
sitting at HPG [Hyde Park Gate] in mind. He must have been 65; I 15 or
16, then; & why I dont know, but I became enraptured, though not exactly interested, but the sight of the large yellow page entranced me. I
used to read it & dream of those obscure adventurers, & no doubt prac-
tised their style in my copy books. (December 8, 1929; *Diary*, 3:271)

Here the discovery of adventure is remembered as an exorbitant
and weighty gift of love—remembered, more than thirty years later,
"with some sentiment." Woolf describes her reading experience as an
affair of the passions rather than the intellect ("I became enraptured,
though not exactly interested"). Rapture, stirrings, wild passions—the
"obscurity" Woolf refers to is transferred from her own Oedipal feelings to the adventures of the Elizabethans, swerving from biological
father to aesthetic ones. This swerve generates a receptive erotics of
discovery for both adventurer and reader. The chastening of this rapture into schoolroom exercise ("no doubt [I] practiced their style in
my copy books") is an unusually strict image of art as sublimation,
for in almost all Woolf's writings on this literature of discovery, erotic
tropes occur, albeit transformed in the service of nonsexual activity.
Thus, in these descriptions, she displaces riches upward but retains
the erotic cast of discovery.

It is important to point out, however, that the image of conquest is
rejected by Woolf in favor of an image of desire that never climaxes
in "marvelous possession," to use Stephen Greenblatt's term for the
complex of awe and mastery that defined New World narratives (*Marvelous Possessions*, 9–20). This desire maintains itself and increases; in
the travel literature, Woolf seeks a certain "attitude of mind, large,
imaginative, unsated. There is a sort of nobleness about them; seen
through their eyes, the world appears fresh and flowing, unexplored,
and of infinite richness" ("Trafficks and Discoveries," 1918, in *Essays*,
2:333). This boon is transferred to the reader who experiences "the
great wealth of good reading in H[akluyt]" (357) and the "lustre of
the [Elizabethan] imagination" ("Sir Walter Raleigh," in *Essays*, 2:92).

These quotations from Woolf's essays reveal the way in which exploration, the narrative of exploration, and the reading of these stories
served Woolf as paradigms for the expansion of consciousness and
imagination. They are a useful reminder of the flexibility of cultural

troping and a caution against too literal an idea of appropriation. Fox's demonstration of Woolf's growing sense of the inapplicability of the elements of adventure to a female protagonist (26–27) ignores the way Woolf extracted from the plot of exploration a myth of imaginative enlargement, an Enlightenment dream of discovery and freedom. This kind of identification with an ethos whose politics, sexual and otherwise, are uncongenial might be instructively compared with Elizabeth Bowen's overpowering reaction to reading Haggard's *She*. Painting her fascination, even obsession, with the novel when she read it at the age of twelve, Bowen says she never identified with either She, the female power in the novel, or with Leo Vincey, the male adventurer. Rather, for her, the book's tremendous significance lay in a realization of the power of fiction.

> I had exhausted the myths of childhood. . . . It was at the height of this, my first winter of discontent, that I came on the novel *She*, by Rider Haggard. . . . This book *She* is for me historic—it stands for the first totally violent impact I ever received from print. After *She*, print was to fill me with apprehension. I was prepared to handle any book like a bomb. It was—did I realize that all the time?—Horace Holly, not ever, really, She-who-must-be-obeyed, who controlled the magic. Writing— that creaking, pedantic, obtrusive, arch, prudish, opaque, over-worded *writing* . . . what it could do! That was the revelation; that was the power in the cave. The power whose inequality dear Holly laments at the opening of every passage. The power of the pen. The inventive pen. (229–37)

It is a similar jolt and revivification that Woolf describes in reading Elizabethan literature, particularly exploration narratives, which liberates, intensifies, and expands her consciousness. Even in her description of reading Spenser, the topos of travel provides a geography of imaginative transport and expansion: "So we feel not shut in, but freed; and take our way in a world which gives expression to sensation more vigorously, more exactly than we can manage ourselves in the flesh. . . . It is a world of astonishing physical brilliance and intensity: sharpened, intensified as objects are in a clearer air, such as we see them . . . now in a landscape, in Ireland or Greece, and now when we think of ourselves, under the more intense ray of poetry; under its sharper, its lovelier light" (*Essays*, 1:18).

The appetitive "I" of the explorer encountering the unknown provides a paradigm for character, writer, and reader. Wonder characterizes this experience as phenomenology and poetry come together in the experience of discovery, a sense of a new poetics of space. The world is seen as if for the first time. In *The Voyage Out*, the metaphor of the New World is played out as a kind of romance of perception; the New World is a phenomenological space where objects come into being for consciousness, as if perception and poetic image could be reinvented for the woman protagonist (just as literary history in *Orlando* must be reinvented for the woman poet after Orlando's sex change and return to England from Turkey). This wonder depends on a receptivity implicit in the genre of adventure. This ethos is meant to contrast with the intellectual and economic plunder of Willoughby, Rachel's father, the cargo ship owner, who in Helen's perception perpetually "rob[bed] a whole continent of mystery" (196).[9]

This emphasis on a sense of space rather than place is felt acutely in *The Voyage Out*, accounting for the lack of particular topographic and geographical description. (Forster, then, is right about the lack of specificity of place.) Ultimately the South American location matters less for constructing cultural difference than for imagining a new, tropical space in which atmosphere is pressure and the visual register of survey (so important in colonial narratives) gives way to a more sensory placement of objects in space according to their distance and intimacy. Space is much more than an attribute of the physical landscape. From our initial view of the ship/female identity as a lonely object in space, unknown to others, the narrative increasingly shifts its focalization to Rachel as vectorized consciousness; we see how space (as opposed to place) is "lived" phenomenologically by the imagination on axes of proximity and distance, accessibility and remoteness.

Critics have remarked the importance of philosophy as content in Woolf's first novel, and indeed, its characters debate and read philosophy.[10] But I am arguing that the topos of travel to the New World— the voyage out—underwrites the self's experiment in confronting the world. In the novel, the borders of Rachel Vinrace's consciousness are

----

[9]See Mary Helms's ethnographic discussion of the relation between cultural distance and cognitive concepts of space in *Ulysses' Sail: An Ethnographic Odyssey of Power, Knowledge, and Geographical Distance*. The Enlightenment theme of the expanding consciousness is itself implicated in the very discourse of conquest that Woolf appropriates in writing her novel.

[10]See, for example, S. P. Rosenbaum, Jaakko Hintikka, and Alan Wilde, "Touching Earth."

continually charted and remapped in relation to her surroundings. Passage after passage painstakingly describes the sensations of her ego as it seems to expand with its knowledge of the world. It is almost a shock to the reader to discover that Rachel is as old as twenty-four, not only because of her naïveté and inexperience, but also because her consciousness is treated experimentally, as if it were a tabula rasa. Indeed, Helen's comments about Rachel implicitly allude to textuality, calling attention to Rachel's birth on the page—Helen calls her "unmarked" and "experimental," words applicable to fictional characters (and to the meaning of the word "character" as inscription): "She really might be six years old," thinks Helen, "referring," the narrator tells us, "to the smooth unmarked outline of the girl's face" (25). This arrested development is figured in historical terms that reimport the idea of Renaissance exploration: "Her mind," the narrator says, "was in the state of an intelligent man's in the beginning of the reign of Queen Elizabeth; she would believe practically anything she was told, invent reasons for anything she said" (34).

Rachel is Minerva, sprung from the pages of the novel; successive revisions of the manuscript seem to have erased rather than consolidated her memories, thus strengthening the sense of her fledgling encounters with the world (and making any kind of psychoanalytic reading more difficult because the manuscript changes in a sense efface the memory of past traumas that might be repeated in the present). It is neither a question of the depth of the character nor her verisimilitude that arises from this erasure; it is a question of the way this first novel thematizes Rachel's journey as textual experimentation. The trope of exploration figures the trajectory of the character's ego. Centrifugal and centripetal movements record acts of the ego's expansion and consolidation, its confrontation with other objects (human and otherwise) in space.

As she wanders through the lush vegetation, a route that sometimes produces a disconcerting loss of bearings, Rachel is often startled by something with which she must suddenly deal. " 'Here's shade,' began Hewet, when Rachel suddenly stopped dead. They saw a man and a woman lying on the ground beneath them, rolling slightly this way and that as the embrace tightened and slackened" (140). The sudden sight of Susan and Arthur embracing is experienced by Rachel as a violation of her own world, an intrusion from which she longs to get free: "But Rachel was still agitated; she could not get away from the sight they had just seen" (140). Her defense is momentarily to mimic a colonial (and omnipotent) survey. A Gulliver-like lord of all she surveys, she tries to gain distance through visual scrutiny.

> It pleased her to scrutinise this inch of the soil of South America so minutely that she noticed every grain of earth and made it into a world where she was endowed with the supreme power. She bent a blade of grass, and set an insect on the utmost tassel of it, and wondered if the insect realised his strange adventure, and thought how strange it was that she should have bent that tassel rather than any other of the million tassels. (141)

Even here the magisterial survey is mixed with a curious detachment from her own actions, as if her choices were a profound mystery to her. The myth of control over her environment quickly gives way to the feeling that she moves through it at its mercy. The adventure of consciousness is tinged with the danger that, in expanding to include the world, the self will lose the sense of its own boundaries. The dilation of Rachel's ego in relation to the world is charted as a kind of "problem" in space, a threat that the self will be overwhelmed by the stimuli it seeks to incorporate and will instead suffer a dissolution of boundaries. This is the "world without a self" that has figured so prominently in the analysis of Woolf's work, the impression that the self, instead of incorporating the world, is submerged, even drowned in it.[11]

The force of the movement out from the self to the world, natural and human, and the counterforce of the world impinging on the self create the sense of atmosphere as pressure. Space is not empty, but full; like the humidity of the jungle, of which the characters complain, the air itself is conceived as force and resistance, a medium of exchange. (Ultimately, the oppressive heat of the jungle, which has an effect on the characters' consciousness, gives way to the image of the sea surrounding Rachel's consciousness in her illness.)[12] At times in *The Voyage Out*, this feeling of space as pressure produces moments

---

[11]See James Naremore's important book *The World without a Self: Virginia Woolf and the Novel*.

[12]This feeling of the vitality of space and of the importance of the subject's relation to the object of its consciousness might be thought of as a spatial alternative to the Bergsonian *durée*. In this novel, there is less sense of the immersion of consciousness in the haze of memory than in most of Woolf's work. Rather, the "medium" of space (and its poetics) takes precedence over diachrony.

of awareness of what Freud was later to call the "bodily ego" as projected in space.

> Meanwhile the steady beat of her own pulse represented the hot current
> of feeling that ran down beneath; beating, struggling, fretting. For the
> time, her own body was the source of all the life in the world, which
> tried to burst forth here—there—and was repressed now by Mr. Bax,
> now by Evelyn, now by the imposition of ponderous stupidity—the
> weight of the entire world. . . . She was no longer able to see the world
> as a town laid out beneath her. It was covered instead by a haze of
> feverish red mist. . . . Thinking was no escape. Physical movement was
> the only refuge, in and out of rooms, in and out of peoples' minds,
> seeking she knew not what. (258–59)

Agitated movement and a nearsighted haziness replace the masterful survey. If this passage sounds more like D. H. Lawrence than Virginia Woolf, it is because Woolf's first novel struggles to represent the
urgency and "quickness" of the self in relation to a mundane world
composed of recalcitrant, almost immovable objects. Convention is figured as an almost physical resistance, growth, as an incursion into
different spaces. Paradoxically, "physical movement" is "the only refuge"—the poles of travel and home curiously merge. No residence of
the self is approached through mere consolidation; the voyage out of
the bodily ego is a necessary risk. Although he did not write "The
Ego and the Id" (1923) until after Woolf wrote her novel, Freud captures what Woolf seems to be doing fictionally in his description of
the contributions of psychophysiology to an understanding of the ego.

> A person's own body, and above all its surface, is a place from which
> both external and internal perceptions may spring. It is *seen* like any
> other object, but to the *touch* it yields two kinds of sensations, one of
> which may be equivalent to an internal perception. Psycho-physiology
> has fully discussed the manner in which a person's own body attains its
> special position among other objects in the world of perception. Pain,
> too, seems to play a part in the process, and the way in which we gain
> new knowledge of our organs during painful illnesses is perhaps a model
> of the way by which in general we arrive at the idea of our body.
>
> The ego is first and foremost a bodily ego; it is not merely a surface
> entity, but is itself the projection of a surface. (636–37)

I will return to the topic of illness and the body's sensation of itself in pain, which Woolf develops in the final sections of the novel, for reading these sections in relation to the development of the bodily ego allows us to see the ending not as a breaking off of the trajectory of the narrative but as an extension of it. But I want to emphasize here the perception of the ego as a bounded space, a projected surface. The ego is an image of how the self takes in and fends off the world.[13]

But to speak purely in terms of Freud's bodily ego or the directionality of consciousness is to ignore the significance of the gendering of Rachel's bodily self in the world, that is, the way that female identity presents a particular problem to the poetics of space and to the representation of the self in language. Although Freud refers not to the body but to the bodily ego, this "ego" is itself a function of self-representation; in Woolf's novel the mental image of the body's boundaries is gendered. In other words, the "poetics of space" (to use Gaston Bachelard's term) in regard to the bodily ego is not immune from the workings of culture, particularly gender difference. Notwithstanding his protests about the freedom of the poetic image from cultural determinants, Bachelard's highly imaginative discussion of topophilia ("the space we love," xxxi) genders subjectivity male.[14] Rachel's coming to consciousness and her lived experience of space *are* inextricably bound up with the gendering of this psychic voyage out, and with the poetic as well as the narrative difference that gender makes. In Rachel's subjectivity, distance, proximity, pressure, immensity, and intensity—the poeticizing of space in relation to the bodily ego—are constructed in terms of expansion and transgression. Specifically, the excitements and terrors of consciousness spring most vividly from heterosexual intimacies.

I speak of the excitements, as well as the terrors, because the adventure of the bodily ego involves a search for intimacy as much as self-possession; it has an exogamous, not merely a xenophobic, dimension. Love itself is configured as a topographical problem—of

---

[13]In Freudian terms, this "taking in" involves a number of processes of identification, including introjection and incorporation, in which mental processes are represented as bodily. For a fascinating discussion of Freud's essay, see Leo Bersani's *Freudian Body: Psychoanalysis and Art*, 92–101.

[14]"For nothing," he says in his introduction, "prepares a poetic image, especially not culture, in the literary sense, and especially not perception, in the psychological sense" (xx). Although I would agree that nothing "prepares" the poetic image in the sense of fully determining it, I would disagree with Bachelard's description of just how "free" from tradition this representation is.

excursions and intrusions, of unbridgeable distances and claustrophobic narrowings. Christine Froula's otherwise excellent discussion of the novel seems to me to treat this search for intimacy as wholly prescribed by patriarchal culture in opposition to female self-possession. "On the one hand, Woolf's story of the semi-autobiographical Rachel Vinrace shows how the paradigms of female initiation encourage the young woman to identify with nature rather than culture and to imagine marriage and maternity as the destiny that will fulfill her life. On the other hand, Woolf endows Rachel with a powerful desire to evade or transcend this culturally determined destiny. . . . Neither the strength nor the resources of Rachel's desire are equal to the powerful cultural currents that oppose it, however, and the history of Woolf's heroine ends not in triumph but in death" (63). Yet this dichotomous view of submission or escape ignores Woolf's exploration of intimacy as potentially transformative. Austen's "tight-plaited" domesticity, as Rachel sees it, does indeed represent a too-confining plot/plait (58); much of *The Voyage Out* explores Rachel's quest for a new kind of intimacy (and thus, a new sort of Mr. and Mrs.) in a different psychic and literary space than England provides. In this way, the novel resembles Lawrence's *Women in Love*, which it curiously anticipates, with its brittle and awkwardly insistent dialogues about marriage and literary discussions about the domestic novel.[15] As in Lawrence's narrative, in *The Voyage Out* the pressure to articulate a new type of intimacy all but threatens to collapse the grammar of the sentences: "There was something between them which had to be spoken of" (270–71)—the preposition hangs in the air just as does Terence and Rachel's discomfort. In the novel, love, like travel, is envisioned as a force that tests the borders of the ego and transfigures the mundane world. The novel stages a quest for poetry as well as plot (at the height of their relationship, Rachel and Terence "speak of poetry more than sex" [299]). That love presents a particular challenge to the vulnerable, unformed, and virginal ego of Rachel Vinrace is evidenced by the anxieties that the poetics of space betrays throughout the narrative as well as by the swerve of the plot from the possibility of erotic knowledge to the staging of Rachel's "knowledge" of death.

[15]Although a full discussion would take us too far afield of the present argument, it is worth observing that the travel within Lawrence's novel is also a dead end for the characters—Birkin and Ursula basically fade out of the novel once they arrive on the Continent, and Gudrun and Gerald are devastated by the German proto-Fascist form of the "new" that they discover in Loerke.

The question that hangs over the narrative of *The Voyage Out* concerns the economy of the return trip. Can the promise of the journey be fulfilled in a "profit" returned, so to speak, to the traveler? On one level, this question is one of plot and genre—Can the poetry of adventure come home to the more ordinary realm of the domestic novel and be treasured hearthside back in England? Can intimacy be a part of Rachel's voyage out, retrievable for the continuation of the plot? But on another level, this question is one about the ultimate riskiness of travel. As Georges Van Den Abbeele puts it, travel involves an economy of anxiety and risk, both necessary and inevitable, "that the limit to the motion of the *anthropos* is to be found in the limit to the latter's existence: 'le *grand* voyage' " (xvi). Can this different "limit" be recorded as a "profit" of knowledge?

The possibility of integrating intimacy and the ego's adventures at home in England preoccupied Virginia Stephen as she composed her travel novel. For writing and revising the latter drafts of the novel coincided with her personal dilemma regarding marriage, particularly her decision to accept Leonard Woolf's proposal of marriage (she had already received three marriage proposals by the time Woolf proposed in January 1912 [*Letters of Virginia Woolf*, 1:483]). In a letter to Clive Bell, who was traveling in Turkey with Vanessa (April 1911), Woolf announces she has rewritten a third of the novel (*Melymbrosia*) and has brought her characters "within sight of the South American shore" (1:461). Sounding more like one of Austen's Bennet sisters or Evelyn Murgatroyd in her own novel, Woolf gossips and speculates about the love life of those at home: "What news is there to fill the page? I'm not engaged; the affairs of Ray and Olive are, I suppose, at a standstill" (1:462). In her letters to Vanessa she gossips about proposals, relationships, and women and men in love: "Here comes a piece of gossip which you *must* keep private. Talking of Oliver Strachey, [Ray Costello] said, 'I can quite imagine falling in love with him' " (1:456). Woolf struggled in her letters to frame her own ambivalent feelings about the institutionalization of sentiment in marriage. To Leonard, she strives to articulate her feelings for him: "There is some feeling which is permanent, and growing. You want to know of course whether it will ever make me marry you. How can I say. . . . I'm half afraid of myself. I sometimes feel that no one ever has or ever can share something. . . . Again, I want everything—love, children, adventure, intimacy, work" (1:496). Louise DeSalvo explicitly connects Woolf's desires and fears about her relationship to Leonard with revisions, made during the second half of 1912, to the descriptions of Terence and Rachel's relationship and to the scene of Rachel's death (7): "Woolf was experiencing in her own life, the counterparts of the events she was revising for her fiction" (75).

In *Beginning Again*, written many years later, Leonard Woolf describes their shared desire to escape from London to some new world of feeling. This, too, sounds like a Lawrentian notion. After Virginia accepts his marriage proposal, they take a train into the countryside, hire a boat at Maidenhead, and feel "a strange happiness of being for a moment alone together in an empty universe" (69). Virginia Woolf's exploration of Rachel's ambivalent quest for connection must be seen in regard to the different type of man that Leonard was—not crass Richard Dalloway patriotically spouting on about England's glory in India, but a gentler, psychologically astute man who chose his relationship with Virginia over his political future (the figure that Terence Hewet comes to be). In 1911 Leonard resigned from the Ceylon Civil Service to pursue his relationship with Virginia at home in England.

Indeed, Leonard, potential partner in intimacy, was also Leonard the writer, whose own "voyage out" to Ceylon and travel records, fictional and nonfictional, figured prominently in Virginia Woolf's life and imagination as she struggled to revise her first novel. The first chapter of his autobiography, *Growing* (published in 1961), is entitled "The Voyage Out," the phrase most commonly applied to the colonial "work" of the English male civil servant—Leonard's work at the time Woolf was writing her novel. Just as both Harold Nicolson and Vita Sackville-West as travelers and writers provided Virginia Woolf with material for her representation of Orlando's travel to Turkey, so Leonard Woolf's voyage out and representations of his travel could have served Virginia in her first novel. On the Woolfs' honeymoon, they both devoted mornings to the task of writing five hundred words; while Virginia worked on *The Voyage Out*, Leonard wrote stories set in the Eastern jungle (*Letters of Leonard Woolf*, 158). On his return to England, he wrote *The Village in the Jungle*, the novel that established him as a writer of importance. The jungle in Leonard Woolf's work conventionally serves as a metaphor for disorientation of a most frightening kind. His stories, in particular, portray women characters as succumbing to the intense, claustrophobic power of the jungle, which often leads to their forced acceptance of sexuality and subsequent madness. Woolf's models for her voyage of exploration *au féminin* are overdetermining—Conrad's *Heart of Darkness*, which telescopes an inner journey with a journey to geographical extremity; Elizabethan travel narratives; the *Odyssey*; and, more biographical, Leonard Woolf's Eastern texts as well.

Why does Rachel's destiny so briefly include love, adventure, and intimacy but never children and work—the "everything," as she writes to Leonard, that Woolf craves? When the "curtain" is finally removed between Terence and Rachel in the unveiling suggested at the narrative's beginning, why does the curtain rise on a scene of death? Why is Rachel unable to return from the heightened interiority of her inward voyage during her illness? To understand why and how the trajectory of travel ends not with a return to England but in the final destination of Rachel's death, we must look at the way the issue of "return" is rehearsed in the narrative. This rehearsal is twofold: it pertains to the lovers' attempted return to the realm of the mundane after the intensity of their journey upriver (an element of the novel's symbolic geography) and also to a verbal transport (or metaphor), that is, the articulation of this extremity in language. It is the Conradian journey upriver that provides the narrative occasion for the round-trip transportation from mundanity to extremity and back again, from "ordinary" language to a language charged with emotionally concentrated experience and then to the ordinary once more. The voyage *in*, within the voyage out, is cast in the symbolic register of the "primitive," the uncanny voyage into the jungle found in the fiction of Conrad as well as Leonard Woolf.

> As they passed into the depths of the forest the light grew dimmer, and the noises of the ordinary world were replaced by those creaking and sighing sounds which suggest to the traveller in a forest that he is walking at the bottom of the sea. The path narrowed and turned; it was hedged in by dense creepers which knotted tree to tree, and burst here and there into star-shaped crimson blossoms. The sighing and creaking up above were broken every now and then by the jarring cry of some startled animal. (270)

The claustrophobia figured in the density of the jungle, with its bursting blossoms and jarring cries, evokes a familiar erotic topos. Indeed, the unarticulated attraction that Terence and Rachel feel toward each other is displaced onto the landscape—as intimacy becomes unavoidable. Yet both metaphor and grammar suggest the inadequacy or inapplicability of the more "standard" literary theme of the erotic journey. In the imagination of the traveler, the humidity of the forest gives way to the palpable liquid medium of the sea, a trope that intensifies the sense of how the body is impinged on by its surroundings. The surprising shift in grammar from plural ("they") to singular pronoun (the masculine pronoun at that) records a persistent anxiety. Is this a journey toward erotic intimacy or merely a parallel journey that cannot be shared? Can the two almost unbearably sentient travelers find the means, linguistic and psychic, to recoup their intense experience in language? "To speak or to be silent was equally an effort, for when they were silent they were keenly conscious of each other's presence, and yet words were either too trivial or too large" (280). Language is conceived as a problem of distance and proportion; increasingly, words are inadequate projectiles hurled into the gulf that divides them. "We love each other," Terence and Rachel repeat, one after the other. "We sat upon the ground" (282), they echo each other as they struggle to twist ordinary words into significant statement, to transform this journey into communication. Yet the erotics remain unconvincing, halfhearted. There is something curiously parallel instead of intimately connected about their experiences, as if they were two young children living through the same intense moment side by side (which anticipates the soliloquies of *The Waves*). At the "heart" of this representation of erotic otherness, of intimacy and connection, Terence and Rachel seem redundant, as if rather than representing the intimate contact of an erotic pair, they narcissistically identify with each other as different facets of the same character.[16]

In this staged round-trip voyage within the larger journey, the "lovers" reenter the mundane space of other people's lives. In what feels like a respite from the charge of its own symbolic spaces such as the jungle and the sea, the narrative returns to the comforting *domus* of the ordinary. Indeed, the characters momentarily lose their designa-

---

[16]The episode ends with probably the strangest and most erotic narrative moment in the novel: Helen's felling of Rachel, Rachel's dreamlike sense of Helen and Terence above her, laughing and kissing, and her sense of Helen's "strong and hospitable arms, and happiness swelling and breaking in one vast wave" (284). In this confused and confusing passage, the object of Rachel's desire seems to be more Helen than Terence in a cross between a maternal and lesbian erotics (even more prominent in earlier drafts of the novel). The moment suggests conflicting rivalries and loyalties—parental, sibling, heterosexual, and homosexual—as if the narrative were testing Rachel's narcissistic identifications. This representation of free-floating libido is revised in *Orlando*'s voyage out in Woolf's 1928 novel.

tion as travelers: "They were no longer embarrassed, or half-choked with meaning which could not express itself; they were not afraid of each other, or, like travellers down a twisting river, dazzled with sudden beauties when the corner is turned; the unexpected happened, but even the ordinary was lovable, and in many ways preferable to the ecstatic and mysterious, for it was refreshingly solid, and called out effort, and effort under such circumstances was not effort but delight" (290–91). The twisting river of the symbolic landscape is eschewed for the landscape of the mundane. Significantly, at this point the novel rehearses a round trip in the larger plot, as Terence and Rachel imagine their return to an England revivified by their relationship. He "sketched for her portraits which fascinated her of what other men and women might be supposed to be thinking and feeling, so that she became very anxious to go back to England, which was full of people, where she could merely stand in the streets and look at them" (299). Even Terence's novel thematically rehearses the possibility of transporting their new knowledge back to England: his characters' marriage fails when they leave their romantic Swiss holiday and return to the drudgery of life at home (this failure his narrator attributes to the "gulf which separates the needs and desires of the male from the needs and desires of the female" [296]).

It is not only that London would be unreceptive to the transformation of relationship that Terence and Rachel seek, for the narrative's uneasiness suggests something is missing, gone awry, even here in this potentially paradisal place of refreshment. The novel, I would contend, is vague about the causes of this gap and presents a number of possibilities, including interpretations by the characters themselves, all invitations to different critical readings. Helen's anxiety over Rachel and Terence's developing relationship, which figures in her imagination as resembling the earth's terrible movement, provides a Faustian argument. They know too much; like MacKenzie, the explorer who "went farther inland than any one's been yet" (277), the two young people, according to Helen, have upset the order of things with their knowledge. On the other hand, Terence says to Rachel, thus anticipating Lawrentian unease about the limits of relationship, "I don't satisfy you in the way you satisfy me. . . . There's something I can't get hold of in you" (302), as though to suggest that Rachel, like Birkin after her, cannot sustain the transformation of reality through only her relationship with a man. Finally, Christine Froula's compelling reading of the novel assigns the "blame" for Rachel's demise to the violence of the patriarchal culture and the way it immures women in their bodies, therefore leaving Rachel with no choice but to die rather than submit to her culturally prescribed fate. How one chooses a "reading" depends in part on one's interpretation of Rachel's illness and death in relation to the earlier parts of the story: Do they represent a reversal, a withdrawal from the world and relationship, or an intensification of the journey of the self?

Rather than reflecting a breakdown in the economy of the journey, the novel's ending struggles to register a "profit" recuperated at the intersection of interiority and exteriority. Rachel's illness and death become the final limit to the trajectory of the self's phenomenological expansion. As Freud suggests in *The Ego and the Id*, illness is a pattern for, rather than an exception to, the ego's conception of itself as bounded and living in the world. Through her illness, Rachel becomes keenly aware of the boundaries of her own body: "Every object in the room, and the bed itself, and her own body with its various limbs and their different sensations were more and more important each day. She was completely cut off, and unable to communicate with the rest of the world, isolated alone with her body" (330). And, "She found that her heat and discomfort had put a gulf between her world and the ordinary world which she could not bridge" (329).

In her famous essay on illness and its language, written many years later, Woolf notes:

> Literature does its best to maintain that its concern is with the mind; that the body is a sheet of plain glass through which the soul looks straight and clear, and, save for one or two passions such as desire and greed, is null, and negligible and non-existent. On the contrary, the very opposite is true. All day, all night the body intervenes; blunts or sharpens, colours or discolours, turns to wax in the warmth of June, hardens to tallow in the murk of February. The creature within can only gaze through the pane—smudged or rosy; it cannot separate off from the body. ("On Being Ill," 193)

She adds, "Yet it is not only a new language that we need, more primitive, more sensual, more obscene, but a new hierarchy of the passions; love must be deposed in favor of a temperature of 104" (194–95).

One could say that in *The Voyage Out*, sexual love is deposed in favor of "a temperature of 104." Rachel's "unexampled" experience of her bodily consciousness is apotheosized in her illness and death, not in Lawrentian intimacy. The heightened subjectivity of her illness defines Rachel's unformed, experimental character. She passes out of the plot of the novel with eyes opened and is translated from character to reader of the narrative: "It needed all her attention to follow the hot, red, quick sights which passed incessantly before her eyes. . . . The sights were all concerned in some plot, some adventure, some escape" (340–41). Rachel's detachment is problematic—she is no longer connected to the plot of her own adventure in the world. Unlike Orlando in the later novel, Rachel does not return from her own intense interiority, her own voyage in. Death brutally cuts off the plot of the bildungsroman; a sense of premature loss pervades the narrative. Yet to view Rachel's death merely in terms of the truncation of plot ignores the continuity of Rachel's and Woolf's imaginative quests. In the record of Rachel's final moments of consciousness, Woolf riskily challenges herself to join the radical interiority caused by Rachel's illness and the radical exteriority of death, which is always beyond the tropings of the imagination. As Garrett Stewart points out, she does this partly through the figure of drowning, which extrapolates the earlier image of the traveler at the bottom of the sea: "As troped toward sheer psychology in some of the major texts of the English tradition, drowning consciously endured is the self as pure subject intersecting, sunk in, the world as pure object. Drowning provides in this way the spectacle of identity reviewing itself as it is given over, given back, to the realm of insentience" (257). As she returns to the "realm of insentience" rather than to the ordinary world, we witness the spectacle of identity reviewing itself. In these passages, the narrative reaches the limits of its own excursus.

Yet some "knowledge" is transmitted to Terence, for empathy binds Terence and Rachel in the end as passion could not: "He had never realised before that underneath every action, underneath the life of every day, pain lies, quiescent, but ready to devour; he seemed to be able to see suffering, as if it were a fire, curling up over the edges of all action, eating away the lives of men and women" (344–45). A metaphoric transfer occurs between Rachel and Terence. Instead of the lover as other, however, Terence seems to function as Rachel's double—novelist and sometimes feminist (seen by Evelyn as having something of a woman about him). He serves as a figure who might translate corpse into corpus, memory into narrative—he might, that is, produce a book about Silence. It is not until Orlando's voyage out that Woolf will rewrite the Terence (writer) and Rachel (voyager) pair as the sexually and textually active traveler/poet Orlando. It is in the protracted textual survival of Orlando that Woolf completes Rachel's and Terence's voyages out in a new key.

In the midst of her South American journey, Rachel dreams of being "a Persian princess far from civilisation, riding her horse upon the mountains alone, and making her women sing to her in the evening, far from all this, from the strife and men and women" (155). In the midst of one journey, she imagines another, a greater escape from the problems of heterosexual intimacy, an exotic woman's world of song. In 1915, Woolf could not have foreseen Sackville-West's trip to Persia, which she recorded in *Passenger to Teheran* and countless letters to her sympathetic partner back in England, or the "orientalizing" of her desire for Sackville-West in the love letter/travel letter that is the novel *Orlando*. In *Orlando*, the protagonist's voyage in is also a voyage back. The pair of Rachel and Terence is replaced by the transsexual Orlando; the death of Rachel is rewritten as the death and rebirth of Orlando in Turkey. If the South American spaces of Woolf's first novel failed to provide a "new world" of heterosexual desire, the Eastern locale of Orlando's sex change served as a gateway to the representation of plural forms of desire. Woolf writes a fantasy of androgyny, bisexuality, and homosexuality, in which Orlando completes Rachel's voyage out, returning to England as a woman who can love both men and women.

The wandering heroes are phallic heroes, in a permanent state of erection; pricking o'er the plain. The word coition presents genital sexuality as walking; but the converse is also true: all walking, or wandering in the labyrinth, is genital-sexual. All movement is phallic, all intercourse sexual. Hermes, the phallus, is the god of roads, of doorways, of all goings-in and comings-out, all goings-on. (Brown, *Love's Body*, 50)

Orlando (1928) stages the mobility of fantasy and desire; it is a narrative of boundary crossings—those of time, space, gender, and sex. A novel that remaps the topography of love's body, *Orlando* exchanges Hermes, the phallic god of the crossroads, for Hermaphroditus (the child of Hermes and Aphrodite). In this satiric biography of a poet who begins life as a man in the late 1500s in England and who metamorphoses into a woman while on a diplomatic mission to Turkey, desire is polymorphous, the heterosexual paradigm of adventure destabilized. The novel's sexual/textual "intercourse" revises phallic economy, and not only in plotting polymorphous sexual possibilities for its nonphallic picaro. For love's textual body is altered in Woolf's revisionary narrative labyrinth, its holes "big enough to put your finger through" (119).[17]

In the beginning, the novel seems to suggest the adequacy of the phallic narrative of lunging and plunging. Orlando prepares for adventure, practicing to be a man's man, engaged in the martial arts that enable English conquest. We see him "slicing at the head of a Moor" (13). "Since he was sixteen only, and too young to ride with them [the patriarchs] in Africa or France, he would steal away from his mother and the peacocks in the garden and go to his attic room and there lunge and plunge and slice the air with his blade" (13): this preliminary flight from the maternal is necessary for Orlando to take his place in the line of male tradition.[18] Yet it soon becomes apparent that the rather androgynous-looking boy finds the Oedipal plots of adventure inadequate. Although he "listened to sailors' stories of hardship and horror and cruelty on the Spanish main" and "their songs of the Azores" (29), he begins to find their plots limited. The narrator–biographer sums up Orlando's weariness with the plots available to male and female: "But when he had heard a score of times how Jakes had lost his nose and Sukey her honour—and they told the stories admirably, it must be admitted—he began to be a little weary of the repetition, for a nose can only be cut off in one way and maidenhood lost in another—or so it seemed to him" (31). Castration threats and defloration—these are the plots that elaborate sexual difference, plots that Woolf, along with Orlando, rejects in favor of a more fluid bisexuality.

[17]Although this phrase of the narrator/biographer refers to the official manuscripts that record Orlando's sojourn in Turkey, I believe it applies generally to the elliptical narrative of the novel. Not only the narrative, with its multiple holes or orifices, but Orlando's writing, too, is suggestively identified with the body of the female despite the dominant patriarchal gendering of literary history: "Stealing away from talk and games, he had hidden himself behind curtains, in priest's holes, or in the cupboard behind his mother's bedroom which had a great hole in the floor and smelt horribly of starling's dung, with an inkhorn in one hand, a pen in another, and on his knee, a roll of paper" (76). Although the roles of both parents are strangely muted in the narrative, this vignette suggests an associative complex linking Orlando's writing with the smelly hole of nature he spies as he hides near his mother's bedroom.

[18]See Paul Zweig's provocative reading of the structure of adventure, which traces the male adventurer's flight from the body of the mother and reencounter with the body of the female in the terrain of his adventures.

One could say that *Orlando* wrenches these phallic paradigms of male adventure into a comic, feminist version of the Freudian narrative of bisexuality adumbrated in "The Ego and the Id" (1923) (and further developed in "Femininity" [1933]). As Elizabeth Abel demonstrates, although Woolf claimed not to have read Freud thoroughly until 1939, her novels of the twenties and thirties engaged "the set of terms that generated the debates [unfolding within British psychoanalysis]" (xvi). The Freudian pre-Oedipal child is bisexual, the little girl is a little man until she "falls" into sexual division, a trajectory comically revised in Orlando's protracted psychosexual development.[19] The first hundred pages, which explore the development of the male Orlando, might be regarded as a prologue to the momentous birth of female subjectivity. Beginning life as a "little man," he suddenly—mysteriously—becomes a woman. In Woolf's version, however, two things happen. First, the polymorphous possibilities of bisexuality continue to circulate. They put into play new types of female narcissism and homoeroticism, ones freed from the shadow of Freudian judgment and represented in a series of mirroring pairs of androgynous lovers. Second, in unveiling the "truth" of Orlando's "castration," Woolf presents a comic deflation of the horrors of the Freudian paradigm: "Orlando looked himself up and down in a long looking-glass, without showing any signs of discomposure, and went, presumably, to his bath" (138). Moreover, the stagy unveiling of Orlando as a woman parodically addresses male fascination, including Freud's, with the enigma of female sexuality. The "erotic life . . . of women," Freud writes in "Three Essays on the Theory of Sexuality" (1905), "partly owing to the stunting effect of civilized conditions and partly owing to their conventional secretiveness and insincerity—is still veiled in an impenetrable obscurity" (248).

Woolf's revisionary gesture of lifting the veil of the "truth" of Orlando's womanhood is deliberately "orientalized." Orlando's sex change is situated in Turkey, where Orlando, the English ambassador,

---

[19]In "The Ego and the Id" Freud writes: "For one gets an impression that the simple Oedipus complex is by no means its commonest form, but rather represents a simplification or schematization which, to be sure, is often enough justified for practical purposes. Closer study usually discloses the more complete Oedipus complex, which is twofold, positive and negative, and is due to the bisexuality originally present in children. . . . It may even be that the ambivalence displayed in the relations to the parents should be attributed entirely to bisexuality and that it is not, as I have represented above, developed out of identification in consequence of rivalry" (641). See Abel's discussion of Woolf's relation to Freud in *Virginia Woolf and the Fictions of Psychoanalysis*.

awakens from a seven-day sleep to discover that he is a woman. It is worth asking why, in a fantasy of a transsexual life lived over more than three hundred years, it seemed necessary to plot the text's most radical event outside of England, specifically, in the Levant. The inclusion of the topos of travel within the general representation of the mobility of desire suggests that English soil is inimical to the emergence of female subjectivity and sexuality. This centrifugal impulse in the narrative is reminiscent of Rachel Vinrace's voyage out for new models of desire. Even from his first meeting with Sasha, Orlando longs for "another landscape, and another tongue. English was too frank, too candid, too honeyed a speech for Sasha. For in all she said, however open she seemed and voluptuous, there was something hidden; in all she did, however daring, there was something concealed" (47). Early in the text, Sasha, the Russian princess, introduces the orientalizing of sexual mystery, along with the trope of androgyny (for Sasha's Eastern dress makes her sex ambiguous), but it is during the trip to Turkey that female subjectivity and sexuality emerge, as it were, behind an oriental veil. As in the actual case of James Morris, the British travel writer who went to Casablanca in 1972 for a sex change operation, Orlando's journey suggests that gender crossing is imagined as a cultural border crossing as well.[20]

In the rest of this chapter, I will discuss the significance of Orlando's round-trip journey to the East in relation to the mobility of desire. In plotting Orlando's diplomatic journey to Turkey (as male), his sojourn with the gypsies, and his return trip to England (as female), Woolf drew on a series of erotic and political projections onto the East in British cultural texts of all kinds. Orlando's voyage out from England initially seems designed to fulfill the dictates of male colonial adventure, as Orlando sublimates eros in diplomatic service. (Orlando's "cover story" for leaving England is his desire to flee the temptations of the Archduchess Harriet.) The East quickly serves, however, as a liminal site of erotic freedom. But this escape is eschewed; Orlando repatriates—as a woman—to England and to English tradition. Exploring an alternative culture with the wandering gypsies, Orlando ultimately decides to face the poetic and cultural legacy she inherits.

---

[20]See Marjorie Garber's discussion of Morris's autobiography, *Conundrum*, in *Vested Interests: Cross-Dressing and Cultural Anxiety*: "For Morris, who had journeyed so extensively in Africa, North and South, Casablanca was a special, liminal place, the geographic counterpart of his/her psychological and physiological condition" (336).

Unlike Rachel Vinrace in *The Voyage Out*, Orlando, the woman, makes a round-trip journey. The dual trajectories of the narrative—centrifugal and liberating, centripetal and domesticating—create a complex cultural politics and poetics. To extrapolate the fantasy of sexual boundary crossings, the narrative mines the overdetermined figure of Eastern travel, yet ultimately repatriates erotic, comic possibilities onto English soil.

I begin with the important relationship between travel and female desire—and particularly the orientalizing of this desire—as it is textualized in the letters exchanged by Vita Sackville-West (the "model" for Orlando) and Virginia Woolf as Woolf began to conceptualize *Orlando*.[21] The "longest and most charming love letter in literature," as Nigel Nicolson called it (202), might be said to have originated in the letters that passed between these two writers during Sackville-West's Eastern trips, the first in 1926 and the second in 1927. From January to May of both years, she settled for a few months in Teheran, where Harold Nicolson had been posted since 1925.[22] During both absences, the two women exchanged correspondence, which consists of love letters, letters of friendship, travel letters, and gossip. "But listen; suppose Orlando turns out to be Vita," Woolf writes to her, "and its all about you and the lusts of your flesh and the lure of your mind" (October 9, 1927; *Letters of Virginia Woolf*, 3:428–29). The lusts of Vita's flesh and the lure of her mind were first textualized by Woolf in their letters. Woolf conceived the first sketch for the novel that ultimately became *Orlando* as she waited impatiently for Vita's letters from her second trip to Teheran. *Orlando* originates, along with other "letters

[21]The publication of the letters between Vita Sackville-West and Virginia Woolf has spawned reevaluations of *Orlando* as a lesbian text that reflects the two women's intense relationship. To Sherron Knopp, the novel "celebrates Virginia's love for Vita" (24) and is "the first positive, and still unsurpassed, sapphic portrait in literature" (33); Susan Squier views it as "the consummation of her love for Vita" (175). Barbara Fassler, Jean Love, and, most recently, Suzanne Raitt find the fictionalizing of Sackville-West and Woolf's relationship in *Orlando* to betray hate as well as love, anger as well as admiration.

[22]Sackville-West's first voyage out to Teheran was documented in *Passenger to Teheran*, published by Hogarth Press in 1926; her second voyage formed the basis of the travel narrative *Twelve Days*. Her first trip took her to Egypt, Iraq, Persia, India, and Russia. During this journey to the Middle East, she completed her poem *The Land*, on which Orlando's poem "The Oak Tree" is based. Although Virginia Woolf herself had traveled to Turkey in 1906, she seems to have drawn on her own experience very little, relying instead on Sackville-West's and Nicolson's more recent experiences in the East. For Woolf's diary entries on her own early trip to Turkey, see *A Passionate Apprentice*.

of desire," in Vita's absence and figures the other as peripatetic, active, and elusive. Like Wollstonecraft's *Letters*, *Orlando* is both private and public, directed to an audience of one and of many. Moreover, it is part of an erotic exchange in which travel and absence play a crucial imaginative role. And again like Wollstonecraft's travel book, Woolf's letters of desire acknowledge that the lover's absence is also potentially the lover's infidelity. (On her second trip abroad, Sackville-West was accompanied by Dorothy Wellesley, and after her return from the Orient, Woolf discovered that she was involved with Mary Campbell as well. Woolf writes to Sackville-West, "If you've given yourself to Campbell, I'll have no more to do with you and so it shall be written, plainly, for all the world to read in *Orlando*" [October 13, 1927; *Letters of Virginia Woolf*, 3:431].) These texts of desire (the erotic letters exchanged by the two women as well as *Orlando* as love letter) bring a renewal of intimacy and a means of figuring (and thereby controlling) the body of the lover. The lover's body is imprinted in and by the textual "body" of the writing. This imprinting was implicitly acknowledged by Woolf in her description of the proofs of *Passenger to Teheran*, Vita's own travel book to be published by Hogarth Press: "The whole book is full of nooks and corners which I enjoy exploring. Sometimes one wants a candle in one's hand though—Thats my only criticism— you've left (I daresay in haste) one or two dangling dim places. Its a delicious method, and one that takes the very skin of your shape, this dallying discursive one. . . . [The book] gives this sense of your being away, travelling, not in any particular geographical country: but travelling far away. Now I see . . . what a great affair going to Persia is" (September 15, 1926; *Letters of Virginia Woolf*, 3:291). Eros pervades both the travel and the travel book. The spaces of the text offer a delicious invitation; the book of exploration becomes the country to explore.

In *A Lover's Discourse*, Roland Barthes allegorizes the plot of absence and waiting in gendered terms: "Historically, the discourse of absence is carried on by the Woman: Woman is sedentary, Man hunts, journeys; Woman is faithful (she waits), man is fickle (he sails away, he cruises)" (13). Even before Sackville-West departs for Teheran, Woolf figures her as the one who travels abroad, while she herself circulates closer to home, but she transforms Barthes's wandering male lover into the image of a maternal voyager. She writes in her diary, "There is her maturity & full breastedness: her being so much in full sail on the high tide; where I am coasting down backwaters" (December 21,

1925; *Diary of Virginia Woolf*, 3:52). Vita's body and character are figured in the full-breastedness. The *Euphrosyne* of *The Voyage Out* is supplanted by a more exuberant vehicle of female power and attraction. (To her husband, Shelmerdine, Orlando's name means "a ship in full sail coming with the sun on it proudly sweeping across the Mediterranean from the South Seas" [251].) In her letters to Sackville-West during the latter's Eastern travels, Woolf constructs herself sometimes playfully, sometimes anxiously as Barthes's "woman who waits," but now Vita is pictured exotically: "But Teheran is exciting me too much. I believe, at this moment, more in Teheran than in Tavistock Square. I see you, somehow in long coat and trousers, like an Abyssinian Empress, stalking over those barren hills. . . . And the affectionate letter—whens that coming?" (February 3, 1926; *Letters of Virginia Woolf*, 3: 238).[23] Casting herself as the woman who waits and Vita as the traveler allowed them both the room for fantasy, which, like travel, is rooted in distance and absence. Distance allows both women the pleasure of picturing each other in writing, of dressing (and undressing) each other exotically for the imagination. (A pleasure that is curiously repeated in the photograph portraits of Orlando and his/her lovers, sumptuously arrayed, drawn from the Sackville-West family gallery and album [of male and female subjects], which accompany the text of the novel.) The lover's body is eroticized as textual corpus.[24]

Woolf wrote to Sackville-West as she worked on *Orlando*: "Orlando will be a little book, with pictures and a map or two. I make it up in bed at night, as I walk the streets, everywhere. I want to see you in the lamplight, in your emeralds" (October 13, 1927; *Letters of Virginia Woolf*, 3:430). What is represented here is not just the erotic setting of the writing (Woolf in bed, composing) but also a desire one might call topographic—a desire to plot the geography of the relationship, to

[23]Sackville-West, for her part, coaxed this sense of suspense in her correspondent, transforming future destinations into promises of renewed intimacy in writing: "My next letter will be posted at Baghdad and written in the Persian Gulf. It will be all about Virginia. Indeed it may arrive before this one, as it will go part of the way by air" (*Letters of Vita Sackville-West*, 105).

[24]Sackville-West was both thrilled at and yet fearful of what this textual body might look like, given Woolf's teasing suggestions of using the novel to exact revenge for Sackville-West's infidelities. On October 11, 1927, she writes: "My God, Virginia, if ever I was thrilled and terrified it is at the prospect of being projected into the shape of Orlando. What fun for you; what fun for me. . . . You have my full permission. Only I think that having drawn and quartered me, unwound and retwisted me, or whatever it is that you intend to do, you ought to dedicate it to your victim" (quoted in *Letters of Virginia Woolf*, 3:429 n. 1).

graph the lovers precisely in a particular erotic space. For her part, Vita's erotic imagination shades into exoticism; she writes of the desire to abduct Virginia, to place her among other exotic objects. From Luxor, Egypt, she writes: "The wish to steal Virginia overcomes me,—steal her, take her away, and put her in the sun among the objects mentioned alphabetically above. You know you liked Greece. You know you liked Spain. Well, then? If I can get myself to Africa and Asia, why can't you? (But with *me*, please.)" (*Letters of Vita Sackville-West*, 94). Here, "Virginia" is swept away to find a place among the Eastern objects already collected. The third-person address ("the wish to steal Virginia"), like the exoticism, functions as a displacement that incites desire.

It is clear that a very literary and even stagy orientalism of abduction, seduction, and disguise fuels these textual fantasies. As Sackville-West travels through the Middle East, Richard Burton's "sotadic zone," documenting her adventures in her letters and travel narrative, she and Woolf draw on a discourse of orientalism associated with an eroticism of masquerade.[25] The erotic possibilities suggested by androgynous Turkish clothes and the association of these garments with the titillation of role playing fuel these fantasies, for they contribute to fascination in *Orlando* with dress-up and cross-dressing. The possibility of shifting roles in these orientalized scenarios, even the very staginess of the topos, seems to propel the imagination, as if Shakespeare's Rosalind had entered *The Arabian Nights*. More than a decade earlier the theatricality of this romantic orientalism, its conduciveness to elaborate sexual role playing, was already a part of Sackville-West's milieu. During the First Balkan War, while Nicolson was serving in Constantinople (right before their marriage), she performed *An Eastern Fantasy* ("a Persian play") in the Great Hall at Knole. She played the part of the Caliph loved by two dancing girls in a production replete with "yashmaks, veils, and flowing drapery" (Lees-Milne, 60). And in her 1928 poem *The Land*, on which *Orlando*'s "Oak Tree" is based, Sackville-West links the image of the Orient to a lesbian passion both desired and feared.

> Sullen and foreign-looking, the snaky flower,
> Scarfed in dull purple, like Egyptian girls

[25]See Burton's essay on homosexuality, originally appended to his translation of *Arabian Nights*.

Camping among the furze, staining the waste
With foreign colour, sulky, dark, and quaint,
Dangerous too, as a girl might sidle up,
An Egyptian girl, with an ancient snaring spell,
Throwing a net, soft round the limbs and heart,
Captivity soft and abhorrent, a close-meshed net. (49)

As Barbara Fassler shows, the Orient functioned for Bloomsbury—
and more generally in late nineteenth- and early twentieth-century
discourse—as a code for androgyny, bisexuality, and homosexuality.[26]
In the love letters of Woolf and Sackville-West, the trappings of orientalism abet fantasies in which femininity and masculinity are put
on and taken off. In one letter, Woolf even pictures herself as a eunuch, divested of the props of sexuality and thus privy to the secrets
of the harem: "D'you know its a great thing being a eunuch as I am:
that is not knowing what's the right side of a skirt: women confide in
one. One pulls a shade over the fury of sex; and then all the veins
and marbling, which, between women, are so fascinating, show out.
Here in my cave I see lots of things you blazing beauties make invis-
ible by the light of your own glory" (January 31, 1927; *Letters of Virginia Woolf*, 3:320). The phallus becomes a prop to be put on and
removed at will, like a skirt, the prop of femininity. Grafting Sackville-
West's Eastern travel onto the Western philosophical tradition, Woolf
is both the wise Platonic philosopher and the eunuch in the harem,
out of the game of sexuality. The "shade" pulled over the fury of sex
suggests that woman's erotic body can best be viewed and represented obliquely—in shadow—by the "safe," sexless observer in the
harem.[27]

Disguise, despotism, the harem—these are the familiar elements of
the orientalism that projected political and erotic fantasies onto the
East. The discourse of orientalism that I have been tracing is recog-

[26]The association of orientalism with an erotics of masquerade of course extends a
Byronic tradition begun even earlier in the century with the cross-dressing of Don Juan
in Turkey and is one more strand in the overdetermined context of Woolf's orientalism.
See also Sara Suleri's *Rhetoric of English India* for a discussion of how Forster rewrites
the orientalist paradigm as a "homoerotics of race" in *A Passage to India* (135).

[27]This "covering" gesture, this adoption of a safe distance from which to contemplate
the body of the lover, may be linked to the persona of the narrator/biographer in
Orlando, a male observer/screen interposed between female writer and female body of
the lover. A full discussion of the narrator/biographer in the erotic dynamics of the
text is beyond the scope of this chapter.

nizably one strand in the complex imaginative geography that scholars, from Edward Said on, have documented in European travel narratives and anthropology. This discourse, as more recent scholars have shown, is not monolithic but heterogeneous in its mappings of gender and race.[28] Woolf's orientalism in *Orlando* draws on a diverse array of cultural sources, from the arts, literature, and politics. Said compares orientalism and "male gender dominance, or patriarchy, in metropolitan societies: the Orient was routinely described as feminine, its riches as fertile, its main symbols the sensual woman, the harem, and the despotic—but curiously attractive—ruler" ("Orientalism Reconsidered," 225). But as Peter Wollen points out in "Fashion/Orientalism/the Body," during the twenties orientalism in the arts, in particular, served a different gender politics, which included redefinition of the "image of the female body" (5). Popular versions of orientalism—in the Russian ballet (exemplified by Diaghilev's *Cleopatra* and *Scheherezade;* Woolf attended performances of the latter at least twice),[29] in opera, and in fashion (in the styles of Paul Poiret, who introduced oriental fashion to Paris)—rewrote the Oedipal scenario in terms of female fantasy. The sexual and political are imbricated in *Scheherezade,* which, notes Wollen, reflects "both a crisis in the state and a crisis in the family (female desire, homosexuality)" (18).

This spectacle of orientalism, so much a part of the European cultural scene of the twenties, is an important source for the textual fantasies produced in the epistolary exchange between Vita and Virginia and in the writing of the "love letter," *Orlando. Orlando* is a put-on, a comic fantasy in costume that elaborates female desire in various forms of masquerade. Indeed, on reading the novel, Vita likened Woolf's act of writing to a scene of erotic and exotic dress-up.

> I feel like one of those wax figures in a shop window, on which you have hung a robe stitched with jewels. It is like being alone in a dark room with a treasure chest full of rubies and nuggets and brocades. Darling, I don't know and scarcely even like to write, so overwhelmed am

[28]In *Critical Terrains: French and British Orientalisms,* Lisa Lowe considers how Said's important work on orientalism presents the gendering of the colonizing discourse as static and plots the Western observer as invariably male.

[29]Woolf records her attendance at a performance of the Diaghilev Ballet Company's *Scheherezade* in October 1918 (*Diary,* 1:201n) and again in July 1919. At the latter performance, Woolf saw Lydia Lopokova dance. Lopokova, who married Maynard Keynes in 1925, became a "type," in Woolf's words, for Rezia in *Mrs. Dalloway* (*Diary,* 2:265).

I, how you could have hung so splendid a garment on so poor a peg. Really this isn't false humility; really it isn't. . . . Also, you have invented a new form of Narcissism,—I confess,—I am in love with Orlando— this is a complication I had not foreseen. (*Letters of Vita Sackville-West,* 288–89)

Woolf's rich imagination produces the textual/sexual embellishment of Sackville-West in *Orlando,* bestowing on her treasures worthy of *The Arabian Nights.* But if the novel is a loving gesture, expressing homoerotic desire, it is also an invitation to female autoeroticism; Woolf's lavish dress-up of Vita allows the latter to find pleasure in her own jewels, "alone in a dark room" with her treasure.[30] It is as if Woolf produced Vita's erotic and exotic textual body and gave it back to her as gift, thus allowing Vita to eroticize her own self-contact.

One can see how homoeroticism was associated with orientalism in Woolf's earliest conception of *Orlando,* which was recorded in her diary (and juxtaposed prominently with Vita's absence): "Although annoyed that I have not heard from Vita by this post nor yet last week, annoyed sentimentally, & partly from vanity—still I must record the conception last night between 12 & one of a new book" (March 14, 1927; *Diary,* 3:130–31). Her first idea is to write a picaresque à la Defoe about a penniless and unattractive woman who goes to Europe.[31] Suddenly, however, a different fantasy comes to mind, a doubling of women in a book called "The Jessamy Brides."

Two women, poor, solitary at the top of a house. One can see anything (for this is all fantasy) the Tower Bridge, clouds, aeroplanes. Also old men listening in the room over the way. Everything is to be tumbled in pall mall. It is to be written as I write letters at the top of my speed: on the ladies of Llangollen; on Mrs Fladgate; on people passing. No attempt is to be made to realise the character. Sapphism is to be suggested. Satire

---

[30]Luce Irigaray describes this homoeroticism as a form of autoeroticism, a way for a woman to get in touch with herself through the other (the "self-same," she calls the other). As Irigaray points out, in the discourse of psychoanalysis "nothing of the special nature of desire between women has been unveiled or stated. That a woman might desire a woman 'like' herself, someone of the 'same' sex, that she might also have auto- and homosexual appetites [*sic*] is simply incomprehensible to Freud, and indeed inadmissible" (101). For an interesting essay on female narcissism in *Orlando,* based on Kristeva's *Tales of Love,* see Ellen Carol Jones, "The Flight of a Word: Narcissism and the Masquerade of Writing in Virginia Woolf's *Orlando.*"

[31]See Susan Squier's essay "Tradition and Revision in Woolf's *Orlando*: Defoe and 'The Jessamy Brides' " on Woolf's revision of Defoe in *Orlando.*

is to be the main note—satire & wildness. The Ladies are to have Constantinople in view. Dreams of golden domes. My own lyric vein is to be satirised. Everything mocked. And it is to end with three dots . . . so. For the truth is I feel the need of an escapade after these serious poetic experimental books whose form is always so closely considered. (131)

Woolf's idea for her novel is a Pisgah sight of Constantinople, a specular and speculative dream of the libidinous East for two English Sapphists. In her diary, she alludes to the aristocratic Irish pair, the "ladies of Llangollen," who together eloped at the end of the eighteenth century, capturing the imaginations of the public and of writers such as Byron (see Mavor). "Desire is a wonderful telescope and Pisgah the best observatory," Robert Louis Stevenson once wrote (266); Mrs. Fladgate (Is floodgate suggested but restrained here?) is only on the threshold of adventure.[32] As Susan Squier points out, the transgressive sexuality of the book that was to become *Orlando* was predicted in the title of Woolf's sketch[33] (and the pair of foppish brides she had envisioned replaced with the series of androgynous pairs in the novel).

In her revised conception of the novel, however, Woolf literalized the Western fantasy of the libidinous East. In a sense, she plotted a time-out in the midst of the novel, which resembles the relief she imagined "The Jessamy Brides" as a whole might provide—"an escapade after these serious poetic experimental books whose form is always so closely considered." The excursus to Turkey, with all its

[32]Compare Woolf's sketch to Stephen Dedalus's "Parable of the Plums," also entitled "A Pisgah Sight of Palestine," in *Ulysses*: "Two Dublin vestals, Stephen said, elderly and pious, have lived fifty and fiftythree years in Fumbally's lane. . . . They want to see the views of Dublin from the top of Nelson's pillar. . . . But they are afraid the pillar will fall, Stephen went on. They see the roofs and argue about where the different churches are" (Joyce, 119, 121).

[33]Quoting Woolf's diary, Squier says that "Jessamy" is "a man who scents himself with perfume or who wears a sprig of Jessamine in his buttonhole . . . a dandy, a fop" (174). Squier goes on to say that by the time Woolf planned the novel, the word "Jessamy" also suggested a parallel term of transgressive sexuality, "Amazon": "In its evocation of the gender line crossings embodied by a foppish male bride, a feminine man, and an 'Amazonian' woman, the initial title for Orlando prefigures Woolf's progatonist [sic], who in the course of a long life loved both sexes passionately, contracted a marriage to a man whom she jokingly suspected of being a woman (and who entertained the corresponding suspicion that Orlando was a man), and who at the novel's conclusion summons herself ('Orlando?') only to be answered by a multiplicity of selves—of both genders and sexual orientations" (174).

"satire and wildness," must be understood in relation to the sexual and textual problems Orlando experiences in England. For England, the biographer tells us, has become "uninhabitable" for Orlando, as he experiences both poetic and sexual blockages. During the "age of prose," Orlando strives to produce "The Oak Tree, A Poem": "But as he scratched out as many lines as he wrote in, the sum of them was often, at the end of the year, rather less than at the beginning, and it looked as if in the process of writing the poem would be completely unwritten" (113). In frustration the struggling poet unintentionally repeats Penelope's strategy of weaving and unweaving, but to no purpose. Having redecorated his home and apostrophized "his house and race in terms of the most moving eloquence" (107), Orlando faces a domestic dead end.

It is at this point that the Archduchess Harriet appears to provide the alibi needed for Orlando's Eastern adventure, and this alibi is lust. Orlando flees the clutches of a woman in love; thus, his request for the ambassadorship seems to confirm adventure's pattern of the flight from women. Yet this flight is a cover story that displaces a more radical kind of "gender trouble,"[34] the specter of homoerotic desire that surfaces and is repressed before Orlando's sex change. Harriet's appearance is not the first occasion for this specter, which is introduced with the oriental Sasha, whose sex is indeterminate for Orlando. She/he is seen as "a figure, which, whether boy's or woman's, for the loose tunic and trousers of the Russian fashion served to disguise the sex, filled him with the highest curiosity. . . . But these details were obscured by the extraordinary seductiveness which issued from the whole person" (37). (Here Woolf borrows a Shakespearean model of trans- or supersexual attractiveness.) Orlando feels a homoerotic attraction to this seductive figure and ruefully imagines that he desires one of his own sex: "When the boy, for alas, it must be—no woman could skate with such speed and vigour—swept almost on tiptoe past him, Orlando was ready to tear his hair with vexation that the person was of his own sex, and thus all embraces were out of the question" (38). But what begins as a kind of mirroring between Orlando and his beloved, a same-sex attraction facilitated by Sasha's clothing, is then channeled into a more conventional heterosexual plot in which the

[34] I borrow the term from Judith Butler's book on feminism and the subversion of identity.

androgynous figure is "othered" into the metaphysical tradition of
Petrarchan love poetry: "She was a woman. Orlando stared; trembled;
turned hot; turned cold" (38).

This specter of homoeroticism resurfaces with Harriet (who we later
learn is really a man), first in the incestuous impetus behind Harriet's
quest for Orlando, for she has seen his picture, which is the image of
her dead sister (115). (Thus she seeks in her lover the image of her
sister.) But homosexual love is disguised and revealed as well in the
allegory of Love's anatomy. Love is figured as having "two faces; one
white, the other black; two bodies; one smooth, the other hairy. It has
two hands, two feet . . . two, indeed, of every member and each one
is the exact opposite of the other. Yet, so strictly are they joined together that you cannot separate them." The narrator tells us that Love,
the "bird of beauty," flies nearer and nearer toward Orlando, yet "all
of a sudden (at the sight of the Archduchess presumably) she [the
bird] wheeled about, turned the other way round; showed herself
black, hairy, brutish; and it was Lust, the vulture, not Love, the Bird
of Paradise" (117–18). This "dung-bedraggled fowl" settles on Orlando's writing table, thus making it impossible for him to continue his
poetic career. In a book in which figures of rhetoric as well as fashion
can obscure the body's parts, this Manichean personification of love
comes dangerously close to suggesting anal eroticism (Love shows not
the back of the head or the back of the brain, but the "behind"). Because the Archduchess will reveal herself as the Archduke, a man who
dresses as a woman to obtain Orlando's love, it is possible that the
figures clothe homoerotic passion, a love that dare not yet speak its
name in the novel. It is this lust and its effect on Orlando's writing
career that propel him into the ambassadorship to Turkey: "Thus real-
ising that his home was uninhabitable, and that steps must be taken
to end the matter instantly, he did what any other young man would
have done in his place, and asked King Charles to send him as Ambassador Extraordinary to Constantinople" (118).[35]

This decision to leave England is the culmination of Orlando's meditation on the vexed relation between sexuality and poetry. For Orlando has been preoccupied with the nature of love and how it might
be captured metaphorically in poetry. He is continually frustrated by
the literary tradition he inherits, which fails to provide adequate lan-

[35]This passage is a sly rewriting of the flight from women encoded in narratives of
adventure; it also suggests the prevalence of male homoeroticism in the colonial service.

guage to represent love: "Every single thing, once he tried to dislodge it from its place in his mind, he found thus cumbered with other matter like the lump of glass which, after a year at the bottom of the sea, is grown about with bones and dragon-flies, and coins and the tresses of drowned women" (101). Even this figure for the workings of the metaphoric tradition is immediately reconsidered by a frustrated Orlando, who (like Penelope) weaves and unweaves his own art: " 'A figure like that is manifestly untruthful,' he argued, 'for no dragon-fly, unless under very exceptional circumstances, could live at the bottom of the sea. And if literature is not the Bride and Bedfellow of Truth, what is she? Confound it all,' he cried, 'why say Bedfellow when one's already said Bride?' " (101). But this question itself is disingenuous, for bedfellow and bride, as Orlando soon discovers through his experience with Harriet, are two quite different aspects of love, and indeed, the confusion of the sex of the partner (bride or bed*fellow*) is displaced onto the semantic debate. To "propitiate" the "austere spirit of poetry," Orlando tries to renounce metaphor—"the sky is blue," "the grass is green"—but this, too, is ineffectual. "Looking up, he saw that, on the contrary, the sky is like the veils which a thousand Madonnas have let fall from their hair; and the grass fleets and darkens like a flight of girls fleeing the embraces of hairy satyrs from enchanted woods" (102). The figures of sexuality return. Orlando's plight leads his biographer to provide a figure for the would-be poet that further complicates this "gender trouble": "When it came to a question of poetry, or his own competence in it, he was as shy as a little girl behind her mother's cottage door" (102). Brides, bedfellows, male poets as little girls—the flight from women that occasions Orlando's trip to Turkey covers more radical instabilities.

Yet if the impulse behind Orlando's adventures in the Levant is flight from the difficulties of women and poetry, Constantinople quickly becomes a place of "satire and wildness," of political and sexual upheaval. Critics have pointed out the coincidence between the political revolution (the overthrow of the sultan) that disrupts Orlando's tenure as ambassador and his private sexual metamorphosis, but they have neglected to discuss the way Woolf satirizes the mapping of gender onto the colonial adventure. In a way that suggests the fragmented form of Wilkie Collins's *Moonstone*—a detective story in which officials try to piece together the events surrounding the theft of an oriental jewel—Woolf represents the "policing of the orient" (as Ronald Thomas has called it) as the policing of sexuality, an effort

that is disrupted by revolution.³⁶ In depicting Orlando's ambas-
sadorial experience, Woolf complicated the gender politics of her
own biographical impulse, representing in Orlando not only Vita
Sackville-West, but Harold Nicolson as well. (Of course, the sexual
politics here are complicated by Nicolson's own homosexuality.) Nicolson served as third secretary in the British Embassy in Constantinople; the fictional "revolution" against the sultan in Orlando draws
on the "Young Turks" coup that Nicolson experienced in the Levant
in January 1913. Nicolson found himself amidst a frenzy over im-
pending massacres. "The city was thrown into turmoil. A massacre
ensued. The Daoud Pasha barracks were in flames. . . . Fearsome ru-
mours were rife" (Lees-Milne, 60.)³⁷

Orlando begins his stint in Turkey as a paper-pushing bureaucrat
but quickly discovers that the English mission of protecting white
women from the potential abuse of the colonial male is not wholly
congenial to him. Like some of Conrad's characters, Orlando finds
himself attracted to the ethos of the other, rather than disposed to
regulate it. Although Orlando is said to have had "a finger in some
of the most delicate negotiations between King Charles and the Turks"
(119), he seems to have had his fingers elsewhere as well. The sign of
the relaxation of military male purpose is Orlando's slumming in disguise among the "natives"; this renunciation of discipline is confirmed
in his marriage to Rosina Pepita, a Spanish dancer ("a dancer, father
unknown, but reputed a gipsy, mother also unknown but reputed a
seller of old iron in the marketplace" [132–33]). This match, witnessed
by a washerwoman, suggests illegitimacy, a departure from the aristocratic, patriarchal Englishness of Orlando's upbringing. In this an-
titraditionalist and anti-imperialist representation, Woolf drew on
popular and literary (and orientalist) stereotypes of the gypsy as care-
free, defiant, and outside history as well as on Vita Sackville-West's
own family background.³⁸

³⁶See Thomas's fascinating discussion of the significance of the Indian Mutiny in The
Moonstone in his Dreams of Authority: Freud and the Fictions of the Unconscious, 203–19.
³⁷Virginia Woolf's attitude toward ambassadorships, particularly Harold Nicolson's,
is captured in a letter from her to Sackville-West: "I am ashamed that any friend of
mine should marry a man who may be an ambassador" (quoted in Trautmann, 36).
³⁸Vita Sackville-West's Pepita (1937), the story of her maternal grandmother, expresses some of the relish with which she approached this gypsy "detour" in her family
history. For Orlando's struggle to recover her legitimate inheritance after her sex
change, Woolf might have been drawing on the whole issue of inheritance raised by
Pepita's relationship with Lionel Sackville-West, who, at the age of twenty, entered the

But Woolf's most direct parody of "official" British orientalist discourse in *Orlando* is exemplified in the discovered "documents" regarding the revolution. The diary of John Fenner Brigge, an English naval officer, provides one record of the troubling events that classically displays the sexual/political nexus of British imperialism: " 'When the rockets began to soar into the air, there was considerable uneasiness among us lest the native population . . . fraught with unpleasant consequences to all, . . . English ladies in the company, . . . I own that my hand went to my cutlass' " (127: ellipses in original). Brigge continues to describe the "superiority of the British." When the "natives" become restless, according to another record, the British bluejackets quell the disturbance, and Orlando begins his seven-day sleep (during which time the duke's secretaries find a certificate of his marriage to Rosina Pepita; on the seventh day, the revolution against the sultan commences, and all foreigners are killed). "A few English managed to escape; but, as might have been expected [the narrator says], the gentlemen of the British Embassy preferred to die in defence of their red boxes, or, in extreme cases, to swallow bunches of keys rather than let them fall into the hands of the Infidel" (133).[39]

Policing the Orient and policing female sexuality are parallel projects, a connection that is most evident in the scene in which Purity, Chastity, and Modesty, the three "graces," uphold the laws of female

---

English Foreign Office and met Pepita in Albolote, Spain. Sackville-West writes in the first chapter: "The papers which have provided the material for the first part of this book owe their existence to the fact that in 1896 it became legally expedient for my grandfather's solicitors to take the evidence of a number of people in Spain who, some forty years earlier, had been acquainted with the principal characters involved. The point, in short, was the necessity of proving whether my grandmother, Pepita, had ever been married to my grandfather or not. Several issues were at stake: an English peerage, and an historic inheritance. . . . They dealt with them in their usual dry practical way, little foreseeing that this body of evidence collected in 1896 from voluble Spanish peasants, servants, villagers, dancers and other theatrical folk, would in 1936 be re-read in stacks of dusty typescript by someone closely connected, who saw therein a hotch-potch of discursiveness, frequently irrelevant but always fascinating" (5). For a very good discussion of this form of Orientalism in the Western imagination, see also Katie Trumpener's "Time of the Gypsies: A 'People without History' in the Narratives of the West."

[39] In a provocative rereading of *The Waves*, Jane Marcus analyzes the fusion of Woolf's feminism and her critique of British imperialism. This critique is found in *Orlando* as well, particularly in the parody of the official discourses of British orientalism quoted above. Marcus goes on to argue that *The Waves* is "about the ideology of white British colonialism and the Romantic literature that sustains it. Its parody and irony mock the complicity of the hero and the poet in the creation of a collective national subject through an elegy for imperialism" (145). As I will show, Woolf's relation to Romanticism in *Orlando* is revisionary, but not parodic.

behavior and decorum. Specifically, they "cast their veils over the mouths of the trumpets" that introduce Orlando's female body (136), but to no avail. This prophylaxis, the official British veiling of female sexuality, is comically undone in the startling transformation of Orlando, which occurs, like the return of the repressed, during his trancelike sleep. The scene of Orlando's unveiling reveals the contradictory impulses that underlie the male troping of the female "behind" the veil, the impulse at once to hide female sexuality (and with it, according to Freudian paradigm, the knowledge of her castration) and to penetrate its enigma, that is, to lift the veil of the truth of female sexuality. In orientalizing Orlando's sex change, Woolf parodied literary, philosophical and psychoanalytic discourses that represent woman as a veiled mystery which the male imagination seeks to penetrate.[40] This orientalizing of the mysterious "truth" of female sexuality is evident in Freud's essay "Femininity," in which he says, "Throughout history people have knocked their heads against the riddle of the nature of femininity." He then quotes some lines from a poem by Heine in illustration: "Heads in hieroglyphic bonnets / Heads in turbans and black birettas / Heads in wigs and thousand other / Wretched, sweating heads of humans" (113n). The mystery of female sexuality is allusively linked here, through the lines of the poem, to the riddle of the Sphinx, to the origin of mystery itself.[41] In locating Orlando's sex change in Turkey—in employing the theatrical

[40]In "Veiling Over Desire: Close-ups of the Woman," Mary Ann Doane offers an excellent overview of the trope of the veil in Western philosophical discourse. The structure of the veil, she says, is "clearly complicit with the tendency to specify the woman's position in relation to knowledge as that of enigma" (118). The veiled woman maps onto sexual difference the dialectic of truth and appearance; in the discourse of metaphysics, Doane says, "the function of the veil is to make truth profound, to ensure that there is a depth that lurks behind the surface of things" (118–19). Doane maintains that even in the antimetaphysical discourse of Nietzsche and Derrida, which deconstructs the opposition of truth and appearance, woman still functions tropologically much as she does in the metaphysical tradition that these philosophers are deconstructing. For a fascinating analysis of the function of the veil in a non-Western context, see Malek Alloula's *Colonial Harem*. Alloula studies postcards picturing veiled Algerian women that were sent by French soldiers during the Algerian War. He analyzes the function of the veil as an extension of "an imaginary harem whose inviolability haunts the photographer-voyeur" (13).

[41]Jane Gallop comments on this passage from Freud in *The Daughter's Seduction: Feminism and Psychoanalysis*: "The enigmatic 'hieroglyphic bonnet' suggests Egypt and in this riddle context reminds us of the riddle of the Sphinx. We think of Oedipus and the way solving riddles leads to blindness. A 'solved' riddle is the reduction of heterogeneous material to logic, to the homogeneity of logical thought, which produces a blind spot, the inability to see the otherness that gets lost in the reduction" (61). See

unveiling of the female body in this oriental surrounding—Woolf bur-
lesques the quest for Isis unveiled (and perhaps Rider Haggard's *She*
and other such narratives were also on her mind).[42]

Woolf also revises the Freudian narrative of female sexual difference.

> The sound of the trumpets died away and Orlando stood stark naked.
> No human being, since the world began, has ever looked more ravishing.
> His form combined in one the strength of a man and a woman's grace.
> As he stood there, the silver trumpets prolonged their note, as if reluctant
> to leave the lovely sight which their blast had called forth; and Chastity,
> Purity, and Modesty, inspired, no doubt, by Curiosity, peeped in at the
> door and threw a garment like a towel at the naked form which, unfor-
> tunately, fell short by several inches. Orlando looked himself up and
> down in a long looking-glass, without showing any signs of discompo-
> sure, and went, presumably, to his bath.
>
> . . . Orlando had become a woman—there is no denying it. But in every
> other respect, Orlando remained precisely as he had been. The change
> of sex, though it altered their future, did nothing whatever to alter their
> identity. Their faces remained, as their portraits prove, practically the
> same. (138)

Orlando comically deflates the symbolic power and horror of the
sight of castration on which psychoanalysis builds its theory of sexual
difference. Orlando glances in the mirror "without showing any signs
of discomposure." Chastity, Purity, and Modesty throw "a garment
like a towel at the naked form which, unfortunately, fell short by
several inches." What is it that falls short by several inches? The referent of the pronoun "which" is ambiguous and suggests that the
narrative here parodically invokes the inadequacy of female genitalia
in the Oedipal narrative. Orlando's glance is a double rewriting: of
Freud's male child confronting in horror the sight of the female genitalia, and of Freud's "bisexual" girl confronting the inadequacy of

the different signifying pattern of the veil in Arab culture (its resistance to the scopic
drive) in Alloula's analysis.

[42]See, in particular, the chapter "Ayesha Unveils" in *She*. The burlesque quality of
Orlando's unveiling is more reminiscent of the scenes in Joyce's vaudevillian rendition
of sex changes in the Circean world of *Ulysses*. "Hide! Hide! Hide!" the three modest
sisters shout, like the witches in *Macbeth*, just as Bloom cheers on Boylan and Molly
("Show! Hide! Show!" [462]).

her own genitalia. Discussing Freud's notion of the bisexuality of the little girl, who begins life as a little boy, Luce Irigaray writes:

> All that remains is to assign her sexual function to this "little boy" with no penis, or at least no penis of any recognized value. Inevitably, the trial of "castration" must be undergone. This "little boy," who was, in all innocence and ignorance of sexual difference, *phallic*, notices how ridiculous "his" sex organ looks. "He" *sees* the disadvantage for which "he" is anatomically destined: "he" has only a tiny little sex organ, no sex organ at all, really, an almost invisible sex organ. . . . The humiliation of being so badly equipped, of cutting such a poor figure, in comparison with the penis, with *the* sex organ can only lead to a desire to "have something like it too," and Freud claims that this desire will form the basis for "normal womanhood." (48–49)[43]

Yet if Woolf mimes the unveiling of female sexuality, she refuses to replace the "truth" of phallocentric narrative with a corresponding "truth" of female sexuality. Although the narrator/biographer, always seeking a clarification that eludes him, announces that "Orlando had become a woman—there is no denying it," the truth of female sexuality is anything but plain, as is evident in the strain on the pronominal grammar of the sentences announcing the transformation: "We have no choice left but confess—*he* was a woman. . . . Orlando remained precisely as *he* had been. The change of sex, though it altered

---

[43]Irigaray describes Freud's narrative of the relationship of women to the mirror and to narcissism in the following way: "The flat mirror reflects the greater part of women's sexual organs only as a hole" (89n). Is this the "hole" in the manuscript big enough to put one's finger through? By comparing Irigaray's mimicry of Freud (in *Speculum of the Other Woman* [1974]) with Woolf's playful revision of sexual/textual orifices, I mean to suggest that "postmodernism" is a misnomer because much of the work associated with it is an extension of modernist concerns. Lest this comparison seem anachronistic, it is instructive to regard *Orlando* in relation to another satiric "biography," *Ladies Almanack*, published privately in 1928 by Djuna Barnes. Barnes's slim volume, like *Orlando*, was considered a *roman à clef*, of sorts—in Barnes's case, a mythopoeic biography of Natalie Barney and the mostly lesbian circle of women writers in Paris in the twenties. *Ladies Almanack* parodies the Freudian phallic economy in satiric terms similar to those of *Orlando* but with more explicit address: " 'And even at that, what have These Scriveners said of her [the woman of genius] but that she must have had a Testes of sorts, however wried and awander; that indeed she was called forth a Man, and when answering, by some Mischance, or monstrous Fury of Fate, stumbled over a Womb, and was damned then and forever to drag it about, like a Prisoner his Ball and Chain, whether she would or no. . . .' 'They cannot let her be, or proclaim her just good Distaff Stuff, but will admit her to sense through the masculine Door only' " (53).

their future, did nothing whatever to alter *their* identity" (137–38: emphasis added). Questions of mixed gender (apparent in the grammar) and sexuality remain. Despite the intervention of "Truth," obscurity still functions. Even though the narrator says summarily "the simple fact" was that "Orlando was a man till the age of thirty; when he became a woman and has remained so ever since" (139), what is figured in the moment of unveiling is a more androgynous fantasy of the elimination of the truth of sexual difference. Orlando, like Botticelli's Venus, reveals herself to the viewer's (and reader's) eye, the most "ravishing" and, in a sense, *complete* form in history: "His form combined in one the strength of a man and a woman's grace. As he stood there, the silver trumpets prolonged their note, as if reluctant to leave the lovely sight which their blast had called forth." As Francette Pacteau points out: "Androgyny cannot be circumscribed as belonging to some being; it is more a question of a relation between a look and appearance, in other words *psyche* and *image*. I do not encounter an 'androgyne' in the street; rather I encounter a figure whom I 'see as' androgynous" (62). Orlando is described only in terms of perceptions of her (those of the prurient muses, now themselves transformed into peeping Toms; the reader; Orlando, gazing at herself in the mirror).[44] The difference between the hermaphrodite and the androgyne, Pacteau says, is that the former is visible, combining male and female anatomical characteristics, whereas the latter exists in the realm of the imagination as clothed, masculinity and femininity both operating as masquerade (71–77). Woolf takes sexual difference out of the realm of the indicative, despite the narrator's assertions (Orlando is a woman), and into that of the subjunctive. Notwithstanding the apparent disrobing of the body, Orlando's image displays the instability of sexual difference to the viewer. The remainder of the novel focuses heavily on Orlando's clothes, her dress-up as one sex or the other (or in androgynous clothing, such as the gypsies wear), and the

[44]Drawing on the work of J.-B. Pontalis, Pacteau says: "To be assigned to one sex deprives one of the powers of the other and conjures up castration. The androgyne would represent the possession of both 'maternal and paternal phallus'; in disavowing the difference, both sexes regain their 'lost half' and the power that comes with it. Pontalis seems to propose a parallel route to the androgynous resolution for woman and man until he comes to the conclusion that 'The positive androgyne cannot exist outside myth. Incarnated, seen, it is effectively and simultaneously castrated man and woman' " (70). As I have suggested, Woolf narrativizes the myth of androgyny in an alternative "script" to Pontalis's Freud. See also Maria DiBattista's fine discussion of androgyny as comedy in *Virginia Woolf's Major Novels: The Fables of Anon.*

way in which both masculinity and femininity are historically constructed.[45]

Ironically, the narrator appeals to photographic representations of Orlando in order to establish that essentially he/she has not changed ("Their faces remained, as their portraits prove, practically the same"). Attempting to dispel confusion, the biographer "proves" instead that one cannot go behind the representation, the iconic image. *Orlando* is Woolf's only novel with photographs; it presents us with portraits of Orlando as male and female, which Woolf painstakingly chose, in consultation with Vita, from the Sackville-West family album of male and female ancestors. Beneath the persistent family resemblance, gender slides from masculine to feminine, thus creating an androgynous portrait—historically, male and female Sackvilles go into the making of Orlando.[46] (The caption, "Orlando as a boy," suggests this emphasis on his convertible appearance, simulating first one gender, then another.)

Thus the old love plot of the self and the other must be radically rewritten. The old plots—of castration (cutting off the noses) and chastity—are dismissed.

> In normal circumstances a lovely young woman alone would have thought of nothing else [but preserving her chastity]; the whole edifice of female government is based on that foundation stone; chastity is their jewel, their centre piece, which they run mad to protect, and die when ravished of. But if one has been a man for thirty years or so, and an Ambassador into the bargain . . . one does not perhaps give such a very great start about that. (153–54)

The new plot includes polymorphous desire, expressed in the attraction of Orlando to androgynous men and to other women—that is, to a set of "mirroring" lovers of both sexes. It is, however, within a female economy that this desire finds its representation.

---

[45]See Sandra Gilbert and Susan Gubar's discussion of Orlando's sex change as "a shift in fashion" (*Sexchanges*, 344).

[46]See the letters from Woolf to Sackville-West of October 30, 1927, and November 6, 1927 (in *Letters*, 3:434–35), which describe Woolf's efforts to assemble illustrations for the novel: she had Sackville ancestral portraits photographed, drew on extant photographs of Sackville-West and had Sackville-West pose for other photographs for the second part of the book.

And as all Orlando's loves had been women, now, through the culpable laggardry of the human frame to adapt itself to convention, though she herself was a woman, it was still a woman she loved; and if the consciousness of being of the same sex had any effect at all, it was to quicken and deepen those feelings which she had had as a man. (161)

Yet if the very possibility of this polymorphous sexuality burgeons with Orlando's experience in Turkey, first in the sex change and then in the androgynous life shared with the gypsies, still, Orlando returns to England. If the journey to Turkey epitomizes the excursive, fantastic nature of the imagination, what of Orlando's repatriation? I would suggest that as significant as the centrifugal movement in the trip to Turkey and the fantasy of multiple sexual possibilities is the centripetal movement staged in Orlando's return home and in the "conservation" of English literary tradition that it signals. It is partly this rootedness that lends itself to at least a questioning of textual/sexual subversions at play in the fantasy. As Van Den Abbeele postulates:

In order to be able to have an economy of travel, some fixed point of reference must be posited. The economy of travel requires an *oikos* (the Greek for "home" from which is derived "economy") in relation to which any wandering can be *comprehended* (enclosed as well as understood). In other words, a home(land) must be posited from which one leaves on the journey and to which one hopes to return—whether one actually makes it back home changes nothing, from this perspective. The positing of an *oikos*, or *domus* . . . is what domesticates the voyage by ascribing certain limits to it. (xvii–xviii)

As Van Den Abbeele says, this oikos is a feature of all travel, regardless of how figuratively the return trip occurs. Yet this suggestion of a conservation, of a bringing back to England the lessons learned abroad, is crucial to understanding the fulcrum that the Eastern journey provides in *Orlando*. This return, like the departure, involves the exigencies of the poetic imagination (and, ultimately, its troping of love). As in her last novel, *Between the Acts*, Woolf satirized, parodied, and revised the English literary tradition but still represented the inevitable confrontation between this patriarchal tradition and the woman poet. Orlando's return to England, a return that Rachel Vinrace cannot make for a number of reasons, signals the repatriation of the imagination, its domestication. By "domestic," I mean to suggest a particular (Coleridgean) Romantic ethos that figures the mating of the poetical genius with the *genius loci* of English nature. This tradition, as Geoffrey Hartman shows, domesticates the high Miltonic, excursive sublime in an accommodation "of the visionary temperament to an English milieu." In this poetic tradition, we find a "meditation on English landscape as alma mater—where landscape is storied England, its legends, history, and rural-reflective spirit" ("Romantic Poetry and the Genius Loci," 319). If radical freedom seems first imaginable outside England, ultimately there is something too nomadic about the East, its rootlessness emblematized by the gypsies with whom Orlando cavorts after being liberated from the patriarchal shackles of his diplomatic position. Unlimited freedom of movement has a negative side; Orlando discovers that the lack of attachment is inimical both to poetry and to intimacy of the kind the novel's androgynous pairings explore.[47]

Specifically, what Orlando discovers is the gypsies' resistance to figuration, a too literal, demystified view of nature that inhibits poetry. For as vexingly cluttered as the English tradition proved, in the world of the gypsies nothing attaches to anything else; everything is itself and nothing else—simile, metaphor (in short, figuration) are curtailed. It is not merely the particular English disease of the love of Nature, as the narrator describes it, that separates Orlando from the gypsies, but also the poetic imagination itself: "She [Orlando] likened the hills to ramparts, and the plains to the flanks of kine. . . . Everything, in fact, was something else" (143). Ironically, the trope of the East, traditionally the site of extravagant mystery and lavish figuration, now, in Orlando's sojourn with the gypsies, suggests a nightmare of literalization, of nature resistant to troping. Orlando, in contrast, returns to meditating on the nature of the imagination (in Romantic fashion, she considers whether beauty resides in "things themselves, or only in herself"[145]). The gypsies, whose freedom from materialism enables a total freedom of physical movement, nevertheless regard Orlando's poeticizing as evidence of a seditious (and antiutilitarian) restlessness of the spirit. For Orlando, nature is not self-

---

[47]Contrast this stance with that of Isabelle Eberhardt, the "passionate nomad" of the modern French tradition: "A nomad I was even when I was very small and would stare at the road, that white spellbinding road headed straight for the unknown . . . a nomad I will remain for life, in love with distant and uncharted places" (96). *Orlando* is placed in a decidedly comic English tradition; as Maria DiBattista points out, Orlando's return is implied in the pattern of comedy itself.

evident but potentially revelatory, mysterious. It is this view of nature (and, hence, of the material body) on which his poetic credo is formed, for the "truth" of poetry, too, is obscure, difficult, not obvious. Truth, as well as Candour and Honesty, we might remember from Orlando's mock unveiling, are "austere Gods" for poets as well as biographers. These gods yield their message clothed in figures of thought and speech. ("Obscurity," we are told early in the narrative, "wraps about a man like a mist; obscurity is dark, ample and free; obscurity lets the mind take its way unimpeded" [104].) It is not on the open plains of Turkey but in the peculiarly English weather, with its mists and clouds (one is reminded of the relation between nuance and *nuée*, or "cloud"), that Orlando's poetic vocation is nurtured. The oak tree, although solid and rooted, grows underground as well as above, its sinewy lines of connection hidden from view.

As Kate Trumpener has shown in an essay on the literary and cultural history of allegorical representations of the gypsies (as she points out, a particular form of orientalism), the gypsies have traditionally functioned as the type of perennial homelessness and freedom (exclusion) from history. This tradition is evident in Woolf's ambivalent representation in *Orlando*—they represent a longed-for freedom from the constraints of the West and yet a threat to history and narrative itself. For in this discourse, the gypsies represent a time-out from history and culture, a "timeless 'natural' culture" divided from "culture-bearing, narrative-bearing nations," Trumpener says (884); this old, old culture represents "transmission without 'tradition' " (860). Orlando realizes how recent is the culture of her own great English house during his/her sojourn with the gypsies, yet it is precisely the threat of falling outside time and tradition that impels Orlando and the narrative back to England. Trumpener notes that "everywhere the Gypsies appear in nineteenth-century narratives, they begin to hold up ordinary life, inducing local amnesias," a "time banditry" (869). We might regard Orlando's sojourn with the gypsies and subsequent return to England as a fascinating revision of the threat of Calypso to the adventurer. Orlando as woman must return to England and the genius loci of Romanticism for the narrative to record the history of the woman poet and her sexual/textual productions.[48]

---

[48]Although "holes" in the text occur before Orlando's travel to Turkey, the *lapsus* in the text surrounding Orlando's sex change is the most stunning example of textual evasion, of a gap in the fabric of the narrative. Michel de Certeau's description of the

This Romantic repatriation of the imagination that I describe seems similar in many ways to a conservative gesture, a chastening of the imagination in which it runs the risk of being redomesticated within the kinds of familiar patterns that threaten its annihilation.[49] Indeed, the potentially subversive possibilities of fantasy, as described by Rosemary Jackson, for example, would seem to suffer from such a reining in of desire. Does the turn back to English nature, the "alma mater," as Hartman describes it in gendered terms ("Romantic Poetry," 319), reinscribe the novel in a poetic tradition and in a Romantic sexual/textual politics that would cripple, rather than spur, the imagination? Furthermore, the completion of the poem "The Oak Tree" (a synecdoche, as Maria DiBattista puts it, for Orlando's country estate [113]) might seem to confirm an aristocratic relation between the poetic estate and the country estate, thus capitulating to the most conservative impulses of pastoral rootedness.

Yet Orlando's "homecoming" of the imagination is anything but cozy. She is forced to endure the reading of her new sexual identity, which, indeed, becomes a matter for the English courts. Orlando temporarily loses her estate and hides her manuscript—her sex change not only occasions her loss of property but drastically alters her relation to poetic inheritance as well. Like Lady Mary Wortley Montagu, who returned from Turkey in the early eighteenth century to encounter ridicule from the pen of Pope, Orlando must watch her step in the

---

function of the "primitive" in the writing of Western history is almost uncannily germane to this lapsus in Woolf's novel: "The profit 'brought back' through writing appears to delimit a 'remainder' which, although it is unwritten, will also define the primitive. . . . Léry's 'ravishments,' the Tupi festivals . . . are ephemeral and irrecoupable, unexploitable moments that will neither be regained nor redeemed. These moments rend holes in the fabric of the traveler's time, as if the Tupis' festive organization were beyond all economy of history" (*Writing of History*, 227).

[49]In *The Country and the City*, Raymond Williams traces the development of the literary genre of the pastoral, describing the original scene of Theocritus's pastoral as the landscape of the Greek islands and Egypt. As Williams shows, the pastoral was originally concerned with the work and days of the shepherd and goatherd, and with maintaining a connection with the "working year and with the real social conditions of country life" (16). *Orlando* taps this particular form of working-class pastoral in the vignette of Orlando's sojourn with the gypsies, but the narrative leaves this highly stylized view of "wildness" behind in favor of a more cultivated, English milieu. Trumpener points out the "chronotopically anachronistic role" of the gypsies, who are associated, as they are in much nineteenth-century literature, with an older form of pastoral (873). In the march through historical and literary styles in the narrative of *Orlando*, the gypsies function as just such an impediment to the progression of styles, anachronistic even in the seventeenth-century period of Orlando's travels.

age of Pope's rapier wit, flickering tongue ("like a lizard"), and flash-
ing eyes (*Orlando*, 209).[50] The biographer's treatment of Orlando in the
nineteenth century almost skips the period of Romanticism (presumably more congenial to Orlando's art) and focuses on Victorian domesticity, replete with the ideology of the angel-in-the-house that
threatens the pen of the woman writer.

Orlando's repatriation illustrates more than the hostile climate encountered by a woman writer; it represents a revisionary Romanticism. Woolf tries nothing less than to rewrite the Romantic marriage
of genius loci and poetic genius, with a woman writer in the latter
role, a woman whose ties to the aesthetic traditions are highly problematic. For the generative powers of the Romantic imagination, its
Coleridgean rootedness in the "genial spirit," is gendered male. Indeed, the Indo-European root of "geniality," "genius," "gender," and
"genre" is "gen," which means, "to beget," a male function.[51] Yet
Orlando completes and publishes her poem (as well as giving birth
to a son). The final sections end on a note of the domestic sublime, in
which a kind of grace descends on the language of poetry, as Orlando
continues her struggle to express her sense of attachment to the objects
she loves. Out of the helter-skelter furnishings of the mind (" 'What
a phantasmagoria the mind is and meeting-place of dissemblables' "
[176]), Orlando tries to "fabricate" something that mirrors her deepest
attachments. Sitting by the oak tree ("She liked to attach herself to
something hard" [324]), Orlando redomesticates her imagination, but
with a difference.

> Was not writing poetry a secret transaction, a voice answering a voice?
> . . . What could have been more secret, she thought, more slow, and like
> the intercourse of lovers, than the stammering answer she had made all
> these years to the old crooning song of the woods, and the farms and
> the brown horses standing at the gate, neck to neck, and the smithy and
> the kitchen and the fields, so laboriously bearing wheat, turnips, grass,
> and the gardens blowing irises and fritillaries? (325)

[50]Indeed, Lady Mary Wortley Montagu might be another source behind Woolf's representation of Orlando's ambassadorship, since Edward Wortley Montagu held an ambassadorship to Turkey during roughly the period of Orlando's tenure there.

[51]Christine Brooke-Rose discusses the representation of genius in the Western tradition: "The really mysterious creative force, however, is genius. . . . Plato called it divine madness, Longinus called it ecstasy . . . the Romantics Imagination but also Genius.
And whatever the name it belongs to man" (*Stories, Theories, and Things*, 255).

Poetry is "a voice answering a voice"—this echoing voice is that of both nature and the "self-same" lover, voices that reflect Orlando to herself. The final ecstatic moment (" 'Ecstasy!' she cried, 'ecstasy!' " [327]) in which Orlando "produces" the name of her lover (" 'Marmaduke Bonthrop Shelmerdine!' she cried, standing by the oak tree. The beautiful, glittering name fell out of the sky like a steel blue feather" [327]) refigures Romantic sublimity. One might think here of another modernist, Gertrude Stein, who imagined poetry as an embrace in language: "Anybody knows how anybody calls out the name of anybody one loves. And so that is poetry really loving the name of anything and that is not prose" (232). Shelmerdine is for Orlando what she has always already known, as she is for him; yet the "otherness" of this self-same lover, figured by travel, suggests that the "self-same" (to return to Irigaray's term) brings something different to the lover from abroad. Orlando's name means to Shel "a ship in full sail coming with the sun on it proudly sweeping across the Mediterranean from the South Seas," and he (a captain) has a name that is a "wild, dark-plumed name—a name which had in her mind, the steel blue gleam of rooks' wings . . . the snake-like twisting descent of their feathers in a silver pool" (250–51).

At the end of the novel, it is 1928; in these modern times, Shel descends in an airplane to Orlando—ironically, the woman who waits. She remembers the words of the gypsy who admonished her love of her patriarchal inheritance (" 'What do you need with four hundred bedrooms and silver lids on all the dishes, and housemaids dusting?' " [326]). Woolf does not negate the property struggles of her poet-protagonist, the agony of (female) Orlando fighting to retain her relation to her inheritance, as Sackville-West tried to do (indeed, in fiction, Woolf reinstates Vita's rightful inheritance). Culture is not elided in the round-trip journey of the narrative; rather, the voyage out enables a return to the scene of home in which home itself is transformed by the return of Shakespeare's sister, the survivor. For in this representation of a woman writer (unlike that in *A Room of One's Own*), Orlando is a poet with both "world enough and time." I have tried to show that, as excursive and fantastic as Orlando's imagination is, Woolf represents the necessity both of confronting one's "inheritance" and of transforming it through new paradigms of female desire.

5

Postmodern
"Vessels of Conception":
Brooke-Rose and Brophy

Penelope's Voyage ends with the trope and plot of the journey in post-modern experimental fiction. Christine Brooke-Rose's novel *Between* (1968) and Brigid Brophy's *In Transit* (1969) are prime examples of the scandalous, "writerly" text hypothesized by Roland Barthes in *S/Z* (1970): "What would be the narrative of a journey in which it was said that one stays somewhere without having departed—in which it was never said that, having departed, one arrives or fails to arrive? Such a narrative would be a scandal, the extenuation, by hemorrhage, of readerliness" (105). Indeed, they anticipate his hypothetical conjecture about a new kind of narrative based on the trope of the journey. These multilinguistic narratives, which, as their titles suggest, thematize travel and translation, present both narratives *of* and narratives *as* journeys severed from origin and *telos*. In other words, these particular novels thematize, in their travel plots, their own experiments with the traditional shape of the journey that underwrites the trajectory of many classic narratives. In the discontinuities and gaps of their own narratives, Brooke-Rose and Brophy do not reject the crucial role of narrative and narrative journey but propose, with Barthes, a new logic for it.

Barthes identifies what he calls the "readerly" text, that is, classic realist narrative, as based on the model of a well-plotted journey, a traditional sequence of events of which he says: "To depart/to travel/to arrive/to stay: the journey is saturated" (105). Like a well-guided tour, this type of narrative leads the reader from place to place, establishing an illusion of continuity in the fullness of its presentation: "To end, to fill, to join, to unify—one might say this is the basic requirement of the *readerly,* as though it were prey to some obsessive fear: that of omitting a connection. Fear of forgetting engenders the appearance of a logic of actions; terms and the links between them are posited (invented) in such a way that they unite, duplicate each other, create an illusion of continuity. . . as if the *readerly* abhors a vacuum" (105). In contrast, the "writerly" text is a "scandal," a "hemorrhage," language that suggests the violation or wounding from within of the classic text, thus destroying its "logic of actions." This text disseminates meaning rather than fixing it in place. This journey without origin or telos thus serves as Barthes's paradigm for a psychological freedom from the compulsion and anxiety betrayed in the figure of the "saturated" journey as sequentially plotted. The journey now funds an optimistic theorizing of a narrative mobility that, unlike conventional narrative, does not circumscribe the movement of desire and free play. According to Barthes, there are pleasures, for writer and reader, in the discontinuities and silences of this "writerly" text.[1]

Published two years before the French publication of *S/Z*, Brooke-Rose's novel anticipates Barthes's new kind of narrative journey, with its break from the logic of beginning, middle, and end. This is not surprising, given Brooke-Rose's own dual vocation as theorist and novelist. An international phenomenon herself, born in Geneva, the daughter of an English father and a half-Swiss, half-American mother, Brooke-Rose has lived in France since 1968 and taught at the experimental Vincennes campus of the University of Paris. She is one of the few contemporary English writers thoroughly "at home" with Continental theory, which her essays and fiction perspicaciously address. In her critical writings and interviews, she refers approvingly to Barthes's notion of the writerly as privileged over the readerly. In her own description of realism in *A Rhetoric of the Unreal,* based on the account of the French critic Philippe Harmon, she analyzes it as a kind of saturation. She says that realist texts deploy two strategies that are sometimes contradictory: the circulation of a great deal of information and a readability and clearness that depend on "semiotic compensa-

---

[1] This is not the place for airing my reservations about Barthes's basic binary schema, which seems to characterize types of reading rather than offer a typology of texts. My point in setting Barthes's model against and with Brooke-Rose's own project is to show her position vis-à-vis French poststructuralist theory. For a helpful discussion of Barthes's model, see Kaja Silverman, "Re-Writing the Classic Text," chapter 6 of *The Subject of Semiotics.*

tion," that is, a variety of ways to make meaningful the load of information. In Brooke-Rose's description of her own experimental style in *Between*, the journey figures a freedom from conventional syntax, an errancy or wandering that resembles Barthes's general idea of the writerly: "The syntax of *Between* is free-ranging in that a sentence can start in one place or time, continue correctly, but by the end of the sentence one is elsewhere" (*Stories, Theories, and Things,* 7). Syntax engages in transgressive travel in an unpredictable trajectory, a metonymic slide from here to there that produces a sense of random movement rather than purposeful direction.[2] In an interview in the *Edinburgh Review*, Brooke-Rose represents the experimentalism of her style in terms of an exploration that is not a quest but a magical and pleasurable crossing of boundaries. As a writer she finds herself "on the frontier of something and I must twist language in some way to pass the frontier, and that's the pleasure" (Turner, 31). The pleasure of the text resides in (or, more properly, lambently circulates in) a style that could pass the electronic screening at the airport, a sly smuggling across conventional borders.

In lieu of a "saturated" narrative journey, the entirely present-tense narration in *Between* offers reiterated passages of dialogue and description in several European languages (with English the hegemonic medium). The narrative settles on the European travels of an unnamed female translator of French and German parentage who "travel[s] in simultaneous interpretation" (408, 494), translating mostly from French to German. Narrative continuity is replaced by replays and repetitions, with iterated scenes generally not clearly marked as having *taken place*, either temporally or spatially. We hear a dialogue about annulment: a marriage is inferred. One hotel room, one plane ride, one lover blends into another. Informational or semantic gaps occur to disrupt the logic of narrative continuity.

---

[2]In an excellent article on Brooke-Rose's fiction, Robert Caserio discusses the burdens this kind of free play places on the reader, who has to run to keep up with the hectic and unexpected trajectory of the narrative: "The xorandoric text needs a reader who is critically hyperactive. He who runs may not read any longer, unless he runs and reads with an unparalleled quickness to catch up with and catch hold of meanings that are rigorous and self-contradictory, determinate and indeterminate, at crucial points" (293). In speaking of the "hectic mobility" of this type of contemporary fiction, Caserio uses Brooke-Rose's own term, "xorandoric," which refers to semantic disjunctions and incoherences more than to the kind of syntactic displacements described in Brooke-Rose's statement above. *Between* relies on both syntactic errancies and semantic gaps of the sort Barthes describes to create a dizzying dislocation in the reader.

The most persistent scene is the inside of a plane en route to one of many European and, occasionally, Asian cities. The novel begins:

> Between the enormous wings the body of the plane stretches its one hundred and twenty seats or so in threes on either side towards the distant brain way up, behind the dark blue curtain and again beyond no doubt a little door. In some countries the women would segregate still to the left of the aisle, the men less numerous to the right. But all in all and civilisation considered the chromosomes sit quietly mixed among the hundred and twenty seats or so that stretch like ribs as if inside a giant centipede. Or else, inside the whale, who knows, three hours, three days of maybe hell. Between doing and not doing the body floats. (395)

The travelers go places but seem to exist in a limbo of movement and disorientation, traveling, but caught—like Eliot's hollow men, like Jonah in the whale—in an interstitial "between" of time and space ("Between the dawn and the non-existent night the body stretches out its hundred and twenty ribs or so towards the distant brain way up beyond the yellow curtain" [404]). "Welcome aboard this vessel of conception floating upon a pinpoint and kindly sit quietly ensconced in your armchairs, the women to the left of the aisle the men less numerous to the right" (442). The plane is a vehicle of transportation, a vehicle of metaphor (the "vessel of conception") that translates us from one place to another: "Beyond the wooden shutters and way down below the layered floors of stunned consciousnesses waking dreams nightmares lost senses of locality the cars hoot faintly poop-pip-poop the trams tinkle way down below in the grand canyon and an engine revs up in what, French German Portuguese" (396–97). In her collection of essays, Brooke-Rose describes her conception of the novel in a Jamesian "metastory": "The I/central consciousness/non-narrating narrative voice/ is a simultaneous interpreter who travels constantly from congress to conference and whose mind is a whirl of topics and jargons and foreign languages/whose mind is a whirl of worldviews, interpretations, stories, models, paradigms, theories, languages" (*Stories, Theories, and Things*, 6–7).

There are references in the novel to the "freedom of the air" and the "inebriating attractions as the body floats in willing suspension of loyalty to anyone" (461), that is, to the liberating possibilities of such constant airplane travel, but the "intended effect" of the mobile, hectic style and plot, she goes on to say in the above passage, is "mimetic realism—in brief, perpetual motion in my central consciousness, and loss of identity due to her activity" (7). Brooke-Rose, who often cautions her readers against searching for authorial "intention," even the one the author hands you on a plate, serves up a metastory that, in its appeal to mimetic realism, partially tames the "scandal" of the writing. The errant style mimics the theme of anomie and rootlessness (see Herbert, 73), a modern condition, which in the "now" of the writing (1968) is replaced by the banality of late capitalism, the global hegemony of mass culture that turns one European place into another. Like the official voice of the pilot and cabin crew, which originates in some "distant brain" and is amplified over the loudspeaker system, the detached, dispassionate narrative voice announces flatly that "air and other such conditioning . . . prevent any true exchange of thoughts"(399), as the body floats in "this great pressurized solitude" (406).

Translation becomes the central metaphor for the general loss of place in this global village. Despite the disorienting effect of the different languages on the reader and at times on the main character, the rapid language changes in the text suggest an almost frightening fluency of scene, dialogue, character, and relationship. The bilingual interpreter becomes the symptom of this frightening fluency; like the phrases passing through the microphones of simultaneous translation, she herself is a translatable sign. We are meant to hear the double meanings in the phrase "Bright girl, she translates beautifully don't you think? Says the boss" (414). The French/German translator crosses national borders, geographical and linguistic, with such facility and frequency that "home" and the destinations of travel cease to be oppositional—there is always something alien about home and something familiar in the foreign locations.[3] In her "metastory," Brooke-Rose insists that this travel is particularly gendered—the female body transported across national boundaries is also the sign of a passive identity which circulates so freely across boundaries that it loses its

---

[3]Brophy's *In Transit*, published in 1969, also uses air travel as the quintessential metaphor for twentieth-century culture: "I adopt the international airport idiom for my native. Come, be my world-oyster" (28). The narrator accepts the way the pure products of postmodern jet-age culture collapse the foreign into the familiar: "This airport was the happy ape of all other airports. Its display case cased and displayed the perfumes of Arabia and of Paris, packaged in the style to which they have become acCustomed [sic] through the universal Excise of capital letters and full stops in the typography. Every artifact in sight excited me, raised me towards tip-toe. None was everyday. All were exotic. Yet nothing chilled or alienated me, since nothing was unfamiliar. The whole setting belonged to *my* century" (26).

own distinctiveness. In *Stories, Theories, and Things*, Brooke-Rose describes her own false start with the novel, in which the interpreter was conceived as "androgynous."[4] These pages, she tells us, were abandoned when she realized that translation figured a particularly (although not exclusively) "feminine" experience. As she puts it, the novel is entangled "with the notion/imagined experience/theory/ story that simultaneous interpretation is a passive activity, that of translating the ideas of others but giving voice to none of one's own, and therefore a feminine experience" (7). Successful translation signals a loss of identity; the translator becomes a conduit, like the microphone that is the tool of her trade.

This oxymoronic sense of travel as a routine disorientation contrasts sharply with the exciting potential signified by the airplane in Woolf's writing—in *Mrs. Dalloway*, for example, where it figures, as Gillian Beer says, " 'free will' and ecstasy, silent, erotic and absurd" (145), or in *Orlando*, where Shelmerdine's descent in a plane suggests "the free spirit of the modern age" (145). The sense of translation as weary work contrasts as well with the foreign language as a refreshment of the mother tongue, just as it functions for Miriam Henderson as she gazes at a Continental newspaper on her trip to Switzerland in Dorothy Richardson's *Oberland*: "The simple text was enthralling. For years she had not so delighted in any reading. . . . Everything she had read stood clear in her mind that yet, insufficiently occupied with the narrative and its strange emanations, caught up single words and phrases and went off independently touring, climbing to fresh arrangements and interpretations of familiar thought" (58). Brooke-Rose presents a more jaundiced, post–World War II view of the possibilities of discovery and escape, a view that echoes Susan Sontag's description of the symptomatic cultural condition of modernity in her influential essay "The Aesthetics of Silence," published in 1967, an essay Brooke-Rose quotes extensively and approvingly in "Eximplosions," her chapter on modernity in *A Rhetoric of the Unreal*.

> In an overpopulated world being connected by global electronic communication and jet travel at a pace too rapid and violent for an organically sound person to assimilate without shock, people are also suffering from a revulsion at any further proliferation of speech and images. Such

---

[4]In a letter to me, Brooke-Rose specified that this false start consisted of about twenty pages (letter to author, August 5, 1992).

different factors as the unlimited "technological reproduction" and near universal diffusion of printed language and speech as well as images . . . and the degeneration of public language within the realms of politics, advertising and entertainment, have produced, especially among the better-educated inhabitants of modern mass society, a devaluation of language.

Art, Sontag suggests, "becomes a kind of counterviolence, seeking to loosen the grip upon consciousness of the habits of lifeless, static verbalization" (Sontag, 64–65).

Brooke-Rose describes Sontag's essay on modern art as a "still remarkable, elegant essay, in many ways a proleptic summary of much that has been said since" (*Rhetoric of the Unreal*, 343–44) and endorses her assessment that a loss of authenticity is experienced in the modern condition. Much as Dean MacCannell in his now classic study *The Tourist* identifies the tourist as an emblem of modern man in search of authenticity in the face of the discontinuities and alienations of modern society, Brooke-Rose envisions her translator/traveler as caught in a limbolike transit, in which she yearns to submit to something when "belief" itself is suspended.

> The body stretches forth towards some thought some order some command obeyed in the distant brain way up or even an idea that actually means something compels a passion or commitment lost or ungained yet as the wing spreads to starboard motionless on the still blue temperature of minus fifty-one degrees, the metal shell dividing it from this great pressurised solitude. The body floats in a quiet suspension of belief and disbelief, the sky grows dark over the chasms of the unseen Pyrenees. (*Between*, 405–6)

What are we to make of this seeming paradox in Brooke-Rose's address to travel, the contradiction, that is, between travel in the novel as a figure for rootlessness and disappointed yearning, a diagnosis of a contemporary condition, and her descriptions of experimental writing as a new and free kind of writerly narrative journey? And how can one reconcile the way the multilinguistic passages in the text of *Between* mimic a disorientation and loss of identity and also provide the nourishments of a Continental, experimental style? Does the experimentalism of the style represent a "postmodernist" fiddling while Europe burns?

The answer to the final question, I believe, is no; indeed, through the trope and plot of travel and translation, Brooke-Rose subverts the possibility of the kind of insouciant dismissal associated with at least one major version of postmodernism, which sees it as a break from modernist anxiety and a ludic acceptance of the anomie modernism helped to diagnose.[5] Brooke-Rose's novel helps us rethink the abstract theorizing of the mobility of desire expressed by Barthes and even Brooke-Rose herself in the description of her style; it engages the problematic of postmodern circulations and represents mobility as specifically charactered and historicized, with cultural pains and pleasures written into it.[6] The novel thus motivates a significant reappraisal of postmodernism's supposed break with modernism and its subversions, as Linda Hutcheon puts it, "of such principles as value, order, meaning, control, and identity . . . that have been the basic premise of bourgeois liberalism" (13). Brooke-Rose's novel demonstrates a self-critical form of radical experimentation that ultimately refuses this kind of dismissal.[7]

For despite the hectic mobility of both her style and her female traveler, Brooke-Rose provides checkpoints in the fluid movement across boundaries; despite its use of the present tense and abandonment of temporal sequence, *Between* nevertheless produces its "present" moment in relation to a specific European geography and history.

[5]For the fullest and most interesting statement of this change in tone and attitude between modernism and postmodernism, see Alan Wilde's *Horizons of Assent*. For my critique of this approach, see my review of Wilde's book in *Novel*.

[6]See Leo Bersani and Ulysse Dutoit's *Forms of Violence: Narrative in Assyrian Art and Modern Culture* for an antinarrative theory that privileges art that represents the "pleasurable movement" of desire and meaning (105) and Caserio's critique of Bersani in his excellent discussion of Brooke-Rose in "Mobility and Masochism: Christine Brooke-Rose and J. G. Ballard."

[7]In a critique of Ihab Hassan's definitional distinctions between modernism and postmodernism, Brooke-Rose objects to the oppositional structure of his paradigm as much as to the overly broad and simplified categories she discovers in much theorizing of the postmodern: "I find both terms peculiarly unimaginative for a criticism that purports to deal with phenomena of which the most striking feature is imagination, and I shall use them only when discussing critics who use them. For one thing, they are purely historical, period words, and in that sense, traditional" ("Eximplosions," 344). In recent years Brooke-Rose has come to identify her own experimentalism with postmodernism and does make use of the term. Still, her novels, including *Between*, explore the continuity between modernist and postmodernist literature, destroying the neat divisions hypothesized by many theorists. In *Constructing Postmodernism* (which I read after this chapter was written) Brian McHale categorizes *Between* as a modernist novel with a "postmodernist undertow" (215).

The series of displacements through travel paradoxically maps a European place of inescapable historical self-discovery. Brooke-Rose reminds us of the constraints, political and literary, that European history imposes on postmodernism. In terms of the "political," I refer specifically to the way the novel's displacements fix on the nameless translator's movements during World War II, when she is caught in Germany by accident (due to an attack of appendicitis while visiting her fraternal aunt) and begins to translate for the Germans. In arranging and rearranging the border crossings and shifting loyalties of her traveling French/German protagonist, Brooke-Rose creates a palimpsest: the blasé travel of the 1960s, from European capital to capital, illuminates the different border crossings during World War II. Random movements and arbitrary excursions raise questions of loyalty, affiliation, and national identity. Customs agents demanding declarations at the borders signal checkpoints in this flux: "Please declare if you have any plants or parts of plants with you such as love loyalty lust intellect belief of any kind or even simple enthusiasm for which you must pay duty to the Customs and Excise until you come to a standstill" (414). This voice is both frightening and inspiring—it evokes the specter of duty, both a price exacted for all this unlimited circulation and a possibly useful demand for an accounting of obligation and commitment. Writing on an earlier version of customs in Hawthorne's "The Custom-House," which prefaces *The Scarlet Letter*, Brooke-Rose calls the customshouse "a public, institutional place, a place of law and order, where custom and excise must be paid on goods (on pleasure, as cost). It is a threshold. The threshold of narrative" (*Stories, Theories, and Things*, 48).

The history that constrains is, however, literary as well as political, for in superimposing a postmodern internationalism on an earlier, more frightening wartime European geography, Brooke-Rose invokes the inescapable inheritance of modernism, an international phenomenon forced by the events of both world wars to revise its assumption that nationalism was something to be outgrown.[8] The multilinguistic resources of avant-garde experimentalism that sustain Eliot's and Pound's modernist poetry and postmodern novels such as those of Brooke-Rose and Brophy are regarded in *Between* in the light of lin-

---

[8]Reed Way Dasenbrock's Modern Language Association (MLA) paper "Anatomies of Internationalism in *Tarr* and *Howards End*" offers a lively and important discussion of nationalism and internationalism in the related contexts of 1992 and 1912.

guistic hegemony and domination. (Brooke-Rose wrote most of her novel while staying at the castle of Ezra Pound's daughter in the Italian Tirol, where she returned, soon after finishing the novel, to write *A ZBC of Ezra Pound* [see Turner, 22]; Pound's role in Brooke-Rose's thinking is beyond the scope of this chapter, but it is crucial to these issues of how nationalism and internationalism are imbricated in twentieth-century experimental writing.) In addressing the legacy of Eliot and Pound, Brooke-Rose acknowledges postmodernism's debt to modernism and exposes the anxiety of influence in postmodernism's claim to break with its own modernist history, revealing this claim as a kind of travel, a defense against the pull of a certain literary "home." Brooke-Rose's postmodernist "vessel of conception" deliberately, and self-consciously retains the genetic material of modernism.[9]

Thus, despite the freewheeling style and protagonist of *Between*, ideas of placement and mobility, commitment and translatability are deeply touched by the war and its allegiances. The easy availability of European pop culture of the 1960s, constructed from the jargon of advertising, is juxtaposed with the darker memories of the war. Unpleasantly surprised by a waiter or chambermaid who invades the refuge of the hotel room, postwar travelers confront "the fear of something else not ordered" (401), an image of those ambivalently haunted by fear of submission and by fear of nothing to submit to. These postmodern ambivalences are textured and colored, one begins to see, by the memories of war and the forms that order and submission took within it. The postwar mobility and translatability of the unnamed protagonist are fixed (though not through any traditional narrative exposition or even flashback) in a particular bilingualism. The Berlitz-like passages of French and German, which blend with other lines of

---

[9]Brooke-Rose's novel often echoes Eliot's poetry of the twenties, such as *The Waste Land* and *The Hollow Men*, particularly in its insistent litany of "betweens" ("Between doing and not doing the body floats" [395], or as one character says, "We live between ideas, nicht wahr?" [413]). This cadence of the "between" conveys an Eliotic feeling of interstitiality, a sense of waiting for *chronos*, or "ordinary time," to be transformed into *kairos*, or "time redeemed." How to discover the sacred in the detritus of culture—this, the question of both Eliot and Pound—recurs in *Between*. "The gods have left this land says Siegfried now the boss" (431), the jaded former German soldier and past lover of the translator. Near the end of the novel, the anonymous translator and Bertrand, an aging French suitor who writes love letters to her, discuss Eliot's poetry. He asks if she has ever read Eliot's poem "La figlia che piange," which reminds him of her, and he quotes some of its lines. She has only heard of Eliot: "He wrote something called The Waste Land didn't he?" (548–49). "Tired of your still point?" Siegfried taunts the translator when she announces her plans to sell her domestic refuge in Wiltshire.

serviceable tourist discourse in other languages (that of menus, advertisements, airport entrances, exits, restrooms), begin to resonate with the differences of their histories, forming both the personal past of the German-French translator and a historical consciousness in the text.

We learn that at the outbreak of war, the girl was trapped in Germany with her father's relatives by accident. Two particular scenes in Germany haunt the narrative: one set in 1946, after the liberation of Germany and the zoning of Berlin, when the girl works in the French Zone and meets an English airman, whom she marries; the other, an earlier war scene in which she is drafted by the Germans into the press supervisory division of the foreign office after she is stranded in Germany. "You must excuse these questions Fräulein but in view of your French upbringing we must make sure of your undivided loyalty let us see now until the age of Herr Oberstleutnant at that age one has no loyalties" (444). In this context, the passivity of "translating beautifully" is implicated in larger ethical questions of compliance during the war.

Under the powerful umbrella of English, languages conduct a romance and engage in intercultural travel, just as the translator moves from German to British lover: "Husbands lovers wives mistresses of many nationalities . . . help to abolish the frontiers of misunderstanding with frequent changes of partners loyalties convictions, free and easily stepping over the old boundaries of conventions, congresses, commissions, conferences to which welcome back Liebes" (437). The fraternization of and in tourist phrases leaves the traces of history, "as if words fraternised silently beneath the syntax, finding each other funny and delicious in a Misch-Masch of tender fornication, inside the bombed out hallowed structures and the rigid steel glass modern edifices of the brain. Du, do you love me?" (447). The postmodern brain is an architectural palimpsest, the skyscraper rising phoenixlike from the ashes of war. Even the Vichy mineral water so repeatedly ordered and not ordered in the text contains the memory of Vichy complicity. The postwar OMO (cleanser) slogan "whiter than white" is grafted onto an allusion to a Persil-Schein certificate, a reference former Nazis would buy after the war to prove that they had never been Nazis at heart. The narrative does not cleanse the traces of war.

Brooke-Rose's own wartime activity as a decoder and analyzer of codes is "translated" into the figure of the nameless translator and her experience of World War II. During the war, Brooke-Rose worked

for "Ultra," a unit of the British Intelligence Service that helped de-
cipher and analyze German radio messages. Enemy codes were
cracked on a machine called "Enigma," which was based on "three
operational rotors which could be taken out and rearranged, each with
26 letters: this allowed milliards of combinations to be obtained" (Garlinski, 173). Using devices known as "bombes," the decoders would
explore "electro-mechanically (not electronically) a range of alternative possibilities at speeds far beyond the pace of human thought. In
practical terms, what the bombes did has been defined as 'to test all
the possible wheel or rotor orders of the Enigma, all the possible
wheel settings and plug or Stecker connections to discover which of
the possible arrangements would match a prescribed combination of
letters' " (Lewin, 123). Brooke-Rose's acquaintance with such procedures helps us understand a sense of urgency that underlies the postmodern mobility of meaning in the text. Despite the drone of
conference jargon, the connection between word games and war
games and between translations and crisis emerges.

Yet from this short sketch one can see that Brooke-Rose's own wartime loyalties were far less equivocal than the interpreter's. The gestures and mechanics of simultaneous translations are themselves
"translated" from Brooke-Rose's own role as decoder into the interpreter's less fixed position. "I never put myself directly into novels, I
find that boring," Brooke-Rose said in an interview. "So I turn personal experience into metaphor" (Turner, 26). Perhaps the stable
allegiances of Brooke-Rose's own wartime practice of translation
seemed too determinant, too clearcut to supply a metaphor for the
confusions and displacements that make "war like a post-modern
text."[10] I would argue, however, that Brooke-Rose's exploration of
chance, randomness, accident in her text directly relates to the special
significance that the novel claims for the *gendering* of travel and translation. For drift, chance, and passivity, symptomatic of the workings
of history, might offer a new technology of narrative, an alternative
to masculine teleological paradigms: "The same question everywhere
goes unanswered have you anything to declare any plants or parts of
plants growing inside you stifling your strength with their octopus
legs undetachable for the vacuum they form over each cell, clamping
each neurone of your processes in a death-kiss while the new Lord

[10]I am indebted to my colleague Robert Caserio for this notion.

Mayor of Prague promises to take up the challenge in trying to make you commit yourself to one single idea" (413).

The "vessel of conception," the narrative vehicle of transplant and translation, is here figured as a *female* body, and the question is, Can it bear a new idea about history, direction, and destination that is different from either the masculine singleness of purpose and certain destination of the "Lord Mayor" or the jaded opportunism of Siegfried, who tries to manipulate the female translator's sense of drift in order to seduce her? "We merely translate other people's ideas, not to mention platitudes, si-mul-ta-né-ment. No one requires us to have any of our own. . . . —Du liebes Kind, komm, geh' mit mir. Gar schöne Spiele spiel' ich mit dir [Dear child, come with me I'll play very good games with you]" (413). This sinister allusion to Goethe's "Erlkönig" reveals a dark underside to the notion of play, suggesting both seduction and death. Although Brooke-Rose's own loyalties during the war were clearly established, her novel explores the pleasures and dangers of chance occurrence and its role in the process of charting one's course. The similarities between German and English lovers and the telescoping of wartime experiences with pre- and postwar experiences puncture a simplistic view of ideological choice, while the narrative still insists on establishing distinctions.

As I have noted, in her metastory Brooke-Rose insists that the passivity of circulation and translation in the novel is linked to the gender of the protagonist: "It was a cliché, which was nevertheless true enough generally (like all clichés) for the purpose of creating the language of the novel and getting, as I. A. Richards used to say, the 'tone' right" (*Stories, Theories, and Things*, 7). This cliché launches the narrative, but through dislocations of both protagonist and style, Brooke-Rose explores possible alternatives to the clichés of masculine aggression and feminine passivity played out in so many ways in twentieth-century discourse. "Between doing and not doing the body floats," the narrator drones, thus suggesting a middle ground, a middle voice, between passivity and activity. The forays in the novel exit somewhere between action and inaction, accident and purpose.

In *The Writing of the Disaster* (1980), Maurice Blanchot addresses the fate of representation after the Holocaust: "The disaster: break with the star, break with every form of totality, never denying, however, the dialectical necessity of a fulfillment; the disaster: prophecy which announces nothing but the refusal of the prophetic as simply an event to come, but which nonetheless opens, nonetheless discovers the patience of vigilant language" (75; see also Blanchot's exploration of passivity, 14–18). In his insistence on rejecting totality yet retaining a sense of urgency—in using the vocabulary of prophecy while refusing prophecy—and in his emphasis on "vigilant language," Blanchot meshes with Brooke-Rose's method and tone in *Between*. Rejecting the type of totalizing mastery that she associates with masculine hubris, she translates passivity into the patience of vigilant language in a stylistic practice that is both modest and bold. Brooke-Rose says of her work: "Modern philosophy talks a lot about the desire and illusion of mastery. But I never feel that, that's more connected with what has been called the totalising novel, which imposes some kind of global meaning on the reality it describes. . . . My experience has been more one of groping inside language and forms" (Turner, 31).

This "groping inside language and forms," this combination of linguistic risk and vigilance, leads to a style in which "small changes" in often repeated phrases in the narrative subtly suggest the possibility of changes in the plot. Buried amid iterated passages of dialogue are references to such facts as the translator has decided to sell her Wiltshire cottage or to buy a car—these unobtrusive alterations in domicile and transportation are the means by which the circularity of the writing, its beginning and ending in the same linguistic "place" ("Between the enormous wings the body floats"), is amended.

Throughout *Between* one hears the refrain, "What difference does it make?" This reiterated question is meant to burden structuralist and poststructuralist theories of meaning in language with the weight of political implication and consequence. "The vaporetto bumps against the jetty of Santa Maria di Salute at the mouth of the Grand Canal that gives out on to the wider waters between San Marco and the unanswered question which remains unanswered for the non-existent future unless perhaps what difference does it make" (556). The novel checks its own acceptance of the unlimited circulation of language. On the one hand, the narrative seems to endorse the metadiscourse of poststructuralist theory it includes, the iterated and freely circulating jargon and "codes" of conferences and commissions—biological, semiological, semantic, Lacanian. A passage in English and in French from a semiology conference on Saussurean difference emphasizes the arbitrariness and self-enclosure of the language system: "As for example in a dictionary each apparently positive definition contains words which themselves need defining. Et tous les dictionnaires prouvent qu'il n'y a jamais de sens propre, jamais d'objectivité d'un terme [And all the dictionaries prove that there is never a literal meaning, never the objectivity of a term]" (562). This sense of circularity is exacerbated by the easy commerce between French and English. The writing in *Between* accepts this post-Saussurean, poststructuralist position. The novel, like other poststructuralist fiction and nonfiction, is "about" the circulation of signs as much as it is "about" the travel and displacements of the nameless translator and her colleagues.

Yet, on the other hand, in representing the circulation of signifiers in her text, Brooke-Rose shows how small adjustments of and in language make a difference. The notion that language is an arbitrary, closed system does not obviate the possibility, even the necessity, of vigilant language of the kind Blanchot describes. The change from "Idlewilde Airport" to "Kennedy Airport" one hundred pages later is one example of such attention, a subtle reminder of the violent events of the 1960s that produced this change in nomenclature. Brooke-Rose's particular "technology" of the "distant brain" shows how small adjustments in the codes of language have historical, personal, and political consequences.

Thus, even cynicism self-destructs as a confident and fixed position, finding itself vulnerable to a critical displacement and subtle dislodging. "The syntax of *Between* is free-ranging in that a sentence can start in one place or time, continue correctly, but by the end of the sentence one is elsewhere" (*Stories, Theories, and Things*, 7). One of the anonymous conference speakers—at a meeting on DNA—disparages the analogy between the language of codes and the workings of genetics and language. The speaker comments on this analogy as a "seductive hypothesis whose seductive element lies in the fact that we play on words and speak of codes, [which] postulates that the stimulus of environment modifies the sequence of bases, leading to the modification of the code within a cell within a body within a box within a village within a wooded area in an alien land. This would leave a trace" (519). Paradoxically, however, in Brooke-Rose's "traveling" style, this cynicism collapses; the pompous statement "begins somewhere . . . continues correctly," yet it winds up "elsewhere." What begins as abstract academic cynicism somehow winds up in the English location of the Wiltshire cottage (the wooded refuge that the protagonist decides to sell near the end of the novel); this seemingly involuntary travel of the sentence dramatizes the local "truth" of the way memory works to trace personal loss. Everywhere, Brooke-Rose confirms that experimental writing, like travel, is risky business; one can prepare and yet be unprepared for adventures in writing. In this particular example, the errancy of syntax and meaning leads to an "elsewhere" that is, paradoxically, home.

For Brooke-Rose, experimental grammar is never merely a question of the relationship between parts of the sentence but a technique for exploring the fixings and releases of positionality as well. This exploration is signaled in her insistent use of prepositions, beginning with the importance of the title itself to suggest a place that is neither home nor abroad, placement nor escape.[11] This emphasis on fixation and mobility within language is, I believe, inextricably connected to Brooke-Rose's decision to abandon her original idea of an androgynous traveler on finding it to be a false start, a roadblock to the journey of the text: "During the writing of the first draft in 1964 the author became totally blocked until some three years and another novel later, this simultaneous interpreter became a woman" (*Stories, Theories, and Things,* 6). In exploring pre-positions and changes in positions, Brooke-Rose focuses on the mark of gender in the circulation of meaning in language. In a significant way, travel in Brooke-Rose's novel intersects with feminist questions about the possibilities of escape within language, within literature, and within history. The metadiscourse of structuralism and psychoanalysis in the narrative underscores how the mark of gender is carried in the "vessel of conception" that is language in general and this novel in particular. The question, "What difference does it make?" is answered in part with, The difference of gender. For Brooke-Rose, the myth of androgyny seems too much to sponsor an illusory freedom of unlimited circulation. Twenty pages into *Between,* Brooke-Rose eschews this trope of erotic freedom (a trope that both Virginia Woolf and Brigid Brophy, for example, find liberating):

Et comme l'a si bien dit Saussure, la langue peut se contenter de l'opposition de quelque chose avec rien. [And just as Saussure has said very well, language can content itself with the opposition of something to nothing.] The marked term on the one hand, say, the feminine, grand*e*, the unmarked on the other, say, the masculine, grand. Mais notez bien

[11]The importance of prepositions in general can be seen in the titles of Brooke-Rose's other novels as well—*Out* and *Through,* included with *Between* in the four-novel collection *Omnibus.* For a meditation on the sexuality of grammar, see Shari Benstock's *Textualizing the Feminine: On the Limits of Genre.*

que le non-marqué peut deriver du marqué par retranchement, by subtraction, par une absence qui signifie. Je répète, une absence qui signifie
eine Abwesenheit die simultaneously etwas bedeutet. [But note well that
the unmarked term can derive from the marked by reduction, by subtraction, by an absence that signifies. I repeat, an absence that signifies
an absence that simultaneously means something.] (426)

Where when and to whose heart did one do that? Do what and what
difference does it make? None except by subtraction from the marked
masculine and unmarked feminine or vice versa as the language of a
long lost code of zones lying forgotten under layers of thickening sen-
sibilities creeps up from down the years into no more than the distant
brain way up to tickle an idle thought such as where when and to whose
heart did one do that? (468)

Despite the fluid translations from one language to another, the position of the feminine gender is marked in opposition to the normative, "unmarked" masculine. As Monique Wittig says in "The Mark
of Gender," "The abstract form, the general, the universal, this is what
the so-called masculine gender means, for the class of men have appropriated the universal for themselves" (5). In this schema, the feminine is "marked"—gender itself becomes feminine, the other to the
neutrality of the masculine in language, that "other" most visible in
the floating signifier of femininity, the French e (about which Barthes
has written so interestingly in S/Z). Yet one can say that the feminine
is unmarked, missing the mark, missing the phallus and is therefore
the sign of lack in Freudian terms (but this difference comes out in
much the same way). Either way, the signifiers "masculine" and "feminine" are indissolubly paired, as Lacan shows in the now famous
illustration of the signs on the lavatory doors in the train station
("Agency," 151–52), a scene that Brooke-Rose invokes in her own text
("We have no evidence at all that live human beings, let alone the
skirted figurine or high-heeled shoe on the door can so embody the
divine principle descending into matter" [571–72]).

    In the twists in the above passage, however, a potentially different
interpretation suggests itself, a possible reversal—the male as "subtracted" from the female and, hence, the masculine as somehow constructed in defense against the female. Such a reading is pressed in
the following passage: "Solamente un piccolo with insolent eyes and
a great tenderness only to see and touch a little in the narrow passage
between the built-in cupboard painted pink and the rosy glow of the

situation so characteristic in this our masculine-dominated myth un-marked save by subtraction from the feminine with its ambivalence in the double-negation no e no" (508). The male pursuit of the woman in the narrow passageway is an all too familiar topos within the "mas-culine-dominated myth." This scene is "unmarked" or unremarked, appearing "natural," except if one recognizes in this myth an ambiv-alent flight from women and a feeling of lack in the male's "subtrac-tion from the feminine." As the passage on page 468 above suggests, the particular grammar of relationship between subject and object ("when and to whose heart did one do that?") might make a real difference.

Jane Gallop criticizes the feminist attack on Lacanian psychoanalysis for taking the position that these "markings" can ever be escaped: "That effort would place the feminist as observer in some sort of float-ing position outside the structure, a position of omniscience. Such po-sitioning ignores the subject's need to place himself within the signifying chain in order to be any place at all. There is no place for a 'subject', no place to be human, to make sense outside of significa-tion, and language always has specific rules which no subject has the power to decree" (12). I would suggest that in the travel novel *Be-tween*, Brooke-Rose acknowledges that however plush or sparse, fem-inine or masculine, one's location in the "vessel of conception," one cannot float outside the plane of language. The "between" of the novel is a space within, rather than outside of, the signifying chain in which gender is marked. Indeed, the novel illustrates how fantasies of es-cape, provided in literature and philosophy, themselves participate in these gendered markings. Brooke-Rose reminds us how myths and metaphors of flight and travel are indelibly marked in this signifying chain, often through plays on words and conventional phrases. The metaphors of travel are pressed into the service of romance; men are constantly offering to take the unnamed translator "under their wing" ("whatever wing means under which he has taken her auburn blond svelte and dark to their conferences" [434]). And myths of rescue are figured in terms of the woman's being carried away: "Please do not throw into W.C. because one day the man will come and lift you out of your self-containment or absorption rising into the night above the wing par à quelle aile j'vois pas d'aile moi only a red light winking on and off in the blackness" (446). Hollywood fantasies of rescue are mobilized: "Ah yes! The ideas. Here we came in, the hero will now pick up the heroine on a plane about to land in Hollywood and offer

her a contract for life" (460). Even direction is gendered, particularly
the movement up and down that underwrites the narrative journey
(the basic movement of the flight in taking off and landing). The
trope of direction itself allegorizes desire as symbolically gendered.
The yearning for transcendence is represented in the metaphors of
masculine authority: "The body stretches forth towards some thought
some order some command obeyed in the distant brain way up"
(405–6).[12] In contrast, the older mythic geography mentioned above is
suggested to be aboriginal, *beneath* the twentieth-century European
map.

> The visitor's attention turns immediately to the sanctuary of Apollo sit-
> uated on the higher slopes of one of the Phaidriades rocks in five terrace-
> like levels, brilliant with the splendour of its monuments . . . the Temple
> of Apollo beneath which the famous oracle used to sit and utter cryptic
> prophecies to all who came and consulted it on serious matters like war,
> alliances, births and marriages. Finally, a little higher up stands the The-
> atre . . . and beyond the Sanctuary lies the Stadium, where the Pythic
> Games took place to celebrate Apollo's victory over Python, the legen-
> dary monster.
>   The visitor's attention turns immediately to the masculine unmarked
> and situated on the higher slopes in five terraces none of which deserves
> a flow of rash enthusiasm. (430)

According to myth, after killing Python, Apollo seized the oracular
shrine of Mother Earth at Delphi; the cult of Apollo depended on this
female power. Perhaps it is this "long lost code of zones lying forgotten" (464) that surfaces tantalizingly in the text to suggest a different kind of language lying hidden within the chain of signification,
one that would make a difference if rediscovered.

This recovery is problematic, given the power of the "male-
dominated myths" to appropriate it. The voice of a cynical speaker
on passive resistance warns:

> Human beings need to eat, to work, and to this end will either knuckle
> under or, more often, persuade themselves that le mensonge vital die
> Lebenslüge [vital lie] contains sufficient double-negation to reintegrate
> him into totality compared with so many fragile truths and lost mysteries

[12]All sorts of puns on the idea of height circulate in the novel: "I have conducted
my higher education by transmitting other people's ideas," says Siegfried (426).

that surround us in this our masculine-dominated civilization turned upside down into the earphones and out into the mouthpiece with a gulliverisation typical of the giant myths euphemised into a sack, a basket, a container cavern womb belly vase vehicle ship temple sepulchre or holy grail, witness le complexe de Jonas with which the lost vitality of the word goes down into the mouthpiece and out through its exits and entrances. (510)

Although the cynical speaker emphasizes the way the giant male myths are "gulliverised" by female analogy, the passage implicitly recognizes that the "vessels of conception" and transportation in central male myths of the Western tradition co-opt, by troping, female morphology.[13] Despite this thick veneer of disdain, the possibility of rediscovering a "long-lost language" is suggested at certain moments in the text, a language of flowers (or plants and transplants), which is associated with the French love letters sent to the translator by Bertrand: "So the white gladiolus explodes in letter after letter in a language that finds itself delicious and breeds plants or parts of plants inside the seven-terraced tower undoing the magic wall of defence anticlockwise from the distant brain way up the downward path escalating to a death-kiss with a half-visualised old man well fifty-seven and plus the circular dance of simulation vital lies lost mysteries and other excitations to the true end of imagination" (542). In this envoi, this circulation of love *letters*, is the suggestion of a circuit of desire in language not wholly contaminated by overuse, a certain pathetic beauty ironized but not destroyed. Like the Trojan horse, the language of flowers disarms defenses from within. Paradoxically, the exhumation of a buried, archaic past is impelled by a rather silly old man who speaks in romantic clichés, which produce, nevertheless, something "that actually means something compels a passion" (406). The translator suggests something of the sort in her response to Siegfried's ridicule of her for replying to Bertrand's adoring letters: "—The lan-

---

[13]Even the "myths" of deconstruction are caught in this euphemizing, this gendering. In his essay "Des Tours de Babel," Derrida tropes the translator as the male in hot pursuit of the virgin translation: "The always intact, the intangible, the untouchable *(unberührbar)* is what fascinates and orients the work of the translator. He wants to touch the untouchable, that which remains of the text when one has extracted from it the communicable meaning. . . . If one can risk a proposition in appearance so absurd, the text will be even more virgin after the passage of the translator, and the hymen, sign of virginity, more jealous of itself after the other hymen, the contract signed and the marriage consummated" (191–92).

guage, Siegfried. The fact that all this suffering stuff as you call it pours out in French, well, it sort of turns the system inside out" (516).

But meaning, difference, and significance travel in this text and do not arrive at any one place, even a myth of female power, for Brooke-Rose is always suspicious of such a gesture of mere reversal. Theory, including a feminist reversal of hierarchies, is subjected to critical displacements. "Inverting the polarities," Brooke-Rose says, "(writing/voice, nonbeing/being, etc.) produces dizziness and fear (and resistance). But could the ultimate effect not be reequilibration, which should produce (and has produced) flights of creativity and word-game processes as enriching and magical as those produced by the incredibly complex flow-charts and numerical logical operators of computer science?" ("Dissolution of Character," 195).

It is this "flight of creativity" which Brooke-Rose attempts to produce in her novels, and which makes *Between* a story of displacement that depicts neither fixation nor flight. One of the experimental techniques she uses to enrich the possibilities for marking gender is to disrupt the operation of personal pronouns through her use of what she calls, following Bakhtin, free direct discourse. The most striking effect of this technique on the narrative is to destabilize the grammatical category of the personal pronoun and hence the representation of identity and gender. The "nonnarrating" consciousness of the translator is never represented by the pronoun "I" (although there are passages that read like interior monologues) and very rarely in the third person. Occasionally the translator is introduced in general terms, such as in the phrase "a woman of uncertain age" (445). The free direct discourse has the curious effect of turning the character of the translator into a *second-person* pronoun. It seems not quite accurate to say, as Brooke-Rose does, that she is the "central consciousness," as if she were like Eliot's Tiresias, for she does not contain the language but is often its audience, as the "receiver" of the conference jargon that flows through her earphones and out through her mouthpiece or as the addressee of primarily male speakers. She becomes not only a traveler but a conduit or vessel of reception as well, similar to the reader as the recipient of the reams of jargon that pass through the narrative. She is more marked according to her gender than the implied "you" of the reader; yet her gender markings are more unmoored than the stable "personing" found in most narratives, first- and third-person alike.

In "The Mark of Gender," Monique Wittig writes:

Gender takes place in a category of language that is totally unlike any
other and which is called the personal pronoun. Personal pronouns are
the only linguistic instances that, in discourse, designate its locators and
their different and successive situations in relationship to discourse. They
are also the pathways and the means of entrance into language. . . . And
although they are instrumental in activating the notion of gender, [per-
sonal pronouns] pass unnoticed. Not being gender marked themselves
in their subjective form (except in one case) [i.e., the third-person], they
can support the notion of gender while pretending to fulfill another function. In principle they mark the opposition of gender only in the third
person and are not gender bearers, per se, in the other persons. . . . But,
in reality, as soon as gender manifests itself in discourse, there is a kind
of suspension of grammatical form. A direct interpellation of the locator
occurs. The locator is called upon in person. The locator intervenes, in
the order of the pronouns, without mediation, in *its proper sex*—that is,
when the locator is a sociological woman. For it is only then, that the
notion of gender takes its full effect. (5)

Turning the character into the addressee does not bypass the path of
gender Wittig outlines, but it alters a certain predictability both in the
power of the pronoun to enforce gender and in the feminist critique
of the circulation of woman as semiotic object. In her own critique of
semiotics as regressively masculinist, Brooke-Rose castigates semioti-
cians whom she otherwise admires for their inability to escape phallocentric paradigms. In her fiction she wrenches her translator out of
an automatic objectification in the third person. The identity of the
translator changes as a function of the kind of "you" that signifies
her. For example, we know by the addresses made to her that although never described physically in the text, the translator is attractive. During the course of the narrative, she ages, which affects the
"you" she represents (the change in the form of address to her, from
"mademoiselle" to "madame," is only the most overt sign of this
process). Unlike Wittig, who attempts to eliminate gender in her experimental fiction, Brooke-Rose rejects the notion of androgyny. She
explores instead the way the feminine subject (and object) is constituted ·in the signifying chain of language, the way her journey as a
signified and signifier is marked.

In experimenting with "person" in this way, Brooke-Rose neither
places her traveler outside of the "male-dominated" signifying chain
nor imprisons her within it. The language of the narrative becomes a

structure of dis-placement rather than of either placement or escape. In this experiment with pronouns she challenges a traditional mode of representation. The grammatical and syntactic mobility of her language enables both the unfixing of identity in the narrative (in accordance with the mimetic realism she mentions) and a fictional possibility that suggests new ways of thinking about character, a new technique for writing gender.

Style offers, to borrow a line from the novel, "new techniques for living" which emerge from contemporary culture (571). The "distant brain" appropriately replaces the author; twentieth-century fiction cannot retreat into nostalgic forms of realism but must catalyze the new ways of knowing made available through innovative media—the computer, for example. Brooke-Rose has increasingly spoken of the philosophical and methodological possibilities emerging from computer technology, possibilities that might help establish new logics of character as well as a new poetry in postmodern fiction: "Just as the flat characters of romance eventually, through print and the far-reaching social developments connected with it, became rounded and complex, so, if we survive at all, perhaps the computer, after first ushering in (apart from superefficiency) the games and preprogrammed oversimplifications of popular culture, will alter our minds and powers of analysis once again, and enable us to create new dimensions in the deep-down logic of characters" ("Dissolution of Character," 195). "Fictional character has died, or become flat," she maintains, "as had *deus ex machina*. We're left, perhaps, with the faint hope of a ghost in the machine" (193). Brooke-Rose's style consciously locates itself in a particular moment of technological possibility; perhaps the "distant brain" that guides the travel in *Between* is such a ghost (or god) in the machine.[14] The convenient ending of the original deus ex machina is replaced by narrative technique that never reaches resolution (indeed, the narrative journey is circular, ending in much the same place as it began); yet this technique uncovers connections and significances through small adjustments of sentences.

Computer technology, however, seems inadequate as the sole source of regeneration for narrative fiction, for its revolution might be

---

[14]The "distant brain" in *Between* is replaced in Brooke-Rose's most recent novel, *Textermination,* by the "aerobrain"—both a vehicle of transportation on which characters travel (and thus a "vehicle" of plot) and a computer-like memory containing a host of fictional characters from various literary traditions and periods.

stuck, Brooke-Rose suggests, in a binary way of thinking that confirms rather than undermines a phallogocentric ethos. One of the persistent worries Brooke-Rose expresses about various forms of postmodernist writing, from theory to fiction, is its insistent phallocentrism: "With a few notable exceptions, some by women, both the postmodern novel and science fiction, like the utopias of Scholes's structural fabulation, are surprisingly phallocratic. It is as if the return to popular forms or the parody of them, even via the intellectual cognition of utopian models, necessarily entailed the circulation of women as objects, which we find both in those models and in folktales and early cultures" ("Dissolution of Character," 193). Brooke-Rose, who has had a vexed relationship to feminism (see "A Womb of One's Own" for her severe reservations about "writing the body" of the feminine), has become increasingly vocal about this bias in postmodernism. She suggests that a countersource to the computer is necessary to effect a revolution in fiction, which could then aspire to the condition of poetry: "The impetus comes from two apparently contradictory sources, the technological revolution and the feminist revolution" (194). Drawing on Lacan's distinction between the *tout* and the *pas tout*, she envisions a "new psychology" in which "both women and men artists who have rejected the totalization, the *tout*, of traditional and even modernist art and chosen the underdetermination and opaqueness of the *pas tout* may clash in an enriching and strengthening way with the binary, superlogical, and by definition exclusive structures of the electronic revolution" (196).

A cynical conference voice says near the end of *Between*, "We have no evidence at all that live human beings, let alone the skirted figurine or high-heeled shoe on the door can so embody the divine principle descending into matter in a behavior sufficiently organised to prevent the illiterate women of an Indian village taught the natural method with an abacus from pushing all those red balls to the left like a magic spell and all coming back pregnant" (571–72). The deus ex machina given form in the technology of style in the novel, the (holy) ghost of the god in the machine descending and landing into textuality, gives no guarantee or evidence of consequences in the "real" world. Indeed, Brooke-Rose often speaks of the pleasures of technique as sufficient for the writer on the frontiers of language. "I think it was Yeats who spoke about poetry coming out of a mouthful of air. I've always been fascinated by this notion of words and ideas floating up there as in a galaxy, from which the poet draws them down into the text" (Jenny Turner, 26). Yet Brooke-Rose's particular brand of postmodern travel charts a space for the flight of the female imagination while mapping out a specific, historical twentieth-century problematic. As in all the voyages, imagined and otherwise, that we have explored, the circulation of an individual "feminine" signifier cannot be severed from the political order or from a specific history. To explore this history, literary and political, Penelope, both author and character, transforms her domestic vigil of waiting into the vigilant, yet self-surprising language of travel. In Brooke-Rose's postmodern version of travel, the categories of passivity and activity merge in the writing in a purposeful technical wandering that, nevertheless, yields a serendipitous "elsewhere."

Brigid Brophy's *In Transit* (1969) serves as the end point (although not the telos) of our trajectory in *Penelope Voyages*, a postscript and emblem of the errant circulations of women's travel. In it, all *scheduled* flights are canceled, replaced by detour and digression. This cancellation is literal and metaphoric. The would-be traveler, an Irish orphan whose two sets of parents (natural and foster) have been killed in plane crashes, circulates for the duration of the novel within an airport transit lounge, while planes take off unpredictably and, for a while, not at all. "Within this pocket," the narrator says of the airport lounge, "within this fully accounted-for, justified and sewn-up détour in my life line, I can be simultaneously relaxed and efficient. I am on my way yet free to stray" (23). The airport is described in the narrative as "a free-ranging womb"; it is a "vessel of conception" (to return to Brooke-Rose's term) that accelerates the pace at which stable identities of traveler and narrative are unbound. In this vessel of transformation, the traveler is reborn: "Out of that egg, ego too am re-hatched. It no longer matters a damn whether 'I' is masc. or fem. or whether 'you' is sing. or plur." (228). The narrator ponders, "Suppose the structure which, like an organic conveyor belt, has been *transporting* all my thoughts and experiences all these years is but an arbitrary convention?" (217; emphasis added).

The sex of the narrator/traveler and the person of the narrative are shifting and indeterminate; the first-person narration hilariously careens from one gender position to another in a Beckett-like journey in which the protagonist herself/himself cannot remember which sex (if any or only one) she/he is. Indeed, the travel novel turns detective novel as the protagonist tries to determine first which sex she/he is and then to solve the mystery of his own missing phallus, which circulates somewhere in the airport. (The second of four sections is entitled "Sexshuntwo the Case of the Missing [Re]Member.") As mischief-maker and detective, called "Unruly" and "O'Hooligan" (72) on the one hand, and O'Rooley, on the other, the agonistic protagonist alternates between pleasure in free circulation and an attempt to put things in their place.

> Hooligan, I accused myself, o hooligan O'Hooligan: *you*'re the hooligan who by night crept into the hall of sculpture (glided into the gliptotek, you did, hooligan) and vandalised the exhibits by chopping 'em all in two across the waistline, after which you hooligamused yourself by reassorting the demi-torsos and putting the from-the-waist-up of the Venus de Milo on top of the from-the-waist-down of the Hermes of Praxiteles. A grand old mutilation of the sperms, *that* was. Welll'llbeciades. (72)[15]

Rather than blocking Brophy's imagination (as the idea of androgyny did in Brooke-Rose's original conception of *Between*), this hermaphroditic circulation launches a fantastic, punning linguistic journey. In this wild ride of the signifier, Brophy parodies the myth of the phallus as transcendental signifier, the myth that props up all the paradigms of the journey underwriting Western culture. In a final passage that is one of many self-described "ALIENATING INTERLUDE [S]" in the narrative addressed to the reader, we read: "The management trussts [*sic*] the clientele has by now observed that at least one of the hero(in)es immolated throughout these pages is language. However, that's not all there is to it. The work's sub-title is: *Or The Autobiography of Sappho's Penis*" (214). This comic and feminist fantasy of the wandering prick seems to be a cross between Norman O. Brown and Luce Irigaray, a pricking of the myth of the mobile phallus and parodic deflation of phallogocentric theories of language. As the narrator discreetly attempts to investigate his/her/its own gender, wondering if she (for ease of reference) indeed possesses a penis or a lack where the penis should be, the multilingual narrator is stricken with "linguistic leprosy"; her/his languages "drop" off in a mock-castration— French and then German fall away. As the narrator describes it, "My languages gave their first dowser's-twig twitch and I conceived they

---

[15]Mutilation of the *herms* was the crime for which Alcibiades was deprived of command of the Athenian expedition to Sicily during the Peloponnesian War.

might be going to fall off" (12). The transcendental signified anchoring language is exposed as trussed-up fiction.

This "misprinted mistranslated overestimated sadomasturbatory pornofantasy-narrative" (143) is a "juicifixion" (217) that repeatedly (and deliberately) stages a failure to nail down the body of language. " 'And did you suppose, Och,' enquired the Maestro Hugh Bris in his accustomed courteous tones . . . 'that puns such as yours could go unpunished?' " (214). But such prideful masters of language cannot stop its errancy and detours. In the course of the narrative, these masters are mocked, including all "apparatus criticus" for mapping meaning and fixing the "mother tongue" (the character "Oc") in her place:

Damn: not criticus at all; merely that old S.-Mapparatus, the masomachine applied, in the language laboratory, by the sado-mysterious "He". Ritual CatemasOChism:—
Q. Who is Master?
A. I do nothing except on your sado.
Q. Where is Oc's tongue?
A. In her cheek.
Q. Where is ox tongue?
A. At the counter that has the OCcam's-razor-sharp bOCan-slicing apparatus. (142)

Not only are the gendered trajectories of traditional journeys deconstructed, but the impulse to map trajectories, conceived in the above dialogue as a priestly critical function, is figured as sadomasochistic as well. The "story of the tongue of Oc" is a tongue-in-cheek critique of preemptive bindings and mappings, particularly of the meaning of gender. This poststructuralist novel, like Brooke-Rose's *Between*, explores the genetic and generic ancestry of its own gender bending. Continuing in the mode of detective fiction, the narrator asks what could have caused this sudden indeterminacy of gender. The cross-dressings and castrati of baroque opera figure prominently in the history of the novel's sex changes: "For we are not at all sure it was you, after all, o Irish O'Pera, who initially set this sexchange in train. I may quite well have been you, O.Fr (=Old French [signed Scholiast One]), you sly old wench, with your already remarked habit of being coy about what's girl and what's boy and your vicious officious imparting of misinformation about the sex of objects possexed" (143). And, "Quick page (is your name Eros?), unsex me here and strap me into my torso-moulded breastplate whose breasts are neither male nor female but undulate in the papier-mâché landscaped contours of a more-than-Teiresianly-heroic heroic-convention'' (51). (Paradoxically, conventions exist even for fixing the androgynous breasts in place, as revealed in Brophy's overlapping allusions to *Macbeth* and *Antony and Cleopatra*.)

But it is the legacy of Joyce, that "comedichameleon, the old pun gent himself" (36), that Brophy most self-consciously invokes as the forefather of her radical experiment, a father to be first acknowledged and then outgrown (near the end of the novel Pat [one of the names of the protagonist] says "Old Father Finnegan Go-and-don'tsinagain. . . . Well, I saw through you, you old pro-façade, before I was out of my boyhood or girlhood. . . . I can't hear you, ex-father. I've switched me deaf-aid off" [228]). In her errant tale, Brophy addresses the Joyce of both *Ulysses* (the transmogrified tale of that master wanderer) and *Finnegans Wake*. The hero/heroine of *In Transit* is called "Oruleus (latinised as Ulrix and thence rather quaintly englished as Unruly)" (175). "Ulysses," the narrator says at one point, is "the hero who can never accomplish the return of the native, because he isn't one" (35). This Irish/Greek/Roman wanderer is the quintessential exile, the emblem for the condition of language as always already fallen from a "home" or origin. Yet Odysseus and Joyce himself are made to stand for the particular relevance of Irish displacements to the pains and pleasures of twentieth-century decenterings.

> No codding: I think it's because we haven't quite a native language that our tongues tend to trip over their roots.
>
> We speak English as a foreign language, even when we have no other. (This is my foster-mother-tongue, since when I have used no other.) . . . Transplant us further, who are unrooted in the first place, banish us from growth and home, banshe banhe, and we will astonish you by how we run to riot in false flowerings of double-headed counterfeit coinages. Pom-pom. . . . Look what became of my distinguished compatriot when, making, with the Irish predisposition to internationalism, for the first handy free port, he was transplanted to windy Trieste, that evocative Avoca where three streams of vocables meet, where everyone is a foreigner and most are anarchist. (34–35)

During the novel, the anarchy of language, the "counterfeit coinages," in the book's pages leads to a full-scale Joycean revolution of the word (not to mention the more political revolution, a takeover of the airport). The transit lounge suddenly springs "into a new, temporary existence as an art gallery, like a pattern leaping into 3-D when viewed from a new standpoint. . . . What had been litter became exhibits. Detritus, trash, turned into works" (207). This transformation underscores the idea of the postmodern simulacrum. The "revolution" (which begins with lesbian airport workers staging a takeover of their workplace and which is joined by Marxists, academics, and postmodernists alike) becomes a revolution of the word, an updated battle of the books in which hundreds of volumes fall off the bookstall shelves, bombarding (and even killing) the travelers with words. As in *Orlando* (and in such a citational text, the reference to Woolf's fantasy of revolutionary sex change seems likely), "various accounts of this episode were in circulation . . . (here there is a lacuna in the manuscript—Scholiast)" (213).

Jean-François Lyotard's account of how postmodernism puts an end to master narratives is predicted in the novel: "Our programme," the narrator says a few pages earlier, is to "Undo the Normative Conquest[s]" (27). Indeed, the wicked, satiric narrative delights in skewering most shibboleths of "mainstream" culture and undoing all sorts of "Normative Conquests"—sexual, political, linguistic. Yet Brophy's novel reminds us as well that even in the most transgressive, experimental journeys, the host system absorbs the parasite—the static produced becomes a part of the music of the text: "Though you achieve the chemical breakdown of my language into its component parse, my igenwitty syntacks them higher together again betterthaneologism. Deplete me here and I rush up reinforcements. I make shift with periphrases and phrase-make with short shrifts" (217). As Michel Serres puts it, the parasite forces the system to new levels of complexity (*Parasite*, 14). "My marrow can still coin corpuscular hosts in two kinds, scilicet verbal nouns, which cashcade from me in jackpots" (217), says the narrator of *In Transit*. The deconstruction of the journey creates a new "return" (a "cashcade"?), or *nostos*, which is a new profit in the travel. As we have seen throughout *Penelope Voyages*, there is mileage in the calculated risks and surprises of travel, not only for the traveler but for the woman writer as well.

The tonal differences between *In Transit* and *Between* reflect two different theories of the postmodern, the former more congruent with Lyotard's embrace of discontinuity and linguistic play. Brooke-Rose's theorizing of the postmodern through the trope of travel suggests a more cautious and cautionary response to the hectic mobility of contemporary culture, a cross between Jameson's melancholy and Lyotard's insistence on the potentially optimistic role of the local. Brophy seems to endorse Lyotard's belief in the radical potential of aesthetic innovation; Brooke-Rose preserves a more representational interest in her language games, an attention to historical fixations and changes. For both writers, travel serves as a central trope for theorizing about the fate of narrative and its relation to gender. Brooke-Rose retains gender as a category that helps determine the circulations and fixations of the traveler; Brophy demotes the importance of gender, experimenting with multiple transgressions of fixed boundaries and oppositions. Yet despite their differences, Brophy and Brooke-Rose both conduct what Brophy's narrative calls "herm warfare" (220). In this skirmish, the old Hermes, "the phallus . . . the god of roads, of doorways, of all goings-in and comings-out; all goings-on" is remade, as a different sort of traveler supplants the "wandering . . . phallic heroes, in a permanent state of erection; pricking o'er the plain" (Brown, *Love's Body*, 50).

Conclusion:
"Questions of Travel"

Is it right to be watching strangers in a play
in this strangest of theatres?
What childishness is it that while there's a breath of life
in our bodies, we are determined to rush
to see the sun the other way around?
                    (Bishop, "Questions of Travel," 93)

The dialectic and ethics of mobility and fixation that Elizabeth Bishop recognizes—the hectic movement of the traveler who attempts to overcome her own fixation, the narrative fixing of the travel experience in writing, including the cultural fixing of those "strangers" on the foreign stage—have been the subjects of *Penelope Voyages*. Variously, in the travel narratives discussed, the very concepts of mobility and placement yield up their ideological significances. Mary Kingsley's narrative/ethnography, the only text that includes the word "travels" in its title, exemplifies the complexities of the double enterprise of travel and fixing. Adopting the jaunty tonalities of English adventure and its privileged ease of movement, Kingsley's narrative attempts to arrest "African culture" within its pages; yet the seven-hundred-page record constantly subverts its own project of knowledge-gathering as well as a sense of the mastery and autonomy of the first-person traveler.

We have seen many historical and generic variations in the way women write about women who leave their domestic moorings. The genre of exilic fiction introduces an alibi for female adventure as well as a caution about the particular travails of women wandering: in the case of Cavendish's cross-dressed heroine, it provides a framework for the creation of a mobile, improvisational Renaissance personality for women and, in the case of Burney's Incognita, a disruption of the fixations of domestic ideology, such as home and identity—that is, a turning inside out of domestic fiction so that it meets its supposed opposite of adventure. *The Wanderer* revisits ideas of both domesticity and adventure with a woman protagonist to demonstrate something illusory within both the stabilities of domesticity and the freedoms of travel.

The "Female Crusoe," then, crosses adventure with domestic realism to illustrate that for women the two cannot be held distinct; it shows, almost allegorically, that the "safe haven" of domestic fiction is riddled with its own reckless politics and adventure. But if Burney's fiction of wandering demonstrates the centrifugal in the centripetal, I have focused more on the pull of centripetal forces on centrifugal movement; these texts record different systems that brake the free circulation of their women protagonists—for better and for worse. These "fixations" are ideological and formal: I have in mind not only the limiting conceptual framework of the *oikos*, the intellectual habit of domesticating the foreign that is a part of all travel and travel writing, but also the generic laws that bind travel writing, the epistolary form, for example, of Wollstonecraft's travel record, which encodes the presence and absence of "home" in the comings and goings of its address to the reader/lover. Woolf's *Voyage Out* might be said to provide a modern example of a "doubling back," as we move from a voyage out to a voyage in, a representation, that is, of a journey to a geographical and historical extremity (the "new world" of South America) and then of another journey to the limit of the self in death. Woolf's twentieth-century novels use the trope of travel both to historicize and to abstract ideas of mobility. Rachel's voyage out to South America on the *Euphrosyne* and Orlando's diplomatic trip to Turkey place twentieth-century travel in the historical context of English imperialism, a masculinist habit of conquest Woolf seeks to expose; these voyages are also symbolically encoded as potential escapes from a constricting gendered subjectivity. Although Orlando manages to escape the confinements of gender in polymorphous relationships as a male in Turkey and after her sex change, her repatriation functions as a rejection of the nomadic life and a reengagement with centripetal forces. In experimenting with the mode of the domestic sublime,

Woolf, like Wollstonecraft, seeks both to transform domesticity and deliberately to curb free circulation.

As I've been suggesting, the meaning of mobility and travel changes diachronically, yet there are affiliations, generic and temperamental, that link travel texts from different periods. Cavendish's cross-dressed Travelia is linked, via the mode of fantasy, to Brophy's Irish O'Rooley, male/female traveler/detective, and to Orlando. Similarly, Brooke-Rose's representation of the tenacity of nationality in the midst of the hectic mobility of her female protagonist in *Between* can be linked to Woolf's repatriation of Orlando after her Turkish travels. I have also traced the persistent and various representations of the traveler who "passes" in fiction and nonfiction—Travelia, cross-dressed; the Incognita, skin darkened and dressed as a beggar; Lee's male Latino wanderers in Africa (who, in turn, represent the female writer "passing" as male in her adventure fiction); Kingsley, the woman addressed as "Sir"; as well as Orlando and Brophy's O'Rooley. Yet the meaning of particular actions and gestures (for example, of cross-dressing) does not remain constant. If a baroque imagination and generic use of fantasy unite Cavendish and Brophy, the gesture of cross-dressing in the former is still circumscribed by the conventions of romance and imaginary voyage, whereas the lost phallus of the latter's hero/heroine and the revolution of the word in transit locate Brophy's "travel" fiction, in this case, in the poststructuralist ethos of the 1960s. Nevertheless, I have also tried to demonstrate, through the example of Brooke-Rose and Brophy, that historicizing the texts of these writers cannot lead to an automatic politics or ideology of mobility. Whereas Brophy represents a quintessentially playful postgendered, poststructuralist circulation of meaning, Brooke-Rose chooses to fix gender and nationality, treating the mobility of postmodern travel with more reserve and skepticism.

Derrida discusses how the trope of navigation is important to the discourse of European identity:

> The word "cap" (*caput, capitis*) refers . . . to the head or the extremity of the extreme, the aim and the end, the ultimate. . . . It here assigns to navigation the pole, the end, the *telos* of an oriented, calculated, deliberate, voluntary, ordered movement: ordered most often by the *man* in charge. Not by a woman, for in general, and especially in wartime, it is a *man* who decides on the heading, from the advanced point that he himself is, the prow, at the head of the ship or plane that he pilots. Eschatology and

teleology—that is man. It is *he* who gives orders to the crew, he who holds the helm or sits at the controls; he is the headman, there at the head of the crew and the machine. And oftentimes, he is called the *captain*. (*Other Heading*, 14)

In her important essay "Castration or Decapitation?" Hélène Cixous writes of women threatened with decapitation under masculine law. Fantasizing an end to such threats from the captain—the head—she draws on the metaphor of endless circulation to describe the textualizing of the feminine: "What takes place is an endless circulation of desire from one body to another, above and across sexual difference, outside those relations of power and regeneration constituted by the family. . . . This takes the metaphorical form of wandering, excess, risk of the unreckonable" (53). Cixous's description of endlessly circulating desire offers a "beheading," an alternative fiction to the trope of masculine navigation that has so dominated European identity. It is a fiction of a wandering that never arrives anywhere, never fixes. Only Brigid Brophy's *In Transit* seems perfectly represented in this description; it is a fiction coterminous with Cixous's own radical imaginings of freedom. For like Elizabeth Bishop's traveler, scribbling in her notebook at the end of the poem "Questions of Travel," the writers studied in *Penelope Voyages* variously acknowledge that *"Continent, city, country, society: / the choice is never wide and never free"* (ll. 64–65). Yet, in plot and in narrative, all the texts considered experiment with replacing the pilot and his calculated navigation. Even in the most realistic genres of novel and ethnography, which to borrow from Henry James explore "the possibility of hugging the shore of the real" ("The New Novel," 130), these writers play out their fantasies of errancy—risky, rewardingly excessive wandering.

Works Cited

Abel, Elizabeth. *Virginia Woolf and the Fictions of Psychoanalysis.* Chicago: University of Chicago Press, 1989.

Adams, Percy G. *Travel Literature and the Evolution of the Novel.* Lexington: University Press of Kentucky, 1983.

Alloula, Malek. *The Colonial Harem.* Translated by Myrna Godzich and Wlad Godzich. Minneapolis: University of Minnesota Press, 1986.

Altman, Janet Gurkin. *Epistolarity: Approaches to a Form.* Columbus: Ohio State University Press, 1982.

Amin, Samir. *Eurocentricism.* New York: Monthly Review Press, 1989.

Appadurai, Arjun. "Putting Hierarchy in Its Place." In *Rereading Cultural Anthropology,* 34–47. Edited by George E. Marcus. Durham: Duke University Press, 1992.

Armstrong, Nancy. *Desire and Domestic Fiction: A Political History of the Novel.* New York: Oxford University Press, 1987.

Auden, W. H., and Louis MacNeice. *Letters from Iceland.* London: Faber and Faber, 1967.

Auerbach, Nina. *Woman and the Demon: The Life of a Victorian Myth.* Cambridge: Harvard University Press, 1982.

Babcock-Abrahams, Barbara. " 'A Tolerated Margin of Mess': The Trickster and His Tales Reconsidered." *(Indiana) Journal of the Folklore Institute* 11 (March 1975): 147–86.

Bachelard, Gaston. *The Poetics of Space.* Translated by Maria Jolas. Boston: Beacon Press, 1969.

Bagehot, Walter. *Literary Studies.* Vol. 1. London: J. M. Dent & Sons, n.d.

Bakhtin, M. M. "Forms of Time and of the Chronotope in the Novel." In *The Dialogic Imagination,* 84–258. Edited by Michael Holquist. Translated by Caryl Emerson and Michael Holquist. Austin: University of Texas Press, 1981.

Bal, Mieke. Review of Malek Alloula's *The Colonial Harem,* Raymond Corbey's

Wildheid En Beschaving: De Europese Verbeelding Van Afrika, and Sander Gilman's *Difference and Pathology: Stereotypes of Sexuality, Race, and Madness.* *Diacritics* 21 (Spring 1991): 25–45.

Baldanza, Frank. "Orlando and the Sackvilles." *PMLA* 70, no. 1 (1955): 274–79.

Barnes, Djuna. *Ladies Almanack.* Elmwood Park, Ill.: Dalkey Archive Press, 1992.

Barthes, Roland. *A Lover's Discourse: Fragments.* Translated by Richard Howard. New York: Hill and Wang, 1978.

———. *S/Z: An Essay.* Translated by Richard Miller. New York: Hill and Wang, 1974.

Batten, Charles L., Jr. *Pleasurable Instruction: Form and Convention in Eighteenth-Century Travel Literature.* Berkeley: University of California Press, 1978.

Beer, Gillian. "The Island and the Aeroplane: The Case of Virginia Woolf." In *Virginia Woolf,* 132–61. Edited by Rachel Bowlby. London: Longman, 1992.

Benstock, Shari. *Textualizing the Feminine: On the Limits of Genre.* Norman: University of Oklahoma Press, 1991.

Bersani, Leo. *The Freudian Body: Psychoanalysis and Art.* New York: Columbia University Press, 1986.

———. *A Future for Astyanax: Character and Desire in Literature.* Boston: Little, Brown, 1969.

Bersani, Leo, and Ulysse Dutoit. *The Forms of Violence: Narrative in Assyrian Art and Modern Culture.* New York: Schocken Books, 1985.

Bhabha, Homi K. "The Other Question: Difference, Discrimination, and the Discourse of Colonialism." In *Literature, Politics, and Theory: Papers from the Essex Conference, 1976–84,* 148–72. Edited by Francis Barker et al. London: Methuen, 1986.

Birkett, Dea. *Spinsters Abroad: Victorian Lady Explorers.* New York: Basil Blackwell, 1989.

Birkett, Deborah. "West Africa's Mary Kingsley." *History Today* 37 (May 1987): 10–16.

Bishop, Elizabeth. "Brazil, January 1, 1502" and "Questions of Travel." In *The Complete Poems 1927–1979,* 92, 93–94. New York: Farrar, Straus, and Giroux, 1979.

Bjornson, Richard. *The Picaresque Hero in European Fiction.* Madison: University of Wisconsin Press, 1977.

Black, Jeremy. *The British and the Grand Tour.* London: Croom Helm, 1985.

Blackwell, Jeannine. "An Island of Her Own: Heroines of the German Robinsonades from 1720 to 1800." *German Quarterly* 58 (Winter 1985): 5–26.

Blake, Susan L. "A Woman's Trek: What Difference Does Gender Make?" *Women's Studies International Forum* 13, no. 4 (1990): 347–55.

Blanchot, Maurice. *The Writing of the Disaster.* Translated by Ann Smock. Lincoln: University of Nebraska Press, 1986.

Bougainville, Louis de. *A Voyage round the World.* Translated by John Reinhold Forster. New York: Da Capo Press, 1967.

Bowdich, T. Edward. *Excursions in Madeira and Porto Santo, during the Autumn of 1823, While on His Third Voyage to Africa* (includes Mrs. Bowdich's "Narrative"). London: George B. Whittaker, 1825.

——. *Mission from Cape Coast Castle to Ashantee with a Statistical Account of That Kingdom and Geographical Notices of Other Parts of the Interior of Africa.* London: John Murray, 1819.

Bowen, Elizabeth. Broadcast on *She.* In *Seven Winters: Memories of a Dublin Childhood and Afterthoughts: Pieces on Writing,* 228–37. New York: Alfred A. Knopf, 1962.

——. Preface to *Orlando.* In *Seven Winters,* 130–39.

Brantlinger, Patrick. *Rule of Darkness: British Literature and Imperialism, 1830–1914.* Ithaca: Cornell University Press, 1988.

Brontë, Charlotte. *Villette.* New York: Penguin Books, 1979.

Brooke-Rose, Christine. *Between.* In *The Christine Brooke-Rose Omnibus: Four Novels,* 391–575. New York: Carcanet, 1986.

——. "The Dissolution of Character in the Novel." In *Reconstructing Individualism: Autonomy, Individuality, and the Self in Western Thought,* 184–96. Edited by Thomas C. Heller et al. Stanford: Stanford University Press, 1986.

——. *A Rhetoric of the Unreal: Studies in Narrative and Structure, Especially of the Fantastic.* Cambridge: Cambridge University Press, 1981.

——. *Stories, Theories, and Things.* Cambridge: Cambridge University Press, 1991.

——. *Textermination.* New York: New Directions, 1992.

——. "A Womb of One's Own." In *Stories, Theories, and Things,* 223–34.

Brooks, Peter. *Reading for the Plot: Design and Intention in Narrative.* New York: Vintage Books, 1984.

Brophy, Brigid. *In Transit: An Heroi-Cyclic Novel.* New York: G. P. Putnam's Sons, 1969.

Brown, Gillian. "Anorexia, Humanism, and Feminism." *Yale Journal of Criticism* 5, no. 1 (1991): 189–215.

Brown, Laura. "Amazons and Africans: Daniel Defoe." In *Ends of Empire: Women and Ideology in Early Eighteenth-Century English Literature,* 135–69. Ithaca: Cornell University Press, 1993.

——. "Imperial Disclosures: Jonathan Swift." In *Ends of Empire,* 170–200.

Brown, Norman O. *Hermes the Thief: The Evolution of a Myth.* New York: Vintage Books, 1969.

——. *Love's Body.* New York: Random House, 1966.

Brown, Rosellen. "On Not Writing a Novel." *American Poetry Review* 8 (November–December, 1979): 18–20.

Burke, Edmund. *A Philosophical Enquiry into the Origin of Our Ideas of the Sublime and Beautiful.* Edited by James T. Boulton. Oxford: Basil Blackwell, 1987.

Burney, Frances. *Fanny Burney: Selected Letters and Journals.* Edited by Joyce Hemlow. Oxford: Clarendon Press, 1986.

——. *The Journals and Letters of Fanny Burney (Madame D'Arblay).* Vol. 7. Edited by Edward Bloom and Lillian Bloom. Oxford: Clarendon Press, 1978.

——. *The Journals and Letters of Fanny Burney (Madame D'Arblay)*. Vol. 8. Edited by Peter Hughes et al. Oxford: Clarendon Press, 1980.

——. *The Wanderer; Or, Female Difficulties*. Introduction by Margaret Drabble. London: Pandora Press, 1988.

Burton, Sir Richard. *The Sotadic Zone*. Boston: Milford House, 1973.

Butler, Judith. *Gender Trouble: Feminism and the Subversion of Identity*. New York: Routledge, 1990.

Butler, Samuel. *The Authoress of the Odyssey*. Chicago: University of Chicago Press, 1967.

Butor, Michel. "Travel and Writing." *Mosaic* 8 (Fall 1974): 1–16.

Buzard, James. *The Beaten Track: European Tourism, Literature, and the Ways to Culture, 1800–1918*. Oxford: Clarendon Press, 1993.

Byron, George Gordon. *Byron's Letters and Journals*. Vol. 1, *1798–1810*. Edited by Leslie Marchand. Cambridge: Harvard University Press, Belknap Press, 1973.

Calloway, Helen. *Gender, Culture, and Empire: European Women in Colonial Nigeria*. Urbana: University of Illinois Press, 1987.

Caserio, Robert L. "Mobility and Masochism: Christine Brooke-Rose and J. G. Ballard." *Novel* (Winter/Spring 1988): 292–310.

Castle, Terry. *Masquerade and Civilization: The Carnivalesque in Eighteenth-Century English Culture and Fiction*. Stanford: Stanford University Press, 1986.

Cavendish, Margaret. *The Description of a New World, called the Blazing-World*. London: A. Maxwell, 1668.

—— [Newcastle, Margaret Lady]. *Poems, and Fancies*. London: Printed by T. R. for F. Martin, and F. Allestrye at the Bell in Saint Pauls Church Yard, 1653.

—— [Newcastle, Margaret Lady]. Preface and "Assaulted and Pursued Chastity." In *Natures Pictures Drawn by Fancies Pencil to the Life. Book II: Feigned Stories in Prose*. 2d ed. London: A Maxwell, 1671.

—— [Newcastle, Margaret (The Lady Marchioness of)]. *Sociable Letters*. London: Printed by William Wilson, 1664.

Certeau, Michel de. *The Writing of History*. Translated by Tom Conley. New York: Columbia University Press, 1988.

——. "Writing vs. Time: History and Anthropology in the Works of Lafitau." *Yale French Studies* 59 (1980): 37–64.

Chaudhuri, Nupur, and Margaret Strobel, eds. *Western Women and Imperialism: Complicity and Resistance*. Bloomington: Indiana University Press, 1992.

Christensen, Jerome. "Setting Byron Straight: Class, Sexuality, and the Poet." In *Literature and the Body: Essays on Populations and Persons*, 125–59. Edited by Elaine Scarry. Baltimore: Johns Hopkins University Press, 1988.

Cixous, Hélène. "Castration or Decapitation?" Translated by Annette Kuhn. *Signs* 7 (Autumn 1981): 41–55.

Cixous, Hélène, and Catherine Clément. *The Newly Born Woman*. Translated by Betsy Wing. Minneapolis: University of Minnesota Press, 1986.

Clifford, James. "Notes on Theory and Travel." In *Traveling Theorists*, 177–85. Edited by James Clifford and Vivek Dhareshwar. *Inscriptions* 5. Santa Cruz: Center for Cultural Studies, 1989.

——. "On Ethnographic Allegory." In *Writing Culture: The Poetics and Politics of Ethnography*, 98–121. Edited by James Clifford and George E. Marcus. Berkeley: University of California Press, 1986.

——. "On Ethnographic Authority," *Representations* 1 (Spring 1983): 118–46.

——. "On Ethnographic Self-Fashioning: Conrad and Malinowski." In *The Predicament of Culture: Twentieth-Century Ethnography, Literature, and Art*, 92–113. Cambridge: Harvard University Press, 1988.

——. "Traveling Cultures." In *Cultural Studies*, 96–112. Edited by Lawrence Grossberg, Cary Nelson, and Paula A. Treichler. New York: Routledge, 1992.

Cohn, Jan, and Thomas H. Miles. "The Sublime: In Alchemy, Aesthetics, and Psychoanalysis." *Modern Philology* 74 (February 1977): 289–304.

Connell, Evan S. *A Long Desire*. New York: Holt, Rinehart & Winston, 1979.

Coverdale, John F. *The Basque Phase of Spain's First Carlist War*. Princeton: Princeton University Press, 1984.

Coxe, William. *Travels into Poland, Russia, Sweden, and Denmark: Interspersed with Historical Relations and Political Inquiries*. 3 vols. Dublin: Printed for S. Price, R. Moncrieffe . . . , 1784.

Craik, George L. *The Pursuit of Knowledge under Difficulties*. London: Bell and Daldy, 1872.

Crapanzano, Vincent. *Hermes' Dilemma and Hamlet's Desire: On the Epistemology of Interpretation*. Cambridge: Cambridge University Press, 1992.

Crawford, Patricia. "Women's Published Writings, 1600–1700." In *Women in English Society, 1500–1800*, 211–31. Edited by Mary Prior. London: Methuen, 1985.

Curtin, Philip. *The Image of Africa: British Ideas and Action, 1780–1850*. Madison: University of Wisconsin Press, 1964.

Darton, F. J. Harvey. *Children's Books in England: Five Centuries of Social Life*. Cambridge: Cambridge University Press, 1932.

Dasenbrock, Reed Way. "Anatomies of Internationalism in *Tarr* and *Howards End*." Paper presented at the annual meeting of the Modern Language Association, Division on Twentieth-Century English Literature, New York, December 1992.

Day, R. A. *Told in Letters: Epistolary Fiction before Richardson*. Ann Arbor: University of Michigan Press, 1966.

Defoe, Daniel. *A General History of the Robberies and Murders of the Most Notorious Pyrates*. New York: Garland Publishing, 1972.

——. *Robinson Crusoe*. New York: Bantam, 1981.

De Lauretis, Teresa, ed. *Alice Doesn't: Feminism, Semiotics, Cinema*. Bloomington: Indiana University Press, 1984.

——. *Feminist Studies: Critical Studies*. Bloomington: Indiana University Press, 1986.

Derrida, Jacques. "Choreographies." *Diacritics* 12 (1982): 66–76.

——. "Des Tours de Babel." In *Difference in Translation*, 165–207. Translated by Joseph F. Graham. Ithaca: Cornell University Press, 1985.

——. "Envois." In *The Postcard: From Socrates to Freud and Beyond*, 1–256. Translated by Alan Bass. Chicago: University of Chicago Press, 1987.

——. *The Other Heading: Reflections on Today's Europe*. Translated by Pascale-Anne Brault and Michael B. Nass. Bloomington: Indiana University Press, 1992.

——. "White Mythology." In *Margins of Philosophy*, 207–71. Translated by Alan Bass. Chicago: University of Chicago Press, 1982.

DeSalvo, Louise A. *Virginia Woolf's First Voyage: A Novel in the Making*. Totowa, N.J.: Rowman and Littlefield, 1980.

DiBattista, Maria. *Virginia Woolf's Major Novels: The Fables of Anon*. New Haven: Yale University Press, 1980.

Doane, Mary Ann. "Commentary: Post-Utopian Difference." In *Coming to Terms: Feminism, Theory, Politics*, 70–78. New York: Routledge, 1989.

——. *The Desire to Desire: The Woman's Film of the 1940's*. Bloomington: Indiana University Press, 1987.

——. "Veiling Over Desire: Close-ups of the Woman." In *Feminism and Psychoanalysis*, 105–41. Edited by Richard Feldstein and Judith Roof. Ithaca: Cornell University Press, 1989.

Donne, John. "A Valediction forbidding mourning." In *The Complete Poetry of John Donne*, 87–88. Introduction, Notes, and Variants by John T. Shawcross. Garden City, N.Y.: Doubleday, 1967.

Doody, Margaret Anne. *Frances Burney: The Life in the Works*. New Brunswick, N.J.: Rutgers University Press, 1988.

Dugaw, Dianne. *Warrior Women and Popular Balladry, 1650–1850*. Cambridge: Cambridge University Press, 1989.

Duplessis, Rachel Blau. *H.D.: The Career of That Struggle*. Bloomington: Indiana University Press, 1986.

——. *Writing beyond the Ending: Narrative Strategies of Twentieth-Century Women Writers*. Bloomington: Indiana University Press, 1985.

Eagleton, Terry. *The Ideology of the Aesthetic*. Oxford: Basil Blackwell, 1990.

Eberhardt, Isabelle. *The Passionate Nomad: The Diary of Isabelle Eberhardt*. Translated by Nina de Voogd. London: Virago Press, 1987.

Epstein, Julia L. "Fanny Burney's Epistolary Voices." *The Eighteenth Century: Theory and Interpretation* 27 (Spring 1986): 162–79.

——. *The Iron Pen: Frances Burney and the Politics of Women's Writing*. Madison: University of Wisconsin Press, 1989.

——. "Writing the Unspeakable: Fanny Burney's Mastectomy and the Fictive Body." *Representations* 16 (Fall 1986): 131–66.

Fabian, Johannes. *Time and the Other: How Anthropology Makes Its Object*. New York: Columbia University Press, 1983.

Fabricant, Carole. "The Literature of Domestic Tourism and the Public Consumption of Private Property." In *The New Eighteenth Century: Theory, Pol-

itics, English Literature, 254–75. Edited by Felicity Nussbaum and Laura Brown. New York: Methuen, 1987.

Fassler, Barbara. "Theories of Homosexuality as Sources of Bloomsbury's Androgyny." *Signs* 5 (Winter 1979): 237–51.

Ferguson, Frances. "Legislating the Sublime." In *Studies in Eighteenth-Century British Art and Aesthetics*, 128–47. Edited by Ralph Cohen. Berkeley: University of California Press, 1985.

———. "Malthus, Godwin, Wordsworth, and the Spirit of Solitude." In *Literature and the Body: Essays on Populations and Persons*, 106–24. Edited by Elaine Scarry. Baltimore: Johns Hopkins University Press, 1988.

———. "The Sublime of Edmund Burke, or the Bathos of Experience." In *Glyph Eight*, 62–78. Edited by Walter B. Michaels. Textual Studies. Baltimore: Johns Hopkins University Press, 1981.

———. "Wollstonecraft Our Contemporary." In *Gender and Theory: Dialogues on Feminist Criticism*, 51–62. Edited by Linda Kaufman. Oxford: Basil Blackwell, 1989.

Ferguson, Moira. "A 'Wise, Wittie and Learned Lady': Margaret Lucas Cavendish." In *Women Writers of the Seventeenth Century*, 305–40. Edited by Katharina M. Wilson and Frank J. Warnke. Athens: University of Georgia Press, 1989.

Ferguson, Moira, and Janet Todd. *Mary Wollstonecraft*. Boston: Twayne Publishers, 1984.

Flint, J. E. "Mary Kingsley—A Reassessment." *Journal of African History* 4, no. 1 (1963): 95–104.

Foucault, Michel. "The Subject and Power." *Critical Inquiry* 8 (Summer 1982): 777–95.

Fowler, Alastair. *Kinds of Literature: An Introduction to the Theory of Genres and Modes*. Cambridge: Harvard University Press, 1982.

Fox, Alice. *Virginia Woolf and the Literature of the English Renaissance*. Oxford: Clarendon Press, 1990.

Frank, Katherine. *A Voyager Out: The Life of Mary Kingsley*. Boston: Houghton Mifflin, 1986.

———. "Voyages Out: Nineteenth-Century Women Travelers in Africa." In *Gender, Ideology, and Action: Historical Perspectives on Women's Public Lives*, 67–93. Edited by Janet Sharistanian. New York: Greenwood Press, 1986.

Freud, Sigmund. *Beyond the Pleasure Principle*. In *The Freud Reader*, 594–626. Edited by Peter Gay. New York: W. W. Norton, 1989.

———. *The Ego and the Id*. In *The Freud Reader*, 628–58.

———. "Femininity." In *New Introductory Lectures on Psycho-Analysis*, 112–35. Translated and edited by James Strachey. London: Hogarth, 1974.

———. *Three Essays on the Theory of Sexuality*. In *The Freud Reader*, 239–93.

———. "The 'Uncanny.'" In *The Standard Edition of the Complete Works of Sigmund Freud*, vol. 17, 217–52. Edited by James Strachey. London: Hogarth, 1955.

Friedman, Susan Stanford. *Penelope's Web: Gender, Modernity, H.D.'s Fiction*. Cambridge: Cambridge University Press, 1990.

Froula, Christine. "Out of the Chrysalis: Female Initiation and Female Authority in Virginia Woolf's *The Voyage Out*." *Tulsa Studies in Women's Literature* 5 (Spring 1986): 63–90.

Frye, Northrop. *The Secular Scripture: A Study of the Structure of Romance.* Cambridge: Harvard University Press, 1976.

Fussell, Paul, ed. *The Norton Book of Travel.* New York: W. W. Norton, 1987.

Gallagher, Catherine. "Embracing the Absolute: The Politics of the Female Subject in Seventeenth-Century England." *Genders*, no. 1 (Spring 1988): 24–39.

Gallop, Jane. *The Daughter's Seduction: Feminism and Psychoanalysis.* Ithaca: Cornell University Press, 1982.

Garber, Marjorie. *Vested Interests: Cross-Dressing and Cultural Anxiety.* New York: Routledge, 1992.

Gardiner, Judith Kegan. "Singularity of Self: Cavendish's Alternative to Rational Individualism." Paper presented at the annual meeting of the Modern Language Association, Division on Seventeenth-Century English Literature, Toronto, December, 1993.

Garlinski, Józef. Review of Wladyslaw Kozaczuk, *W. kregu Enigmy. New Scientist*, October 16, 1980, 73–74.

Gaunt, Mary. *Alone in West Africa.* New York: Charles Scribner's Sons; London: T. Werner Laurie, 1912.

Gelley, Alexander. *Narrative Crossings: Theory and Pragmatics of Prose Fiction.* Baltimore: Johns Hopkins University Press, 1987.

Gerard, Alexander. *An Essay on Taste (1759) Together with Observations Concerning the Imitative Nature of Poetry.* 3d ed. Gainesville, Fla.: Scholars' Facsimiles and Reprints, 1963.

Gilbert, Sandra M. "Costumes of the Mind: Transvestitism as Metaphor in Modern Literature." *Critical Inquiry* 7 (Winter 1980): 391–418.

Gilbert, Sandra M., and Susan Gubar. *The Madwoman in the Attic: The Woman Writer and the Nineteenth-Century Literary Imagination.* New Haven: Yale University Press, 1979.

———. *No Man's Land: The Place of the Woman Writer in the Twentieth Century.* Vol. 1, *The War of the Words.* New Haven: Yale University Press, 1988.

———. *No Man's Land: The Place of the Woman Writer in the Twentieth Century.* Vol. 2, *Sexchanges.* New Haven: Yale University Press, 1989.

Gilman, Sander L. "Black Bodies, White Bodies: Toward an Iconography of Female Sexuality in Late Nineteenth-Century Art, Medicine, and Literature." *Critical Inquiry* 12 (Autumn 1985): 204–42.

Godwin, William. *Memoirs of the Author of "The Rights of Woman,"* 202–77. Edited by Richard Holmes. Middlesex, England: Penguin Books, 1987.

Goldsmith, Elizabeth C. "Authority, Authenticity, and the Publication of Letters by Women." In *Writing the Female Voice: Essays on Epistolary Literature,* 46–59. Edited by Elizabeth C. Goldsmith. Boston: Northeastern University Press, 1989.

Gordon, Deborah. "Writing Culture, Writing Feminism: The Poetics and Politics of Experimental Ethnography." In *Inscriptions*, nos. 3/4 (1988): 7–24.

Gould, Stephen Jay. *The Mismeasure of Man*. New York: W. W. Norton, 1981.

Gove, Philip Babcock. *The Imaginary Voyage in Prose Fiction*. New York: Arno Press, 1974.

Grant, Douglas. *Margaret the First: A Biography of Margaret Cavendish, Duchess of Newcastle, 1623–1673*. Toronto: University of Toronto Press, 1957.

Graves, Robert. *Homer's Daughter*. Chicago: Academy Chicago, 1982.

Green, Martin. *Dreams of Adventure, Deeds of Empire*. New York: Basic Books, 1979.

——. *The English Novel in the Twentieth Century (The Doom of Empire)*. London: Routledge & Kegan Paul, 1984.

——. *The Robinson Crusoe Story*. University Park: Pennsylvania State University Press, 1990.

Greenblatt, Stephen. "Fiction and Friction." In *Reconstructing Individualism: Autonomy, Individuality, and the Self in Western Thought*, 30–52. Edited by Thomas C. Heller et al. Stanford: Stanford University Press, 1986.

——. *Marvelous Possessions: The Wonder of the New World*. Chicago: University of Chicago Press, 1991.

——. *Renaissance Self-Fashioning: From More to Shakespeare*. Chicago: University of Chicago Press, 1980.

Greenstein, Susan. "Sarah Lee: The Woman Traveller and the Literature of Empire." In *Design and Intent in African Literature*, 133–37. Edited by David F. Dorsey, Phanuel A. Egejuru, and Stephen H. Arnold. Washington, D.C.: Three Continents Press, 1982.

Guerlac, Suzanne. "Longinus and the Subject of the Sublime." *New Literary History* 16 (Winter 1985), 275–89.

Gwynn, Stephen. *The Life of Mary Kingsley*. London: Macmillan, 1933.

Haggard, Rider H. *She*. Oxford: Oxford University Press, 1991.

Hamalian, Leo, ed. *Ladies on the Loose: Women Travellers of the Eighteenth and Nineteenth Centuries*. New York: Dodd, Mead, 1981.

Hammond, Dorothy, and Alta Jablow. *The Myth of Africa*. New York: Library of Social Science, 1977.

Haraway, Donna. *Primate Visions: Gender, Race, and Nature in the World of Modern Science*. New York: Routledge, 1989.

Hartman, Geoffrey H. "Romantic Poetry and the Genius Loci." In *Beyond Formalism: Literary Essays, 1958–1970*, 311–36. New Haven: Yale University Press, 1970.

——. "Wordsworth, Inscriptions, and Romantic Nature Poetry." In *Beyond Formalism*, 206–30.

Haywood, Eliza. *Idalia*. Reprinted in *Masquerade Novels of Eliza Haywood*. Facsimile reproductions and Introduction by Mary Anne Schofield. Delmar, N.Y.: Scholars' Facsimiles and Reprints, 1986.

Hazlitt, William. *The Complete Works of William Hazlitt*. Edited by P. P. Howe. Vol. 6, *Lectures on the English Comic Writers*. London: J. M. Dent and Sons, 1931.

Heineman, Helen. *Mrs. Trollope: The Triumphant Feminine in the Nineteenth Century*. Athens: Ohio University Press, 1979.

Heinzelman, Susan Sage. "Hard Cases, Easy Cases, and Weird Cases: Canon Formation in Law and Literature." *Mosaic* 21 (Spring 1988): 59–72.

Helms, Mary W. *Ulysses' Sail: An Ethnographic Odyssey of Power, Knowledge, and Geographical Distance*. Princeton: Princeton University Press, 1988.

Helsinger, Elizabeth K., Robin Lauterbach Sheets, and William Veeder. *The Woman Question: Society and Literature in Britain and America, 1837–1883*. Vol. 3, *Literary Issues*. New York: Garland Publishing, 1983. Reprint. Chicago: University of Chicago Press, 1989.

Herbert, Christopher. *Culture and Anomie: Ethnographic Imagination in the Nineteenth Century*. Chicago: University of Chicago Press, 1991.

Hintikka, Jaakko. "Virginia Woolf and Our Knowledge of the External World." *Journal of Aesthetics and Art Criticism* 38 (1979): 5–14.

Hipple, Walter John, Jr. *The Beautiful, the Sublime, and the Picturesque in Eighteenth-Century British Aesthetic Theory*. Carbondale: Southern Illinois University Press, 1957.

Hobby, Elaine. *Virtue of Necessity: English Women's Writing, 1649–88*. Ann Arbor: University of Michigan Press, 1989.

Hobson, J. A. *Imperialism: A Study*. London: George Allen & Unwin, 1963.

Holmes, Richard, ed. Introduction and Notes to *Mary Wollstonecraft, "A Short Residence in Sweden, Norway, and Denmark" and William Godwin, "Memoirs of the Author of 'The Rights of Woman,'"* 9–55, 279–308. Middlesex, England: Penguin Books, 1987.

Holt, Edgar. *The Carlist Wars in Spain*. Chester Springs, Pa.: Dufour Editions, 1967.

Homer. *The Odyssey*. Translated by Robert Fitzgerald. New York: Random House, 1990.

Hutcheon, Linda. *A Poetics of Postmodernism: History, Theory, Fiction*. New York: Routledge, 1988.

Irigaray, Luce. *Speculum of the Other Woman*. Translated by Gillian C. Gill. Ithaca: Cornell University Press, 1985.

Jackson, Rosemary. *Fantasy: The Literature of Subversion*. London: Methuen, 1981.

Jacobus, Mary. "The Difference of View." In *Reading Woman: Essays in Feminist Criticism*, 27–40. New York: Columbia University Press, 1986.

James, Henry. "The New Novel." In *Literary Criticism: Essays on Literature, American Writers, English Writers*, 124–59. New York: Library of America, 1984.

——. "Preface to 'Daisy Miller.'" In *The Art of the Novel*, 267–87. New York: Charles Scribner's Sons, 1962.

Jameson, Fredric. *The Political Unconscious: Narrative as a Socially Symbolic Act.* Ithaca: Cornell University Press, 1981.

JanMohamed, Abdul R. "The Economy of Manichean Allegory: The Function of Racial Difference in Colonialist Literature." *Critical Inquiry* 12 (Autumn 1985): 59–87.

Jardine, Lisa. *Still Harping on Daughters: Women and Drama in the Age of Shakespeare.* Sussex: Harvester Press; Barnes & Noble Books, 1983.

Jensen, Katharine A. "Male Models of Feminine Epistolarity; or, How to Write Like a Woman in Seventeenth-Century France." In *Writing the Female Voice: Essays on Epistolary Literature,* 25–45. Edited by Elizabeth C. Goldsmith. Boston: Northeastern University Press, 1989.

Jones, Ellen Carol. "The Flight of a Word: Narcissism and the Masquerade of Writing in Virginia Woolf's *Orlando.*" Unpublished essay.

Jordanova, Ludmilla. *Sexual Visions: Images of Gender in Science and Medicine between the Eighteenth and Twentieth Centuries.* Madison: University of Wisconsin Press, 1989.

Joyce, James. "Daniel Defoe." Edited and translated by Joseph Prescott. *Buffalo Studies* 1 (December 1964): 1–27.

——. *Ulysses.* Edited by Hans Walter Gabler. New York: Random House, 1986.

Kamuf, Peggy. "Penelope at Work: Interruptions in *A Room of One's Own.*" *Novel* 16 (Fall 1982): 5–18.

Kant, Immanuel. *Observations on the Feeling of the Beautiful and Sublime.* Translated by John T. Goldthwait. Berkeley: University of California Press, 1960.

Kaplan, Caren. "Deterritorializations: The Rewriting of Home and Exile in Western Feminist Discourse." *Cultural Critique* 6 (Spring 1987): 187–98.

Kaplan, Cora. "Pandora's Box: Subjectivity, Class, and Sexuality in Socialist Feminist Criticism." In *Making a Difference: Feminist Literary Criticism,* 146–76. Edited by Gayle Greene and Coppelia Kahn. London: Methuen, 1985.

Karl, Frederick Robert. *Joseph Conrad: The Three Lives.* New York: Farrar, Straus, and Giroux, 1979.

Katz, Marylin A. *Penelope's Renown: Meaning and Indeterminacy in "The Odyssey."* Princeton: Princeton University Press, 1991.

Kauffman, Linda S. *Discourses of Desire: Gender, Genre, and Epistolary Fictions.* Ithaca: Cornell University Press, 1986.

Kingsley, Mary H. *Travels in West Africa: Congo Français, Corisco, and Cameroons.* Boston: Beacon Press, 1988.

——. *West African Studies.* London: Frank Cass, 1964.

Kipling, Rudyard. *Mary Kingsley.* Garden City, N.Y.: Doubleday, Doran, 1932.

Knapp, Steven. *Personification and the Sublime: Milton to Coleridge.* Cambridge: Harvard University Press, 1985.

Knoepflmacher, U. C., and G. B. Tennyson. *Nature and the Victorian Imagination.* Berkeley: University of California Press, 1977.

Knopp, Sherron E. " 'If I Saw You Would You Kiss Me?': Sapphism and the

Subversiveness of Virginia Woolf's *Orlando.*" *PMLA* 108 (January 1988): 24–34.

Knox-Shaw, Peter. *The Explorer in English Fiction.* New York: St. Martin's, 1986.

Kolodny, Annette. *The Land before Her: Fantasy and Experience of the American Frontiers, 1630–1860.* Chapel Hill: University of North Carolina Press, 1984.

Lacan, Jacques. "The Agency of the Letter in the Unconscious or Reason since Freud." In *Ecrits: A Selection,* 146–78. Translated by Alan Sheridan. New York: W. W. Norton, 1977.

———. *The Four Fundamental Concepts of Psycho-Analysis.* New York: W. W. Norton, 1978.

Landes, Joan B. *Women and the Public Sphere in the Age of the French Revolution.* Ithaca: Cornell University Press, 1988.

Laplanche, Jean, and J.-B. Pontalis. *The Language of Psycho-Analysis.* Translated by Donald Nicholson-Smith. New York: W. W. Norton, 1973.

Lawrence, Karen. "The Cypher: Disclosure and Reticence in *Villette.*" In *Tradition and the Talents of Women,* 87–101. Edited by Florence Howe. Urbana: University of Illinois Press, 1991.

———. "Joyce and Feminism." In *The Cambridge Companion to James Joyce,* 237–58. Edited by Derek Attridge. Cambridge: Cambridge University Press, 1990.

———. *The Odyssey of Style in "Ulysses."* Princeton: Princeton University Press, 1981.

———. Review of Alan Wilde, *Horizons of Assent. Novel* 16 (Winter 1983): 177–81.

Lee, Sarah (Mrs. R. Lee). *The African Wanderers; or, The Adventures of Carlos and Antonio, Embracing Interesting Descriptions of the Manners and Customs of the Western Tribes, and the Natural Productions of the Country.* 5th ed. London: Griffith & Farran, 1877.

———. "Narrative." Appended to T. E. Bowdich, *Excursions in Madeira and Porto Santo, during the Autumn of 1823, While On His Third Voyage to Africa,* 173–218. London: George B. Whittaker, 1825.

———. *Stories of Strange Lands; and Fragments from the Notes of a Traveller.* London: Edward Moxon, 1835.

Lees-Milne, James. *Harold Nicolson: A Biography, 1886–1929.* London: Chatto & Windus, 1980.

Lewin, Ronald. *Ultra Goes to War: The First Account of World War II's Greatest Secret, Based on Official Documents.* New York: Pocket Books, 1980.

Loomis, Chauncey C. "The Arctic Sublime." In *Nature and the Victorian Imagination,* 95–112. Edited by U. C. Knoepflmacher and G. B. Tennyson. Berkeley: University of California Press, 1977.

Love, Jean O. "*Orlando* and Its Genesis: Venturing and Experimenting in Art, Love, and Sex." In *Virginia Woolf: Revaluation and Continuity,* 189–218. Edited by Ralph Freedman. Berkeley: University of California Press, 1980.

Lowe, Lisa. *Critical Terrains: French and British Orientalisms.* Ithaca: Cornell University Press, 1991.

Lyman, Stanford, and Marvin Scott. "Adventures." In *The Drama of Social Reality*, 147–58. New York: Oxford University Press, 1975.

Macaulay, Thomas Babington. *Critical and Historical Essays*. Vol. 3. Edited by F. C. Montague. London: Methuen, 1903.

MacCannell, Dean. *The Tourist: A New Theory of the Leisure Class*. New York: Schocken, 1976.

McClintock, Anne. "Maidens, Maps, and Mines: The Reinvention of Patriarchy in Colonial South Africa." *South Atlantic Quarterly* 87 (Winter 1988): 147–92.

McHale, Brian. *Constructing Postmodernism*. London: Routledge, 1992.

McKeon, Michael. *The Origins of the English Novel, 1600–1740*. Baltimore: Johns Hopkins University Press, 1987.

MacPherson, C. B. *The Political Theory of Possessive Individualism: Hobbes to Locke*. Oxford: Clarendon Press, 1962.

Mannoni, O. *Prospero and Caliban: The Psychology of Colonization*. Translated by Pamela Powesland. New York: Frederick A. Praeger, 1956.

Marcus, Jane. "Britannia Rules the Waves." In *Decolonizing Tradition: New Views of Twentieth-Century "British" Literature*, 136–62. Edited by Karen R. Lawrence. Urbana: University of Illinois Press, 1992.

Marichal, Carlos. *Spain (1834–1844): A New Society*. London: Tamesis Books, 1977.

Marin, Louis. *Utopics: Spatial Play*. Translated by Robert A. Vollrath. Atlantic Highlands, N.J.: Humanities Press, 1984.

Markley, Robert. "Sentimentality as Performance: Shaftesbury, Sterne, and the Theatrics of Virtue." In *The New Eighteenth Century: Theory, Politics, English Literature*, 210–30. Edited by Felicity Nussbaum and Laura Brown. New York: Methuen, 1987.

Martin, Biddy, and Chandra Talpade Mohanty. "Feminist Politics: What's Home Got to Do with It?" In *Feminist Studies: Critical Studies*, 191–212. Edited by Teresa de Lauretis. Bloomington: Indiana University Press, 1986.

Martineau, Harriet. *Dawn Island: A Tale*. Manchester: J. Gadsby, Newall's-Buildings, 1845.

———. *How to Observe Morals and Manners*. New Brunswick, N.J.: Transaction Publishers, 1989.

Mauss, Marcel. *The Gift: Forms and Functions of Exchange in Archaic Societies*. Translated by Ian Cunnison. New York: W. W. Norton, 1967.

Mavor, Elizabeth, ed. *The Ladies of Llangollen: A Study in Romantic Friendship*. Harmondsworth, Eng.: Penguin Books, 1971.

Melville, Herman. *Moby Dick*. Oxford: Oxford University Press, 1988.

Middleton, Dorothy. *Victorian Lady Travellers*. Chicago: Academy Chicago Press, 1965.

Miller, Christopher L. *Blank Darkness: Africanist Discourse in French*. Chicago: University of Chicago Press, 1985.

Miller, Nancy K. "Arachnologies: The Woman, the Text, and the Critic." In

The Poetics of Gender, 270–95. Edited by Nancy K. Miller. New York: Columbia University Press, 1986.

——. "Emphasis Added: Plots and Plausibilities in Women's Fiction." Reprinted in *The New Feminist Criticism: Essays on Women, Literature, and Theory*, 339–60. Edited by Elaine Showalter. New York: Pantheon, 1985.

Mills, Sara. *Discourses of Difference: An Analysis of Women's Travel Writing and Colonialism*. London: Routledge, 1991.

Milton, John. *The Oxford Authors: John Milton*. Edited by Stephen Orgel and Jonathan Goldberg. Oxford: Oxford University Press, 1990.

Minow-Pinkney, Makiko. *Virginia Woolf and the Problem of the Subject: Feminine Writing in the Major Novels*. New Brunswick, N.J.: Rutgers University Press, 1987.

Monk, Samuel H. *The Sublime: A Study of Critical Theories in Seventeenth-Century England*. New York: Modern Language Association of America, 1935.

Montaigne, Michel de. "Of Idleness." In *The Complete Essays of Montaigne*, 20–21. Translated by Donald M. Frame. Stanford: Stanford University Press, 1965.

Montrose, Louis A. "*A Midsummer Night's Dream* and the Shaping Fantasies of Elizabethan Culture: Gender, Power, Form." In *Rewriting the Renaissance: The Discourses of Sexual Difference in Early Modern Europe*, 65–87. Edited by Margaret W. Ferguson, Maureen Quilligan, and Nancy J. Vickers. Chicago: University of Chicago Press, 1986.

——. "The Work of Gender and Sexuality in the Elizabethan Discourse of Discovery." In *Discourses of Sexuality: From Aristotle to AIDS*, 138–84. Edited by Domna C. Stanton. Ann Arbor: University of Michigan Press, 1992.

Moore, Lisa. Review of Felicity A. Nussbaum, *The Autobiographical Subject: Gender and Ideology in Eighteenth-Century England*. *Diacritics* 21 (Fall 1991): 89–101.

Mudimbe, V. Y. *The Invention of Africa: Gnosis, Philosophy, and the Order of Knowledge*. Bloomington: Indiana University Press, 1988.

Myers, Mitzi. "Mary Wollstonecraft's *Letters Written . . . in Sweden*: Toward Romantic Autobiography." In *Studies in Eighteenth-Century Culture*, vol. 8, 165–85. Edited by Roseann Runte. Madison: University of Wisconsin Press, 1979.

Nandy, Ashis. *The Intimate Enemy: Loss and Recovery of Self under Colonialism*. Delhi: Oxford University Press, 1983.

Naremore, James. *The World without a Self: Virginia Woolf and the Novel*. New Haven: Yale University Press, 1973.

Nashe, Thomas. *The Unfortunate Traveller and Other Works*. Edited by J. B. Steane. New York: Viking Penguin, 1985.

Neely, Carol T. "Loss and Recovery in Margaret Cavendish's *New World, Called the Blazing-World*: A Fetishized Feminist Utopia." Paper presented at the annual meeting of the Modern Language Association, Division on Seventeenth-Century English Literature, Toronto, December, 1993.

Nelson, Claudia. *Boys Will Be Girls: The Feminine Ethic and British Children's Fiction, 1857–1917.* New Brunswick, N.J.: Rutgers University Press, 1991.

Nerlich, Michael. *Ideology of Adventure: Studies in Modern Consciousness, 1100–1750.* Translated by Ruth Crowley. Vols. 1 and 2. Minneapolis: University of Minnesota Press, 1987.

Nicolson, Marjorie Hope. *Voyages to the Moon.* New York: Macmillan, 1948.

Nicolson, Nigel. *Portrait of a Marriage.* New York: Atheneum, 1973.

Nyström, Per. *Mary Wollstonecraft's Scandinavian Journey.* Göteborg: Kungl. Vetenskaps-och Vitterhets-Samhället, 1980.

Oliver, Caroline. *Western Women in Colonial Africa.* Westport, Conn.: Greenwood Press, 1982.

Orgel, Stephen. "Nobody's Perfect: Or Why Did the English Stage Take Boys for Women?" *South Atlantic Quarterly* 88 (Winter 1989): 7–29.

Pacteau, Francette. "The Impossible Referent: Representations of the Androgyne." In *Formations of Fantasy,* 62–84. Edited by Victor Burgin, James Donald, and Cora Kaplan. London: Methuen, 1986.

Paloma, Dolores. "Margaret Cavendish: Defining the Female Self." *Women's Studies* 7 (1980): 55–66.

Parry, Benita. "Problems in Current Theories of Colonial Discourse." *Oxford Literary Review,* 9, nos. 1–2 (1987): 27–58.

Paulson, Ronald. *Representations of Revolution (1789–1820).* New Haven: Yale University Press, 1983.

Pelton, Robert D. *The Trickster in West Africa: A Study of Mythic Irony and Sacred Delight.* Berkeley: University of California Press, 1980.

Perham, Margery, and J. Simmons. *African Discovery: An Anthology of Exploration.* London: Faber and Faber, 1943.

Perry, Ruth. *Women, Letters, and the Novel.* New York: AMS Press, 1980.

Pietz, William. "The Problem of the Fetish, II: The Origin of the Fetish." *Res* 13 (Spring 1987): 23–45.

———. "The Problem of the Fetish, IIIa: Bosman's Guinea and the Enlightenment Theory of Fetishism." *Res* 16 (Autumn 1988): 105–23.

Poole, Roger. *The Unknown Virginia Woolf.* 3d ed. Atlantic Highlands, N.J.: Humanities Press, 1990.

Poovey, Mary. "Fathers and Daughters: The Trauma of Growing Up Female." In *Men by Women,* 39–58. Edited by Janet Todd. New York: Holmes & Meier Publishers, 1981.

———. *The Proper Lady and the Woman Writer: Ideology as Style in the Works of Mary Wollstonecraft, Mary Shelley, and Jane Austen.* Chicago: University of Chicago Press, 1984.

Porter, Dennis. *Haunted Journeys: Desire and Transgression in European Travel Writing.* Princeton: Princeton University Press, 1991.

Pratt, Mary Louise. "Fieldwork in Common Places." In *Writing Culture: The Poetics and Politics of Ethnography,* 27–50. Edited by James Clifford and George E. Marcus. Berkeley: University of California Press, 1986.

——. *Imperial Eyes: Travel Writing and Transculturation*. London: Routledge, 1992.

——. "Scratches on the Face of the Country; or, What Mr. Barrow Saw in the Land of the Bushmen." *Critical Inquiry* 12 (Autumn 1985): 119–43.

Price, Martin. "The Sublime Poem: Pictures and Powers." Reprinted in *Poets of Sensibility and the Sublime*, 31–47. Edited by Harold Bloom. New York: Chelsea House Publishers, 1986.

Ragussis, Michael. *Acts of Naming: The Family Plot in Fiction*. New York: Oxford University Press, 1986.

Raitt, Suzanne. *Vita and Virginia: The Work and Friendship of V. Sackville-West and Virginia Woolf*. Oxford: Clarendon Press, 1993.

Ranger, Terence. "The Invention of Tradition in Colonial Africa." In *The Invention of Tradition*, 211–62. Edited by Eric Hobsbawm and Terence Ranger. Cambridge: Cambridge University Press, 1983.

Reiss, Timothy J. "Revolution in Bounds: Wollstonecraft, Women, and Reason." In *Gender and Theory: Dialogues on Feminist Criticism*, 11–50. Edited by Linda Kauffman. Oxford: Basil Blackwell, 1989.

Richardson, Dorothy M. *Dawn's Left Hand*. In *Pilgrimage*, vol. 4, 131–267. Urbana: University of Illinois Press, 1979.

——. *Oberland*. In *Pilgrimage*, vol. 4, 9–127.

Richetti, John J. "Popular Narrative in the Early Eighteenth Century: Formats and Formulas." In *The First English Novelists: Essays in Understanding*, 3–39. Edited by J. M. Armistead. Knoxville: University of Tennessee Press, 1985.

——. "Robinson Crusoe: The Self as Master." In *Modern Essays on Eighteenth-Century Literature*, 201–36. Edited by Leopold Damrosch, Jr. New York: Oxford University Press, 1988.

Robinson, Lillian. "Canon Fathers and Myth Universe." *New Literary History* 19 (1987–1988): 23–35.

Robinson, Ronald, and John Gallagher, with Alice Denny. *Africa and the Victorians: The Climax of Imperialism in the Dark Continent*. New York: St. Martin's, 1961.

Rogers, John. "New Castles in the Air: Margaret Cavendish and the Ethics of Self-Motion." In *The Matter of Revolution: The Poetics of Materialism in the Age of Milton*. Unpublished manuscript.

Romero, Patricia W., ed. *Women's Voices on Africa: A Century of Travel Writings*. Princeton, N.J.: Markus Wiener Publishing, 1992.

Rose, Phyllis. *Woman of Letters: A Life of Virginia Woolf*. New York: Oxford University Press, 1978.

Rosenbaum, S. P. "The Philosophical Realism of Virginia Woolf." In *English Literature and British Philosophy: A Collection of Essays*, 316–56. Edited by S. P. Rosenbaum. Chicago: University of Chicago Press, 1971.

Russell, Mary. *The Blessings of a Good Thick Skirt: Women Travellers and Their World*. London: Collins, 1986.

Russett, Cynthia Eagle. *Sexual Science: The Victorian Construction of Womanhood*. Cambridge: Harvard University Press, 1989.

Sackville-West, Vita. *The Land*. London: William Heinemann, 1939.

——. *Letters of Vita Sackville-West to Virginia Woolf*. Edited by Louise DeSalvo and Mitchell A. Leaska. New York: William Morrow, 1985.

——. *Passenger to Teheran*. New York: Moyer Bell, 1990.

——. *Pepita*. New York: Doubleday, Doran, 1937.

Said, Edward W. "Orientalism Reconsidered." In *Literature, Politics, and Theory: Papers from the Essex Conference, 1976–84*, 210–29. Edited by Francis Barker et al. London: Methuen, 1986.

——. *The World, the Text, and the Critic*. Cambridge: Harvard University Press, 1983.

St Aubin de Terán, Lisa, ed. *Indiscreet Journeys: Stories of Women on the Road*. Boston: Faber and Faber, 1990.

Schiebinger, Londa. "The Anatomy of Difference." In *Nature's Body: Gender in the Making of Modern Science*, 115–42. Boston: Beacon Press, 1993.

Schor, Naomi. "Dreaming Dissymmetry: Barthes, Foucault, and Sexual Difference." In *Coming to Terms: Feminism, Theory, Politics*, 47–58. Edited by Elizabeth Weed. New York: Routledge, 1989.

Scott, Joan W. "Gender: A Useful Category of Historical Analysis." In *Coming to Terms: Feminism, Theory, Politics*, 81–100. Edited by Elizabeth Weed. New York: Routledge, 1989.

Sedgwick, Eve Kosofsky. "Sexualism and the Citizen of the World: Wycherley, Sterne, and Male Homosocial Desire." *Critical Inquiry* 11 (December 1984): 226–45.

Seidel, Michael. *Exile and the Narrative Imagination*. New Haven: Yale University Press, 1986.

Serres, Michel. *Hermes: Literature, Science, Philosophy*. Edited by Josué V. Harari and David F. Bell. Baltimore: Johns Hopkins University Press, 1982.

——. *The Parasite*. Translated by Lawrence R. Schehr. Baltimore: Johns Hopkins University Press, 1982.

Shaw, W. David. *The Lucid Veil: Poetic Truth in the Victorian Age*. Madison: University of Wisconsin Press, 1987.

Shearman, John. "Mary Kingsley and Rudyard Kipling." *Kipling Journal* 61 (December 1987): 11–24.

Shepherd, Simon. *Amazons and Warrior Women: Varieties of Feminism in Seventeenth-Century Drama*. Sussex: Harvester Press, 1981.

Sieber, Harry. *The Picaresque*. London: Methuen, 1977.

Silberman, Lauren. "Singing Unsung Heroines: Androgynous Discourse in Book 3 of *The Faerie Queene*." In *Rewriting the Renaissance: The Discourses of Sexual Difference in Early Modern Europe*, 259–71. Edited by Margaret W. Ferguson, Maureen Quilligan, and Nancy J. Vickers. Chicago: University of Chicago Press, 1986.

Silverman, Kaja. *The Subject of Semiotics*. New York: Oxford University Press, 1983.

Simmel, George. *The Philosophy of Money*. 2d ed. Edited by David Frisby. Translated by Tom Bottomore and David Frisby. London: Routledge, 1990.

Simons, Judy. *Fanny Burney.* Totowa, N.J.: Barnes & Noble Books, 1987.

Smith, Hilda L. *Reason's Disciples: Seventeenth-Century English Feminists.* Urbana: University of Illinois Press, 1982.

Smith, Sidonie. *A Poetics of Women's Autobiography: Marginality and the Fictions of Self-Representation.* Bloomington: Indiana University Press, 1987.

Sontag, Susan. "The Aesthetics of Silence." In *The Discontinuous Universe: Selected Writings in Contemporary Consciousness,* 50–75. Edited by Sallie Sears and Georgianna W. Lord. New York: Basic Books, 1972.

Spacks, Patricia Meyer. "Dynamics of Fear: Fanny Burney." In *Imagining a Self: Autobiography and Novel in Eighteenth-Century England,* 158–92. Cambridge: Harvard University Press, 1976.

———. "Female Resources: Epistles, Plot, and Power." In *Writing the Female Voice,* 63–76. Edited by Elizabeth C. Goldsmith. Boston: Northeastern University Press, 1989.

Spender, Dale. *Mothers of the Novel.* London: Pandora Press, 1986.

Spengemann, William C. *The Adventurous Muse: The Poetics of American Fiction, 1789–1900.* New Haven: Yale University Press, 1977.

Spivak, Gayatri Chakravorty. "Feminism and Deconstruction, Again: Negotiating with Unacknowledged Masculinism." In *Between Feminism and Psychoanalysis,* 206–23. Edited by Teresa Brennan. London: Routledge, 1989.

———. *In Other Worlds: Essays in Cultural Politics.* New York: Routledge, 1988.

———. "The Political Economy of Women as Seen by a Literary Critic." In *Coming to Terms: Feminism, Theory, Politics,* 218–29. New York: Routledge, 1989.

———. *The Post-Colonial Critic: Interviews, Strategies, Dialogues.* Edited by Sarah Harasym. New York: Routledge, 1990.

———. "Three Women's Texts and a Critique of Imperialism." *Critical Inquiry* 12, no. 2 (1985): 243–61.

Squier, Susan M. "Tradition and Revision in Woolf's *Orlando*: Defoe and 'The Jessamy Brides.'" *Women's Studies* 12, no. 2 (1986): 167–77.

Stanley, Henry M. *My Kalulu, Prince, King, and Slave: A Story of Central Africa.* New York: Negro Universities Press, 1969.

Stein, Gertrude. *Lectures in America.* Boston: Beacon Press, 1935.

Sterne, Laurence. *A Sentimental Journey through France and Italy by Mr. Yorick.* Edited by Gardner D. Stout, Jr. Berkeley: University of California Press, 1967.

Stevenson, Catherine Barnes. *Victorian Women Travel Writers in Africa.* Boston: Twayne Publishers, 1982.

Stevenson, Robert Louis. "A Humble Remonstrance." In *Memories and Portraits,* 254–76. New York: Charles Scribner's Sons, 1907.

Stewart, Garrett. *Death Sentences: Styles of Dying in British Fiction.* Cambridge: Harvard University Press, 1984.

Stocking, George W., Jr. *Victorian Anthropology.* New York: Free Press; London: Collier–Macmillan Publishers, 1987.

Suleri, Sara. *The Rhetoric of English India*. Chicago: The University of Chicago Press, 1992.

Thomas, Ronald R. *Dreams of Authority: Freud and the Fictions of the Unconscious*. Ithaca: Cornell University Press, 1990.

Todd, Janet. *Sensibility: An Introduction*. London: Methuen, 1986.

Tomalin, Claire. *The Life and Death of Mary Wollstonecraft*. New York: Meridian, 1974.

Trautmann, Joanne. *The Jessamy Brides: The Friendship of Virginia Woolf and V. Sackville-West*. Pennsylvania State University Studies no. 36. University Park: Pennsylvania State University, 1973.

Trumpener, Katie. "The Time of the Gypsies: A 'People without History' in the Narratives of the West." *Critical Inquiry* 18 (Summer 1992): 843–84.

Turner, Jenny. "Reclaim the Brain: Christine Brooke-Rose Interviewed." *Edinburgh Review* 84 (1990): 19–40.

Turner, Victor. *Dramas, Fields, and Metaphors: Symbolic Action in Human Society*. Ithaca: Cornell University Press, 1974.

Van Den Abbeele, Georges. *Travel as Metaphor from Montaigne to Rousseau*. Minneapolis: University of Minnesota Press, 1992.

Webster, Steven. "Dialogue and Fiction in Ethnography." *Dialectical Anthropology* 7 (September 1982): 91–114.

Wheelwright, Julie. *Amazons and Military Maids: Women Who Dressed as Men in the Pursuit of Life, Liberty, and Happiness*. London: Pandora Press, 1989.

Wilde, Alan. *Horizons of Assent: Modernism, Postmodernism, and the Ironic Imagination*. Baltimore: Johns Hopkins University Press, 1981.

——. "Touching Earth: Virginia Woolf and the Prose of the World." In *Philosophical Approaches to Literature: New Essays on Nineteenth- and Twentieth-Century Texts*, 140–64. Edited by William E. Cain. Lewisburg, Pa.: Bucknell University Press, 1984.

Williams, Raymond. *The Country and the City*. New York: Oxford University Press, 1973.

Wittig, Monique. "The Mark of Gender." *Feminist Issues* 5 (Fall 1985): 1–12.

Wollen, Peter. "Fashion/Orientalism/The Body." *New Formations* 1 (Spring 1987): 5–33.

Wollstonecraft, Mary. "Letters to Imlay." In *The Works of Mary Wollstonecraft*, vol. 6, 365–438. Edited by Janet Todd and Marilyn Butler. London: William Pickering, 1989.

——. *Letters Written during a Short Residence in Sweden, Norway, and Denmark*. Edited and Introduced by Carol H. Poston. Lincoln: University of Nebraska Press, 1976.

——. *Letters Written during a Short Residence in Sweden, Norway, and Denmark*. In *The Works of Mary Wollstonecraft*, vol. 6, 237–348. Edited by Janet Todd and Marilyn Butler. London: William Pickering, 1989.

——. Review of "Observations on the River Wye, and several Parts of South Wales, etc. relative chiefly to picturesque Beauty, made in the Summer of the Year 1770." *Analytical Review*, vol. 5, 1789. Reprinted in *The Works of Mary Wollstonecraft*, vol. 7, 160–64. Edited by Janet Todd and Marilyn Butler. London: William Pickering, 1989.

——. *A Vindication of the Rights of Woman: An Authoritative Text, Backgrounds, the Wollstonecraft Debate, Criticism*. 2d ed. Edited by Carol H. Poston. New York: W. W. Norton, 1988.

Woolf, Leonard. *Beginning Again: An Autobiography of the Years 1911 to 1918*. New York: Harcourt Brace Jovanovich, 1964.

——. *Diaries in Ceylon, 1908–1911. Ceylon Historical Journal* 9 (July 1959–April 1960): vii–lx.

——. *The Letters of Leonard Woolf*. Edited by Frederic Spotts. San Diego: Harcourt Brace Jovanovich, 1989.

——. *The Village in the Jungle*. Oxford: Oxford University Press, 1981.

Woolf, Virginia. *The Common Reader*. 1st ser. Annotated ed. Edited by Andrew McNeillie. San Diego: Harcourt Brace Jovanovich, 1984.

——. *The Diary of Virginia Woolf*. Edited by Anne Olivier Bell. 5 vols. New York: Harcourt Brace Jovanovich, 1977–84.

——. "The Duchess of Newcastle." In *The Common Reader: First Series, 1925*. Reprinted in *Women and Writing*, 79–88. Edited by Michele Barrett. New York: Harcourt Brace Jovanovich, 1979.

——. *Essays of Virginia Woolf*. Edited by Andrew McNeillie. 3 vols. San Diego: Harcourt Brace Jovanovich, 1986.

——. *The Letters of Virginia Woolf*. Edited by Nigel Nicolson. 6 vols. New York: Harcourt Brace Jovanovich, 1975–80.

——. "On Being Ill." In *Collected Essays*, vol. 4, 93–203. London: Hogarth Press, 1967.

——. *Orlando: A Biography*. New York: Harcourt Brace Jovanovich, 1956.

——. *A Passionate Apprentice: The Early Journals, 1897–1909*. Edited by Mitchell A. Leaska. San Diego: Harcourt Brace Jovanovich, 1990.

——. "Robinson Crusoe." In *The Second Common Reader*. Edited by Andrew McNeillie. San Diego: Harcourt Brace Jovanovich, 1986.

——. *The Voyage Out*. San Diego: Harcourt Brace Jovanovich, 1920.

Yeager, Patricia. "Toward a Female Sublime." In *Gender and Theory: Dialogues on Feminist Criticism*, 191–212. Edited by Linda Kauffman. Oxford: Basil Blackwell, 1989.

Zweig, Paul. *The Adventurer: The Fate of Adventure in the Western World*. Princeton: Princeton University Press, 1974.

Index

Abel, Elizabeth, 181
Adams, Percy, 1–2, 23, 41, 48
Adventure and adventure literature, ix-x,
    1–2, 4–5n.3, 19, 117, 122, 126, 128, 130–
    32, 159, 172; femininity in, 4–7, 8, 52n,
    108n.5, 112–13; masculinity of, 1–7, 51–
    52, 56, 107–8, 110–13, 118–19, 140, 144,
    158, 165, 191, 192n, 193; revision of, by
    women writers, 17–18, 20, 26n.28, 28,
    30, 33, 37–50, 53–55, 68–69, 104, 113–
    14, 118, 122, 124, 131, 134, 152–53, 156,
    162–66, 178–82, 190–91, 203, 237–39.
    See also Exploration; Imperialism and
    colonialism; Wandering
Aesthetics, 80, 89–97, 101–2. See also
    Enlightenment and travel, the;
    Sublime, the
Africa, 18, 23, 41, 103–53. See also
    Ethnography; Imperialism and
    colonialism; Race, the discourse of
Alloula, Malek, 156n.3, 196–97nn.40–41
Alone in West Africa (Gaunt), 111–13
Althusser, Louis, 65
Altman, Janet Gurkin, 80n
Amazon, 4, 41, 190n.33. See also Gender
    bending
Amin, Samir, 11n.13
Appadurai, Arjun, xii, 126
Apuleius, 58n.26
Arabian Nights, The, 186, 189
Arcadia (Sidney), 35
Armstrong, Nancy, 51–52, 56, 132, 147
Auden, W. H., 25–26
Auerbach, Nina, 4, 21–22
Austen, Jane, 171

Bachelard, Gaston, 170
Bagehot, Walter, 24–25
Bakhtin, M. M., 37n.10, 38–39, 47, 58n.26,
    92, 227
Bal, Mieke, 64n. 31
Balkan War, 186
Barnes, Djuna, 198n
Barthes, Roland, 214; *Lover's Discourse, A,*
    ix, 75–76, 81, 184–85; *S/Z*, 207–8, 223
Batten, Charles L., 90
Bedford, Sybille, 25
Beer, Gillian, 212
Belatedness, anxiety of, x, 24–25, 35, 216
Bell, Clive, 172
Bell, David, 7, 9
Bell, Gertrude, 106n
Bell, Vanessa, 172
Benstock, Shari, 222n
Bergson, Henri, 135, 168n.12
Bersani, Leo, 170n.13, 214n.6
Besant, Annie, 106n
Birkett, Dea, 104–6, 126
Bishop, Elizabeth, x, 158, 237, 240
Bishop, Isabella Bird, 105
Bjornson, Richard, 56–57
Black, Jeremy, 74n
Blackwell, Jeannine, 54n.23
Blanchot, Maurice, 219–21
Bloomsbury, 187
Bougainville, Louis de, 43–44n
Bowdich, Mrs. T. E. *See* Lee, Sarah
Bowdich, T. Edward, 113
Bowen, Elizabeth, 165
Brantlinger, Patrick, 17–18, 19–20n.25,
    108, 116n.14, 121, 135, 150n

Reading Women Writing

A SERIES EDITED BY
Shari Benstock and Celeste Schenck